THE PROPHETS

ᴴᴱ BOOKS ᴼᶠ ᴛʜᴇ BIBLE

NEW INTERNATIONAL VERSION

LISTEN TO GOD'S MESSENGERS PROCLAIMING HOPE & TRUTH

ZONDERVAN®

Library of Congress Catalog Card Number 2017936205

18 19 20 21 22 23 /DSC/ 21 20 19 18 17 16 15 14 13 12 11 10 9 8 7 6 5 4 3 2

A portion of the purchase price of your NIV® Bible is provided to Biblica so together we support
the mission of *Transforming lives through God's Word*.

THE DRAMA OF THE BIBLE IN SIX ACTS

The Bible is a collection of letters, poems, stories, visions, prophetic oracles, wisdom and other kinds of writing. The first step to good Bible reading and understanding is to engage these collected works as the different kinds of writing that they are, and to read them as whole books. We encourage you to read big, to not merely take in little fragments of the Bible. The introductions at the start of each book will help you to do this.

But it is also important not to view the Bible as a gathering of unrelated writings. Overall, the Bible is a narrative. These books come together to tell God's true story and his plan to set the world right again. This story of the Bible falls naturally into six key major acts, which are briefly summarized below.

> "I had always felt life first as a story: and if there is a story, there is a story-teller."
>
> G. K. Chesterton

But even more precisely, we can say the story of the Bible is a drama. The key to a drama is that it has to be acted out, performed, lived. It can't remain as only words on a page. A drama is an activated story. The Bible was written so we could enter into its story. It is meant to be lived.

All of us, without exception, live our lives as a drama. We are on stage every single day. What will we say? What will we do? According to which story will we live? If we are not answering these questions with the biblical script, we will follow another. We can't avoid living by someone's stage instructions, even if merely our own.

This is why another key to engaging the Bible well is to recognize that its story has not ended. God's saving action continues. We are all invited to take up our own roles in this ongoing story of redemption and new creation. So, welcome to the drama of the Bible. Welcome to the story of how God intends to renew your life, and the life of the world. God himself is calling you to engage with his word.

ACT 1: GOD'S INTENTION

The drama begins (in the first pages of the book of Genesis) with God already on the stage creating a world. He makes a man and a woman, Adam and Eve, and places them in the Garden of Eden to work it and take care of it. The earth is created to be their home. God's intention is for humanity to be in close, trusting relationship with him and in harmony with the rest of creation that surrounds them.

In a startling passage, the Bible tells us that human beings are God's image-bearers, created to share in the task of bringing God's wise and beneficial rule to the rest of the world. Male and female together, we are significant, decision-making, world-shaping beings. This is our vocation, our purpose as defined in the biblical story.

An equally remarkable part of Act 1 is the description of God as coming into the garden to be with the first human beings. Not only is the earth the God-intended place for humanity, God himself comes to make the beautiful new creation his home as well.

God then gives his own assessment of the whole creation: *God saw all that he had made, and it was very good.* Act 1 reveals God's original desire for the world. It shows us that life itself is a gift from the Creator. It tells us what we were made for and provides the setting for all the action that follows.

ACT 2: EXILE

 Tension and conflict are introduced to the story when Adam and Eve decide to go their own way and seek their own wisdom. They listen to the deceptive voice of God's enemy, Satan, and doubt God's trustworthiness. They decide to live apart from the word that God himself has given them. They decide to be a law to themselves.

The disobedience of Adam and Eve—the introduction of sin into our world—is presented in the Bible as having devastating consequences. Humans were created for healthy, life-giving relationship: with God, with each other, and with the rest of creation. But now humanity must live with the fracturing of all these relations and with the resulting shame, brokenness, pain, loneliness—and death.

Heaven and earth—God's realm and our realm—were intended to be united. God's desire from the beginning was clearly to live with us in the world he made. But now God is hidden. Now it is possible to be in our world and not know him, not experience his presence, not follow his ways, not live in gratitude.

As a result of this rebellion, the first exile in the story takes place. The humans are driven away from God's presence. Their offspring throughout history will seek to find their way back to the source of life. They will devise any number of philosophies and religions, trying to make sense of a fallen, yet haunting world. But death now stalks them, and they will find that they cannot escape it. Having attempted to live apart from God and his good word, humans will find they have neither God nor life.

New questions arise in the drama: Can the curse on creation be overcome and the relationship between God and humanity restored? Can heaven and earth be reunited? Or did God's enemy effectively end the plan and subvert the story?

ACT 3: CALLING ISRAEL TO A MISSION

We see the direction of God's redemptive plan when he calls Abraham, promising to make him into a great nation. God narrows his focus and concentrates on one group of people. But the ultimate goal remains the same: to bless all the peoples on earth and remove the curse from creation.

When Abraham's descendants are enslaved in Egypt, a central pattern in the story is set: God hears their cries for help and comes to set them free. God makes a covenant with this new nation of Israel at Mt. Sinai. Israel is called by God to be a light to the nations, showing the world what it means to follow God's ways for living. If they will do this, he will bless them in their new land and will come to live with them.

However, God also warns them that if they are not faithful to the covenant, he will send them away, just as he did with Adam and Eve. In spite of God's repeated warnings through his prophets, Israel seems determined to break the covenant. So God abandons the holy temple—the sign of his presence with his people—and it is smashed by pagan invaders. Israel's capital city Jerusalem is sacked and burned.

Abraham's descendants, chosen to reverse the failure of Adam, have now apparently also failed. The problem this poses in the biblical story is profound. Israel, sent as the divine answer to Adam's fall, cannot escape Adam's sin. God, however, remains committed to his people and his plan, so he sows the seed of a different outcome. He promises to send a new king, a descendant of Israel's great King David, who will lead the nation back to its destiny. The very prophets who warned Israel of the dire consequences of its wrongdoing also pledge that the good news of God's victory will be heard in Israel once again.

Act 3 ends tragically, with God apparently absent and the pagan nations ruling over Israel. But the hope of a promise remains. There is one true God. He has chosen Israel. He will return to his people to live with them again. He will bring justice, peace and healing to Israel, and then to the world. He will do this in a final and climactic way. God will send his anointed one—the Messiah. He has given his word on this.

ACT 4: THE SURPRISING VICTORY OF JESUS

"He is the god made manifest . . . the universal savior of human life." These words, referring to Caesar Augustus (found in a Roman inscription from 4 BC in Ephesus), proclaim the gospel of the Roman Empire. This version of the good news announces that Caesar is the lord who brings peace and prosperity to the world.

Into this empire a son of David is born, and he announces the gospel of God's kingdom. Jesus of Nazareth brings the good news of the coming of God's reign. He begins to show what God's new creation looks like. He announces the end of Israel's exile and the forgiveness of sins. He heals the sick and raises the dead. He overcomes the dark spiritual powers. He welcomes sinners and those considered unclean. Jesus renews the nation, rebuilding the twelve tribes of Israel around himself in a symbolic way.

But the established religious leaders are threatened by Jesus and his kingdom, so they have him brought before the Roman governor. During the very week that the Jews were remembering and celebrating Passover—God's ancient rescue of his people from slavery in Egypt—the Romans nail Jesus to a cross and kill him as a false king.

But the Bible claims that this defeat is actually God's greatest victory. How? Jesus willingly gives up his life as a sacrifice on behalf of the nation, on behalf of the world. Jesus takes onto himself the full force of evil and empties it of its power. In this surprising way, Jesus fights and wins Israel's ultimate battle. The real enemy was never Rome, but the spiritual powers that lie behind Rome and every other kingdom whose weapon is death. Through his blood Jesus pays the price and reconciles everything in heaven and on earth to God.

God then publicly declares this victory by reversing Jesus' death sentence and raising him back to life. The resurrection of Israel's king shows that the great enemies of God's creation—sin and death—really have been defeated. The resurrection is the great sign that the new creation has begun.

Jesus is the fulfillment of Israel's story and a new start for the entire human race. Death came through the first man, Adam. The resurrection of the dead comes through the new man, Jesus. God's original intention is being reclaimed.

ACT 5: THE RENEWED PEOPLE OF GOD

If the key victory has already been secured, why is there an Act 5? The answer is that God wants the victory of Jesus to spread to all the nations of the world. The risen Jesus says to his disciples, *"Peace be with you! As the Father has sent me, I am sending you."* So this new act in the drama tells the story of how the earliest followers of Jesus began to spread the good news of God's reign.

According to the New Testament, all those who belong to Israel's Messiah are children of Abraham, heirs of both the ancient promises and the ancient mission. The task of bringing blessing to the peoples of the world has been given again to Abraham's family. Their mission is to live out the liberating message of the good news of God's kingdom.

God is gathering people from all around the world and forming them into assemblies of Jesus-followers—his church. Together they are God's new temple, the place where his Spirit lives. They are the community of those who have pledged their allegiance to Jesus as the true Lord of the world. They have crossed from death into new life, through the power of God's Spirit. They demonstrate God's love across the usual boundaries of race, class, tribe and nation.

Forgiveness of sins and reconciliation with God can now be announced to all. Following in the steps of Jesus, his followers proclaim this gospel in both word and deed. The power of this new, God-given life breaking into the world is meant to be shown by the real-world actions of the Christian community. But the message also has a warning. When the Messiah returns, he will come as the rightful judge of the world.

The Bible is the story of the central struggle weaving its way through the history of the world. And now the story arrives at our own time, enveloping us in its drama.

So the challenge of a decision confronts us. What will we do? How will we fit into this story? What role will we play? God is inviting us to be a part of his mission of re-creation—of bringing restoration, justice and forgiveness. We are to join in the task of making things new, to be a living sign of what is to come when the drama is complete.

ACT 6: GOD COMES HOME

 God's future has come into our world through the work of Jesus the Messiah. But for now, the present evil age also continues. Brokenness, wrongdoing, sickness and even death remain. We live in the time of the overlap of the ages, the time of in-between. The final Act is coming, but it has not yet arrived.

We live in the time of invitation, when the call of the gospel goes out to every creature. Of course, many still live as though God doesn't exist. They do not acknowledge the rule of the Messiah. But the day is coming when Jesus will return to earth and the reign of God will become an uncontested reality throughout the world.

God's presence will be fully and openly with us once again, as it was at the beginning of the drama. God's plan of redemption will reach its goal. The creation will experience its own Exodus, finding freedom from its bondage to decay. Pain and tears, regret and shame, suffering and death will be no more.

When the day of resurrection arrives God's people will find that their hope has been realized. The dynamic force of an indestructible life will course through their bodies. Empowered by the Spirit, and unhindered by sin and death, we will pursue our original vocation as a renewed humanity. We will be culture makers, under God but over the world. Having been remade in the image of Christ, we will share in bringing his wise, caring rule to the earth.

At the center of it all will be God himself. He will return and make his home with us, this time in a new heaven and a new earth. We, along with the rest of creation, will worship him perfectly and fulfill our true calling. God will be all in all, and the whole world will be full of his glory.

WHAT NOW?

The preceding overview of the drama of the Bible is meant to give you a framework so you can begin to read the books that make up the story. The summary we've provided is merely an invitation for you to engage the sacred books themselves.

Many people today follow the practice of reading only small, fragmentary snippets of the Bible—verses—and often in isolation from the books of which they are a part. This does not lead

Go deep and read big.

to good Bible understanding. We encourage you instead to take in whole books, the way their authors wrote them. This is really the only way to gain deep insight to the Scriptures.

The more you immerse yourself in the script of this drama, the better you will be able to find your own place in the story. The following page, called *Living the Script*, will help you with practical next steps for taking up your role in the Bible's drama of renewal.

LIVING
THE SCRIPT

From the beginning God made it clear that he intends for us to be significant players in his drama. No doubt, it is first and foremost God's story. But we can't passively sit back and just watch what happens. At every stage he invites humans to participate with him.

Here are three key steps to finding your place in the drama:

1. IMMERSE YOURSELF IN THE BIBLE

If we are unfamiliar with the text of the drama itself, there's no chance of living our parts well. Only when we read both deeply and widely in the Bible, marinating in it and letting it soak into our lives, will we be prepared to effectively take up our roles. The more we read the Bible, the better readers we will become. Rather than skimming the surface, we will become skilled at interpreting and practicing what we read.

2. COMMIT TO FOLLOW JESUS

We've all taken part in the brokenness and wrongdoing that came into the story in Act 2. The victory of Jesus in Act 4 now offers us the opportunity to have our lives turned around. Our sins can be forgiven. We can become part of God's story of new creation.

Turn away from your wrongdoing. God has acted through the death and resurrection of the Messiah to deal decisively with evil—in your life and in the life of the world. His death was a sacrifice, and his resurrection a new beginning. Acknowledge that Jesus is the rightful ruler of the world, and commit to follow him and join with God's people.

3. LIVE YOUR PART

Followers of Jesus are gospel players in local communities living out the biblical drama together. But we do not have an exact script for our lines and actions in the drama today. Our history has not yet been written. And we can't just repeat lines from earlier acts in the drama. So what do we do?

We read the Bible to understand what God has already done, especially through Jesus the Messiah, and to know how we carry this story forward. The Bible helps us answer the key question about everything we say and do: Is this an appropriate and fitting way to live out the story of Jesus today? This is how we put the Scriptures into action. Life's choices can be messy, but God has given us his word and promised us his Spirit to guide us on the way. You are God's artwork, created to do good works. May your life be a gift of beauty back to him.

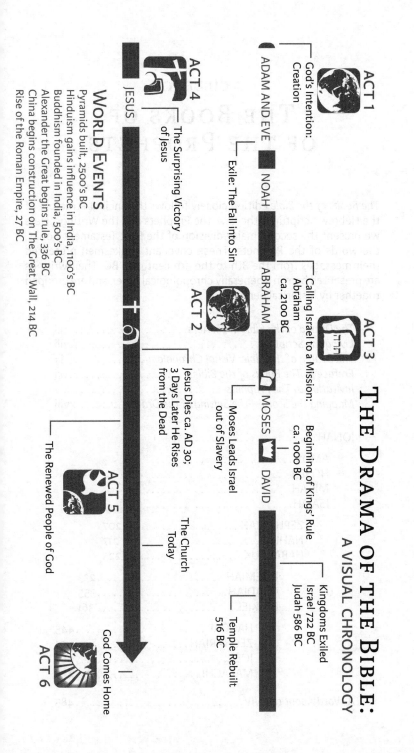

THE DRAMA OF THE BIBLE:
A VISUAL CHRONOLOGY

ACT 1

God's Intention: Creation

ADAM AND EVE

Exile: The Fall into Sin

NOAH

ACT 3

Calling Israel to a Mission: Abraham
ca. 2100 BC

ABRAHAM

Beginning of Kings' Rule
ca. 1000 BC

ACT 2

Moses Leads Israel out of Slavery

MOSES

DAVID

Kingdoms Exiled
Israel 722 BC
Judah 586 BC

Temple Rebuilt
516 BC

ACT 4

The Surprising Victory of Jesus

JESUS

Jesus Dies ca. AD 30;
3 Days Later He Rises from the Dead

The Church Today

ACT 5

The Renewed People of God

ACT 6

God Comes Home

WORLD EVENTS

Pyramids built, 2500's BC
Hinduism gains influence in India, 1100's BC
Buddhism founded in India, 500's BC
Alexander the Great begins rule, 336 BC
China begins construction on The Great Wall, 214 BC
Rise of the Roman Empire, 27 BC

A GUIDE TO

THE BOOKS OF
OF THE PROPHETS

The Books of the Bible edition closely follows the ancient structure of the Hebrew Scriptures: the Law, the Prophets and the Writings. Here we present the second major division of the First Testament books, the words of the Prophets. These covenant spokesmen presented their messages from the 8th to the 5th centuries BC. Their writings are presented here in a generally chronological order, and are grouped together by historical period.

PREFACE TO
THE BOOKS
OF THE BIBLE

The Bible isn't a single book. It's a collection of many books that were written, preserved and gathered together so that they could be shared with new generations of readers. Reading, of course, is not an end in itself. Especially in the case of the Bible, reading is a means of entering into the story. Overall, the Bible is an invitation to the reader first to view the world in a new way, and then to become an agent of the world's renewal. Reading is a step in this journey. *The Books of the Bible* is intended to help readers have a more meaningful encounter with the sacred writings and to read with more understanding, so they can take their places more readily within this story of new creation.

Just as the Bible is not a single book, the Bible is more than bare words. Those who wrote its books chose to put them in particular forms, using the literary conventions appropriate to those forms. Many different kinds of writing are found in the Bible: poetry, narrative, wisdom collections, letters, law codes, apocalyptic visions and more. All of these forms must be read as the literature they really are, or else misunderstanding and distortion of meaning are bound to follow. In order to engage the text on its own terms, good readers will honor the agreement between themselves and the biblical writers implied by the choices of particular forms. Good readers will respect the conventions of these forms. In other words, they'll read poetry as poetry, songs as songs, stories as stories, and so forth.

Unfortunately, for some time now the Bible has been printed in a format that hides its literary forms under a mask of numbers. These break the text into bits and sections that the authors never intended. And so *The Books of the Bible* seeks instead to present the books in their distinctive literary forms and structures. It draws on the key insight that visual presentation can be a crucial aid to right reading, good understanding and a better engagement with the Bible.

Specifically, this edition of the Bible differs from the most common current format in several significant ways:

: chapter and verse numbers have been removed from the text;
: the books are presented instead according to the internal divisions that we believe their authors have indicated;
: a single-column setting is used to present the text more clearly and naturally, and to avoid disrupting the intended line breaks in poetry;
: footnotes, section headings and any other additional materials have been removed from the pages of the sacred text;

: individual books that later tradition divided into two or more parts are put back together again; and

: the books have been placed in an order that we hope will help readers understand them better.

Why have we made these changes? First of all, the chapters and verses in the Bible weren't put there by the original authors. The present system of chapter divisions was devised in the thirteenth century, and our present verse divisions weren't added until the sixteenth. Chapters and verses have imposed a foreign structure on the Bible and made it more difficult to read with understanding. Chapter divisions typically don't correspond with the actual divisions of thought. They require readers to make sense of only part of a longer discussion as if it were complete in itself, or else to try to combine two separate discussions into one coherent whole. Moreover, because the Bible's chapters are all roughly the same length, they can at best only indicate sections of a certain size. This hides the existence of both larger and smaller units of thought within biblical books.

When verses are treated as intentional units (as their numbering suggests they should be), they encourage the Bible to be read as a giant reference book, perhaps as a collection of rules or as a series of propositions. Also, when "Bible verses" are treated as independent and free-standing statements, they can be taken selectively out of context and arranged in such a way as to suggest that the Bible supports beliefs and positions that it really doesn't.

It is true that chapter and verse numbers allow ease of reference. But finding passages at this speed may be a dubious benefit since this can encourage ignoring the text *around* the sought out citation. In order to encourage greater understanding and more responsible use of the Bible, we've removed chapter and verse numberings from the text entirely. (A chapter-and-verse range is included at the bottom of each page.)

Because the biblical books were handwritten, read out loud and then hand-copied long before standardized printing, their authors and compilers needed a way to indicate divisions within the text itself. They often did this by repeating a phrase or expression each time they made a transition from one section to another. We can confirm that particular phrases are significant in this way by observing how their placement reinforces a structure that can already be recognized implicitly from other characteristics of a book, such as changes in topic, movement in place or time, or shifts from one kind of writing to another. Through line spacing, we've marked off sections of varying sizes. The smallest are indicated by one blank line, the next largest by two lines, and so on, up to four-line breaks in the largest books. We've also indicated key divisions with a large initial capital letter of new sections. Our goal is to encourage meaningful units to be read in their entirety and so with greater appreciation and understanding.

Footnotes, section headings and other supplemental materials have been removed from the page in order to give readers a more direct and immediate experience of the word of God. At the beginning of each biblical book we've included an invitation to that particular writing with background information on why it was written and how we understand it to be put together. Beyond this, we encourage readers to study the Bible in community. We believe that if they do, they and their teachers, leaders and peers will provide one another with much more information and many more insights than could ever be included in notes added by publishers.

The books of the Bible were written or recorded individually. When they were gathered together, they were placed into a variety of orders. Unfortunately, the order in which today's readers typically encounter these books is yet another factor that hinders their understanding. Paul's letters, for example, have been put in order of length. They are badly out of historical order, and this makes it difficult to read them with an appreciation for where they fit in the course of his life or how they express the development of his thought. The traditional order of the biblical books can also encourage misunderstandings of what kind of writing a particular work is. For example, the book of James has strong affinities with other biblical books in the wisdom tradition. But it's typically placed within a group of letters, suggesting that it, too, should be read as a letter. To help readers overcome such difficulties, we've sought to order the books so that their literary types, their circumstances of composition and the theological traditions they reflect will be evident. Our introductions to each of the different parts of the Bible will explain how we have ordered the books in these sections, and why.

Just as the work of Bible translation is never finished, the work of formatting the Bible on the principles described here will never be completed. Advances in the literary interpretation of the biblical books will undoubtedly enable the work we've begun here to be extended and improved in the years ahead. Yet the need to help readers overcome the many obstacles inherent in the Bible's current format is urgent, so we humbly offer the results of our work to those seeking an improved visual presentation of its sacred books.

We gratefully acknowledge the assistance of many lay people, clergy, scholars and people engaged in active Scripture outreach who've reviewed our work. They've shared their considerable knowledge and expertise with us and continue to provide valuable insights and guidance. However, final responsibility for all of the decisions in this format rests with us. We trust that readers will gain a deeper appreciation for, and a greater understanding of, these sacred texts. Our hope and prayer is that their engagement with *The Books of the Bible* will enable them to take up their own roles in God's great drama of redemption.

The Bible Design Group
Biblica
Colorado Springs, Colorado
March 2011

INVITATION TO THE
THE PROPHETS

The books of the prophets make up the second major division of the First Testament. These books account for about a third of the First Testament, and one quarter of the whole Bible. The prophets were people chosen by God to bring the word of the Lord to Israel at urgent times in the life of that nation. Though they came from many different walks of life and lived under different historical conditions, the prophets nevertheless speak with a single voice. Indeed, they understand themselves to be speaking within a living tradition. Many of them refer self-consciously to the words of the prophets who came before them.

The prophets typically delivered their messages by composing poetic oracles and reciting them in public settings. Many of these oracles may actually have been sung: the prophets sometimes refer to their oracles as "songs" or "laments," and the closing oracle of Habakkuk actually bears musical notations. But the prophets also used a wide variety of other means of communication, such as writing letters, giving sermons, explaining the meaning of signs that they observed or created, challenging the people with questions and then engaging them in dialogue, and sharing the content of visions that God gave them. While most of their communication was initially oral, it was preserved in writing and safeguarded by their followers. Their message was finally embraced by a repentant nation and included in the Scriptures, where it still speaks to us today.

The prophets whose words have been collected for us in the Bible were active from around 750 BC to about 450 BC. Their activity is clustered around a few key periods. (We learn elsewhere in the scriptures that other prophets, both men and women, spoke to the people both before and after these times.)

: Jonah, Amos, Hosea, Micah and Isaiah prophesied as the empire of Assyria was growing so strong that it threatened and ultimately conquered the northern kingdom of Israel. The southern kingdom of Judah narrowly escaped being conquered itself at this time.

: Nahum, Zephaniah and Habakkuk spoke to a later situation, when the Assyrian empire was crumbling and the Babylonians and Egyptians were jockeying to become rulers of the region.

: Jeremiah, Obadiah and Ezekiel lived at the time when the Babylonians conquered Judah and deported much of its population.

: And Haggai, Zechariah and Malachi brought their messages to the community that had returned from Babylon to Judea under Persian rule. The prophecies in the second part of the book of Isaiah also speak to this situation of return and restoration.

: It's difficult to determine precisely when the prophet Joel lived. Scholars place him anywhere from the 800s to the 400s BC. Therefore, while we've presented the other prophets in what we feel is plausibly their historical order, we've put the book of Joel near the end of the group, where it can be understood in light of the prophetic tradition as a whole.

The foundation of everything the prophets said was the covenant bond between Israel and the Lord. They urged the people of Israel to be faithful to this covenant by not turning away from him to worship false gods, by living lives of moral purity, and by maintaining social and economic justice, especially in their care for the poor and the needy. The essential theme of their message, which can be seen in the actual sequence of oracles built into many of the prophetic books, is first judgment on the house of Israel for the failure to follow God's ways, then judgment on the other nations, and finally a promise of future restoration and hope. Many of the prophets use the technique of a "covenant lawsuit," gathering witnesses and marshaling evidence to demonstrate clearly that Israel has disobeyed the requirements of the bond between God and his people. Yet the Lord's promises will prove to be resilient, overcoming even the nation's stubborn wrongdoing.

These promises had a partial fulfillment in the return of Israel from exile in Babylon. But the prophets themselves speak of a hope that is both deeper and wider, a grand and universal salvation that extends beyond Israel, to the nations of the world and finally even to the creation itself. All things will be made new. The realization of this hope lies beyond these prophetic books, beyond the First Testament itself. The prophets looked to later events concerning one who will take Israel's suffering and exile onto himself, facing the crisis of judgment to find vindication for a renewed Israel in the surprising ways of their faithful God.

God's covenant spokesmen,
HIS SERVANTS THE PROPHETS,
bring the word of the Lord
TO HIS PEOPLE ISRAEL,
announcing a message
OF CLEANSING JUDGMENT
AS WELL AS HOPE AND RENEWAL
for all of God's good creation,

THE PROPHETS

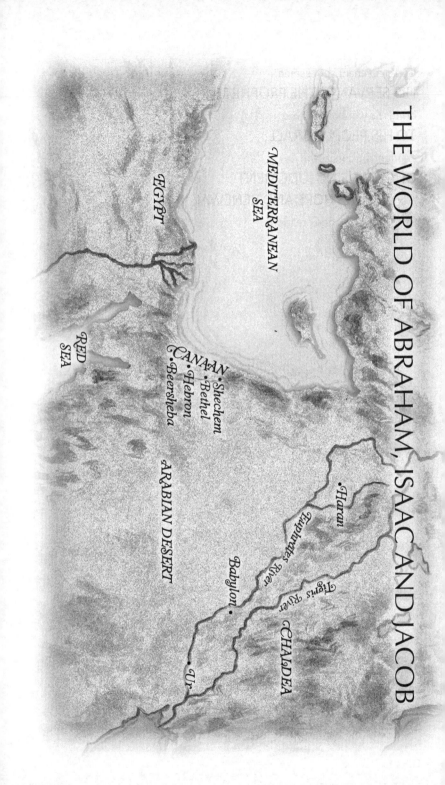

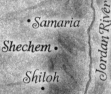

THE KINGDOM OF ISRAEL
and Surrounding Nations

Damascus •

MEDITERRANEAN SEA

• *Samaria*

Shechem •

Shiloh •

Bethel •

Jerusalem •

Bethlehem •

Jordan River

AMMON

• *Jericho*

PHILISTIA

• *Gaza*   *Hebron* •

Beersheba •

MOAB

EDOM

David Thomason 2010

INVITATION TO
JONAH

This book relates how God sent the prophet Jonah, who lived during the reign of Jeroboam II (783–743 or 793–753 BC), to warn the people of Nineveh that their city was about to be destroyed. This book's form is unique among all the prophetic books. It presents a narrative about a prophet, rather than a collection of his oracles. In this whole book there's only one sentence of prophecy: *Forty more days and Nineveh will be overthrown.*

The book of Jonah is written with a great deal of literary care. It's structured into two main acts, with two scenes each. The repetition of God's command to Jonah, *Go to the great city of Nineveh,* marks the beginning of each act. Act one, scene one is set on a ship at sea as Jonah tries to avoid the mission God has sent him on. The second scene takes place in the belly of a huge fish that has swallowed Jonah. Both scenes of the next act are associated with the city of Nineveh. Act two, scene one takes place within the city itself as Jonah preaches and Nineveh repents. Scene two takes place just outside the city as Jonah struggles to accept God's grace and mercy for others.

Biblical scholars offer varying estimates of when the book of Jonah was written. Because it relates several significant episodes from the life of a prophet who lived in the eighth century BC, in this edition it's placed with the books that record the words of other prophets who lived at that time. But these episodes from Jonah's life may actually be recounted in order to speak to the situation of a later generation. In the book, Jonah seems to represent the attitude that many people in Israel took at various times toward other nations. This is not a minor matter but concerns Israel's original calling to be God's agent for bringing blessing to the world. Instead of recognizing their mission to help these nations come to know the true God, they considered them their enemies and expected God to destroy them. And so God's question to Jonah at the end of the book—*should I not have concern for the great city of Nineveh?*—is also being posed to any readers who share Jonah's hostile attitude to foreigners.

This suggests that Jonah may represent Israel more generally in the book. God did tell some of the other prophets to act out signs in which they represented their nation. For example, Ezekiel lived on rationed food to show that Jerusalem would come under siege (pp. 368–369).

If Jonah's role in the story is to represent Israel, then his experience of being swallowed by the great fish may have an additional symbolic meaning that can help us get a general idea of the book's date. Even when he is still inside the fish, Jonah sings a song of thanksgiving, which is the centerpiece of the book. While he isn't yet safe on dry land, he has already been delivered from the engulfing waters. This may indicate that the book's author and audience are in exile: they're not yet back in their own land, but they have been spared from destruction. On the other hand, Jonah's argument with God, in which the book's message is heard most clearly, takes place after he is back on dry land. Once again, if Jonah is playing a symbolic role, this may suggest that the book was written after the return from exile.

But we don't need to know exactly when the book was written in order to appreciate its message. The people of God are always called to the mission of helping others come into the light and truth of the world's Creator. Those of us living in a later act of the biblical drama should also avoid viewing those outside the believing community as enemies, hoping only for God to trample them down. Instead, we should rejoice in—and certainly not resent—the fact that we serve a gracious and compassionate God, slow to anger and abounding in love, a God who relents from sending calamity. This mercy and love extends beyond the borders of Israel to include all nations, indeed, to the whole creation.

JONAH

The word of the LORD came to Jonah son of Amittai: "Go to the great city of Nineveh and preach against it, because its wickedness has come up before me."

But Jonah ran away from the LORD and headed for Tarshish. He went down to Joppa, where he found a ship bound for that port. After paying the fare, he went aboard and sailed for Tarshish to flee from the LORD.

Then the LORD sent a great wind on the sea, and such a violent storm arose that the ship threatened to break up. All the sailors were afraid and each cried out to his own god. And they threw the cargo into the sea to lighten the ship.

But Jonah had gone below deck, where he lay down and fell into a deep sleep. The captain went to him and said, "How can you sleep? Get up and call on your god! Maybe he will take notice of us so that we will not perish."

Then the sailors said to each other, "Come, let us cast lots to find out who is responsible for this calamity." They cast lots and the lot fell on Jonah. So they asked him, "Tell us, who is responsible for making all this trouble for us? What kind of work do you do? Where do you come from? What is your country? From what people are you?"

He answered, "I am a Hebrew and I worship the LORD, the God of heaven, who made the sea and the dry land."

This terrified them and they asked, "What have you done?" (They knew he was running away from the LORD, because he had already told them so.)

The sea was getting rougher and rougher. So they asked him, "What should we do to you to make the sea calm down for us?"

"Pick me up and throw me into the sea," he replied, "and it will become calm. I know that it is my fault that this great storm has come upon you."

Instead, the men did their best to row back to land. But they could not, for the sea grew even wilder than before. Then they cried out to the LORD, "Please, LORD, do not let us die for taking this man's life. Do not hold us accountable for killing an innocent man, for you, Lord, have done as you pleased." Then they took Jonah and threw him overboard, and the raging sea grew calm. At this the men greatly feared the Lord, and they offered a sacrifice to the Lord and made vows to him.

Now the Lord provided a huge fish to swallow Jonah, and Jonah was in the belly of the fish three days and three nights. From inside the fish Jonah prayed to the Lord his God. He said:

> "In my distress I called to the Lord,
>   and he answered me.
> From deep in the realm of the dead I called
>   for help,
>   and you listened to my cry.
> You hurled me into the depths,
>   into the very heart of the seas,
>   and the currents swirled about me;
> all your waves and breakers
>   swept over me.
> I said, 'I have been banished
>   from your sight;
> yet I will look again
>   toward your holy temple.'
> The engulfing waters threatened me,
>   the deep surrounded me;
>   seaweed was wrapped around my head.
> To the roots of the mountains I sank down;
>   the earth beneath barred me in forever.
> But you, Lord my God,
>   brought my life up from the pit.
>
> "When my life was ebbing away,
>   I remembered you, Lord,
> and my prayer rose to you,
>   to your holy temple.
>
> "Those who cling to worthless idols
>   turn away from God's love for them.
> But I, with shouts of grateful praise,
>   will sacrifice to you.

What I have vowed I will make good.
I will say, 'Salvation comes from the LORD.'"

And the LORD commanded the fish, and it vomited Jonah onto dry land.

Then the word of the LORD came to Jonah a second time: "Go to the great city of Nineveh and proclaim to it the message I give you."

Jonah obeyed the word of the LORD and went to Nineveh. Now Nineveh was a very large city; it took three days to go through it. Jonah began by going a day's journey into the city, proclaiming, "Forty more days and Nineveh will be overthrown." The Ninevites believed God. A fast was proclaimed, and all of them, from the greatest to the least, put on sackcloth.

When Jonah's warning reached the king of Nineveh, he rose from his throne, took off his royal robes, covered himself with sackcloth and sat down in the dust. This is the proclamation he issued in Nineveh:

"By the decree of the king and his nobles:

Do not let people or animals, herds or flocks, taste anything; do not let them eat or drink. But let people and animals be covered with sackcloth. Let everyone call urgently on God. Let them give up their evil ways and their violence. Who knows? God may yet relent and with compassion turn from his fierce anger so that we will not perish."

When God saw what they did and how they turned from their evil ways, he relented and did not bring on them the destruction he had threatened.

But to Jonah this seemed very wrong, and he became angry. He prayed to the LORD, "Isn't this what I said, LORD, when I was still at home? That is what I tried to forestall by fleeing to Tarshish. I knew that you are a gracious and compassionate God, slow to anger and abounding in love, a God who relents from sending calamity. Now, LORD, take away my life, for it is better for me to die than to live."

But the LORD replied, "Is it right for you to be angry?"

Jonah had gone out and sat down at a place east of the city. There he made himself a shelter, sat in its shade and waited to see what would happen to the city. Then the LORD God provided a leafy plant and made it grow up over Jonah to give shade for his head to ease his discomfort, and Jonah was very happy about the plant. But at dawn the next day God provided a worm, which chewed the plant so that it withered. When the sun rose, God provided a scorching east wind, and the sun blazed on Jonah's head so that he grew faint. He wanted to die, and said, "It would be better for me to die than to live."

But God said to Jonah, "Is it right for you to be angry about the plant?"

"It is," he said. "And I'm so angry I wish I were dead."

But the LORD said, "You have been concerned about this plant, though you did not tend it or make it grow. It sprang up overnight and died overnight. And should I not have concern for the great city of Nineveh, in which there are more than a hundred and twenty thousand people who cannot tell their right hand from their left — and also many animals?"

INVITATION TO
AMOS

The northern kingdom of Israel reached its greatest height during the forty-year reign of Jeroboam II (783–743 or 793–753 BC). He took back much of the territory that Israel had lost to surrounding nations, conquering additional lands in the process. These victories led the people of his kingdom to anticipate what they called *the day of the LORD*. This was how they described the time when they expected God to strike down all the enemies that still surrounded them and establish their nation as the undisputed ruler of the region.

In addition to their military victories, the Israelites drew confidence from their own dedication to worship. They believed that God would surely favor a nation that lavished such attention on him. They went frequently to shrines at places like Gilgal, and traveled to the great royal temple at Bethel for festivals three times a year. They were careful not to do any business on the sabbath or during new moon festivals, and they regularly brought sacrifices and offerings to the temple. They also knew that God had delivered their ancestors from slavery in Egypt and had driven out mighty nations before them, and they were sure that this same God would still want to help them. Confident in their former victories, their worship, and their heritage, they adopted the motto, "God is with us!"

Into this atmosphere of overconfident nationalism stepped a man from the southern kingdom of Judah. His name was Amos. By his own admission, he wasn't a prophet, but a shepherd. Nevertheless, he claimed that God had shown him a series of visions revealing that Israel's confidence was misplaced. Amos stood in the royal temple at Bethel and announced that the nation would not prevail against its enemies. Instead, it would soon be conquered by a nation that God would stir up against it, and its people would be uprooted from their land. *The day of the LORD*, he insisted, *will be darkness, not light*.

Amos argued that God wasn't impressed that Israel had a strong army, or that the Israelites were descended from the people he had brought out of Egypt, or even that they were so devout in their religious observances. What God cared about, Amos insisted, was justice. And there was no justice in Israel under Jeroboam II. Even those who had legitimate cases didn't win in court, because judges could be bribed. In the end, people stopped speaking up for the innocent entirely, knowing they'd only get in trouble themselves. The wealthy and powerful took advantage of the poor and landless through every means they could think of. They used the money they extorted from the poor to fund their self-indulgent lives. So long as this continued, Amos insisted, God would not bless the nation. He called the nation to repentance as the only way to avoid destruction. *Seek good, not evil,* he cried, *that you may live. Then the* LORD *God Almighty will be with you, just as you say he is. Hate evil, love good; maintain justice in the courts. Perhaps the* LORD *God Almighty will have mercy.*

Amos' message caused an uproar. Amaziah, the high priest at Bethel, accused him of treason and conspiracy. He banished him from the kingdom, likely with the personal approval of King Jeroboam II. But it is probably because Amos was expelled from Israel that he wrote his oracles down, thus creating one of the earliest collections we have from any Hebrew prophet. In this time when only a few people could read, anyone with an urgent message to communicate would not write a book, but rather go to an influential location to speak, as Amos did. However, when his message was rejected, it appears that he (or perhaps his followers) recorded his words to show that he'd faithfully carried out his assignment from God. His words were also recorded so that when the events he foretold came to pass, their meaning would be understood in light of what he'd said.

The book of Amos consists of about three dozen separate oracles and vision reports, plus the story of his expulsion from the northern kingdom. It opens with eight oracles against the nations, first addressing those which circle around the northern kingdom, but then unexpectedly turning its sights on Israel as well. However, in general the book's oracles aren't necessarily presented in the same order that Amos delivered them. They don't seem to be grouped thematically, either. And three stanzas of a hymn that praises God as creator have been inserted into the book at different places—one of them apparently right in the middle of an oracle. So the book as a whole is loosely assembled. In many places oracles seem to have been put together because they have some significant word or phrase in common.

Nevertheless, the book of Amos does possess an essential unity. This unity is created first on the poetic level, as the prophet uses similar images from oracle to oracle, and repeats devices such as plays on the meanings of words. But even more importantly, the book conveys one strong and consistent message: *Let justice roll on like a river, righteousness like a never-failing stream!* The essential word about justice that God conveyed through Amos in the days of Jeroboam II has thus been preserved, and it continues to speak to those of us living in the later acts of the biblical drama.

Amos

The words of Amos, one of the shepherds of Tekoa—the vision he saw concerning Israel two years before the earthquake, when Uzziah was king of Judah and Jeroboam son of Jehoash was king of Israel.

He said:

> "The Lord roars from Zion
> and thunders from Jerusalem;
>
> the pastures of the shepherds dry up,
> and the top of Carmel withers."

This is what the Lord says:

> "For three sins of Damascus,
> even for four, I will not relent.
>
> Because she threshed Gilead
> with sledges having iron teeth,
>
> I will send fire on the house of Hazael
> that will consume the fortresses of Ben-Hadad.
>
> I will break down the gate of Damascus;
> I will destroy the king who is in the Valley of Aven
>
> and the one who holds the scepter in Beth Eden.
> The people of Aram will go into exile to Kir,"
>
> > says the Lord.

This is what the Lord says:

> "For three sins of Gaza,
> even for four, I will not relent.
>
> Because she took captive whole communities
> and sold them to Edom,

I will send fire on the walls of Gaza
that will consume her fortresses.

I will destroy the king of Ashdod
and the one who holds the scepter in Ashkelon.

I will turn my hand against Ekron,
till the last of the Philistines are dead,"
says the Sovereign Lord.

This is what the Lord says:

"For three sins of Tyre,
even for four, I will not relent.

Because she sold whole communities of captives to
Edom,
disregarding a treaty of brotherhood,

I will send fire on the walls of Tyre
that will consume her fortresses."

This is what the Lord says:

"For three sins of Edom,
even for four, I will not relent.

Because he pursued his brother with a sword
and slaughtered the women of the land,

because his anger raged continually
and his fury flamed unchecked,

I will send fire on Teman
that will consume the fortresses of Bozrah."

This is what the Lord says:

"For three sins of Ammon,
even for four, I will not relent.

Because he ripped open the pregnant women
of Gilead
in order to extend his borders,

I will set fire to the walls of Rabbah
that will consume her fortresses

amid war cries on the day of battle,
amid violent winds on a stormy day.

Her king will go into exile,
he and his officials together,"
says the Lord.

This is what the LORD says:

> "For three sins of Moab,
> even for four, I will not relent.
>
> Because he burned to ashes
> the bones of Edom's king,
>
> I will send fire on Moab
> that will consume the fortresses of Kerioth.
>
> Moab will go down in great tumult
> amid war cries and the blast of the trumpet.
>
> I will destroy her ruler
> and kill all her officials with him,"
>
> says the LORD.

This is what the LORD says:

> "For three sins of Judah,
> even for four, I will not relent.
>
> Because they have rejected the law
>   of the LORD
> and have not kept his decrees,
>
> because they have been led astray
>   by false gods,
> the gods their ancestors followed,
>
> I will send fire on Judah
> that will consume the fortresses of
>   Jerusalem."

This is what the LORD says:

> "For three sins of Israel,
> even for four, I will not relent.
>
> They sell the innocent for silver,
> and the needy for a pair of sandals.
>
> They trample on the heads of the poor
> as on the dust of the ground
> and deny justice to the oppressed.
>
> Father and son use the same girl
> and so profane my holy name.
>
> They lie down beside every altar
> on garments taken in pledge.
>
> In the house of their god
> they drink wine taken as fines.

"Yet I destroyed the Amorites before them,
 though they were tall as the cedars
 and strong as the oaks.
I destroyed their fruit above
 and their roots below.
I brought you up out of Egypt
 and led you forty years in the wilderness
 to give you the land of the Amorites.

"I also raised up prophets from among your children
 and Nazirites from among your youths.
Is this not true, people of Israel?"
                                    declares the Lord.
"But you made the Nazirites drink wine
 and commanded the prophets not to prophesy.

"Now then, I will crush you
 as a cart crushes when loaded with grain.
The swift will not escape,
 the strong will not muster their strength,
 and the warrior will not save his life.
The archer will not stand his ground,
 the fleet-footed soldier will not get away,
 and the horseman will not save his life.
Even the bravest warriors
 will flee naked on that day,"
                                    declares the Lord.

Hear this word, people of Israel, the word the Lord has spoken
against you — against the whole family I brought up out of
Egypt:

"You only have I chosen
 of all the families of the earth;
therefore I will punish you
 for all your sins."

Do two walk together
 unless they have agreed to do so?
Does a lion roar in the thicket
 when it has no prey?

Does it growl in its den
when it has caught nothing?
Does a bird swoop down to a trap on the ground
when no bait is there?
Does a trap spring up from the ground
if it has not caught anything?
When a trumpet sounds in a city,
do not the people tremble?
When disaster comes to a city,
has not the Lord caused it?

Surely the Sovereign Lord does nothing
without revealing his plan
to his servants the prophets.

The lion has roared—
who will not fear?
The Sovereign Lord has spoken—
who can but prophesy?

Proclaim to the fortresses of Ashdod
and to the fortresses of Egypt:
"Assemble yourselves on the mountains
of Samaria;
see the great unrest within her
and the oppression among her people."

"They do not know how to do right," declares
the Lord,
"who store up in their fortresses
what they have plundered and looted."

Therefore this is what the Sovereign Lord says:

"An enemy will overrun your land,
pull down your strongholds
and plunder your fortresses."

This is what the Lord says:

"As a shepherd rescues from the lion's mouth
only two leg bones or a piece of an ear,

so will the Israelites living in Samaria be rescued,
with only the head of a bed
and a piece of fabric from a couch."

"Hear this and testify against the descendants of Jacob," declares
the Lord, the Lord God Almighty.

"On the day I punish Israel for her sins,
I will destroy the altars of Bethel;

the horns of the altar will be cut off
and fall to the ground.

I will tear down the winter house
along with the summer house;

the houses adorned with ivory will be destroyed
and the mansions will be demolished,"

declares the Lord.

Hear this word, you cows of Bashan on Mount Samaria,
you women who oppress the poor and crush the needy
and say to your husbands, "Bring us some drinks!"

The Sovereign Lord has sworn by his holiness:
"The time will surely come

when you will be taken away with hooks,
the last of you with fishhooks.

You will each go straight out
through breaches in the wall,
and you will be cast out toward Harmon,"

declares the Lord.

"Go to Bethel and sin;
go to Gilgal and sin yet more.

Bring your sacrifices every morning,
your tithes every three years.

Burn leavened bread as a thank offering
and brag about your freewill offerings—

boast about them, you Israelites,
for this is what you love to do,"

declares the Sovereign Lord.

"I gave you empty stomachs in every city
and lack of bread in every town,
yet you have not returned to me,"
                              declares the LORD.

"I also withheld rain from you
when the harvest was still three months away.

I sent rain on one town,
but withheld it from another.

One field had rain;
another had none and dried up.

People staggered from town to town for water
but did not get enough to drink,
yet you have not returned to me,"
                              declares the LORD.

"Many times I struck your gardens and
        vineyards,
destroying them with blight and mildew.

Locusts devoured your fig and olive trees,
yet you have not returned to me,"
                              declares the LORD.

"I sent plagues among you
as I did to Egypt.

I killed your young men with the sword,
along with your captured horses.

I filled your nostrils with the stench of your camps,
yet you have not returned to me,"
                              declares the LORD.

"I overthrew some of you
as I overthrew Sodom and Gomorrah.

You were like a burning stick snatched from
        the fire,
yet you have not returned to me,"
                              declares the LORD.

"Therefore this is what I will do to you, Israel,
and because I will do this to you, Israel,
prepare to meet your God."

He who forms the mountains,
who creates the wind,
and who reveals his thoughts to mankind,

who turns dawn to darkness,
and treads on the heights of the earth—
the Lord God Almighty is his name.

Hear this word, Israel, this lament I take up concerning you:

"Fallen is Virgin Israel,
never to rise again,
deserted in her own land,
with no one to lift her up."

This is what the Sovereign Lord says to Israel:

"Your city that marches out a thousand strong
will have only a hundred left;
your town that marches out a hundred strong
will have only ten left."

This is what the Lord says to Israel:

"Seek me and live;
do not seek Bethel,
do not go to Gilgal,
do not journey to Beersheba.
For Gilgal will surely go into exile,
and Bethel will be reduced to nothing."

Seek the Lord and live,
or he will sweep through the tribes of Joseph like a fire;
it will devour them,
and Bethel will have no one to quench it.

There are those who turn justice into bitterness
and cast righteousness to the ground.

He who made the Pleiades and Orion,
who turns midnight into dawn
and darkens day into night,
who calls for the waters of the sea
and pours them out over the face of the land—
the Lord is his name.
With a blinding flash he destroys the
         stronghold
and brings the fortified city to ruin.

There are those who hate the one who upholds
         justice in court
and detest the one who tells the truth.

You levy a straw tax on the poor
and impose a tax on their grain.
Therefore, though you have built stone mansions,
you will not live in them;
though you have planted lush vineyards,
you will not drink their wine.
For I know how many are your offenses
and how great your sins.

There are those who oppress the innocent
         and take bribes
and deprive the poor of justice in the courts.
Therefore the prudent keep quiet in such times,
for the times are evil.

Seek good, not evil,
that you may live.
Then the Lord God Almighty will be with you,
just as you say he is.
Hate evil, love good;
maintain justice in the courts.
Perhaps the Lord God Almighty will have mercy
on the remnant of Joseph.

Therefore this is what the Lord, the Lord God Almighty, says:

> "There will be wailing in all the streets
> and cries of anguish in every public square.
>
> The farmers will be summoned to weep
> and the mourners to wail.
>
> There will be wailing in all the vineyards,
> for I will pass through your midst,"

says the Lord.

> Woe to you who long
> for the day of the Lord!
>
> Why do you long for the day of the Lord?
> That day will be darkness, not light.
>
> It will be as though a man fled from a lion
> only to meet a bear,
>
> as though he entered his house
> and rested his hand on the wall
> only to have a snake bite him.
>
> Will not the day of the Lord be darkness,
>   not light—
> pitch-dark, without a ray of brightness?

> "I hate, I despise your religious festivals;
> your assemblies are a stench to me.
>
> Even though you bring me burnt offerings and grain
>   offerings,
> I will not accept them.
>
> Though you bring choice fellowship offerings,
> I will have no regard for them.
>
> Away with the noise of your songs!
> I will not listen to the music of your harps.
>
> But let justice roll on like a river,
> righteousness like a never-failing stream!

> "Did you bring me sacrifices and offerings
> forty years in the wilderness, people of Israel?

You have lifted up the shrine of your king,
the pedestal of your idols,
the star of your god —
which you made for yourselves.

Therefore I will send you into exile beyond Damascus,"
says the Lord, whose name is God Almighty.

Woe to you who are complacent in Zion,
and to you who feel secure on Mount Samaria,

you notable men of the foremost nation,
to whom the people of Israel come!

Go to Kalneh and look at it;
go from there to great Hamath,
and then go down to Gath in Philistia.

Are they better off than your two kingdoms?
Is their land larger than yours?

You put off the day of disaster
and bring near a reign of terror.

You lie on beds adorned with ivory
and lounge on your couches.

You dine on choice lambs
and fattened calves.

You strum away on your harps like David
and improvise on musical instruments.

You drink wine by the bowlful
and use the finest lotions,
but you do not grieve over the ruin of Joseph.

Therefore you will be among the first to go into exile;
your feasting and lounging will end.

The Sovereign Lord has sworn by himself — the Lord God Almighty
declares:

"I abhor the pride of Jacob
and detest his fortresses;

I will deliver up the city
and everything in it."

If ten people are left in one house, they too will die. And if the
relative who comes to carry the bodies out of the house to burn

them asks anyone who might be hiding there, "Is anyone else with you?" and he says, "No," then he will go on to say, "Hush! We must not mention the name of the LORD."

> For the LORD has given the command,
> and he will smash the great house into pieces
> and the small house into bits.

> Do horses run on the rocky crags?
> Does one plow the sea with oxen?

> But you have turned justice into poison
> and the fruit of righteousness into bitterness—

> you who rejoice in the conquest of Lo Debar
> and say, "Did we not take Karnaim by our own
> strength?"

> For the LORD God Almighty declares,
> "I will stir up a nation against you, Israel,

> that will oppress you all the way
> from Lebo Hamath to the valley of the Arabah."

This is what the Sovereign LORD showed me: He was preparing swarms of locusts after the king's share had been harvested and just as the late crops were coming up. When they had stripped the land clean, I cried out, "Sovereign LORD, forgive! How can Jacob survive? He is so small!"

So the LORD relented.

"This will not happen," the LORD said.

This is what the Sovereign LORD showed me: The Sovereign LORD was calling for judgment by fire; it dried up the great deep and devoured the land. Then I cried out, "Sovereign LORD, I beg you, stop! How can Jacob survive? He is so small!"

So the LORD relented.

"This will not happen either," the Sovereign LORD said.

This is what he showed me: The Lord was standing by a wall that had been built true to plumb, with a plumb line in his hand. And the LORD asked me, "What do you see, Amos?"

"A plumb line," I replied.

Then the Lord said, "Look, I am setting a plumb line among my people Israel; I will spare them no longer.

> "The high places of Isaac will be destroyed
> and the sanctuaries of Israel will be ruined;
> with my sword I will rise against the house of Jeroboam."

Then Amaziah the priest of Bethel sent a message to Jeroboam king of Israel: "Amos is raising a conspiracy against you in the very heart of Israel. The land cannot bear all his words. For this is what Amos is saying:

> " 'Jeroboam will die by the sword,
> and Israel will surely go into exile,
> away from their native land.' "

Then Amaziah said to Amos, "Get out, you seer! Go back to the land of Judah. Earn your bread there and do your prophesying there. Don't prophesy anymore at Bethel, because this is the king's sanctuary and the temple of the kingdom."

Amos answered Amaziah, "I was neither a prophet nor the son of a prophet, but I was a shepherd, and I also took care of sycamore-fig trees. But the LORD took me from tending the flock and said to me, 'Go, prophesy to my people Israel.' Now then, hear the word of the LORD. You say,

> " 'Do not prophesy against Israel,
> and stop preaching against the descendants of Isaac.'

"Therefore this is what the LORD says:

> " 'Your wife will become a prostitute in the city,
> and your sons and daughters will fall by the sword.
>
> Your land will be measured and divided up,
> and you yourself will die in a pagan country.
>
> And Israel will surely go into exile,
> away from their native land.' "

This is what the Sovereign LORD showed me: a basket of ripe fruit. "What do you see, Amos?" he asked.

"A basket of ripe fruit," I answered.

Then the Lᴏʀᴅ said to me, "The time is ripe for my people Israel; I will spare them no longer.

"In that day," declares the Sovereign Lᴏʀᴅ, "the songs in the temple will turn to wailing. Many, many bodies—flung everywhere! Silence!"

H ear this, you who trample the needy
and do away with the poor of the land,

saying,

"When will the New Moon be over
that we may sell grain,

and the Sabbath be ended
that we may market wheat?"—

skimping on the measure,
boosting the price
and cheating with dishonest scales,

buying the poor with silver
and the needy for a pair of sandals,
selling even the sweepings with the wheat.

The Lᴏʀᴅ has sworn by himself, the Pride of Jacob: "I will never forget anything they have done.

"Will not the land tremble for this,
and all who live in it mourn?

The whole land will rise like the Nile;
it will be stirred up and then sink
like the river of Egypt.

"In that day," declares the Sovereign Lᴏʀᴅ,

"I will make the sun go down at noon
and darken the earth in broad daylight.

I will turn your religious festivals into mourning
and all your singing into weeping.

I will make all of you wear sackcloth
and shave your heads.

I will make that time like mourning for
an only son
and the end of it like a bitter day.

"The days are coming," declares the Sovereign LORD,
　"when I will send a famine through the land —

not a famine of food or a thirst for water,
　but a famine of hearing the words of the LORD.

People will stagger from sea to sea
　and wander from north to east,

searching for the word of the LORD,
　but they will not find it.

"In that day

"the lovely young women and strong young men
　will faint because of thirst.

Those who swear by the sin of Samaria —
　who say, 'As surely as your god lives, Dan,'
or, 'As surely as the god of Beersheba lives' —
　they will fall, never to rise again."

I saw the Lord standing by the altar, and he said:

"Strike the tops of the pillars
　so that the thresholds shake.

Bring them down on the heads of all
　　the people;
those who are left I will kill with the sword.

Not one will get away,
　none will escape.

Though they dig down to the depths below,
　from there my hand will take them.

Though they climb up to the heavens above,
　from there I will bring them down.

Though they hide themselves on the top
　　of Carmel,
there I will hunt them down and seize them.

Though they hide from my eyes at the bottom
　　of the sea,
there I will command the serpent to bite them.

Though they are driven into exile by their
enemies,
there I will command the sword to slay them.

"I will keep my eye on them
for harm and not for good."

The Lord, the LORD Almighty—

he touches the earth and it melts,
and all who live in it mourn;

the whole land rises like the Nile,
then sinks like the river of Egypt;

he builds his lofty palace in the heavens
and sets its foundation on the earth;

he calls for the waters of the sea
and pours them out over the face of the land—
the LORD is his name.

"Are not you Israelites
the same to me as the Cushites?"

declares the LORD.

"Did I not bring Israel up from Egypt,
the Philistines from Caphtor
and the Arameans from Kir?

"Surely the eyes of the Sovereign LORD
are on the sinful kingdom.

I will destroy it
from the face of the earth.

Yet I will not totally destroy
the descendants of Jacob,"

declares the LORD.

"For I will give the command,
and I will shake the people of Israel
among all the nations

as grain is shaken in a sieve,
and not a pebble will reach the ground.

All the sinners among my people
will die by the sword,

all those who say,
'Disaster will not overtake or meet us.'

"In that day

"I will restore David's fallen shelter —
I will repair its broken walls
and restore its ruins —
and will rebuild it as it used to be,

so that they may possess the remnant of Edom
and all the nations that bear my name,"
declares the Lord, who will do these things.

"The days are coming," declares the Lord,

"when the reaper will be overtaken by the plowman
and the planter by the one treading grapes.

New wine will drip from the mountains
and flow from all the hills,
and I will bring my people Israel back from exile.

"They will rebuild the ruined cities and live in them.
They will plant vineyards and drink their wine;
they will make gardens and eat their fruit.

I will plant Israel in their own land,
never again to be uprooted
from the land I have given them,"

says the Lord your God.

HOSEA

The prophet Hosea spoke to the northern kingdom of Israel during the last years of Jeroboam II (who ruled from 783–743 or 793–753 BC) and throughout the period of great instability that followed his reign. Israel had six different kings in the twenty-two years after Jeroboam died. Four were assassinated and the last was forced off the throne. These weak, briefly-reigning kings kept changing their foreign policies. Sometimes they tried to appease the rising empire of Assyria by paying tribute and surrendering territory. At other times, they tried to get Egypt to protect them from Assyria. Eventually, Israel and its neighbor Syria formed an alliance against Assyria. They invaded the southern kingdom of Judah to try to get it to join them. But in response, the Assyrians invaded Israel. By 722 BC they had completely conquered the nation and carried off most of its population into exile.

Throughout the period of instability after Jeroboam II, the people of Israel remained devoted to worshipping the Lord. They thought this would guarantee them prosperity and victory. But they no longer saw the Lord as the God who'd brought them out of slavery in Egypt and established his covenant with them. Instead, they identified him with Baal, a Canaanite nature god. This identification may have begun innocently enough. The word *baal* simply means "master," and the Lord was, after all, the one who really gave Israel the blessings of nature. But by the time of Hosea, the people were worshiping the Lord as if he were Baal. They visited temple and shrine prostitutes, and they adopted the magical practices of fertility cults. These cults immersed the people in the rhythms of the changing seasons and led them to forget the way God had intervened in history and established social justice through the law of Moses.

In his messages, Hosea repeatedly condemned this corrupted worship as spiritual prostitution. He also condemned the nation's foolish foreign intrigues, its rejection of the moral law, and its callous greed. *There is no faithfulness, no love, no acknowledgment of God in the land,* he protested. *There is only cursing, lying and murder, stealing and adultery . . . . The merchant uses dishonest scales; and loves to defraud.* The people rejected Hosea's warnings, however, and simply mocked him. *The prophet is considered a fool,* he marveled. But when Hosea's message was rejected, his oracles were set down in writing, like the oracles of Amos, so they'd remain as a testimony against those who had refused them, and so that he'd be vindicated when his predictions later came true.

The book of Hosea has two main parts. The messages in the first and much shorter part seem to have been delivered when Jeroboam II was still alive. They describe a period of prosperity, speaking of *the grain, the new wine and oil . . . the silver and gold*, and they refer to God's judgment on *the house of Jehu*, Jeroboam's dynasty, as a future event. This part of the book tells how God commanded Hosea to marry Gomer, a woman who was unfaithful to him. She represented the way that Israel, like an adulterous wife, was guilty of unfaithfulness to the Lord. Gomer bore several children to Hosea, and God told him to give them symbolic names. The first was called Jezreel, to show that God would repay the blood the nation had shed. (Jezreel was the place where a man named Jehu began the cycle of assassinations in Israel.) The second and third children were given names that showed God had rejected the nation: Lo-Ruhamah, meaning *not loved,* and Lo-Ammi, meaning *not my people*. But when Hosea, at God's command, publicly took his wife back after her unfaithfulness, he demonstrated that God's purposes were nevertheless to bring Israel back to himself. *I will say to those called "Not my people," "You are my people"; and they will say, "You are my God."* And so the prophet's own life provided a picture of God's intentions toward the wayward kingdom.

The second and longer part of the book contains oracles that were delivered in the period of instability and decline after Jeroboam. These oracles are grouped loosely together. They refer to the series of assassinations: *they devour their rulers* and *all their kings fall*. They describe the constantly shifting foreign policy: *Ephraim is . . . easily deceived and senseless—now calling to Egypt, now turning to Assyria.* And they allude to the way the last king was forced off the throne by the Assyrians: *Where is your king, that he may save you?* The earlier oracles in this section are generally more concerned with the fertility cult, while the later ones concentrate more on the history of God's relationship with Israel.

The kingdom's main problem, which Hosea speaks to in both parts of the book, was that its people were finding so much security in their institutions (the worship system and the monarchy) that they had become spiritually complacent. The solution to this problem was for the Israelites to go back to their time in the wilderness, when they lived in direct relationship with God and recognized their complete dependence on him. This uprooting could only be accomplished through the drastic measure of conquest and exile. But then the LORD and his "bride" could begin their relationship anew, and the bride could recognize the true foundations of her "marriage" covenant. Once this had been accomplished, there could be a happy return from exile. Hosea foresees this return in the hopeful oracles that are placed right alongside his other oracles of woe and impending judgment. As hope and doom alternate, God, speaking through the prophet, dramatically portrays himself wrestling with his own heart, as he both threatens and pleads with the kingdom of Israel in the last years before its exile.

HOSEA

T he word of the LORD that came to Hosea son of Beeri during the reigns of Uzziah, Jotham, Ahaz and Hezekiah, kings of Judah, and during the reign of Jeroboam son of Jehoash king of Israel:

W hen the LORD began to speak through Hosea, the LORD said to him, "Go, marry a promiscuous woman and have children with her, for like an adulterous wife this land is guilty of unfaithfulness to the LORD." So he married Gomer daughter of Diblaim, and she conceived and bore him a son.

Then the LORD said to Hosea, "Call him Jezreel, because I will soon punish the house of Jehu for the massacre at Jezreel, and I will put an end to the kingdom of Israel. In that day I will break Israel's bow in the Valley of Jezreel."

Gomer conceived again and gave birth to a daughter. Then the LORD said to Hosea, "Call her Lo-Ruhamah (which means "not loved"), for I will no longer show love to Israel, that I should at all forgive them. Yet I will show love to Judah; and I will save them—not by bow, sword or battle, or by horses and horsemen, but I, the LORD their God, will save them."

After she had weaned Lo-Ruhamah, Gomer had another son. Then the LORD said, "Call him Lo-Ammi (which means "not my people"), for you are not my people, and I am not your God.

"Yet the Israelites will be like the sand on the seashore, which cannot be measured or counted. In the place where it was said to them, 'You are not my people,' they will be called 'children of the living God.' The people of Judah and the people of Israel will come together; they will appoint one leader and will come up out of the land, for great will be the day of Jezreel.

"Say of your brothers, 'My people,' and of your sisters, 'My loved one.'

"Rebuke your mother, rebuke her,
for she is not my wife,
and I am not her husband.

Let her remove the adulterous look from her face
and the unfaithfulness from between her breasts.

Otherwise I will strip her naked
and make her as bare as on the day she was born;

I will make her like a desert,
turn her into a parched land,
and slay her with thirst.

I will not show my love to her children,
because they are the children of adultery.

Their mother has been unfaithful
and has conceived them in disgrace.

She said, 'I will go after my lovers,
who give me my food and my water,
my wool and my linen, my olive oil and my drink.'

Therefore I will block her path with thornbushes;
I will wall her in so that she cannot find her way.

She will chase after her lovers but not catch them;
she will look for them but not find them.

Then she will say,
'I will go back to my husband as at first,
for then I was better off than now.'

She has not acknowledged that I was the one
who gave her the grain, the new wine and oil,

who lavished on her the silver and gold—
which they used for Baal.

"Therefore I will take away my grain when it ripens,
and my new wine when it is ready.

I will take back my wool and my linen,
intended to cover her naked body.

So now I will expose her lewdness
before the eyes of her lovers;
no one will take her out of my hands.

I will stop all her celebrations:
her yearly festivals, her New Moons,
her Sabbath days—all her appointed festivals.

I will ruin her vines and her fig trees,
which she said were her pay from her
    lovers;
I will make them a thicket,
and wild animals will devour them.

I will punish her for the days
she burned incense to the Baals;
she decked herself with rings and jewelry,
and went after her lovers,
but me she forgot,"
                         declares the LORD.

"Therefore I am now going to allure her;
I will lead her into the wilderness
and speak tenderly to her.

There I will give her back her vineyards,
and will make the Valley of Achor a door of hope.
There she will respond as in the days of her youth,
as in the day she came up out of Egypt.

"In that day," declares the LORD,
"you will call me 'my husband';
you will no longer call me 'my master.'
I will remove the names of the Baals from
    her lips;
no longer will their names be invoked.

In that day I will make a covenant for them
with the beasts of the field, the birds in the sky
and the creatures that move along the ground.
Bow and sword and battle
I will abolish from the land,
so that all may lie down in safety.

I will betroth you to me forever;
I will betroth you in righteousness and justice,
in love and compassion.
I will betroth you in faithfulness,
and you will acknowledge the LORD.

"In that day I will respond,"
declares the LORD —
"I will respond to the skies,
and they will respond to the earth;

and the earth will respond to the grain,
the new wine and the olive oil,
and they will respond to Jezreel.

I will plant her for myself in the land;
I will show my love to the one I called 'Not my loved one.'

I will say to those called 'Not my people,' 'You are my
    people';
and they will say, 'You are my God.'"

The LORD said to me, "Go, show your love to your wife again, though she is loved by another man and is an adulteress. Love her as the LORD loves the Israelites, though they turn to other gods and love the sacred raisin cakes."

So I bought her for fifteen shekels of silver and about a homer and a lethek of barley. Then I told her, "You are to live with me many days; you must not be a prostitute or be intimate with any man, and I will behave the same way toward you."

For the Israelites will live many days without king or prince, without sacrifice or sacred stones, without ephod or household gods. Afterward the Israelites will return and seek the LORD their God and David their king. They will come trembling to the LORD and to his blessings in the last days.

Hear the word of the LORD, you Israelites,
because the LORD has a charge to bring
against you who live in the land:

"There is no faithfulness, no love,
no acknowledgment of God in the land.

There is only cursing, lying and murder,
stealing and adultery;

they break all bounds,
and bloodshed follows bloodshed.

Because of this the land dries up,
and all who live in it waste away;

the beasts of the field, the birds in the sky
and the fish in the sea are swept away.

"But let no one bring a charge,
let no one accuse another,

for your people are like those
who bring charges against a priest.

You stumble day and night,
and the prophets stumble with you.

So I will destroy your mother —
my people are destroyed from lack of knowledge.

"Because you have rejected knowledge,
I also reject you as my priests;

because you have ignored the law of your God,
I also will ignore your children.

The more priests there were,
the more they sinned against me;
they exchanged their glorious God for something
    disgraceful.

They feed on the sins of my people
and relish their wickedness.

And it will be: Like people, like priests.
I will punish both of them for their ways
and repay them for their deeds.

"They will eat but not have enough;
they will engage in prostitution but not flourish,

because they have deserted the LORD
to give themselves to prostitution;

old wine and new wine
take away their understanding.

My people consult a wooden idol,
and a diviner's rod speaks to them.

A spirit of prostitution leads them astray;
they are unfaithful to their God.

They sacrifice on the mountaintops
and burn offerings on the hills,

under oak, poplar and terebinth,
where the shade is pleasant.
Therefore your daughters turn to prostitution
and your daughters-in-law to adultery.

"I will not punish your daughters
when they turn to prostitution,

nor your daughters-in-law
when they commit adultery,

because the men themselves consort with harlots
and sacrifice with shrine prostitutes —
a people without understanding will come to ruin!

"Though you, Israel, commit adultery,
do not let Judah become guilty.

"Do not go to Gilgal;
do not go up to Beth Aven.
And do not swear, 'As surely as the LORD lives!'

The Israelites are stubborn,
like a stubborn heifer.

How then can the LORD pasture them
like lambs in a meadow?

Ephraim is joined to idols;
leave him alone!

Even when their drinks are gone,
they continue their prostitution;
their rulers dearly love shameful ways.

A whirlwind will sweep them away,
and their sacrifices will bring them shame.

"Hear this, you priests!
Pay attention, you Israelites!

Listen, royal house!
This judgment is against you:

You have been a snare at Mizpah,
a net spread out on Tabor.

The rebels are knee-deep in slaughter.
I will discipline all of them.

I know all about Ephraim;
Israel is not hidden from me.

Ephraim, you have now turned to prostitution;
Israel is corrupt.

"Their deeds do not permit them
to return to their God.

A spirit of prostitution is in their heart;
they do not acknowledge the Lord.

Israel's arrogance testifies against them;
the Israelites, even Ephraim, stumble in their sin;
Judah also stumbles with them.

When they go with their flocks and herds
to seek the Lord,

they will not find him;
he has withdrawn himself from them.

They are unfaithful to the Lord;
they give birth to illegitimate children.

When they celebrate their New Moon feasts,
he will devour their fields.

"Sound the trumpet in Gibeah,
the horn in Ramah.

Raise the battle cry in Beth Aven;
lead on, Benjamin.

Ephraim will be laid waste
on the day of reckoning.

Among the tribes of Israel
I proclaim what is certain.

Judah's leaders are like those
who move boundary stones.

I will pour out my wrath on them
like a flood of water.

Ephraim is oppressed,
trampled in judgment,
intent on pursuing idols.

I am like a moth to Ephraim,
like rot to the people of Judah.

"When Ephraim saw his sickness,
and Judah his sores,

then Ephraim turned to Assyria,
and sent to the great king for help.

But he is not able to cure you,
not able to heal your sores.

For I will be like a lion to Ephraim,
like a great lion to Judah.

I will tear them to pieces and go away;
I will carry them off, with no one to rescue them.

Then I will return to my lair
until they have borne their guilt
and seek my face —

in their misery
they will earnestly seek me."

"Come, let us return to the Lord.

He has torn us to pieces
but he will heal us;

he has injured us
but he will bind up our wounds.

After two days he will revive us;
on the third day he will restore us,
that we may live in his presence.

Let us acknowledge the Lord;
let us press on to acknowledge him.

As surely as the sun rises,
he will appear;

he will come to us like the winter rains,
like the spring rains that water the earth."

"What can I do with you, Ephraim?
What can I do with you, Judah?

Your love is like the morning mist,
like the early dew that disappears.

Therefore I cut you in pieces with my prophets,
I killed you with the words of my mouth —
then my judgments go forth like the sun.

For I desire mercy, not sacrifice,
and acknowledgment of God rather than burnt
offerings.

As at Adam, they have broken the covenant;
they were unfaithful to me there.

Gilead is a city of evildoers,
stained with footprints of blood.

As marauders lie in ambush for a victim,
so do bands of priests;

they murder on the road to Shechem,
carrying out their wicked schemes.

I have seen a horrible thing in Israel:
There Ephraim is given to prostitution,
Israel is defiled.

"Also for you, Judah,
a harvest is appointed.

"Whenever I would restore the fortunes of my people,
whenever I would heal Israel,

the sins of Ephraim are exposed
and the crimes of Samaria revealed.

They practice deceit,
thieves break into houses,
bandits rob in the streets;

but they do not realize
that I remember all their evil deeds.

Their sins engulf them;
they are always before me.

"They delight the king with their wickedness,
the princes with their lies.

They are all adulterers,
burning like an oven

whose fire the baker need not stir
from the kneading of the dough till it rises.

On the day of the festival of our king
the princes become inflamed with wine,
and he joins hands with the mockers.

Their hearts are like an oven;
they approach him with intrigue.

Their passion smolders all night;
in the morning it blazes like a flaming fire.

All of them are hot as an oven;
they devour their rulers.

All their kings fall,
and none of them calls on me.

"Ephraim mixes with the nations;
Ephraim is a flat loaf not turned over.

Foreigners sap his strength,
but he does not realize it.

His hair is sprinkled with gray,
but he does not notice.

Israel's arrogance testifies against him,
but despite all this

he does not return to the Lord his God
or search for him.

"Ephraim is like a dove,
easily deceived and senseless—

now calling to Egypt,
now turning to Assyria.

When they go, I will throw my net over them;
I will pull them down like the birds in the sky.

When I hear them flocking together,
I will catch them.

Woe to them,
because they have strayed from me!

Destruction to them,
because they have rebelled against me!

I long to redeem them
but they speak about me falsely.

They do not cry out to me from their hearts
but wail on their beds.

They slash themselves, appealing to their gods
for grain and new wine,
but they turn away from me.

I trained them and strengthened their arms,
but they plot evil against me.

They do not turn to the Most High;
they are like a faulty bow.

Their leaders will fall by the sword
because of their insolent words.

For this they will be ridiculed
in the land of Egypt.

"Put the trumpet to your lips!
An eagle is over the house of the Lord
because the people have broken
my covenant
and rebelled against my law.

Israel cries out to me,
'Our God, we acknowledge you!'

But Israel has rejected what is good;
an enemy will pursue him.

They set up kings without my consent;
they choose princes without my approval.

With their silver and gold
they make idols for themselves
to their own destruction.

Samaria, throw out your calf-idol!
My anger burns against them.

How long will they be incapable of purity?
They are from Israel!

This calf—a metalworker has made it;
it is not God.

It will be broken in pieces,
that calf of Samaria.

"They sow the wind
and reap the whirlwind.

The stalk has no head;
it will produce no flour.

Were it to yield grain,
foreigners would swallow it up.

Israel is swallowed up;
now she is among the nations
like something no one wants.

For they have gone up to Assyria
like a wild donkey wandering alone.
Ephraim has sold herself to lovers.

Although they have sold themselves among
    the nations,
I will now gather them together.

They will begin to waste away
under the oppression of the mighty king.

"Though Ephraim built many altars for sin offerings,
these have become altars for sinning.

I wrote for them the many things of my law,
but they regarded them as something foreign.

Though they offer sacrifices as gifts to me,
and though they eat the meat,
the LORD is not pleased with them.

Now he will remember their wickedness
and punish their sins:
They will return to Egypt.

Israel has forgotten their Maker
and built palaces;
Judah has fortified many towns.

But I will send fire on their cities
that will consume their fortresses."

Do not rejoice, Israel;
do not be jubilant like the other nations.

For you have been unfaithful to your God;
you love the wages of a prostitute
at every threshing floor.

Threshing floors and winepresses will not feed
    the people;
the new wine will fail them.

They will not remain in the LORD's land;
Ephraim will return to Egypt
and eat unclean food in Assyria.

They will not pour out wine offerings to the LORD,
nor will their sacrifices please him.

Such sacrifices will be to them like the bread of
    mourners;
all who eat them will be unclean.

This food will be for themselves;
it will not come into the temple of the LORD.

What will you do on the day of your appointed
    festivals,
on the feast days of the LORD?

Even if they escape from destruction,
Egypt will gather them,
and Memphis will bury them.

Their treasures of silver will be taken over by briers,
and thorns will overrun their tents.

The days of punishment are coming,
the days of reckoning are at hand.
Let Israel know this.

Because your sins are so many
and your hostility so great,

the prophet is considered a fool,
the inspired person a maniac.

The prophet, along with my God,
is the watchman over Ephraim,

yet snares await him on all his paths,
and hostility in the house of his God.

They have sunk deep into corruption,
as in the days of Gibeah.
God will remember their wickedness
and punish them for their sins.

"When I found Israel,
it was like finding grapes in the desert;

when I saw your ancestors,
it was like seeing the early fruit on the fig tree.

But when they came to Baal Peor,
they consecrated themselves to that shameful idol
and became as vile as the thing they loved.

Ephraim's glory will fly away like a bird —
no birth, no pregnancy, no conception.

Even if they rear children,
I will bereave them of every one.

Woe to them
when I turn away from them!

I have seen Ephraim, like Tyre,
planted in a pleasant place.

But Ephraim will bring out
their children to the slayer."

Give them, Lord —
what will you give them?
Give them wombs that miscarry
and breasts that are dry.

"Because of all their wickedness in Gilgal,
I hated them there.
Because of their sinful deeds,
I will drive them out of my house.
I will no longer love them;
all their leaders are rebellious.
Ephraim is blighted,
their root is withered,
they yield no fruit.
Even if they bear children,
I will slay their cherished offspring."

My God will reject them
because they have not obeyed him;
they will be wanderers among the nations.

Israel was a spreading vine;
he brought forth fruit for himself.
As his fruit increased,
he built more altars;
as his land prospered,
he adorned his sacred stones.
Their heart is deceitful,
and now they must bear their guilt.
The Lord will demolish their altars
and destroy their sacred stones.

Then they will say, "We have no king
because we did not revere the Lord.
But even if we had a king,
what could he do for us?"
They make many promises,
take false oaths
and make agreements;

therefore lawsuits spring up
like poisonous weeds in a plowed field.

The people who live in Samaria fear
for the calf-idol of Beth Aven.

Its people will mourn over it,
and so will its idolatrous priests,

those who had rejoiced over its splendor,
because it is taken from them into exile.

It will be carried to Assyria
as tribute for the great king.

Ephraim will be disgraced;
Israel will be ashamed of its foreign alliances.

Samaria's king will be destroyed,
swept away like a twig on the surface of the waters.

The high places of wickedness will be destroyed—
it is the sin of Israel.

Thorns and thistles will grow up
and cover their altars.

Then they will say to the mountains, "Cover us!"
and to the hills, "Fall on us!"

"Since the days of Gibeah, you have sinned, Israel,
and there you have remained.

Will not war again overtake
the evildoers in Gibeah?

When I please, I will punish them;
nations will be gathered against them
to put them in bonds for their double sin.

Ephraim is a trained heifer
that loves to thresh;

so I will put a yoke
on her fair neck.

I will drive Ephraim,
Judah must plow,
and Jacob must break up the ground.

Sow righteousness for yourselves,
reap the fruit of unfailing love,

and break up your unplowed ground;
for it is time to seek the Lord,

until he comes
and showers his righteousness on you.

But you have planted wickedness,
you have reaped evil,
you have eaten the fruit of deception.

Because you have depended on your own strength
and on your many warriors,

the roar of battle will rise against your people,
so that all your fortresses will be devastated—

as Shalman devastated Beth Arbel on the day
of battle,
when mothers were dashed to the ground with
their children.

So will it happen to you, Bethel,
because your wickedness is great.
When that day dawns,
the king of Israel will be completely destroyed.

"When Israel was a child, I loved him,
and out of Egypt I called my son.

But the more they were called,
the more they went away from me.

They sacrificed to the Baals
and they burned incense to images.

It was I who taught Ephraim to walk,
taking them by the arms;

but they did not realize
it was I who healed them.

I led them with cords of human kindness,
with ties of love.

To them I was like one who lifts
a little child to the cheek,
and I bent down to feed them.

"Will they not return to Egypt
and will not Assyria rule over them
because they refuse to repent?

A sword will flash in their cities;
it will devour their false prophets
and put an end to their plans.

My people are determined to turn from me.
Even though they call me God Most High,
I will by no means exalt them.

"How can I give you up, Ephraim?
How can I hand you over, Israel?

How can I treat you like Admah?
How can I make you like Zeboyim?

My heart is changed within me;
all my compassion is aroused.

I will not carry out my fierce anger,
nor will I devastate Ephraim again.

For I am God, and not a man—
the Holy One among you.
I will not come against their cities.

They will follow the Lord;
he will roar like a lion.

When he roars,
his children will come trembling from
        the west.

They will come from Egypt,
trembling like sparrows,
from Assyria, fluttering like doves.

I will settle them in their homes,"
declares the Lord.

Ephraim has surrounded me with lies,
Israel with deceit.

And Judah is unruly against God,
even against the faithful Holy One

Ephraim feeds on the wind;
he pursues the east wind all day
and multiplies lies and violence.

He makes a treaty with Assyria
and sends olive oil to Egypt.

The Lord has a charge to bring against Judah;
he will punish Jacob according to his ways
and repay him according to his deeds.

In the womb he grasped his brother's heel;
as a man he struggled with God.

He struggled with the angel and overcame him;
he wept and begged for his favor.

He found him at Bethel
and talked with him there—

the Lord God Almighty,
the Lord is his name!

But you must return to your God;
maintain love and justice,
and wait for your God always.

The merchant uses dishonest scales
and loves to defraud.

Ephraim boasts,
"I am very rich; I have become wealthy.

With all my wealth they will not find in me
any iniquity or sin."

"I have been the Lord your God
ever since you came out of Egypt;

I will make you live in tents again,
as in the days of your appointed festivals.

I spoke to the prophets,
gave them many visions
and told parables through them."

Is Gilead wicked?
Its people are worthless!

Do they sacrifice bulls in Gilgal?
Their altars will be like piles of stones
on a plowed field.

Jacob fled to the country of Aram;
Israel served to get a wife,
and to pay for her he tended sheep.

The Lord used a prophet to bring Israel up from Egypt,
by a prophet he cared for him.

But Ephraim has aroused his bitter anger;
his Lord will leave on him the guilt of his bloodshed
and will repay him for his contempt.

When Ephraim spoke, people trembled;
he was exalted in Israel.
But he became guilty of Baal worship and died.

Now they sin more and more;
they make idols for themselves from their silver,

cleverly fashioned images,
all of them the work of craftsmen.

It is said of these people,
"They offer human sacrifices!
They kiss calf-idols!"

Therefore they will be like the morning mist,
like the early dew that disappears,
like chaff swirling from a threshing floor,
like smoke escaping through a window.

"But I have been the Lord your God
ever since you came out of Egypt.

You shall acknowledge no God but me,
no Savior except me.

I cared for you in the wilderness,
in the land of burning heat.

When I fed them, they were satisfied;
when they were satisfied, they became proud;
then they forgot me.

So I will be like a lion to them,
like a leopard I will lurk by the path.

Like a bear robbed of her cubs,
I will attack them and rip them open;

like a lion I will devour them—
a wild animal will tear them apart.

"You are destroyed, Israel,
because you are against me, against your helper.

Where is your king, that he may save you?
Where are your rulers in all your towns,

of whom you said,
'Give me a king and princes'?

So in my anger I gave you a king,
and in my wrath I took him away.

The guilt of Ephraim is stored up,
his sins are kept on record.

Pains as of a woman in childbirth come to him,
but he is a child without wisdom;

when the time arrives,
he doesn't have the sense to come out of the womb.

"I will deliver this people from the power of the grave;
I will redeem them from death.

Where, O death, are your plagues?
Where, O grave, is your destruction?

"I will have no compassion,
even though he thrives among his brothers.

An east wind from the LORD will come,
blowing in from the desert;

his spring will fail
and his well dry up.

His storehouse will be plundered
of all its treasures.

The people of Samaria must bear their guilt,
because they have rebelled against their God.

They will fall by the sword;
their little ones will be dashed to the ground,
their pregnant women ripped open."

Return, Israel, to the LORD your God.
Your sins have been your downfall!

Take words with you
and return to the LORD.

Say to him:
"Forgive all our sins

and receive us graciously,
that we may offer the fruit of our lips.

Assyria cannot save us;
we will not mount warhorses.

We will never again say 'Our gods'
to what our own hands have made,
for in you the fatherless find compassion."

"I will heal their waywardness
and love them freely,
for my anger has turned away from them.

I will be like the dew to Israel;
he will blossom like a lily.

Like a cedar of Lebanon
he will send down his roots;
his young shoots will grow.

His splendor will be like an olive tree,
his fragrance like a cedar of Lebanon.

People will dwell again in his shade;
they will flourish like the grain,

they will blossom like the vine—
Israel's fame will be like the wine of Lebanon.

Ephraim, what more have I to do with idols?
I will answer him and care for him.

I am like a flourishing juniper;
your fruitfulness comes from me."

Who is wise? Let them realize these things.
Who is discerning? Let them understand.
The ways of the Lord are right;
the righteous walk in them,
but the rebellious stumble in them.

INVITATION TO
MICAH

The prophet Micah spoke to the southern kingdom of Judah *during the reigns of Jotham, Ahaz and Hezekiah*, that is, from around 740 BC until some time after 700 BC. He foresaw that Samaria and Jerusalem, the capital cities of Israel and Judah, would be destroyed because of their injustice and religious corruption. The complaints that Micah delivered in God's name were essentially the same ones that Amos and Hosea brought a generation earlier. The people had abandoned their covenant with God and taken up the pagan religious practices of the Canaanites. Micah speaks of witchcraft, spells, idols, sacred stones and Asherah poles. He describes how the rich and powerful were ignoring the law of Moses and ruthlessly exploiting the poor: *They covet fields and seize them, and houses, and take them; her leaders judge for a bribe;* they use *dishonest scales* and *false weights*. Micah warned that in punishment for their unfaithfulness and injustice, both kingdoms would be invaded, conquered and exiled. Just as he predicted, Samaria fell to the Assyrians in 722 BC and Jerusalem fell to the Babylonians in 587 or 586 BC.

But Micah's prophecies actually alternate between warnings of destruction and promises of restoration. Micah foresees that in forgiveness, compassion and covenant faithfulness, God will preserve a remnant of the people, purify them, and bring them back from exile. In their own land, they'll be ruled by a righteous king and become a beacon to the whole world. They'll become a kingdom that will show all nations the ways of God. The Lord will help Israel find its place in the biblical drama.

Micah's prophecies of doom and hope alternate in a much more systematic way than Hosea's. In the book of Micah there are three groups of oracles. Each one begins with a series of judgments, and then each one concludes with promises of restoration. Thus the book is organized thematically. But even so, its oracles aren't in exact historical order. For example, its first two oracles are paired together in an opening judgment section, but they date from different periods in Micah's ministry. The first oracle comes from some time before the destruction of Samaria, which took place in 722 BC, but the second oracle was delivered twenty years later, during the Assyrian invasion of Judah.

This Assyrian invasion was ultimately unsuccessful. Jerusalem was spared the fate of Samaria, at least for a time. This seems to have been due at least in part to Micah himself. Nearly 150 years after he lived, the prophet Jeremiah was threatened with death for declaring Jerusalem would be destroyed. But some of the elders of Israel defended him by recalling that Micah had once said the same thing (see p. 295). These elders noted that Micah's prophecies had prompted King Hezekiah to *fear the* Lord *and seek his favor,* and that this had led the Lord to *relent, so that he did not bring the disaster he pronounced against them.* This shows that Micah helped encourage the reforms that took place in Judah under Hezekiah, and that he enabled the people of Judah discover in his own day that God does *not stay angry forever but delight[s] to show mercy.*

Micah

The word of the Lord that came to Micah of Moresheth during the reigns of Jotham, Ahaz and Hezekiah, kings of Judah—the vision he saw concerning Samaria and Jerusalem.

Hear, you peoples, all of you,
listen, earth and all who live in it,

that the Sovereign Lord may bear witness against you,
the Lord from his holy temple.

Look! The Lord is coming from his dwelling place;
he comes down and treads on the heights of the earth.

The mountains melt beneath him
and the valleys split apart,

like wax before the fire,
like water rushing down a slope.

All this is because of Jacob's transgression,
because of the sins of the people of Israel.

What is Jacob's transgression?
Is it not Samaria?

What is Judah's high place?
Is it not Jerusalem?

"Therefore I will make Samaria a heap of rubble,
a place for planting vineyards.

I will pour her stones into the valley
and lay bare her foundations.

All her idols will be broken to pieces;
all her temple gifts will be burned with fire;
I will destroy all her images.

Since she gathered her gifts from the wages of
  prostitutes,
as the wages of prostitutes they will again be used."

Because of this I will weep and wail;
I will go about barefoot and naked.

I will howl like a jackal
and moan like an owl.

For Samaria's plague is incurable;
it has spread to Judah.

It has reached the very gate of my people,
even to Jerusalem itself.

Tell it not in Gath;
weep not at all.

In Beth Ophrah
roll in the dust.

Pass by naked and in shame,
you who live in Shaphir.

Those who live in Zaanan
will not come out.

Beth Ezel is in mourning;
it no longer protects you.

Those who live in Maroth writhe in pain,
waiting for relief,

because disaster has come from the LORD,
even to the gate of Jerusalem.

You who live in Lachish,
harness fast horses to the chariot.

You are where the sin of Daughter Zion began,
for the transgressions of Israel were found in you.

Therefore you will give parting gifts
to Moresheth Gath.

The town of Akzib will prove deceptive
to the kings of Israel.

I will bring a conqueror against you
who live in Mareshah.

The nobles of Israel
will flee to Adullam.

Shave your head in mourning
for the children in whom you delight;

make yourself as bald as the vulture,
for they will go from you into exile.

Woe to those who plan iniquity,
to those who plot evil on their beds!

At morning's light they carry it out
because it is in their power to do it.

They covet fields and seize them,
and houses, and take them.

They defraud people of their homes,
they rob them of their inheritance.

Therefore, the LORD says:

"I am planning disaster against this people,
from which you cannot save yourselves.

You will no longer walk proudly,
for it will be a time of calamity.

In that day people will ridicule you;
they will taunt you with this mournful song:

'We are utterly ruined;
my people's possession is divided up.

He takes it from me!
He assigns our fields to traitors.'"

Therefore you will have no one in the assembly
of the LORD
to divide the land by lot.

"Do not prophesy," their prophets say.
"Do not prophesy about these things;
disgrace will not overtake us."

You descendants of Jacob, should it be said,
"Does the LORD become impatient?
Does he do such things?"

"Do not my words do good
to the one whose ways are upright?

Lately my people have risen up
like an enemy.

You strip off the rich robe
from those who pass by without a care,
like men returning from battle.

You drive the women of my people
from their pleasant homes.

You take away my blessing
from their children forever.

Get up, go away!
For this is not your resting place,

because it is defiled,
it is ruined, beyond all remedy.

If a liar and deceiver comes and says,
'I will prophesy for you plenty of wine and beer,'
that would be just the prophet for this people!

"I will surely gather all of you, Jacob;
I will surely bring together the remnant of Israel.

I will bring them together like sheep in a pen,
like a flock in its pasture;
the place will throng with people.

The One who breaks open the way will go up before
        them;
they will break through the gate and go out.

Their King will pass through before them,
the Lord at their head."

T hen I said,

"Listen, you leaders of Jacob,
you rulers of Israel.

Should you not embrace justice,
you who hate good and love evil;

who tear the skin from my people
and the flesh from their bones;

who eat my people's flesh,
strip off their skin
and break their bones in pieces;

who chop them up like meat for the pan,
like flesh for the pot?"

Then they will cry out to the LORD,
but he will not answer them.

At that time he will hide his face from them
because of the evil they have done.

This is what the LORD says:

"As for the prophets
who lead my people astray,

they proclaim 'peace'
if they have something to eat,

but prepare to wage war against anyone
who refuses to feed them.

Therefore night will come over you, without visions,
and darkness, without divination.

The sun will set for the prophets,
and the day will go dark for them.

The seers will be ashamed
and the diviners disgraced.

They will all cover their faces
because there is no answer from God."

But as for me, I am filled with power,
with the Spirit of the LORD,
and with justice and might,

to declare to Jacob his transgression,
to Israel his sin.

Hear this, you leaders of Jacob,
you rulers of Israel,

who despise justice
and distort all that is right;

who build Zion with bloodshed,
and Jerusalem with wickedness.

Her leaders judge for a bribe,
her priests teach for a price,
and her prophets tell fortunes for money.
Yet they look for the Lord's support and say,
"Is not the Lord among us?
No disaster will come upon us."

Therefore because of you,
Zion will be plowed like a field,

Jerusalem will become a heap of rubble,
the temple hill a mound overgrown with thickets.

In the last days

the mountain of the Lord's temple will be established
as the highest of the mountains;

it will be exalted above the hills,
and peoples will stream to it.

Many nations will come and say,

"Come, let us go up to the mountain of the Lord,
to the temple of the God of Jacob.

He will teach us his ways,
so that we may walk in his paths."

The law will go out from Zion,
the word of the Lord from Jerusalem.

He will judge between many peoples
and will settle disputes for strong nations far and wide.

They will beat their swords into plowshares
and their spears into pruning hooks.

Nation will not take up sword against nation,
nor will they train for war anymore.

Everyone will sit under their own vine
and under their own fig tree,

and no one will make them afraid,
for the Lord Almighty has spoken.

All the nations may walk
in the name of their gods,

but we will walk in the name of the Lord
our God for ever and ever.

"In that day," declares the Lord,

> "I will gather the lame;
> I will assemble the exiles
> and those I have brought to grief.

> I will make the lame my remnant,
> those driven away a strong nation.

> The Lord will rule over them in Mount Zion
> from that day and forever.

> As for you, watchtower of the flock,
> stronghold of Daughter Zion,

> the former dominion will be restored to you;
> kingship will come to Daughter Jerusalem."

> Why do you now cry aloud—
> have you no king?

> Has your ruler perished,
> that pain seizes you like that of a woman in labor?

> Writhe in agony, Daughter Zion,
> like a woman in labor,

> for now you must leave the city
> to camp in the open field.

> You will go to Babylon;
> there you will be rescued.

> There the Lord will redeem you
> out of the hand of your enemies.

> But now many nations
> are gathered against you.

> They say, "Let her be defiled,
> let our eyes gloat over Zion!"

> But they do not know
> the thoughts of the Lord;

> they do not understand his plan,
> that he has gathered them like sheaves to
> the threshing floor.

> "Rise and thresh, Daughter Zion,
> for I will give you horns of iron;

> I will give you hooves of bronze,
> and you will break to pieces many nations."

You will devote their ill-gotten gains to the Lord,
their wealth to the Lord of all the earth.

Marshal your troops now, city of troops,
for a siege is laid against us.
They will strike Israel's ruler
on the cheek with a rod.

"But you, Bethlehem Ephrathah,
though you are small among the clans of Judah,
out of you will come for me
one who will be ruler over Israel,
whose origins are from of old,
from ancient times."

Therefore Israel will be abandoned
until the time when she who is in labor bears a son,
and the rest of his brothers return
to join the Israelites.

He will stand and shepherd his flock
in the strength of the Lord,
in the majesty of the name of the Lord his God.
And they will live securely, for then his greatness
will reach to the ends of the earth.

And he will be our peace
when the Assyrians invade our land
and march through our fortresses.
We will raise against them seven shepherds,
even eight commanders,
who will rule the land of Assyria with the sword,
the land of Nimrod with drawn sword.
He will deliver us from the Assyrians
when they invade our land
and march across our borders.

The remnant of Jacob will be
in the midst of many peoples

like dew from the LORD,
like showers on the grass,

which do not wait for anyone
or depend on man.

The remnant of Jacob will be among the nations,
in the midst of many peoples,
like a lion among the beasts of the forest,
like a young lion among flocks of sheep,

which mauls and mangles as it goes,
and no one can rescue.

Your hand will be lifted up in triumph over your
enemies,
and all your foes will be destroyed.

"In that day," declares the LORD,

"I will destroy your horses from among you
and demolish your chariots.

I will destroy the cities of your land
and tear down all your strongholds.

I will destroy your witchcraft
and you will no longer cast spells.

I will destroy your idols
and your sacred stones from among you;

you will no longer bow down
to the work of your hands.

I will uproot from among you your Asherah poles
when I demolish your cities.

I will take vengeance in anger and wrath
on the nations that have not obeyed me."

Listen to what the LORD says:

"Stand up, plead my case before the mountains;
let the hills hear what you have to say.

"Hear, you mountains, the LORD's accusation;
listen, you everlasting foundations of the earth.

For the Lord has a case against his people;
he is lodging a charge against Israel.

"My people, what have I done to you?
How have I burdened you? Answer me.

I brought you up out of Egypt
and redeemed you from the land of slavery.

I sent Moses to lead you,
also Aaron and Miriam.

My people, remember
what Balak king of Moab plotted
and what Balaam son of Beor answered.

Remember your journey from Shittim to Gilgal,
that you may know the righteous acts of the Lord."

With what shall I come before the Lord
and bow down before the exalted God?

Shall I come before him with burnt offerings,
with calves a year old?

Will the Lord be pleased with thousands of rams,
with ten thousand rivers of olive oil?

Shall I offer my firstborn for my transgression,
the fruit of my body for the sin of my soul?

He has shown you, O mortal, what is good.
And what does the Lord require of you?

To act justly and to love mercy
and to walk humbly with your God.

Listen! The Lord is calling to the city—
and to fear your name is wisdom—
"Heed the rod and the One who appointed it.

Am I still to forget your ill-gotten treasures, you wicked
house,
and the short ephah, which is accursed?

Shall I acquit someone with dishonest scales,
with a bag of false weights?

Your rich people are violent;
your inhabitants are liars
and their tongues speak deceitfully.

Therefore, I have begun to destroy you,
to ruin you because of your sins.

You will eat but not be satisfied;
your stomach will still be empty.

You will store up but save nothing,
because what you save I will give to the sword.

You will plant but not harvest;
you will press olives but not use the oil,
you will crush grapes but not drink the wine.

You have observed the statutes of Omri
and all the practices of Ahab's house;
you have followed their traditions.

Therefore I will give you over to ruin
and your people to derision;
you will bear the scorn of the nations."

What misery is mine!
I am like one who gathers summer fruit
at the gleaning of the vineyard;
there is no cluster of grapes to eat,
none of the early figs that I crave.

The faithful have been swept from the land;
not one upright person remains.

Everyone lies in wait to shed blood;
they hunt each other with nets.

Both hands are skilled in doing evil;
the ruler demands gifts,

the judge accepts bribes,
the powerful dictate what they desire —
they all conspire together.

The best of them is like a brier,
the most upright worse than a thorn hedge.

The day God visits you has come,
the day your watchmen sound the alarm.
Now is the time of your confusion.

Do not trust a neighbor;
put no confidence in a friend.

Even with the woman who lies in your embrace
guard the words of your lips.

For a son dishonors his father,
a daughter rises up against her mother,

a daughter-in-law against her mother-in-law—
a man's enemies are the members of his own household.

But as for me, I watch in hope for the LORD,
I wait for God my Savior;
my God will hear me.

Do not gloat over me, my enemy!
Though I have fallen, I will rise.

Though I sit in darkness,
the LORD will be my light.

Because I have sinned against him,
I will bear the LORD's wrath,

until he pleads my case
and upholds my cause.

He will bring me out into the light;
I will see his righteousness.

Then my enemy will see it
and will be covered with shame,

she who said to me,
"Where is the LORD your God?"

My eyes will see her downfall;
even now she will be trampled underfoot
like mire in the streets.

The day for building your walls will come,
the day for extending your boundaries.

In that day people will come to you
from Assyria and the cities of Egypt,

even from Egypt to the Euphrates
and from sea to sea
and from mountain to mountain.

The earth will become desolate because of its
inhabitants,
as the result of their deeds.

Shepherd your people with your staff,
the flock of your inheritance,

which lives by itself in a forest,
in fertile pasturelands.

Let them feed in Bashan and Gilead
as in days long ago.

"As in the days when you came out of Egypt,
I will show them my wonders."

Nations will see and be ashamed,
deprived of all their power.

They will put their hands over their mouths
and their ears will become deaf.

They will lick dust like a snake,
like creatures that crawl on the ground.

They will come trembling out of their dens;
they will turn in fear to the Lord our God
and will be afraid of you.

Who is a God like you,
who pardons sin and forgives the transgression
of the remnant of his inheritance?

You do not stay angry forever
but delight to show mercy.

You will again have compassion on us;
you will tread our sins underfoot
and hurl all our iniquities into the depths of the sea.

You will be faithful to Jacob,
and show love to Abraham,

as you pledged on oath to our ancestors
in days long ago.

INVITATION TO
Isaiah

The prophet Isaiah spoke to the kingdom of Judah for forty years, beginning *in the year that King Uzziah died* (around 740 BC) and continuing at least until the Assyrian siege of Jerusalem in 701 BC. Isaiah emphasized many of the same themes as Amos, Hosea and Micah: God didn't want merely formal worship; he wanted justice throughout the land. But Isaiah also had personal access to Judah's kings and brought them counsel during national crises.

The first crisis came in 734 BC when Israel and Syria invaded Judah. Isaiah assured King Ahaz he could trust God for deliverance, but the king wanted to appeal to Assyria instead. Isaiah warned that once the Assyrians subdued Israel and Syria, they would turn against Judah. But Ahaz refused to listen, so Isaiah withdrew from public life. He wrote down his oracles and left them with his followers for safekeeping.

Isaiah's predictions came true. The Assyrians put down the revolt, destroying Syria and overrunning most of Israel. Even so, Israel revolted again. So in 722 BC the Assyrians destroyed its capital city, Samaria, and deported most of the population. Judah's new king, Hezekiah, served the Assyrians at first. But eventually he joined an Egyptian-led rebellion against them. In 701 BC the emperor Sennacherib led a huge army that quashed this rebellion. Hezekiah tried to appease him with tribute, but he overran most of Judah, besieged Jerusalem and demanded Hezekiah's surrender.

The king asked Isaiah (who had returned to public life and royal favor under this godly king) how he should respond. Isaiah assured Hezekiah the Assyrians would never take the city. Once again, his predictions came true. *The angel of the LORD* wiped out Sennacherib's army, the city was delivered, and Hezekiah's faith was vindicated.

Much of the book of Isaiah can be understood against the background of these events.

: The first section presents oracles that condemn greed, extortion and religious corruption in Judah. They threaten divine judgment but also promise mercy and restoration. This section includes an account of Isaiah's calling to be a prophet and describes his counsel to Ahaz (pp. 73–96).

: The oracles in the second section address kingdoms and empires beyond Israel's borders. They speak to a variety of situations, both within Isaiah's lifetime and many years afterwards (pp. 96–115).

: The third section applies the themes of the preceding oracles on a larger scale. God's judgments become cosmic, as if creation itself is undone. But then the people of Israel will return to their land, and God will reign over them in Jerusalem (pp. 115–122).

: The oracles in the fourth section pronounce woes on Judah for cultivating international alliances instead of relying on God. These oracles likely come from the years leading up to Sennacherib's invasion. They condemn the people's greed, drunkenness, complacency and misplaced confidence but also include promises of restoration (pp. 122–136).

: The fifth section also describes God's judgments in cosmic terms. Its first oracle depicts the general destruction of the wicked; its second portrays a universal renewal culminating in the return of Judah's exiles (pp. 134–139).

: The sixth section narrates two historical episodes. It first describes the siege of Jerusalem during Sennacherib's invasion. It then tells how Hezekiah recovered from a near-fatal illness. This actually happened ten years before the invasion. But it's told afterwards to help introduce the themes of the rest of the book. When the king of Babylon sent messengers to congratulate Hezekiah on his recovery, he showed them the treasures of his kingdom. Isaiah predicted these treasures would one day be carried off to Babylon, and they were, as great empires rose and fell in the years ahead (pp. 139–146).

The rest of the book addresses later historical events. The Assyrian empire slowly crumbled over the next century. Its capital Nineveh was destroyed in 612 BC by a Babylonian-led coalition. The Babylonians then defeated the Egyptians to become the uncontested rulers of the region. When Judah rebelled against them, they destroyed Jerusalem and exiled most of the population. But the Babylonians were displaced, in turn, by the Persians under Cyrus, who captured the city of Babylon in 539 BC. In all the territories he conquered, Cyrus allowed exiled populations to return to their homelands. As soon as they could anticipate his victory over the Babylonians, many of the exiled Judeans began to believe that the promises of their restoration might soon come true. The final two sections of the book of Isaiah speak to these later developments.

: In the seventh section, the people are told their *hard service has been completed*, and they're promised a return to Judea. The later oracles in this section introduce a servant figure with a complex identity. Sometimes he's the prophet, who says, the LORD *formed me in the womb to be his servant to bring Jacob back to him and gather Israel to himself*. But he's also the nation, *Israel, my servant, Jacob, whom I have chosen, you descendants of Abraham my friend*. Cyrus is sometimes described as this servant. But the figure will also bear *the sin of many* and make *intercession for the transgressors*. He will remove Israel's shame and end the curse on creation: *instead of the thornbush will grow the juniper*. God's good promise will not return empty, but will accomplish all that he desires—Israel's, and ultimately the whole world's, return from exile (pp. 146–183).

: The eighth section contains oracles addressed to the Judean community after its return from exile. The city walls and temple are being rebuilt. The people have their own rulers again. But they have to be warned to maintain justice. This last section culminates with a vision the book has presented several times before: Jerusalem will be rebuilt in splendor and Israel will fulfill its calling to be God's agent in bringing blessing to the world (pp. 183–205).

The book of Isaiah speaks to two different situations 150 years apart. Nevertheless, it presents a unified vision. It teaches that God will use conquest and exile to purify the people from complacency, idolatry and injustice, and then he will bring them back to their homeland. There they will become a *light for the Gentiles,* and the *glory of the Lord* will be seen throughout the earth. The book looks ahead to the coming of the *Wonderful Counselor, Mighty God, Everlasting Father, Prince of Peace* who will establish God's reign over *new heavens and a new earth*.

ISAIAH

The vision concerning Judah and Jerusalem that Isaiah son of Amoz saw during the reigns of Uzziah, Jotham, Ahaz and Hezekiah, kings of Judah.

Hear me, you heavens! Listen, earth!
For the Lord has spoken:

"I reared children and brought them up,
but they have rebelled against me.

The ox knows its master,
the donkey its owner's manger,

but Israel does not know,
my people do not understand."

Woe to the sinful nation,
a people whose guilt is great,

a brood of evildoers,
children given to corruption!

They have forsaken the Lord;
they have spurned the Holy One of Israel
and turned their backs on him.

Why should you be beaten anymore?
Why do you persist in rebellion?

Your whole head is injured,
your whole heart afflicted.

From the sole of your foot to the top of your head
there is no soundness—

only wounds and welts
and open sores,

not cleansed or bandaged
or soothed with olive oil.

Your country is desolate,
your cities burned with fire;

your fields are being stripped by foreigners
right before you,
laid waste as when overthrown by strangers.

Daughter Zion is left
like a shelter in a vineyard,

like a hut in a cucumber field,
like a city under siege.

Unless the LORD Almighty
had left us some survivors,

we would have become like Sodom,
we would have been like Gomorrah.

Hear the word of the LORD,
you rulers of Sodom;

listen to the instruction of our God,
you people of Gomorrah!

"The multitude of your sacrifices—
what are they to me?" says the LORD.

"I have more than enough of burnt offerings,
of rams and the fat of fattened animals;

I have no pleasure
in the blood of bulls and lambs and goats.

When you come to appear before me,
who has asked this of you,
this trampling of my courts?

Stop bringing meaningless offerings!
Your incense is detestable to me.

New Moons, Sabbaths and convocations—
I cannot bear your worthless assemblies.

Your New Moon feasts and your appointed festivals
I hate with all my being.

They have become a burden to me;
I am weary of bearing them.

When you spread out your hands in prayer,
I hide my eyes from you;

even when you offer many prayers,
I am not listening.

Your hands are full of blood!

Wash and make yourselves clean.
Take your evil deeds out of my sight;
stop doing wrong.

Learn to do right; seek justice.
Defend the oppressed.

Take up the cause of the fatherless;
plead the case of the widow.

"Come now, let us settle the matter,"
says the LORD.

"Though your sins are like scarlet,
they shall be as white as snow;

though they are red as crimson,
they shall be like wool.

If you are willing and obedient,
you will eat the good things of the land;

but if you resist and rebel,
you will be devoured by the sword."

For the mouth of the LORD has spoken.

See how the faithful city
has become a prostitute!

She once was full of justice;
righteousness used to dwell in her —
but now murderers!

Your silver has become dross,
your choice wine is diluted with water.

Your rulers are rebels,
partners with thieves;

they all love bribes
and chase after gifts.

They do not defend the cause of the fatherless;
the widow's case does not come before them.

Therefore the Lord, the LORD Almighty,
the Mighty One of Israel, declares:

"Ah! I will vent my wrath on my foes
and avenge myself on my enemies.

I will turn my hand against you;
I will thoroughly purge away your dross
and remove all your impurities.

I will restore your leaders as in days of old,
your rulers as at the beginning.

Afterward you will be called
the City of Righteousness,
the Faithful City."

Zion will be delivered with justice,
her penitent ones with righteousness.

But rebels and sinners will both be broken,
and those who forsake the LORD will perish.

"You will be ashamed because of the sacred oaks
in which you have delighted;

you will be disgraced because of the gardens
that you have chosen.

You will be like an oak with fading leaves,
like a garden without water.

The mighty man will become tinder
and his work a spark;

both will burn together,
with no one to quench the fire."

This is what Isaiah son of Amoz saw concerning Judah and Jerusalem:

In the last days

the mountain of the LORD's temple will be established
as the highest of the mountains;

it will be exalted above the hills,
and all nations will stream to it.

Many peoples will come and say,

"Come, let us go up to the mountain of the LORD,
to the temple of the God of Jacob.

He will teach us his ways,
so that we may walk in his paths."

The law will go out from Zion,
the word of the Lord from Jerusalem.

He will judge between the nations
and will settle disputes for many peoples.

They will beat their swords into plowshares
and their spears into pruning hooks.

Nation will not take up sword against nation,
nor will they train for war anymore.

Come, descendants of Jacob,
let us walk in the light of the Lord.

You, Lord, have abandoned your people,
the descendants of Jacob.

They are full of superstitions from the East;
they practice divination like the Philistines
and embrace pagan customs.

Their land is full of silver and gold;
there is no end to their treasures.

Their land is full of horses;
there is no end to their chariots.

Their land is full of idols;
they bow down to the work of their hands,
to what their fingers have made.

So people will be brought low
and everyone humbled—
do not forgive them.

Go into the rocks, hide in the ground
from the fearful presence of the Lord
and the splendor of his majesty!

The eyes of the arrogant will be humbled
and human pride brought low;
the Lord alone will be exalted in that day.

The Lord Almighty has a day in store
for all the proud and lofty,

for all that is exalted
(and they will be humbled),

for all the cedars of Lebanon, tall and lofty,
and all the oaks of Bashan,

for all the towering mountains
and all the high hills,

for every lofty tower
and every fortified wall,

for every trading ship
and every stately vessel.

The arrogance of man will be brought low
and human pride humbled;

the Lord alone will be exalted in that day,
and the idols will totally disappear.

People will flee to caves in the rocks
and to holes in the ground

from the fearful presence of the Lord
and the splendor of his majesty,
when he rises to shake the earth.

In that day people will throw away
to the moles and bats

their idols of silver and idols of gold,
which they made to worship.

They will flee to caverns in the rocks
and to the overhanging crags

from the fearful presence of the Lord
and the splendor of his majesty,
when he rises to shake the earth.

Stop trusting in mere humans,
who have but a breath in their nostrils.
Why hold them in esteem?

See now, the Lord,
the Lord Almighty,

is about to take from Jerusalem and Judah
both supply and support:

all supplies of food and all supplies of water,
the hero and the warrior,

the judge and the prophet,
the diviner and the elder,

the captain of fifty and the man of rank,
the counselor, skilled craftsman and clever enchanter.

"I will make mere youths their officials;
children will rule over them."

People will oppress each other —
man against man, neighbor against neighbor.

The young will rise up against the old,
the nobody against the honored.

A man will seize one of his brothers
in his father's house, and say,

"You have a cloak, you be our leader;
take charge of this heap of ruins!"

But in that day he will cry out,
"I have no remedy.

I have no food or clothing in my house;
do not make me the leader of the people."

Jerusalem staggers,
Judah is falling;

their words and deeds are against the Lord,
defying his glorious presence.

The look on their faces testifies against them;
they parade their sin like Sodom;
they do not hide it.

Woe to them!
They have brought disaster upon themselves.

Tell the righteous it will be well with them,
for they will enjoy the fruit of their deeds.

Woe to the wicked!
Disaster is upon them!

They will be paid back
for what their hands have done.

Youths oppress my people,
women rule over them.

My people, your guides lead you astray;
they turn you from the path.

The LORD takes his place in court;
he rises to judge the people.

The LORD enters into judgment
against the elders and leaders of his people:

"It is you who have ruined my vineyard;
the plunder from the poor is in your houses.

What do you mean by crushing my people
and grinding the faces of the poor?"
declares the Lord, the LORD Almighty.

The LORD says,
"The women of Zion are haughty,

walking along with outstretched necks,
flirting with their eyes,

strutting along with swaying hips,
with ornaments jingling on their ankles.

Therefore the Lord will bring sores on the heads of the
women of Zion;
the LORD will make their scalps bald."

In that day the Lord will snatch away their finery: the bangles
and headbands and crescent necklaces, the earrings and bracelets
and veils, the headdresses and anklets and sashes, the perfume bot-
tles and charms, the signet rings and nose rings, the fine robes and
the capes and cloaks, the purses and mirrors, and the linen garments and tiaras and shawls.

Instead of fragrance there will be a stench;
instead of a sash, a rope;

instead of well-dressed hair, baldness;
instead of fine clothing, sackcloth;
instead of beauty, branding.

Your men will fall by the sword,
your warriors in battle.

The gates of Zion will lament and mourn;
destitute, she will sit on the ground.

In that day seven women
will take hold of one man

and say, "We will eat our own food
and provide our own clothes;
only let us be called by your name.
Take away our disgrace!"

In that day the Branch of the LORD will be beautiful and glorious,
and the fruit of the land will be the pride and glory of the survivors
in Israel. Those who are left in Zion, who remain in Jerusalem, will
be called holy, all who are recorded among the living in Jerusalem.
The Lord will wash away the filth of the women of Zion; he will
cleanse the bloodstains from Jerusalem by a spirit of judgment and
a spirit of fire. Then the LORD will create over all of Mount Zion and
over those who assemble there a cloud of smoke by day and a glow
of flaming fire by night; over everything the glory will be a canopy.
It will be a shelter and shade from the heat of the day, and a refuge
and hiding place from the storm and rain.

I will sing for the one I love
a song about his vineyard:
My loved one had a vineyard
on a fertile hillside.
He dug it up and cleared it of stones
and planted it with the choicest vines.
He built a watchtower in it
and cut out a winepress as well.
Then he looked for a crop of good grapes,
but it yielded only bad fruit.

"Now you dwellers in Jerusalem and people of Judah,
judge between me and my vineyard.
What more could have been done for my vineyard
than I have done for it?
When I looked for good grapes,
why did it yield only bad?
Now I will tell you
what I am going to do to my vineyard:
I will take away its hedge,
and it will be destroyed;
I will break down its wall,
and it will be trampled.

I will make it a wasteland,
neither pruned nor cultivated,
and briers and thorns will grow there.

I will command the clouds
not to rain on it."

The vineyard of the Lord Almighty
is the nation of Israel,

and the people of Judah
are the vines he delighted in.

And he looked for justice, but saw bloodshed;
for righteousness, but heard cries of distress.

Woe to you who add house to house
and join field to field

till no space is left
and you live alone in the land.

The Lord Almighty has declared in my hearing:

"Surely the great houses will become desolate,
the fine mansions left without occupants.

A ten-acre vineyard will produce only a bath of wine;
a homer of seed will yield only an ephah of grain."

Woe to those who rise early in the morning
to run after their drinks,

who stay up late at night
till they are inflamed with wine.

They have harps and lyres at their banquets,
pipes and timbrels and wine,

but they have no regard for the deeds of the Lord,
no respect for the work of his hands.

Therefore my people will go into exile
for lack of understanding;

those of high rank will die of hunger
and the common people will be parched with thirst.

Therefore Death expands its jaws,
opening wide its mouth;

into it will descend their nobles and masses
with all their brawlers and revelers.

So people will be brought low
and everyone humbled,
the eyes of the arrogant humbled.

But the Lord Almighty will be exalted by his justice,
and the holy God will be proved holy by his righteous
    acts.

Then sheep will graze as in their own pasture;
lambs will feed among the ruins of the rich.

Woe to those who draw sin along with cords of deceit,
and wickedness as with cart ropes,

to those who say, "Let God hurry;
let him hasten his work
so we may see it.
The plan of the Holy One of Israel—
let it approach, let it come into view,
so we may know it."

Woe to those who call evil good
and good evil,

who put darkness for light
and light for darkness,

who put bitter for sweet
and sweet for bitter.

Woe to those who are wise in their own eyes
and clever in their own sight.

Woe to those who are heroes at drinking wine
and champions at mixing drinks,

who acquit the guilty for a bribe,
but deny justice to the innocent.

Therefore, as tongues of fire lick up straw
and as dry grass sinks down in the flames,

so their roots will decay
and their flowers blow away like dust;

for they have rejected the law of the Lord Almighty
and spurned the word of the Holy One of Israel.

Therefore the Lord's anger burns against his people;
his hand is raised and he strikes them down.

The mountains shake,
and the dead bodies are like refuse in the streets.

Yet for all this, his anger is not turned away,
his hand is still upraised.

He lifts up a banner for the distant nations,
he whistles for those at the ends of the earth.
Here they come,
swiftly and speedily!
Not one of them grows tired or stumbles,
not one slumbers or sleeps;
not a belt is loosened at the waist,
not a sandal strap is broken.

Their arrows are sharp,
all their bows are strung;
their horses' hooves seem like flint,
their chariot wheels like a whirlwind.

Their roar is like that of the lion,
they roar like young lions;
they growl as they seize their prey
and carry it off with no one to rescue.

In that day they will roar over it
like the roaring of the sea.

And if one looks at the land,
there is only darkness and distress;
even the sun will be darkened by clouds.

In the year that King Uzziah died, I saw the Lord, high and exalted, seated on a throne; and the train of his robe filled the temple. Above him were seraphim, each with six wings: With two wings they covered their faces, with two they covered their feet, and with two they were flying. And they were calling to one another:

"Holy, holy, holy is the LORD Almighty;
the whole earth is full of his glory."

At the sound of their voices the doorposts and thresholds shook and the temple was filled with smoke.

"Woe to me!" I cried. "I am ruined! For I am a man of unclean lips, and I live among a people of unclean lips, and my eyes have seen the King, the LORD Almighty."

Then one of the seraphim flew to me with a live coal in his hand, which he had taken with tongs from the altar. With it he touched my mouth and said, "See, this has touched your lips; your guilt is taken away and your sin atoned for."

Then I heard the voice of the Lord saying, "Whom shall I send? And who will go for us?"

And I said, "Here am I. Send me!"

He said, "Go and tell this people:

> " 'Be ever hearing, but never understanding;
> be ever seeing, but never perceiving.'

> Make the heart of this people calloused;
> make their ears dull
> and close their eyes.

> Otherwise they might see with their eyes,
> hear with their ears,
> understand with their hearts,

> and turn and be healed."

Then I said, "For how long, Lord?"

And he answered:

> "Until the cities lie ruined
> and without inhabitant,

> until the houses are left deserted
> and the fields ruined and ravaged,
> until the LORD has sent everyone far away
> and the land is utterly forsaken.

> And though a tenth remains in the land,
> it will again be laid waste.

> But as the terebinth and oak
> leave stumps when they are cut down,
> so the holy seed will be the stump in the land."

When Ahaz son of Jotham, the son of Uzziah, was king of Judah, King Rezin of Aram and Pekah son of Remaliah king of Israel marched up to fight against Jerusalem, but they could not overpower it.

Now the house of David was told, "Aram has allied itself with Ephraim"; so the hearts of Ahaz and his people were shaken, as the trees of the forest are shaken by the wind.

Then the LORD said to Isaiah, "Go out, you and your son Shear-Jashub, to meet Ahaz at the end of the aqueduct of the Upper Pool, on the road to the Launderer's Field. Say to him, 'Be careful, keep calm and don't be afraid. Do not lose heart because of these two smoldering stubs of firewood — because of the fierce anger of Rezin and Aram and of the son of Remaliah. Aram, Ephraim and Remaliah's son have plotted your ruin, saying, "Let us invade Judah; let us tear it apart and divide it among ourselves, and make the son of Tabeel king over it." Yet this is what the Sovereign LORD says:

> " 'It will not take place,
> it will not happen,
> for the head of Aram is Damascus,
> and the head of Damascus is only Rezin.
>
> Within sixty-five years
> Ephraim will be too shattered to be a people.
> The head of Ephraim is Samaria,
> and the head of Samaria is only Remaliah's son.
>
> If you do not stand firm in your faith,
> you will not stand at all.' "

Again the LORD spoke to Ahaz, "Ask the LORD your God for a sign, whether in the deepest depths or in the highest heights."

But Ahaz said, "I will not ask; I will not put the LORD to the test."

Then Isaiah said, "Hear now, you house of David! Is it not enough to try the patience of humans? Will you try the patience of my God also? Therefore the Lord himself will give you a sign: The virgin will conceive and give birth to a son, and will call him Immanuel. He will be eating curds and honey when he knows enough to reject the wrong and choose the right, for before the boy knows enough to reject the wrong and choose the right, the land of the two kings you dread will be laid waste. The LORD will bring on you and on your people and on the house of your father a time unlike any since Ephraim broke away from Judah — he will bring the king of Assyria."

In that day the LORD will whistle for flies from the Nile delta in Egypt and for bees from the land of Assyria. They will all come and settle in the steep ravines and in the crevices in the rocks, on all the thornbushes and at all the water holes. In that day the Lord will use a razor hired from beyond the Euphrates River — the king of Assyria — to shave your head and private parts, and to cut off your beard also. In that day, a person will keep alive a young cow and two goats. And because of the abundance of the milk they give, there will be curds to eat. All who remain in the land will eat curds and honey. In that day, in every place where there were a thousand vines worth a thousand silver shekels, there will be only briers and thorns. Hunters will go there with bow and arrow, for the land will be covered with briers and thorns. As for all the hills once cultivated by the hoe, you will no longer go there for fear of the briers and thorns; they will become places where cattle are turned loose and where sheep run.

The Lord said to me, "Take a large scroll and write on it with an ordinary pen: Maher-Shalal-Hash-Baz." So I called in Uriah the priest and Zechariah son of Jeberekiah as reliable witnesses for me. Then I made love to the prophetess, and she conceived and gave birth to a son. And the Lord said to me, "Name him Maher-Shalal-Hash-Baz. For before the boy knows how to say 'My father' or 'My mother,' the wealth of Damascus and the plunder of Samaria will be carried off by the king of Assyria."

The Lord spoke to me again:

> "Because this people has rejected
> the gently flowing waters of Shiloah
> and rejoices over Rezin
> and the son of Remaliah,
>
> therefore the Lord is about to bring against them
> the mighty floodwaters of the Euphrates—
> the king of Assyria with all his pomp.
>
> It will overflow all its channels,
> run over all its banks
>
> and sweep on into Judah, swirling over it,
> passing through it and reaching up to the neck.
>
> Its outspread wings will cover the breadth of your land,
> Immanuel!"
>
> Raise the war cry, you nations, and be shattered!
> Listen, all you distant lands.
>
> Prepare for battle, and be shattered!
> Prepare for battle, and be shattered!
>
> Devise your strategy, but it will be thwarted;
> propose your plan, but it will not stand,
> for God is with us.

This is what the Lord says to me with his strong hand upon me, warning me not to follow the way of this people:

"Do not call conspiracy
everything this people calls a conspiracy;
do not fear what they fear,
and do not dread it.
The Lord Almighty is the one you are to regard as holy,
he is the one you are to fear,
he is the one you are to dread.
He will be a holy place;
for both Israel and Judah he will be
a stone that causes people to stumble
and a rock that makes them fall.
And for the people of Jerusalem he will be
a trap and a snare.
Many of them will stumble;
they will fall and be broken,
they will be snared and captured."

Bind up this testimony of warning
and seal up God's instruction among my disciples.
I will wait for the Lord,
who is hiding his face from the descendants of Jacob.
I will put my trust in him.

Here am I, and the children the Lord has given me. We are
signs and symbols in Israel from the Lord Almighty, who dwells
on Mount Zion.

When someone tells you to consult mediums and spiritists,
who whisper and mutter, should not a people inquire of their God?
Why consult the dead on behalf of the living? Consult God's instruction and the testimony of warning. If anyone does not speak
according to this word, they have no light of dawn. Distressed and
hungry, they will roam through the land; when they are famished,
they will become enraged and, looking upward, will curse their king
and their God. Then they will look toward the earth and see only
distress and darkness and fearful gloom, and they will be thrust
into utter darkness.

Nevertheless, there will be no more gloom for those who were in
distress. In the past he humbled the land of Zebulun and the land
of Naphtali, but in the future he will honor Galilee of the nations,
by the Way of the Sea, beyond the Jordan —

The people walking in darkness
have seen a great light;
on those living in the land of deep darkness
a light has dawned.

You have enlarged the nation
and increased their joy;
they rejoice before you
as people rejoice at the harvest,
as warriors rejoice
when dividing the plunder.

For as in the day of Midian's defeat,
you have shattered
the yoke that burdens them,
the bar across their shoulders,
the rod of their oppressor.

Every warrior's boot used in battle
and every garment rolled in blood
will be destined for burning,
will be fuel for the fire.

For to us a child is born,
to us a son is given,
and the government will be on his shoulders.

And he will be called
Wonderful Counselor, Mighty God,
Everlasting Father, Prince of Peace.

Of the greatness of his government and peace
there will be no end.

He will reign on David's throne
and over his kingdom,
establishing and upholding it
with justice and righteousness
from that time on and forever.

The zeal of the LORD Almighty
will accomplish this.

The Lord has sent a message against Jacob;
it will fall on Israel.

All the people will know it —
Ephraim and the inhabitants of Samaria —

who say with pride
and arrogance of heart,

"The bricks have fallen down,
but we will rebuild with dressed stone;

the fig trees have been felled,
but we will replace them with cedars."

But the Lord has strengthened Rezin's foes against them
and has spurred their enemies on.

Arameans from the east and Philistines from the west
have devoured Israel with open mouth.

Yet for all this, his anger is not turned away,
his hand is still upraised.

But the people have not returned to him who struck
them,
nor have they sought the Lord Almighty.

So the Lord will cut off from Israel both head and tail,
both palm branch and reed in a single day;

the elders and dignitaries are the head,
the prophets who teach lies are the tail.

Those who guide this people mislead them,
and those who are guided are led astray.

Therefore the Lord will take no pleasure in the young
men,
nor will he pity the fatherless and widows,

for everyone is ungodly and wicked,
every mouth speaks folly.

Yet for all this, his anger is not turned away,
his hand is still upraised.

Surely wickedness burns like a fire;
it consumes briers and thorns,

it sets the forest thickets ablaze,
so that it rolls upward in a column of smoke.

By the wrath of the Lord Almighty
the land will be scorched

and the people will be fuel for the fire;
they will not spare one another.

On the right they will devour,
but still be hungry;

on the left they will eat,
but not be satisfied.

Each will feed on the flesh of their own offspring:
Manasseh will feed on Ephraim, and Ephraim on
    Manasseh;
together they will turn against Judah.

Yet for all this, his anger is not turned away,
his hand is still upraised.

Woe to those who make unjust laws,
to those who issue oppressive decrees,

to deprive the poor of their rights
and withhold justice from the oppressed of my people,

making widows their prey
and robbing the fatherless.

What will you do on the day of reckoning,
when disaster comes from afar?
To whom will you run for help?
Where will you leave your riches?

Nothing will remain but to cringe among the captives
or fall among the slain.

Yet for all this, his anger is not turned away,
his hand is still upraised.

"Woe to the Assyrian, the rod of my anger,
in whose hand is the club of my wrath!
I send him against a godless nation,
I dispatch him against a people who anger me,
to seize loot and snatch plunder,
and to trample them down like mud in the streets.
But this is not what he intends,
this is not what he has in mind;
his purpose is to destroy,
to put an end to many nations.
'Are not my commanders all kings?' he says.
'Has not Kalno fared like Carchemish?
Is not Hamath like Arpad,
and Samaria like Damascus?

As my hand seized the kingdoms of the idols,
kingdoms whose images excelled those of Jerusalem and
Samaria —
shall I not deal with Jerusalem and her images
as I dealt with Samaria and her idols?' "

When the Lord has finished all his work against Mount Zion
and Jerusalem, he will say, "I will punish the king of Assyria for the
willful pride of his heart and the haughty look in his eyes. For he
says:

" 'By the strength of my hand I have done this,
and by my wisdom, because I have understanding.
I removed the boundaries of nations,
I plundered their treasures;
like a mighty one I subdued their kings.
As one reaches into a nest,
so my hand reached for the wealth of the nations;
as people gather abandoned eggs,
so I gathered all the countries;
not one flapped a wing,
or opened its mouth to chirp.' "

Does the ax raise itself above the person who
swings it,
or the saw boast against the one who uses it?
As if a rod were to wield the person who lifts it up,
or a club brandish the one who is not wood!
Therefore, the Lord, the LORD Almighty,
will send a wasting disease upon his sturdy
warriors;
under his pomp a fire will be kindled
like a blazing flame.
The Light of Israel will become a fire,
their Holy One a flame;
in a single day it will burn and consume
his thorns and his briers.
The splendor of his forests and fertile fields
it will completely destroy,
as when a sick person wastes away.
And the remaining trees of his forests will be so few
that a child could write them down.

In that day the remnant of Israel,
the survivors of Jacob,

will no longer rely on him
who struck them down

but will truly rely on the Lord,
the Holy One of Israel.

A remnant will return, a remnant of Jacob
will return to the Mighty God.

Though your people be like the sand by the sea,
Israel,
only a remnant will return.

Destruction has been decreed,
overwhelming and righteous.

The Lord, the Lord Almighty, will carry out
the destruction decreed upon the whole land.

Therefore this is what the Lord, the Lord Almighty, says:

"My people who live in Zion,
do not be afraid of the Assyrians,

who beat you with a rod
and lift up a club against you, as Egypt did.

Very soon my anger against you will end
and my wrath will be directed to their destruction."

The Lord Almighty will lash them with a whip,
as when he struck down Midian at the rock of Oreb;

and he will raise his staff over the waters,
as he did in Egypt.

In that day their burden will be lifted from your
shoulders,
their yoke from your neck;

the yoke will be broken
because you have grown so fat.

They enter Aiath;
they pass through Migron;
they store supplies at Mikmash.

They go over the pass, and say,
"We will camp overnight at Geba."

Ramah trembles;
Gibeah of Saul flees.

Cry out, Daughter Gallim!
Listen, Laishah!
Poor Anathoth!

Madmenah is in flight;
the people of Gebim take cover.

This day they will halt at Nob;
they will shake their fist

at the mount of Daughter Zion,
at the hill of Jerusalem.

See, the Lord, the Lord Almighty,
will lop off the boughs with great power.

The lofty trees will be felled,
the tall ones will be brought low.

He will cut down the forest thickets with an ax;
Lebanon will fall before the Mighty One.

A shoot will come up from the stump of Jesse;
from his roots a Branch will bear fruit.

The Spirit of the Lord will rest on him—
the Spirit of wisdom and of understanding,
the Spirit of counsel and of might,
the Spirit of the knowledge and fear of the Lord—

and he will delight in the fear of the Lord.

He will not judge by what he sees with his eyes,
or decide by what he hears with his ears;

but with righteousness he will judge the needy,
with justice he will give decisions for the poor of the
    earth.

He will strike the earth with the rod of his mouth;
with the breath of his lips he will slay the wicked.

Righteousness will be his belt
and faithfulness the sash around his waist.

The wolf will live with the lamb,
the leopard will lie down with the goat,

the calf and the lion and the yearling together;
and a little child will lead them.

The cow will feed with the bear,
their young will lie down together,
and the lion will eat straw like the ox.

The infant will play near the cobra's den,
and the young child will put its hand into the viper's
nest.

They will neither harm nor destroy
on all my holy mountain,

for the earth will be filled with the knowledge
of the Lord
as the waters cover the sea.

In that day the Root of Jesse will stand as a banner for the peoples; the nations will rally to him, and his resting place will be glorious. In that day the Lord will reach out his hand a second time to reclaim the surviving remnant of his people from Assyria, from Lower Egypt, from Upper Egypt, from Cush, from Elam, from Babylonia, from Hamath and from the islands of the Mediterranean.

He will raise a banner for the nations
and gather the exiles of Israel;

he will assemble the scattered people of Judah
from the four quarters of the earth.

Ephraim's jealousy will vanish,
and Judah's enemies will be destroyed;

Ephraim will not be jealous of Judah,
nor Judah hostile toward Ephraim.

They will swoop down on the slopes of Philistia to the
west;
together they will plunder the people to the east.

They will subdue Edom and Moab,
and the Ammonites will be subject to them.

The Lord will dry up
the gulf of the Egyptian sea;

with a scorching wind he will sweep his hand
over the Euphrates River.

He will break it up into seven streams
so that anyone can cross over in sandals.

There will be a highway for the remnant of his people
that is left from Assyria,

as there was for Israel
when they came up from Egypt.

In that day you will say:

> "I will praise you, LORD.
> Although you were angry with me,
>
> your anger has turned away
> and you have comforted me.
>
> Surely God is my salvation;
> I will trust and not be afraid.
>
> The LORD, the LORD himself, is my strength and
>   my defense;
> he has become my salvation."
>
> With joy you will draw water
> from the wells of salvation.

In that day you will say:

> "Give praise to the LORD, proclaim his name;
> make known among the nations what he has done,
> and proclaim that his name is exalted.
>
> Sing to the LORD, for he has done glorious things;
> let this be known to all the world.
>
> Shout aloud and sing for joy, people of Zion,
> for great is the Holy One of Israel among you."

A prophecy against Babylon that Isaiah son of Amoz saw:

> Raise a banner on a bare hilltop,
> shout to them;
>
> beckon to them
> to enter the gates of the nobles.
>
> I have commanded those I prepared for battle;
> I have summoned my warriors to carry out my wrath —
> those who rejoice in my triumph.
>
> Listen, a noise on the mountains,
> like that of a great multitude!
>
> Listen, an uproar among the kingdoms,
> like nations massing together!

The LORD Almighty is mustering
an army for war.

They come from faraway lands,
from the ends of the heavens—

the LORD and the weapons of his wrath—
to destroy the whole country.

Wail, for the day of the LORD is near;
it will come like destruction from the Almighty.

Because of this, all hands will go limp,
every heart will melt with fear.

Terror will seize them,
pain and anguish will grip them;
they will writhe like a woman in labor.

They will look aghast at each other,
their faces aflame.

See, the day of the LORD is coming
—a cruel day, with wrath and fierce anger—
to make the land desolate
and destroy the sinners within it.

The stars of heaven and their constellations
will not show their light.

The rising sun will be darkened
and the moon will not give its light.

I will punish the world for its evil,
the wicked for their sins.

I will put an end to the arrogance of the haughty
and will humble the pride of the ruthless.

I will make people scarcer than pure gold,
more rare than the gold of Ophir.

Therefore I will make the heavens tremble;
and the earth will shake from its place

at the wrath of the LORD Almighty,
in the day of his burning anger.

Like a hunted gazelle,
like sheep without a shepherd,

they will all return to their own people,
they will flee to their native land.

Whoever is captured will be thrust through;
all who are caught will fall by the sword.

Their infants will be dashed to pieces before their eyes;
their houses will be looted and their wives violated.

See, I will stir up against them the Medes,
who do not care for silver
and have no delight in gold.

Their bows will strike down the young men;
they will have no mercy on infants,
nor will they look with compassion on children.

Babylon, the jewel of kingdoms,
the pride and glory of the Babylonians,

will be overthrown by God
like Sodom and Gomorrah.

She will never be inhabited
or lived in through all generations;

there no nomads will pitch their tents,
there no shepherds will rest their flocks.

But desert creatures will lie there,
jackals will fill her houses;

there the owls will dwell,
and there the wild goats will leap about.

Hyenas will inhabit her strongholds,
jackals her luxurious palaces.

Her time is at hand,
and her days will not be prolonged.

The Lord will have compassion on Jacob;
once again he will choose Israel
and will settle them in their own land.

Foreigners will join them
and unite with the descendants of Jacob.

Nations will take them
and bring them to their own place.

And Israel will take possession of the nations
and make them male and female servants in the Lord's
land.

They will make captives of their captors
and rule over their oppressors.

On the day the LORD gives you relief from your suffering and turmoil and from the harsh labor forced on you, you will take up this taunt against the king of Babylon:

> How the oppressor has come to an end!
> How his fury has ended!

> The LORD has broken the rod of the wicked,
> the scepter of the rulers,

> which in anger struck down peoples
> with unceasing blows,

> and in fury subdued nations
> with relentless aggression.

> All the lands are at rest and at peace;
> they break into singing.

> Even the junipers and the cedars of Lebanon
> gloat over you and say,

> "Now that you have been laid low,
> no one comes to cut us down."

> The realm of the dead below is all astir
> to meet you at your coming;

> it rouses the spirits of the departed to greet you—
> all those who were leaders in the world;

> it makes them rise from their thrones—
> all those who were kings over the nations.

> They will all respond,
> they will say to you,

> "You also have become weak, as we are;
> you have become like us."

> All your pomp has been brought down to the grave,
> along with the noise of your harps;

> maggots are spread out beneath you
> and worms cover you.

> How you have fallen from heaven,
> morning star, son of the dawn!

> You have been cast down to the earth,
> you who once laid low the nations!

> You said in your heart,
> "I will ascend to the heavens;

I will raise my throne
above the stars of God;
I will sit enthroned on the mount of assembly,
on the utmost heights of Mount Zaphon.
I will ascend above the tops of the clouds;
I will make myself like the Most High."
But you are brought down to the realm of the dead,
to the depths of the pit.

Those who see you stare at you,
they ponder your fate:
"Is this the man who shook the earth
and made kingdoms tremble,
the man who made the world a wilderness,
who overthrew its cities
and would not let his captives go home?"

All the kings of the nations lie in state,
each in his own tomb.
But you are cast out of your tomb
like a rejected branch;
you are covered with the slain,
with those pierced by the sword,
those who descend to the stones of the pit.
Like a corpse trampled underfoot,
you will not join them in burial,
for you have destroyed your land
and killed your people.

Let the offspring of the wicked
never be mentioned again.
Prepare a place to slaughter his children
for the sins of their ancestors;
they are not to rise to inherit the land
and cover the earth with their cities.

"I will rise up against them,"
declares the Lord Almighty.
"I will wipe out Babylon's name and survivors,
her offspring and descendants,"
declares the Lord.

"I will turn her into a place for owls
and into swampland;

I will sweep her with the broom of destruction,"
declares the Lord Almighty.

The Lord Almighty has sworn,

"Surely, as I have planned, so it will be,
and as I have purposed, so it will happen.

I will crush the Assyrian in my land;
on my mountains I will trample him down.

His yoke will be taken from my people,
and his burden removed from their shoulders."

This is the plan determined for the whole world;
this is the hand stretched out over all nations.

For the Lord Almighty has purposed, and who can
thwart him?

His hand is stretched out, and who can turn it back?

This prophecy came in the year King Ahaz died:

Do not rejoice, all you Philistines,
that the rod that struck you is broken;

from the root of that snake will spring up a viper,
its fruit will be a darting, venomous serpent.

The poorest of the poor will find pasture,
and the needy will lie down in safety.

But your root I will destroy by famine;
it will slay your survivors.

Wail, you gate! Howl, you city!
Melt away, all you Philistines!

A cloud of smoke comes from the north,
and there is not a straggler in its ranks.

What answer shall be given
to the envoys of that nation?

"The Lord has established Zion,
and in her his afflicted people will find refuge."

A prophecy against Moab:

> Ar in Moab is ruined,
> destroyed in a night!
>
> Kir in Moab is ruined,
> destroyed in a night!
>
> Dibon goes up to its temple,
> to its high places to weep;
> Moab wails over Nebo and Medeba.
>
> Every head is shaved
> and every beard cut off.
>
> In the streets they wear sackcloth;
> on the roofs and in the public squares
> they all wail,
> prostrate with weeping.
>
> Heshbon and Elealeh cry out,
> their voices are heard all the way to Jahaz.
>
> Therefore the armed men of Moab cry out,
> and their hearts are faint.
>
> My heart cries out over Moab;
> her fugitives flee as far as Zoar,
> as far as Eglath Shelishiyah.
>
> They go up the hill to Luhith,
> weeping as they go;
>
> on the road to Horonaim
> they lament their destruction.
>
> The waters of Nimrim are dried up
> and the grass is withered;
>
> the vegetation is gone
> and nothing green is left.
>
> So the wealth they have acquired and stored up
> they carry away over the Ravine of the Poplars.
>
> Their outcry echoes along the border of Moab;
> their wailing reaches as far as Eglaim,
> their lamentation as far as Beer Elim.
>
> The waters of Dimon are full of blood,
> but I will bring still more upon Dimon —

a lion upon the fugitives of Moab
and upon those who remain in the land.

Send lambs as tribute
to the ruler of the land,
from Sela, across the desert,
to the mount of Daughter Zion.

Like fluttering birds
pushed from the nest,
so are the women of Moab
at the fords of the Arnon.

"Make up your mind," Moab says.
"Render a decision.

Make your shadow like night —
at high noon.
Hide the fugitives,
do not betray the refugees.

Let the Moabite fugitives stay with you;
be their shelter from the destroyer."

The oppressor will come to an end,
and destruction will cease;
the aggressor will vanish from the land.

In love a throne will be established;
in faithfulness a man will sit on it —
one from the house of David —
one who in judging seeks justice
and speeds the cause of righteousness.

We have heard of Moab's pride —
how great is her arrogance! —
of her conceit, her pride and her insolence;
but her boasts are empty.

Therefore the Moabites wail,
they wail together for Moab.
Lament and grieve
for the raisin cakes of Kir Hareseth.

The fields of Heshbon wither,
the vines of Sibmah also.

The rulers of the nations
have trampled down the choicest vines,

which once reached Jazer
and spread toward the desert.

Their shoots spread out
and went as far as the sea.

So I weep, as Jazer weeps,
for the vines of Sibmah.

Heshbon and Elealeh,
I drench you with tears!

The shouts of joy over your ripened fruit
and over your harvests have been stilled.

Joy and gladness are taken away from the orchards;
no one sings or shouts in the vineyards;

no one treads out wine at the presses,
for I have put an end to the shouting.

My heart laments for Moab like a harp,
my inmost being for Kir Hareseth.

When Moab appears at her high place,
she only wears herself out;

when she goes to her shrine to pray,
it is to no avail.

This is the word the LORD has already spoken concerning Moab. But now the LORD says: "Within three years, as a servant bound by contract would count them, Moab's splendor and all her many people will be despised, and her survivors will be very few and feeble."

A prophecy against Damascus:

"See, Damascus will no longer be a city
but will become a heap of ruins.

The cities of Aroer will be deserted
and left to flocks, which will lie down,
with no one to make them afraid.

The fortified city will disappear from Ephraim,
and royal power from Damascus;

the remnant of Aram will be
like the glory of the Israelites,"
                        declares the LORD Almighty.

"In that day the glory of Jacob will fade;
　the fat of his body will waste away.

It will be as when reapers harvest the standing grain,
　gathering the grain in their arms —

as when someone gleans heads of grain
　in the Valley of Rephaim.

Yet some gleanings will remain,
　as when an olive tree is beaten,

leaving two or three olives on the topmost branches,
　four or five on the fruitful boughs,"
　　　　　　declares the Lord, the God of Israel.

In that day people will look to their Maker
　and turn their eyes to the Holy One of Israel.

They will not look to the altars,
　the work of their hands,

and they will have no regard for the Asherah poles
　and the incense altars their fingers have made.

In that day their strong cities, which they left because of the Israelites, will be like places abandoned to thickets and undergrowth. And all will be desolation.

You have forgotten God your Savior;
　you have not remembered the Rock, your fortress.

Therefore, though you set out the finest plants
　and plant imported vines,

though on the day you set them out, you make them
　　　　grow,
and on the morning when you plant them, you bring
　　　　them to bud,

yet the harvest will be as nothing
　in the day of disease and incurable pain.

Woe to the many nations that rage —
　they rage like the raging sea!

Woe to the peoples who roar —
　they roar like the roaring of great waters!

Although the peoples roar like the roar of surging
　　　　waters,
when he rebukes them they flee far away,

driven before the wind like chaff on the hills,
like tumbleweed before a gale.

In the evening, sudden terror!
Before the morning, they are gone!

This is the portion of those who loot us,
the lot of those who plunder us.

Woe to the land of whirring wings
along the rivers of Cush,

which sends envoys by sea
in papyrus boats over the water.

Go, swift messengers,

to a people tall and smooth-skinned,
to a people feared far and wide,

an aggressive nation of strange speech,
whose land is divided by rivers.

All you people of the world,
you who live on the earth,

when a banner is raised on the mountains,
you will see it,

and when a trumpet sounds,
you will hear it.

This is what the LORD says to me:
"I will remain quiet and will look on from
        my dwelling place,

like shimmering heat in the sunshine,
like a cloud of dew in the heat of harvest."

For, before the harvest, when the blossom
        is gone
and the flower becomes a ripening grape,

he will cut off the shoots with pruning knives,
and cut down and take away the spreading
        branches.

They will all be left to the mountain birds
        of prey
and to the wild animals;

the birds will feed on them all summer,
the wild animals all winter.

At that time gifts will be brought to the Lord Almighty

> from a people tall and smooth-skinned,
> from a people feared far and wide,
> an aggressive nation of strange speech,
> whose land is divided by rivers —

the gifts will be brought to Mount Zion, the place of the Name of the Lord Almighty.

A prophecy against Egypt:

> See, the Lord rides on a swift cloud
> and is coming to Egypt.
> The idols of Egypt tremble before him,
> and the hearts of the Egyptians melt with fear.
>
> "I will stir up Egyptian against Egyptian —
> brother will fight against brother,
> neighbor against neighbor,
> city against city,
> kingdom against kingdom.
> The Egyptians will lose heart,
> and I will bring their plans to nothing;
> they will consult the idols and the spirits of the dead,
> the mediums and the spiritists.
> I will hand the Egyptians over
> to the power of a cruel master,
> and a fierce king will rule over them,"
> declares the Lord, the Lord Almighty.
>
> The waters of the river will dry up,
> and the riverbed will be parched and dry.
> The canals will stink;
> the streams of Egypt will dwindle and dry up.
> The reeds and rushes will wither,
> also the plants along the Nile,
> at the mouth of the river.
> Every sown field along the Nile
> will become parched, will blow away and be no more.
> The fishermen will groan and lament,
> all who cast hooks into the Nile;

those who throw nets on the water
will pine away.

Those who work with combed flax will despair,
the weavers of fine linen will lose hope.

The workers in cloth will be dejected,
and all the wage earners will be sick at heart.

The officials of Zoan are nothing but fools;
the wise counselors of Pharaoh give senseless advice.

How can you say to Pharaoh,
"I am one of the wise men,
a disciple of the ancient kings"?

Where are your wise men now?
Let them show you and make known
what the Lord Almighty
has planned against Egypt.

The officials of Zoan have become fools,
the leaders of Memphis are deceived;
the cornerstones of her peoples
have led Egypt astray.

The Lord has poured into them
a spirit of dizziness;
they make Egypt stagger in all that she does,
as a drunkard staggers around in his vomit.

There is nothing Egypt can do —
head or tail, palm branch or reed.

In that day the Egyptians will become weaklings. They will shudder with fear at the uplifted hand that the Lord Almighty raises against them. And the land of Judah will bring terror to the Egyptians; everyone to whom Judah is mentioned will be terrified, because of what the Lord Almighty is planning against them.

In that day five cities in Egypt will speak the language of Canaan and swear allegiance to the Lord Almighty. One of them will be called the City of the Sun.

In that day there will be an altar to the Lord in the heart of Egypt, and a monument to the Lord at its border. It will be a sign and witness to the Lord Almighty in the land of Egypt. When they cry out to the Lord because of their oppressors, he will send them a savior and defender, and he will rescue them. So the Lord will make himself known to the Egyptians, and in that day they will acknowledge the Lord. They will worship with sacrifices and grain offerings; they will make vows to the Lord and keep them. The Lord will strike Egypt with a plague; he will strike them and heal them. They will turn to the Lord, and he will respond to their pleas and heal them.

In that day there will be a highway from Egypt to Assyria. The Assyrians will go to Egypt and the Egyptians to Assyria. The Egyptians and Assyrians will worship together. In that day Israel will be the third, along with Egypt and Assyria, a blessing on the earth. The Lord Almighty will bless them, saying, "Blessed be Egypt my people, Assyria my handiwork, and Israel my inheritance."

In the year that the supreme commander, sent by Sargon king of Assyria, came to Ashdod and attacked and captured it — at that time the Lord spoke through Isaiah son of Amoz. He said to him, "Take off the sackcloth from your body and the sandals from your feet." And he did so, going around stripped and barefoot.

Then the Lord said, "Just as my servant Isaiah has gone stripped and barefoot for three years, as a sign and portent against Egypt and Cush, so the king of Assyria will lead away stripped and barefoot the Egyptian captives and Cushite exiles, young and old, with buttocks bared — to Egypt's shame. Those who trusted in Cush and boasted in Egypt will be dismayed and put to shame. In that day the people who live on this coast will say, 'See what has happened to those we relied on, those we fled to for help and deliverance from the king of Assyria! How then can we escape?'"

A prophecy against the Desert by the Sea:

> Like whirlwinds sweeping through the southland,
>   an invader comes from the desert,
>   from a land of terror.
>
> A dire vision has been shown to me:
>   The traitor betrays, the looter takes loot.
>
> Elam, attack! Media, lay siege!
>   I will bring to an end all the groaning she caused.
>
> At this my body is racked with pain,
>   pangs seize me, like those of a woman in labor;
>
> I am staggered by what I hear,
>   I am bewildered by what I see.
>
> My heart falters,
>   fear makes me tremble;

the twilight I longed for
has become a horror to me.

They set the tables,
they spread the rugs,
they eat, they drink!
Get up, you officers,
oil the shields!

This is what the Lord says to me:

"Go, post a lookout
and have him report what he sees.
When he sees chariots
with teams of horses,
riders on donkeys
or riders on camels,
let him be alert,
fully alert."

And the lookout shouted,

"Day after day, my lord, I stand on the watchtower;
every night I stay at my post.
Look, here comes a man in a chariot
with a team of horses.
And he gives back the answer:
'Babylon has fallen, has fallen!
All the images of its gods
lie shattered on the ground!'"

My people who are crushed on the threshing floor,
I tell you what I have heard
from the LORD Almighty,
from the God of Israel.

A prophecy against Dumah:

Someone calls to me from Seir,
"Watchman, what is left of the night?
Watchman, what is left of the night?"
The watchman replies,
"Morning is coming, but also the night.

> If you would ask, then ask;
> and come back yet again."

A prophecy against Arabia:

> You caravans of Dedanites,
> who camp in the thickets of Arabia,
> bring water for the thirsty;
>
> you who live in Tema,
> bring food for the fugitives.
>
> They flee from the sword,
> from the drawn sword,
>
> from the bent bow
> and from the heat of battle.

This is what the Lord says to me: "Within one year, as a servant bound by contract would count it, all the splendor of Kedar will come to an end. The survivors of the archers, the warriors of Kedar, will be few." The Lord, the God of Israel, has spoken.

A prophecy against the Valley of Vision:

> What troubles you now,
> that you have all gone up on the roofs,
>
> you town so full of commotion,
> you city of tumult and revelry?
>
> Your slain were not killed by the sword,
> nor did they die in battle.
>
> All your leaders have fled together;
> they have been captured without using the bow.
>
> All you who were caught were taken prisoner together,
> having fled while the enemy was still far away.
>
> Therefore I said, "Turn away from me;
> let me weep bitterly.
>
> Do not try to console me
> over the destruction of my people."
>
> The Lord, the Lord Almighty, has a day
> of tumult and trampling and terror
> in the Valley of Vision,
>
> a day of battering down walls
> and of crying out to the mountains.

Elam takes up the quiver,
with her charioteers and horses;
Kir uncovers the shield.

Your choicest valleys are full of chariots,
and horsemen are posted at the city gates.

The Lord stripped away the defenses of Judah,
and you looked in that day
to the weapons in the Palace of the Forest.

You saw that the walls of the City of David
were broken through in many places;
you stored up water
in the Lower Pool.

You counted the buildings in Jerusalem
and tore down houses to strengthen the wall.

You built a reservoir between the two walls
for the water of the Old Pool,
but you did not look to the One who made it,
or have regard for the One who planned it long ago.

The Lord, the LORD Almighty,
called you on that day
to weep and to wail,
to tear out your hair and put on sackcloth.

But see, there is joy and revelry,
slaughtering of cattle and killing of sheep,
eating of meat and drinking of wine!

"Let us eat and drink," you say,
"for tomorrow we die!"

The LORD Almighty has revealed this in my hearing: "Till your dying day this sin will not be atoned for," says the Lord, the LORD Almighty.

This is what the Lord, the LORD Almighty, says:

"Go, say to this steward,
to Shebna the palace administrator:

What are you doing here and who gave you
permission
to cut out a grave for yourself here,

hewing your grave on the height
and chiseling your resting place in the rock?

"Beware, the LORD is about to take firm hold of you
and hurl you away, you mighty man.

He will roll you up tightly like a ball
and throw you into a large country.

There you will die
and there the chariots you were so proud of
will become a disgrace to your master's house.

I will depose you from your office,
and you will be ousted from your position.

"In that day I will summon my servant, Eliakim son of Hilkiah. I will clothe him with your robe and fasten your sash around him and hand your authority over to him. He will be a father to those who live in Jerusalem and to the people of Judah. I will place on his shoulder the key to the house of David; what he opens no one can shut, and what he shuts no one can open. I will drive him like a peg into a firm place; he will become a seat of honor for the house of his father. All the glory of his family will hang on him: its offspring and offshoots — all its lesser vessels, from the bowls to all the jars.

"In that day," declares the LORD Almighty, "the peg driven into the firm place will give way; it will be sheared off and will fall, and the load hanging on it will be cut down." The LORD has spoken.

A prophecy against Tyre:

Wail, you ships of Tarshish!
For Tyre is destroyed
and left without house or harbor.

From the land of Cyprus
word has come to them.

Be silent, you people of the island
and you merchants of Sidon,
whom the seafarers have enriched.

On the great waters
came the grain of the Shihor;

the harvest of the Nile was the revenue of Tyre,
and she became the marketplace of the nations.

Be ashamed, Sidon, and you fortress of the sea,
for the sea has spoken:

"I have neither been in labor nor given birth;
I have neither reared sons nor brought
    up daughters."

When word comes to Egypt,
they will be in anguish at the report from Tyre.

Cross over to Tarshish;
wail, you people of the island.

Is this your city of revelry,
the old, old city,

whose feet have taken her
to settle in far-off lands?

Who planned this against Tyre,
the bestower of crowns,

whose merchants are princes,
whose traders are renowned in the earth?

The Lord Almighty planned it,
to bring down her pride in all her splendor
and to humble all who are renowned on the earth.

Till your land as they do along the Nile,
Daughter Tarshish,
for you no longer have a harbor.

The Lord has stretched out his hand over the sea
and made its kingdoms tremble.

He has given an order concerning Phoenicia
that her fortresses be destroyed.

He said, "No more of your reveling,
Virgin Daughter Sidon, now crushed!

"Up, cross over to Cyprus;
even there you will find no rest."

Look at the land of the Babylonians,
this people that is now of no account!

The Assyrians have made it
a place for desert creatures;

they raised up their siege towers,
they stripped its fortresses bare
and turned it into a ruin.

Wail, you ships of Tarshish;
your fortress is destroyed!

At that time Tyre will be forgotten for seventy years, the span of a king's life. But at the end of these seventy years, it will happen to Tyre as in the song of the prostitute:

> "Take up a harp, walk through the city,
> you forgotten prostitute;
>
> play the harp well, sing many a song,
> so that you will be remembered."

At the end of seventy years, the LORD will deal with Tyre. She will return to her lucrative prostitution and will ply her trade with all the kingdoms on the face of the earth. Yet her profit and her earnings will be set apart for the LORD; they will not be stored up or hoarded. Her profits will go to those who live before the LORD, for abundant food and fine clothes.

S ee, the LORD is going to lay waste the earth
and devastate it;

he will ruin its face
and scatter its inhabitants —

it will be the same
for priest as for people,
for the master as for his servant,
for the mistress as for her servant,
for seller as for buyer,
for borrower as for lender,
for debtor as for creditor.

The earth will be completely laid waste
and totally plundered.
The LORD has spoken this word.

The earth dries up and withers,
the world languishes and withers,
the heavens languish with the earth.

The earth is defiled by its people;
they have disobeyed the laws,

violated the statutes
and broken the everlasting covenant.

Therefore a curse consumes the earth;
its people must bear their guilt.

Therefore earth's inhabitants are burned up,
and very few are left.

The new wine dries up and the vine withers;
all the merrymakers groan.

The joyful timbrels are stilled,
the noise of the revelers has stopped,
the joyful harp is silent.

No longer do they drink wine with a song;
the beer is bitter to its drinkers.

The ruined city lies desolate;
the entrance to every house is barred.

In the streets they cry out for wine;
all joy turns to gloom,
all joyful sounds are banished from the earth.

The city is left in ruins,
its gate is battered to pieces.

So will it be on the earth
and among the nations,

as when an olive tree is beaten,
or as when gleanings are left after the grape harvest.

They raise their voices, they shout for joy;
from the west they acclaim the Lord's majesty.

Therefore in the east give glory to the Lord;
exalt the name of the Lord, the God of Israel,
in the islands of the sea.

From the ends of the earth we hear singing:
"Glory to the Righteous One."

But I said, "I waste away, I waste away!
Woe to me!
The treacherous betray!
With treachery the treacherous betray!"

Terror and pit and snare await you,
people of the earth.

Whoever flees at the sound of terror
will fall into a pit;

whoever climbs out of the pit
will be caught in a snare.

The floodgates of the heavens are opened,
the foundations of the earth shake.

The earth is broken up,
the earth is split asunder,
the earth is violently shaken.

The earth reels like a drunkard,
it sways like a hut in the wind;

so heavy upon it is the guilt of its rebellion
that it falls — never to rise again.

In that day the Lᴏʀᴅ will punish
the powers in the heavens above
and the kings on the earth below.

They will be herded together
like prisoners bound in a dungeon;

they will be shut up in prison
and be punished after many days.

The moon will be dismayed,
the sun ashamed;

for the Lᴏʀᴅ Almighty will reign
on Mount Zion and in Jerusalem,
and before its elders — with great glory.

Lᴏʀᴅ, you are my God;
I will exalt you and praise your name,

for in perfect faithfulness
you have done wonderful things,
things planned long ago.

You have made the city a heap of rubble,
the fortified town a ruin,

the foreigners' stronghold a city no more;
it will never be rebuilt.

Therefore strong peoples will honor you;
cities of ruthless nations will revere you.

You have been a refuge for the poor,
a refuge for the needy in their distress,

a shelter from the storm
and a shade from the heat.

For the breath of the ruthless
is like a storm driving against a wall
and like the heat of the desert.

You silence the uproar of foreigners;
as heat is reduced by the shadow
of a cloud,
so the song of the ruthless is stilled.

On this mountain the LORD Almighty
will prepare
a feast of rich food for all peoples,
a banquet of aged wine—
the best of meats and the finest of wines.

On this mountain he will destroy
the shroud that enfolds all peoples,
the sheet that covers all nations;
he will swallow up death forever.

The Sovereign LORD will wipe away
the tears
from all faces;
he will remove his people's disgrace
from all the earth.

The LORD has spoken.

In that day they will say,

"Surely this is our God;
we trusted in him, and he saved us.

This is the LORD, we trusted in him;
let us rejoice and be glad in his salvation."

The hand of the LORD will rest on
this mountain;
but Moab will be trampled in their land
as straw is trampled down in the manure.

They will stretch out their hands in it,
as swimmers stretch out their hands
to swim.

God will bring down their pride
despite the cleverness of their hands.

He will bring down your high fortified walls
and lay them low;

he will bring them down to the ground,
to the very dust.

In that day this song will be sung in the land of Judah:

> We have a strong city;
> God makes salvation
> its walls and ramparts.

> Open the gates
> that the righteous nation may enter,
> the nation that keeps faith.

> You will keep in perfect peace
> those whose minds are steadfast,
> because they trust in you.

> Trust in the LORD forever,
> for the LORD, the LORD himself, is the Rock eternal.

> He humbles those who dwell on high,
> he lays the lofty city low;

> he levels it to the ground
> and casts it down to the dust.

> Feet trample it down—
> the feet of the oppressed,
> the footsteps of the poor.

> The path of the righteous is level;
> you, the Upright One, make the way of the righteous
>   smooth.

> Yes, LORD, walking in the way of your laws,
> we wait for you;

> your name and renown
> are the desire of our hearts.

> My soul yearns for you in the night;
> in the morning my spirit longs for you.

> When your judgments come upon the earth,
> the people of the world learn righteousness.

> But when grace is shown to the wicked,
> they do not learn righteousness;

> even in a land of uprightness they go on
>   doing evil
> and do not regard the majesty of the LORD.

> LORD, your hand is lifted high,
> but they do not see it.

Let them see your zeal for your people and be put
to shame;
let the fire reserved for your enemies consume them.

Lord, you establish peace for us;
all that we have accomplished you have done for us.

Lord our God, other lords besides you have ruled
over us,
but your name alone do we honor.

They are now dead, they live no more;
their spirits do not rise.

You punished them and brought them to ruin;
you wiped out all memory of them.

You have enlarged the nation, Lord;
you have enlarged the nation.

You have gained glory for yourself;
you have extended all the borders of the land.

Lord, they came to you in their distress;
when you disciplined them,
they could barely whisper a prayer.

As a pregnant woman about to give birth
writhes and cries out in her pain,
so were we in your presence, Lord.

We were with child, we writhed in labor,
but we gave birth to wind.

We have not brought salvation to the earth,
and the people of the world have not come to life.

But your dead will live, Lord;
their bodies will rise —

let those who dwell in the dust
wake up and shout for joy —

your dew is like the dew of the morning;
the earth will give birth to her dead.

Go, my people, enter your rooms
and shut the doors behind you;

hide yourselves for a little while
until his wrath has passed by.

See, the Lord is coming out of his dwelling
to punish the people of the earth for their sins.

The earth will disclose the blood shed on it;
the earth will conceal its slain no longer.

In that day,

the LORD will punish with his sword—
his fierce, great and powerful sword—
Leviathan the gliding serpent,
Leviathan the coiling serpent;
he will slay the monster of the sea.

In that day—

"Sing about a fruitful vineyard:
I, the LORD, watch over it;
I water it continually.
I guard it day and night
so that no one may harm it.
I am not angry.
If only there were briers and thorns confronting me!
I would march against them in battle;
I would set them all on fire.
Or else let them come to me for refuge;
let them make peace with me,
yes, let them make peace with me."

In days to come Jacob will take root,
Israel will bud and blossom
and fill all the world with fruit.

Has the LORD struck her
as he struck down those who struck her?
Has she been killed
as those were killed who killed her?
By warfare and exile you contend with her—
with his fierce blast he drives her out,
as on a day the east wind blows.
By this, then, will Jacob's guilt be atoned for,
and this will be the full fruit of the removal
of his sin:
When he makes all the altar stones
to be like limestone crushed to pieces,

no Asherah poles or incense altars
will be left standing.

The fortified city stands desolate,
an abandoned settlement, forsaken like
    the wilderness;

there the calves graze,
there they lie down;
they strip its branches bare.

When its twigs are dry, they are broken off
and women come and make fires with them.

For this is a people without understanding;
so their Maker has no compassion on them,
and their Creator shows them no favor.

In that day the LORD will thresh from the flowing Euphrates to the Wadi of Egypt, and you, Israel, will be gathered up one by one. And in that day a great trumpet will sound. Those who were perishing in Assyria and those who were exiled in Egypt will come and worship the LORD on the holy mountain in Jerusalem.

W oe to that wreath, the pride of Ephraim's
    drunkards,
to the fading flower, his glorious beauty,

set on the head of a fertile valley —
to that city, the pride of those laid low by wine!

See, the Lord has one who is powerful and strong.
Like a hailstorm and a destructive wind,

like a driving rain and a flooding downpour,
he will throw it forcefully to the ground.

That wreath, the pride of Ephraim's drunkards,
will be trampled underfoot.

That fading flower, his glorious beauty,
set on the head of a fertile valley,

will be like figs ripe before harvest —
as soon as people see them and take them in hand,
they swallow them.

In that day the LORD Almighty
will be a glorious crown,

a beautiful wreath
for the remnant of his people.

He will be a spirit of justice
to the one who sits in judgment,

a source of strength
to those who turn back the battle at the gate.

And these also stagger from wine
and reel from beer:

Priests and prophets stagger from beer
and are befuddled with wine;

they reel from beer,
they stagger when seeing visions,
they stumble when rendering decisions.

All the tables are covered with vomit
and there is not a spot without filth.

"Who is it he is trying to teach?
To whom is he explaining his message?

To children weaned from their milk,
to those just taken from the breast?

For it is:
Do this, do that,
a rule for this, a rule for that;
a little here, a little there."

Very well then, with foreign lips and strange tongues
God will speak to this people,

to whom he said,
"This is the resting place, let the weary rest";

and, "This is the place of repose" —
but they would not listen.

So then, the word of the Lord to them will become:
Do this, do that,
a rule for this, a rule for that;
a little here, a little there —

so that as they go they will fall backward;
they will be injured and snared and captured.

Therefore hear the word of the Lord, you scoffers
who rule this people in Jerusalem.

You boast, "We have entered into a covenant with death,
with the realm of the dead we have made an agreement.

When an overwhelming scourge sweeps by,
it cannot touch us,

for we have made a lie our refuge
and falsehood our hiding place."

So this is what the Sovereign LORD says:

"See, I lay a stone in Zion, a tested stone,
a precious cornerstone for a sure foundation;

the one who relies on it
will never be stricken with panic.

I will make justice the measuring line
and righteousness the plumb line;

hail will sweep away your refuge, the lie,
and water will overflow your hiding place.

Your covenant with death will be annulled;
your agreement with the realm of the dead will not
        stand.

When the overwhelming scourge sweeps by,
you will be beaten down by it.

As often as it comes it will carry you away;
morning after morning, by day and by night,
it will sweep through."

The understanding of this message
will bring sheer terror.

The bed is too short to stretch out on,
the blanket too narrow to wrap around you.

The LORD will rise up as he did at Mount Perazim,
he will rouse himself as in the Valley of Gibeon —

to do his work, his strange work,
and perform his task, his alien task.

Now stop your mocking,
or your chains will become heavier;

the Lord, the LORD Almighty, has told me
of the destruction decreed against the whole land.

Listen and hear my voice;
pay attention and hear what I say.

When a farmer plows for planting, does he plow
    continually?
Does he keep on breaking up and working the soil?

When he has leveled the surface,
does he not sow caraway and scatter cumin?

Does he not plant wheat in its place,
barley in its plot,
    and spelt in its field?

His God instructs him
and teaches him the right way.

Caraway is not threshed with a sledge,
nor is the wheel of a cart rolled over cumin;

caraway is beaten out with a rod,
and cumin with a stick.

Grain must be ground to make bread;
so one does not go on threshing it forever.

The wheels of a threshing cart may be rolled over it,
but one does not use horses to grind grain.

All this also comes from the Lord Almighty,
whose plan is wonderful,
    whose wisdom is magnificent.

Woe to you, Ariel, Ariel,
the city where David settled!

Add year to year
and let your cycle of festivals go on.

Yet I will besiege Ariel;
she will mourn and lament,
    she will be to me like an altar hearth.

I will encamp against you on all sides;
I will encircle you with towers
    and set up my siege works against you.

Brought low, you will speak from the ground;
your speech will mumble out of the dust.

Your voice will come ghostlike from the earth;
out of the dust your speech will whisper.

But your many enemies will become like fine dust,
the ruthless hordes like blown chaff.

Suddenly, in an instant,
the LORD Almighty will come

with thunder and earthquake and great noise,
with windstorm and tempest and flames of a devouring
fire.

Then the hordes of all the nations that fight against
Ariel,
that attack her and her fortress and besiege her,

will be as it is with a dream,
with a vision in the night —

as when a hungry person dreams of eating,
but awakens hungry still;

as when a thirsty person dreams of drinking,
but awakens faint and thirsty still.

So will it be with the hordes of all the nations
that fight against Mount Zion.

Be stunned and amazed,
blind yourselves and be sightless;

be drunk, but not from wine,
stagger, but not from beer.

The LORD has brought over you a deep sleep:
He has sealed your eyes (the prophets);
he has covered your heads (the seers).

For you this whole vision is nothing but words sealed in a
scroll. And if you give the scroll to someone who can read, and say,
"Read this, please," they will answer, "I can't; it is sealed." Or if you
give the scroll to someone who cannot read, and say, "Read this,
please," they will answer, "I don't know how to read."

The Lord says:

"These people come near to me with their mouth
and honor me with their lips,
but their hearts are far from me.

Their worship of me
is based on merely human rules they have been taught.

Therefore once more I will astound these people
with wonder upon wonder;

the wisdom of the wise will perish,
the intelligence of the intelligent will vanish."

Woe to those who go to great depths
to hide their plans from the LORD,

who do their work in darkness and think,
"Who sees us? Who will know?"

You turn things upside down,
as if the potter were thought to be like the clay!

Shall what is formed say to the one who formed it,
"You did not make me"?

Can the pot say to the potter,
"You know nothing"?

In a very short time, will not Lebanon be turned into a
    fertile field
and the fertile field seem like a forest?

In that day the deaf will hear the words of the scroll,
and out of gloom and darkness
the eyes of the blind will see.

Once more the humble will rejoice in the LORD;
the needy will rejoice in the Holy One of Israel.

The ruthless will vanish,
the mockers will disappear,
and all who have an eye for evil will be cut down—

those who with a word make someone out to be guilty,
who ensnare the defender in court
and with false testimony deprive the innocent of justice.

Therefore this is what the LORD, who redeemed Abraham, says
to the descendants of Jacob:

"No longer will Jacob be ashamed;
no longer will their faces grow pale.

When they see among them their children,
the work of my hands,

they will keep my name holy;
they will acknowledge the holiness of the Holy One
    of Jacob,
and will stand in awe of the God of Israel.

Those who are wayward in spirit will gain
    understanding;
those who complain will accept instruction."

"Woe to the obstinate children,"
declares the LORD,

"to those who carry out plans that are not mine,
forming an alliance, but not by my Spirit,
heaping sin upon sin;

who go down to Egypt
without consulting me;

who look for help to Pharaoh's protection,
to Egypt's shade for refuge.

But Pharaoh's protection will be to your shame,
Egypt's shade will bring you disgrace.

Though they have officials in Zoan
and their envoys have arrived in Hanes,

everyone will be put to shame
because of a people useless to them,

who bring neither help nor advantage,
but only shame and disgrace."

A prophecy concerning the animals of the Negev:

Through a land of hardship and distress,
of lions and lionesses,
of adders and darting snakes,

the envoys carry their riches on donkeys' backs,
their treasures on the humps of camels,

to that unprofitable nation,
to Egypt, whose help is utterly useless.

Therefore I call her
Rahab the Do-Nothing.

Go now, write it on a tablet for them,
inscribe it on a scroll,

that for the days to come
it may be an everlasting witness.

For these are rebellious people, deceitful children,
children unwilling to listen to the LORD's instruction.

They say to the seers,
"See no more visions!"

and to the prophets,
"Give us no more visions of what is right!

Tell us pleasant things,
prophesy illusions.

Leave this way,
get off this path,

and stop confronting us
with the Holy One of Israel!"

Therefore this is what the Holy One of Israel says:

"Because you have rejected this message,
relied on oppression
and depended on deceit,

this sin will become for you
like a high wall, cracked and bulging,
that collapses suddenly, in an instant.

It will break in pieces like pottery,
shattered so mercilessly

that among its pieces not a fragment will be found
for taking coals from a hearth
or scooping water out of a cistern."

This is what the Sovereign Lord, the Holy One of Israel, says:

"In repentance and rest is your salvation,
in quietness and trust is your strength,
but you would have none of it.

You said, 'No, we will flee on horses.'
Therefore you will flee!

You said, 'We will ride off on swift horses.'
Therefore your pursuers will be swift!

A thousand will flee
at the threat of one;

at the threat of five
you will all flee away,

till you are left
like a flagstaff on a mountaintop,
like a banner on a hill."

Yet the Lord longs to be gracious to you;
therefore he will rise up to show you compassion.

For the Lord is a God of justice.
Blessed are all who wait for him!

People of Zion, who live in Jerusalem, you will weep no more. How gracious he will be when you cry for help! As soon as he hears, he will answer you. Although the Lord gives you the bread of adversity and the water of affliction, your teachers will be hidden no more; with your own eyes you will see them. Whether you turn to the right or to the left, your ears will hear a voice behind you, saying, "This is the way; walk in it." Then you will desecrate your idols overlaid with silver and your images covered with gold; you will throw them away like a menstrual cloth and say to them, "Away with you!"

He will also send you rain for the seed you sow in the ground, and the food that comes from the land will be rich and plentiful. In that day your cattle will graze in broad meadows. The oxen and donkeys that work the soil will eat fodder and mash, spread out with fork and shovel. In the day of great slaughter, when the towers fall, streams of water will flow on every high mountain and every lofty hill. The moon will shine like the sun, and the sunlight will be seven times brighter, like the light of seven full days, when the Lord binds up the bruises of his people and heals the wounds he inflicted.

See, the Name of the Lord comes from afar,
with burning anger and dense clouds of smoke;
his lips are full of wrath,
and his tongue is a consuming fire.

His breath is like a rushing torrent,
rising up to the neck.

He shakes the nations in the sieve of destruction;
he places in the jaws of the peoples
a bit that leads them astray.

And you will sing
as on the night you celebrate a holy festival;

your hearts will rejoice
as when people playing pipes go up

to the mountain of the Lord,
to the Rock of Israel.

The Lord will cause people to hear his majestic voice
and will make them see his arm coming down
with raging anger and consuming fire,
with cloudburst, thunderstorm and hail.

The voice of the Lord will shatter Assyria;
with his rod he will strike them down.

Every stroke the Lord lays on them
with his punishing club

will be to the music of timbrels and harps,
as he fights them in battle with the blows of his arm.

Topheth has long been prepared;
it has been made ready for the king.

Its fire pit has been made deep and wide,
with an abundance of fire and wood;

the breath of the Lord,
like a stream of burning sulfur,
sets it ablaze.

Woe to those who go down to Egypt for help,
who rely on horses,

who trust in the multitude of their chariots
and in the great strength of their horsemen,

but do not look to the Holy One of Israel,
or seek help from the Lord.

Yet he too is wise and can bring disaster;
he does not take back his words.

He will rise up against that wicked nation,
against those who help evildoers.

But the Egyptians are mere mortals and not God;
their horses are flesh and not spirit.

When the Lord stretches out his hand,
those who help will stumble,
those who are helped will fall;
all will perish together.

This is what the Lord says to me:

"As a lion growls,
a great lion over its prey —

and though a whole band of shepherds
is called together against it,

it is not frightened by their shouts
or disturbed by their clamor —

> so the LORD Almighty will come down
> to do battle on Mount Zion and on its heights.

> Like birds hovering overhead,
> the LORD Almighty will shield Jerusalem;

> he will shield it and deliver it,
> he will 'pass over' it and will rescue it."

Return, you Israelites, to the One you have so greatly revolted against. For in that day every one of you will reject the idols of silver and gold your sinful hands have made.

> "Assyria will fall by no human sword;
> a sword, not of mortals, will devour them.

> They will flee before the sword
> and their young men will be put to forced labor.

> Their stronghold will fall because of terror;
> at the sight of the battle standard their commanders will
> panic,"

> declares the LORD,
> whose fire is in Zion,
> whose furnace is in Jerusalem.

> See, a king will reign in righteousness
> and rulers will rule with justice.

> Each one will be like a shelter from the wind
> and a refuge from the storm,

> like streams of water in the desert
> and the shadow of a great rock in a thirsty land.

> Then the eyes of those who see will no longer be closed,
> and the ears of those who hear will listen.

> The fearful heart will know and understand,
> and the stammering tongue will be fluent and clear.

> No longer will the fool be called noble
> nor the scoundrel be highly respected.

> For fools speak folly,
> their hearts are bent on evil:

> They practice ungodliness
> and spread error concerning the LORD;

> the hungry they leave empty
> and from the thirsty they withhold water.

Scoundrels use wicked methods,
they make up evil schemes

to destroy the poor with lies,
even when the plea of the needy is just.

But the noble make noble plans,
and by noble deeds they stand.

You women who are so complacent,
rise up and listen to me;

you daughters who feel secure,
hear what I have to say!

In little more than a year
you who feel secure will tremble;

the grape harvest will fail,
and the harvest of fruit will not come.

Tremble, you complacent women;
shudder, you daughters who feel secure!

Strip off your fine clothes
and wrap yourselves in rags.

Beat your breasts for the pleasant fields,
for the fruitful vines

and for the land of my people,
a land overgrown with thorns and briers—

yes, mourn for all houses of merriment
and for this city of revelry.

The fortress will be abandoned,
the noisy city deserted;

citadel and watchtower will become a wasteland forever,
the delight of donkeys, a pasture for flocks,

till the Spirit is poured on us from on high,
and the desert becomes a fertile field,
and the fertile field seems like a forest.

The LORD's justice will dwell in the desert,
his righteousness live in the fertile field.

The fruit of that righteousness will be peace;
its effect will be quietness and confidence forever.

My people will live in peaceful dwelling places,
in secure homes,
in undisturbed places of rest.

Though hail flattens the forest
and the city is leveled completely,

how blessed you will be,
sowing your seed by every stream,
and letting your cattle and donkeys range free.

Woe to you, destroyer,
you who have not been destroyed!

Woe to you, betrayer,
you who have not been betrayed!

When you stop destroying,
you will be destroyed;

when you stop betraying,
you will be betrayed.

Lord, be gracious to us;
we long for you.

Be our strength every morning,
our salvation in time of distress.

At the uproar of your army, the peoples flee;
when you rise up, the nations scatter.

Your plunder, O nations, is harvested as by young
locusts;
like a swarm of locusts people pounce on it.

The Lord is exalted, for he dwells on high;
he will fill Zion with his justice and righteousness.

He will be the sure foundation for your times,
a rich store of salvation and wisdom and knowledge;
the fear of the Lord is the key to this treasure.

Look, their brave men cry aloud in the streets;
the envoys of peace weep bitterly.

The highways are deserted,
no travelers are on the roads.

The treaty is broken,
its witnesses are despised,
no one is respected.

The land dries up and wastes away,
Lebanon is ashamed and withers;

Sharon is like the Arabah,
and Bashan and Carmel drop their leaves.

"Now will I arise," says the Lord.
"Now will I be exalted;
now will I be lifted up.

You conceive chaff,
you give birth to straw;
your breath is a fire that consumes you.

The peoples will be burned to ashes;
like cut thornbushes they will be set ablaze."

You who are far away, hear what I have done;
you who are near, acknowledge my power!

The sinners in Zion are terrified;
trembling grips the godless:

"Who of us can dwell with the consuming fire?
Who of us can dwell with everlasting burning?"

Those who walk righteously
and speak what is right,

who reject gain from extortion
and keep their hands from accepting bribes,

who stop their ears against plots of murder
and shut their eyes against contemplating evil—

they are the ones who will dwell on the heights,
whose refuge will be the mountain fortress.

Their bread will be supplied,
and water will not fail them.

Your eyes will see the king in his beauty
and view a land that stretches afar.

In your thoughts you will ponder the former terror:
"Where is that chief officer?

Where is the one who took the revenue?
Where is the officer in charge of the towers?"

You will see those arrogant people no more,
people whose speech is obscure,
whose language is strange and incomprehensible.

Look on Zion, the city of our festivals;
your eyes will see Jerusalem,
a peaceful abode, a tent that will not be moved;

its stakes will never be pulled up,
nor any of its ropes broken.

There the LORD will be our Mighty One.
It will be like a place of broad rivers and streams.

No galley with oars will ride them,
no mighty ship will sail them.

For the LORD is our judge,
the LORD is our lawgiver,

the LORD is our king;
it is he who will save us.

Your rigging hangs loose:
The mast is not held secure,
the sail is not spread.

Then an abundance of spoils will be divided
and even the lame will carry off plunder.

No one living in Zion will say, "I am ill";
and the sins of those who dwell there will be forgiven.

C ome near, you nations, and listen;
pay attention, you peoples!
Let the earth hear, and all that is in it,
the world, and all that comes out of it!

The LORD is angry with all nations;
his wrath is on all their armies.

He will totally destroy them,
he will give them over to slaughter.

Their slain will be thrown out,
their dead bodies will stink;
the mountains will be soaked with their blood.

All the stars in the sky will be dissolved
and the heavens rolled up like a scroll;

all the starry host will fall
like withered leaves from the vine,
like shriveled figs from the fig tree.

My sword has drunk its fill in the heavens;
see, it descends in judgment on Edom,
the people I have totally destroyed.

The sword of the LORD is bathed in blood,
it is covered with fat —

the blood of lambs and goats,
fat from the kidneys of rams.

For the LORD has a sacrifice in Bozrah
and a great slaughter in the land of Edom.

And the wild oxen will fall with them,
the bull calves and the great bulls.

Their land will be drenched with blood,
and the dust will be soaked with fat.

For the LORD has a day of vengeance,
a year of retribution, to uphold Zion's cause.

Edom's streams will be turned into pitch,
her dust into burning sulfur;
her land will become blazing pitch!

It will not be quenched night or day;
its smoke will rise forever.

From generation to generation it will lie desolate;
no one will ever pass through it again.

The desert owl and screech owl will possess it;
the great owl and the raven will nest there.

God will stretch out over Edom
the measuring line of chaos
and the plumb line of desolation.

Her nobles will have nothing there to be called a
kingdom,
all her princes will vanish away.

Thorns will overrun her citadels,
nettles and brambles her strongholds.

She will become a haunt for jackals,
a home for owls.

Desert creatures will meet with hyenas,
and wild goats will bleat to each other;

there the night creatures will also lie down
and find for themselves places of rest.

The owl will nest there and lay eggs,
she will hatch them, and care for her young
under the shadow of her wings;

there also the falcons will gather,
each with its mate.

Look in the scroll of the LORD and read:

> None of these will be missing,
> not one will lack her mate.

> For it is his mouth that has given the order,
> and his Spirit will gather them together.

> He allots their portions;
> his hand distributes them by measure.

> They will possess it forever
> and dwell there from generation to generation.

> The desert and the parched land will be glad;
> the wilderness will rejoice and blossom.

> Like the crocus, it will burst into bloom;
> it will rejoice greatly and shout for joy.

> The glory of Lebanon will be given to it,
> the splendor of Carmel and Sharon;

> they will see the glory of the LORD,
> the splendor of our God.

> Strengthen the feeble hands,
> steady the knees that give way;

> say to those with fearful hearts,
> "Be strong, do not fear;

> your God will come,
> he will come with vengeance;

> with divine retribution
> he will come to save you."

> Then will the eyes of the blind be opened
> and the ears of the deaf unstopped.

> Then will the lame leap like a deer,
> and the mute tongue shout for joy.

> Water will gush forth in the wilderness
> and streams in the desert.

> The burning sand will become a pool,
> the thirsty ground bubbling springs.

> In the haunts where jackals once lay,
> grass and reeds and papyrus will grow.

And a highway will be there;
it will be called the Way of Holiness;
it will be for those who walk on that Way.

The unclean will not journey on it;
wicked fools will not go about on it.

No lion will be there,
nor any ravenous beast;
they will not be found there.

But only the redeemed will walk there,
and those the Lord has rescued will return.

They will enter Zion with singing;
everlasting joy will crown their heads.

Gladness and joy will overtake them,
and sorrow and sighing will flee away.

In the fourteenth year of King Hezekiah's reign, Sennacherib king of Assyria attacked all the fortified cities of Judah and captured them. Then the king of Assyria sent his field commander with a large army from Lachish to King Hezekiah at Jerusalem. When the commander stopped at the aqueduct of the Upper Pool, on the road to the Launderer's Field, Eliakim son of Hilkiah the palace administrator, Shebna the secretary, and Joah son of Asaph the recorder went out to him.

The field commander said to them, "Tell Hezekiah:

"'This is what the great king, the king of Assyria, says: On what are you basing this confidence of yours? You say you have counsel and might for war—but you speak only empty words. On whom are you depending, that you rebel against me? Look, I know you are depending on Egypt, that splintered reed of a staff, which pierces the hand of anyone who leans on it! Such is Pharaoh king of Egypt to all who depend on him. But if you say to me, "We are depending on the Lord our God"—isn't he the one whose high places and altars Hezekiah removed, saying to Judah and Jerusalem, "You must worship before this altar"?

"'Come now, make a bargain with my master, the king of Assyria: I will give you two thousand horses—if you can put riders on them! How then can you repulse one officer of the least of my master's officials, even though you are depending on Egypt for chariots and horsemen? Furthermore, have I come to attack and destroy this land without the Lord? The Lord himself told me to march against this country and destroy it.'"

Then Eliakim, Shebna and Joah said to the field commander, "Please speak to your servants in Aramaic, since we understand it. Don't speak to us in Hebrew in the hearing of the people on the wall."

But the commander replied, "Was it only to your master and you that my master sent me to say these things, and not to the people sitting on the wall—who, like you, will have to eat their own excrement and drink their own urine?"

Then the commander stood and called out in Hebrew, "Hear the words of the great king, the king of Assyria! This is what the king says: Do not let Hezekiah deceive you. He cannot deliver you! Do not let Hezekiah persuade you to trust in the Lord when he says, 'The Lord will surely deliver us; this city will not be given into the hand of the king of Assyria.'

"Do not listen to Hezekiah. This is what the king of Assyria says: Make peace with me and come out to me. Then each of you will eat fruit from your own vine and fig tree and drink water from your own cistern, until I come and take you to a land like your own—a land of grain and new wine, a land of bread and vineyards.

"Do not let Hezekiah mislead you when he says, 'The Lord will deliver us.' Have the gods of any nations ever delivered their lands from the hand of the king of Assyria? Where are the gods of Hamath and Arpad? Where are the gods of Sepharvaim? Have they rescued Samaria from my hand? Who of all the gods of these countries have been able to save their lands from me? How then can the Lord deliver Jerusalem from my hand?"

But the people remained silent and said nothing in reply, because the king had commanded, "Do not answer him."

Then Eliakim son of Hilkiah the palace administrator, Shebna the secretary and Joah son of Asaph the recorder went to Hezekiah, with their clothes torn, and told him what the field commander had said.

When King Hezekiah heard this, he tore his clothes and put on sackcloth and went into the temple of the Lord. He sent Eliakim the palace administrator, Shebna the secretary, and the leading priests, all wearing sackcloth, to the prophet Isaiah son of Amoz. They told him, "This is what Hezekiah says: This day is a day of distress and rebuke and disgrace, as when children come to the moment of birth and there is no strength to deliver them. It may be that the Lord your God will hear the words of the field commander, whom his master, the king of Assyria, has sent to ridicule the living God, and that he will rebuke him for the words the Lord your God has heard. Therefore pray for the remnant that still survives."

When King Hezekiah's officials came to Isaiah, Isaiah said to them, "Tell your master, 'This is what the Lord says: Do not be afraid of what you have heard — those words with which the underlings of the king of Assyria have blasphemed me. Listen! When he hears a certain report, I will make him want to return to his own country, and there I will have him cut down with the sword.'"

When the field commander heard that the king of Assyria had left Lachish, he withdrew and found the king fighting against Libnah.

Now Sennacherib received a report that Tirhakah, the king of Cush, was marching out to fight against him. When he heard it, he sent messengers to Hezekiah with this word: "Say to Hezekiah king of Judah: Do not let the god you depend on deceive you when he says, 'Jerusalem will not be given into the hands of the king of Assyria.' Surely you have heard what the kings of Assyria have done to all the countries, destroying them completely. And will you be delivered? Did the gods of the nations that were destroyed by my predecessors deliver them — the gods of Gozan, Harran, Rezeph and the people of Eden who were in Tel Assar? Where is the king of Hamath or the king of Arpad? Where are the kings of Lair, Sepharvaim, Hena and Ivvah?"

Hezekiah received the letter from the messengers and read it. Then he went up to the temple of the Lord and spread it out before the Lord. And Hezekiah prayed to the Lord: "Lord Almighty, the God of Israel, enthroned between the cherubim, you alone are God over all the kingdoms of the earth. You have made heaven and earth. Give ear, Lord, and hear; open your eyes, Lord, and see; listen to all the words Sennacherib has sent to ridicule the living God.

"It is true, Lord, that the Assyrian kings have laid waste all these peoples and their lands. They have thrown their gods into the fire and destroyed them, for they were not gods but only wood and stone, fashioned by human hands. Now, Lord our God, deliver us from his hand, so that all the kingdoms of the earth may know that you, Lord, are the only God."

Then Isaiah son of Amoz sent a message to Hezekiah: "This is what the Lord, the God of Israel, says: Because you have prayed to me concerning Sennacherib king of Assyria, this is the word the Lord has spoken against him:

> "Virgin Daughter Zion
> despises and mocks you.
> Daughter Jerusalem
> tosses her head as you flee.

Who is it you have ridiculed and blasphemed?
Against whom have you raised your voice

and lifted your eyes in pride?
Against the Holy One of Israel!

By your messengers
you have ridiculed the Lord.

And you have said,
'With my many chariots

I have ascended the heights of the mountains,
the utmost heights of Lebanon.

I have cut down its tallest cedars,
the choicest of its junipers.

I have reached its remotest heights,
the finest of its forests.

I have dug wells in foreign lands
and drunk the water there.

With the soles of my feet
I have dried up all the streams of Egypt.'

"Have you not heard?
Long ago I ordained it.

In days of old I planned it;
now I have brought it to pass,

that you have turned fortified cities
into piles of stone.

Their people, drained of power,
are dismayed and put to shame.

They are like plants in the field,
like tender green shoots,

like grass sprouting on the roof,
scorched before it grows up.

"But I know where you are
and when you come and go
and how you rage against me.

Because you rage against me
and because your insolence has reached my ears,

I will put my hook in your nose
and my bit in your mouth,

and I will make you return
by the way you came.

"This will be the sign for you, Hezekiah:

"This year you will eat what grows by itself,
and the second year what springs from that.
But in the third year sow and reap,
plant vineyards and eat their fruit.
Once more a remnant of the kingdom of Judah
will take root below and bear fruit above.
For out of Jerusalem will come a remnant,
and out of Mount Zion a band of survivors.
The zeal of the Lord Almighty
will accomplish this.

"Therefore this is what the Lord says concerning the king of Assyria:

"He will not enter this city
or shoot an arrow here.
He will not come before it with shield
or build a siege ramp against it.
By the way that he came he will return;
he will not enter this city,"

declares the Lord.

"I will defend this city and save it,
for my sake and for the sake of David my servant!"

Then the angel of the Lord went out and put to death a hundred and eighty-five thousand in the Assyrian camp. When the people got up the next morning—there were all the dead bodies! So Sennacherib king of Assyria broke camp and withdrew. He returned to Nineveh and stayed there.

One day, while he was worshiping in the temple of his god Nisrok, his sons Adrammelek and Sharezer killed him with the sword, and they escaped to the land of Ararat. And Esarhaddon his son succeeded him as king.

In those days Hezekiah became ill and was at the point of death. The prophet Isaiah son of Amoz went to him and said, "This is what the Lord says: Put your house in order, because you are going to die; you will not recover."

Hezekiah turned his face to the wall and prayed to the Lord, "Remember, Lord, how I have walked before you faithfully and with wholehearted devotion and have done what is good in your eyes." And Hezekiah wept bitterly.

Then the word of the LORD came to Isaiah: "Go and tell Hezekiah, 'This is what the LORD, the God of your father David, says: I have heard your prayer and seen your tears; I will add fifteen years to your life. And I will deliver you and this city from the hand of the king of Assyria. I will defend this city.

" 'This is the LORD's sign to you that the LORD will do what he has promised: I will make the shadow cast by the sun go back the ten steps it has gone down on the stairway of Ahaz.' " So the sunlight went back the ten steps it had gone down.

A writing of Hezekiah king of Judah after his illness and recovery:

> I said, "In the prime of my life
> must I go through the gates of death
> and be robbed of the rest of my years?"
> I said, "I will not again see the LORD himself
> in the land of the living;
> no longer will I look on my fellow man,
> or be with those who now dwell in this world.
> Like a shepherd's tent my house
> has been pulled down and taken from me.
> Like a weaver I have rolled up my life,
> and he has cut me off from the loom;
> day and night you made an end of me.
> I waited patiently till dawn,
> but like a lion he broke all my bones;
> day and night you made an end of me.
> I cried like a swift or thrush,
> I moaned like a mourning dove.
> My eyes grew weak as I looked to the heavens.
> I am being threatened; Lord, come to my aid!"
>
> But what can I say?
> He has spoken to me, and he himself has
>   done this.
> I will walk humbly all my years
> because of this anguish of my soul.
> Lord, by such things people live;
> and my spirit finds life in them too.

You restored me to health
and let me live.

Surely it was for my benefit
that I suffered such anguish.

In your love you kept me
from the pit of destruction;

you have put all my sins
behind your back.

For the grave cannot praise you,
death cannot sing your praise;

those who go down to the pit
cannot hope for your faithfulness.

The living, the living—they praise you,
as I am doing today;

parents tell their children
about your faithfulness.

The Lord will save me,
and we will sing with stringed instruments

all the days of our lives
in the temple of the Lord.

Isaiah had said, "Prepare a poultice of figs and apply it to the boil, and he will recover."

Hezekiah had asked, "What will be the sign that I will go up to the temple of the Lord?"

At that time Marduk-Baladan son of Baladan king of Babylon sent Hezekiah letters and a gift, because he had heard of his illness and recovery. Hezekiah received the envoys gladly and showed them what was in his storehouses—the silver, the gold, the spices, the fine olive oil—his entire armory and everything found among his treasures. There was nothing in his palace or in all his kingdom that Hezekiah did not show them.

Then Isaiah the prophet went to King Hezekiah and asked, "What did those men say, and where did they come from?"

"From a distant land," Hezekiah replied. "They came to me from Babylon."

The prophet asked, "What did they see in your palace?"

"They saw everything in my palace," Hezekiah said. "There is nothing among my treasures that I did not show them."

Then Isaiah said to Hezekiah, "Hear the word of the Lord

Almighty: The time will surely come when everything in your palace, and all that your predecessors have stored up until this day, will be carried off to Babylon. Nothing will be left, says the Lord. And some of your descendants, your own flesh and blood who will be born to you, will be taken away, and they will become eunuchs in the palace of the king of Babylon."

"The word of the Lord you have spoken is good," Hezekiah replied. For he thought, "There will be peace and security in my lifetime."

C omfort, comfort my people,
　 says your God.

Speak tenderly to Jerusalem,
and proclaim to her

that her hard service has been completed,
that her sin has been paid for,

that she has received from the Lord's hand
double for all her sins.

A voice of one calling:

"In the wilderness prepare
the way for the Lord;
make straight in the desert
a highway for our God.

Every valley shall be raised up,
every mountain and hill made low;

the rough ground shall become level,
the rugged places a plain.

And the glory of the Lord will be revealed,
and all people will see it together.
　　　For the mouth of the Lord has spoken."

A voice says, "Cry out."
And I said, "What shall I cry?"

"All people are like grass,
and all their faithfulness is like the flowers of the field.

The grass withers and the flowers fall,
because the breath of the Lord blows on them.
Surely the people are grass.

The grass withers and the flowers fall,
but the word of our God endures forever."

You who bring good news to Zion,
go up on a high mountain.

You who bring good news to Jerusalem,
lift up your voice with a shout,

lift it up, do not be afraid;
say to the towns of Judah,
"Here is your God!"

See, the Sovereign Lord comes with power,
and he rules with a mighty arm.

See, his reward is with him,
and his recompense accompanies him.

He tends his flock like a shepherd:
He gathers the lambs in his arms

and carries them close to his heart;
he gently leads those that have young.

Who has measured the waters in the hollow
of his hand,
or with the breadth of his hand marked off
the heavens?

Who has held the dust of the earth in a basket,
or weighed the mountains on the scales
and the hills in a balance?

Who can fathom the Spirit of the Lord,
or instruct the Lord as his counselor?

Whom did the Lord consult to enlighten him,
and who taught him the right way?

Who was it that taught him knowledge,
or showed him the path of understanding?

Surely the nations are like a drop in a bucket;
they are regarded as dust on the scales;
he weighs the islands as though they were fine dust.

Lebanon is not sufficient for altar fires,
nor its animals enough for burnt offerings.

Before him all the nations are as nothing;
they are regarded by him as worthless
and less than nothing.

With whom, then, will you compare God?
To what image will you liken him?

As for an idol, a metalworker casts it,
and a goldsmith overlays it with gold
and fashions silver chains for it.

A person too poor to present such an offering
selects wood that will not rot;
they look for a skilled worker
to set up an idol that will not topple.

Do you not know?
Have you not heard?

Has it not been told you from the beginning?
Have you not understood since the earth
        was founded?

He sits enthroned above the circle of the earth,
and its people are like grasshoppers.

He stretches out the heavens like a canopy,
and spreads them out like a tent to live in.

He brings princes to naught
and reduces the rulers of this world to nothing.

No sooner are they planted,
no sooner are they sown,
no sooner do they take root in the ground,
than he blows on them and they wither,
and a whirlwind sweeps them away like chaff.

"To whom will you compare me?
Or who is my equal?" says the Holy One.

Lift up your eyes and look to the heavens:
Who created all these?

He who brings out the starry host one by one
and calls forth each of them by name.

Because of his great power and mighty strength,
not one of them is missing.

Why do you complain, Jacob?
Why do you say, Israel,

"My way is hidden from the LORD;
my cause is disregarded by my God"?

Do you not know?
Have you not heard?

The LORD is the everlasting God,
the Creator of the ends of the earth.

He will not grow tired or weary,
and his understanding no one can fathom.

He gives strength to the weary
and increases the power of the weak.

Even youths grow tired and weary,
and young men stumble and fall;

but those who hope in the LORD
will renew their strength.

They will soar on wings like eagles;
they will run and not grow weary,
they will walk and not be faint.

"Be silent before me, you islands!
Let the nations renew their strength!

Let them come forward and speak;
let us meet together at the place of judgment.

"Who has stirred up one from the east,
calling him in righteousness to his service?

He hands nations over to him
and subdues kings before him.

He turns them to dust with his sword,
to windblown chaff with his bow.

He pursues them and moves on unscathed,
by a path his feet have not traveled before.

Who has done this and carried it through,
calling forth the generations from the beginning?

I, the LORD — with the first of them
and with the last — I am he."

The islands have seen it and fear;
the ends of the earth tremble.

They approach and come forward;
they help each other
and say to their companions, "Be strong!"

The metalworker encourages the goldsmith,
and the one who smooths with the hammer
spurs on the one who strikes the anvil.

One says of the welding, "It is good."
The other nails down the idol so it will not topple.

"But you, Israel, my servant,
Jacob, whom I have chosen,
you descendants of Abraham my friend,

I took you from the ends of the earth,
from its farthest corners I called you.

I said, 'You are my servant';
I have chosen you and have not rejected you.

So do not fear, for I am with you;
do not be dismayed, for I am your God.

I will strengthen you and help you;
I will uphold you with my righteous right hand.

"All who rage against you
will surely be ashamed and disgraced;

those who oppose you
will be as nothing and perish.

Though you search for your enemies,
you will not find them.

Those who wage war against you
will be as nothing at all.

For I am the Lord your God
who takes hold of your right hand

and says to you, Do not fear;
I will help you.

Do not be afraid, you worm Jacob,
little Israel, do not fear,

for I myself will help you," declares the Lord,
your Redeemer, the Holy One of Israel.

"See, I will make you into a threshing sledge,
new and sharp, with many teeth.

You will thresh the mountains and crush them,
and reduce the hills to chaff.

You will winnow them, the wind will pick them up,
and a gale will blow them away.

But you will rejoice in the Lord
and glory in the Holy One of Israel.

"The poor and needy search for water,
but there is none;
their tongues are parched with thirst.
But I the Lord will answer them;
I, the God of Israel, will not forsake them.

I will make rivers flow on barren heights,
and springs within the valleys.
I will turn the desert into pools of water,
and the parched ground into springs.
I will put in the desert
the cedar and the acacia, the myrtle and the olive.
I will set junipers in the wasteland,
the fir and the cypress together,
so that people may see and know,
may consider and understand,
that the hand of the Lord has done this,
that the Holy One of Israel has created it.

"Present your case," says the Lord.
"Set forth your arguments," says Jacob's King.
"Tell us, you idols,
what is going to happen.
Tell us what the former things were,
so that we may consider them
and know their final outcome.
Or declare to us the things to come,
tell us what the future holds,
so we may know that you are gods.
Do something, whether good or bad,
so that we will be dismayed and filled with fear.
But you are less than nothing
and your works are utterly worthless;
whoever chooses you is detestable.

"I have stirred up one from the north, and he comes —
one from the rising sun who calls on my name.
He treads on rulers as if they were mortar,
as if he were a potter treading the clay.

Who told of this from the beginning, so we could know,
or beforehand, so we could say, 'He was right'?

No one told of this,
no one foretold it,
no one heard any words from you.

I was the first to tell Zion, 'Look, here they are!'
I gave to Jerusalem a messenger of good news.

I look but there is no one—
no one among the gods to give counsel,
no one to give answer when I ask them.

See, they are all false!
Their deeds amount to nothing;
their images are but wind and confusion.

"Here is my servant, whom I uphold,
my chosen one in whom I delight;

I will put my Spirit on him,
and he will bring justice to the nations.

He will not shout or cry out,
or raise his voice in the streets.

A bruised reed he will not break,
and a smoldering wick he will not snuff out.

In faithfulness he will bring forth justice;
he will not falter or be discouraged

till he establishes justice on earth.
In his teaching the islands will put their hope."

This is what God the LORD says—

the Creator of the heavens, who stretches them out,
who spreads out the earth with all that springs from it,
who gives breath to its people,
and life to those who walk on it:

"I, the LORD, have called you in righteousness;
I will take hold of your hand.

I will keep you and will make you
to be a covenant for the people
and a light for the Gentiles,

to open eyes that are blind,
to free captives from prison

and to release from the dungeon those who sit
    in darkness.

"I am the LORD; that is my name!
I will not yield my glory to another
or my praise to idols.

See, the former things have taken place,
and new things I declare;

before they spring into being
I announce them to you."

Sing to the LORD a new song,
    his praise from the ends of the earth,

you who go down to the sea, and all that is in it,
    you islands, and all who live in them.

Let the wilderness and its towns raise their voices;
    let the settlements where Kedar lives rejoice.

Let the people of Sela sing for joy;
    let them shout from the mountaintops.

Let them give glory to the LORD
    and proclaim his praise in the islands.

The LORD will march out like a champion,
    like a warrior he will stir up his zeal;

with a shout he will raise the battle cry
    and will triumph over his enemies.

"For a long time I have kept silent,
    I have been quiet and held myself back.

But now, like a woman in childbirth,
    I cry out, I gasp and pant.

I will lay waste the mountains and hills
    and dry up all their vegetation;

I will turn rivers into islands
    and dry up the pools.

I will lead the blind by ways they have not known,
    along unfamiliar paths I will guide them;

I will turn the darkness into light before them
    and make the rough places smooth.

These are the things I will do;
    I will not forsake them.

But those who trust in idols,
who say to images, 'You are our gods,'
will be turned back in utter shame.

"Hear, you deaf;
look, you blind, and see!

Who is blind but my servant,
and deaf like the messenger I send?

Who is blind like the one in covenant with me,
blind like the servant of the Lord?

You have seen many things, but you pay no attention;
your ears are open, but you do not listen."

It pleased the Lord
for the sake of his righteousness
to make his law great and glorious.

But this is a people plundered and looted,
all of them trapped in pits
or hidden away in prisons.

They have become plunder,
with no one to rescue them;

they have been made loot,
with no one to say, "Send them back."

Which of you will listen to this
or pay close attention in time to come?

Who handed Jacob over to become loot,
and Israel to the plunderers?

Was it not the Lord,
against whom we have sinned?

For they would not follow his ways;
they did not obey his law.

So he poured out on them his burning anger,
the violence of war.

It enveloped them in flames, yet they did not
understand;
it consumed them, but they did not take it to heart.

But now, this is what the Lord says—
he who created you, Jacob,
he who formed you, Israel:

"Do not fear, for I have redeemed you;
I have summoned you by name; you are mine.

When you pass through the waters,
I will be with you;

and when you pass through the rivers,
they will not sweep over you.

When you walk through the fire,
you will not be burned;
the flames will not set you ablaze.

For I am the Lord your God,
the Holy One of Israel, your Savior;

I give Egypt for your ransom,
Cush and Seba in your stead.

Since you are precious and honored in my sight,
and because I love you,

I will give people in exchange for you,
nations in exchange for your life.

Do not be afraid, for I am with you;
I will bring your children from the east
and gather you from the west.

I will say to the north, 'Give them up!'
and to the south, 'Do not hold them back.'
Bring my sons from afar
and my daughters from the ends of the earth—

everyone who is called by my name,
whom I created for my glory,
whom I formed and made."

Lead out those who have eyes but are blind,
who have ears but are deaf.

All the nations gather together
and the peoples assemble.

Which of their gods foretold this
and proclaimed to us the former things?

Let them bring in their witnesses to prove they
were right,
so that others may hear and say, "It is true."

"You are my witnesses," declares the Lord,
"and my servant whom I have chosen,

so that you may know and believe me
and understand that I am he.

Before me no god was formed,
nor will there be one after me.

I, even I, am the LORD,
and apart from me there is no savior.

I have revealed and saved and proclaimed—
I, and not some foreign god among you.

You are my witnesses," declares the LORD, "that I am
God.
Yes, and from ancient days I am he.

No one can deliver out of my hand.
When I act, who can reverse it?"

This is what the LORD says—
your Redeemer, the Holy One of Israel:

"For your sake I will send to Babylon
and bring down as fugitives all the Babylonians,
in the ships in which they took pride.

I am the LORD, your Holy One,
Israel's Creator, your King."

This is what the LORD says—
he who made a way through the sea,
a path through the mighty waters,

who drew out the chariots and horses,
the army and reinforcements together,

and they lay there, never to rise again,
extinguished, snuffed out like a wick:

"Forget the former things;
do not dwell on the past.

See, I am doing a new thing!
Now it springs up; do you not perceive it?

I am making a way in the wilderness
and streams in the wasteland.

The wild animals honor me,
the jackals and the owls,

because I provide water in the wilderness
and streams in the wasteland,

to give drink to my people, my chosen,
the people I formed for myself
that they may proclaim my praise.

"Yet you have not called on me, Jacob,
you have not wearied yourselves for me, Israel.

You have not brought me sheep for burnt offerings,
nor honored me with your sacrifices.

I have not burdened you with grain offerings
nor wearied you with demands for incense.

You have not bought any fragrant calamus for me,
or lavished on me the fat of your sacrifices.

But you have burdened me with your sins
and wearied me with your offenses.

"I, even I, am he who blots out
your transgressions, for my own sake,
and remembers your sins no more.

Review the past for me,
let us argue the matter together;
state the case for your innocence.

Your first father sinned;
those I sent to teach you rebelled against me.

So I disgraced the dignitaries of your temple;
I consigned Jacob to destruction
and Israel to scorn.

"But now listen, Jacob, my servant,
Israel, whom I have chosen.

This is what the LORD says—
he who made you, who formed you in the womb,
and who will help you:

Do not be afraid, Jacob, my servant,
Jeshurun, whom I have chosen.

For I will pour water on the thirsty land,
and streams on the dry ground;

I will pour out my Spirit on your offspring,
and my blessing on your descendants.

They will spring up like grass in a meadow,
like poplar trees by flowing streams.

Some will say, 'I belong to the LORD';
others will call themselves by the name of Jacob;

still others will write on their hand, 'The LORD's,'
and will take the name Israel.

"This is what the LORD says—
Israel's King and Redeemer, the LORD Almighty:

I am the first and I am the last;
apart from me there is no God.

Who then is like me? Let him proclaim it.
Let him declare and lay out before me

what has happened since I established my ancient
people,
and what is yet to come—
yes, let them foretell what will come.

Do not tremble, do not be afraid.
Did I not proclaim this and foretell it long ago?

You are my witnesses. Is there any God besides me?
No, there is no other Rock; I know not one."

All who make idols are nothing,
and the things they treasure are worthless.

Those who would speak up for them are blind;
they are ignorant, to their own shame.

Who shapes a god and casts an idol,
which can profit nothing?

People who do that will be put to shame;
such craftsmen are only human beings.

Let them all come together and take their stand;
they will be brought down to terror and shame.

The blacksmith takes a tool
and works with it in the coals;

he shapes an idol with hammers,
he forges it with the might of his arm.

He gets hungry and loses his strength;
he drinks no water and grows faint.

The carpenter measures with a line
and makes an outline with a marker;

he roughs it out with chisels
and marks it with compasses.

He shapes it in human form,
human form in all its glory,
that it may dwell in a shrine.

He cut down cedars,
or perhaps took a cypress or oak.

He let it grow among the trees of the forest,
or planted a pine, and the rain made it grow.

It is used as fuel for burning;
some of it he takes and warms himself,
he kindles a fire and bakes bread.

But he also fashions a god and worships it;
he makes an idol and bows down to it.

Half of the wood he burns in the fire;
over it he prepares his meal,
he roasts his meat and eats his fill.

He also warms himself and says,
"Ah! I am warm; I see the fire."

From the rest he makes a god, his idol;
he bows down to it and worships.

He prays to it and says,
"Save me! You are my god!"

They know nothing, they understand nothing;
their eyes are plastered over so they cannot see,
and their minds closed so they cannot understand.

No one stops to think,
no one has the knowledge or understanding to say,

"Half of it I used for fuel;
I even baked bread over its coals,
I roasted meat and I ate.

Shall I make a detestable thing from what is left?
Shall I bow down to a block of wood?"

Such a person feeds on ashes; a deluded heart
        misleads him;
he cannot save himself, or say,
"Is not this thing in my right hand a lie?"

"Remember these things, Jacob,
for you, Israel, are my servant.

I have made you, you are my servant;
Israel, I will not forget you.

I have swept away your offenses like a cloud,
your sins like the morning mist.

Return to me,
for I have redeemed you."

Sing for joy, you heavens, for the LORD has done this;
shout aloud, you earth beneath.

Burst into song, you mountains,
you forests and all your trees,

for the LORD has redeemed Jacob,
he displays his glory in Israel.

"This is what the LORD says —
your Redeemer, who formed you in the womb:

I am the LORD,
the Maker of all things,
who stretches out the heavens,
who spreads out the earth by myself,

who foils the signs of false prophets
and makes fools of diviners,

who overthrows the learning of the wise
and turns it into nonsense,

who carries out the words of his servants
and fulfills the predictions of his messengers,

who says of Jerusalem, 'It shall be inhabited,'
of the towns of Judah, 'They shall be rebuilt,'
and of their ruins, 'I will restore them,'

who says to the watery deep, 'Be dry,
and I will dry up your streams,'

who says of Cyrus, 'He is my shepherd
and will accomplish all that I please;

he will say of Jerusalem, "Let it be rebuilt,"
and of the temple, "Let its foundations be laid." '

"This is what the LORD says to his anointed,
to Cyrus, whose right hand I take hold of

to subdue nations before him
and to strip kings of their armor,

to open doors before him
so that gates will not be shut:

I will go before you
and will level the mountains;

I will break down gates of bronze
and cut through bars of iron.

I will give you hidden treasures,
riches stored in secret places,

so that you may know that I am the Lord,
the God of Israel, who summons you by name.

For the sake of Jacob my servant,
of Israel my chosen,

I summon you by name
and bestow on you a title of honor,
though you do not acknowledge me.

I am the Lord, and there is no other;
apart from me there is no God.

I will strengthen you,
though you have not acknowledged me,

so that from the rising of the sun
to the place of its setting

people may know there is none besides me.
I am the Lord, and there is no other.

I form the light and create darkness,
I bring prosperity and create disaster;
I, the Lord, do all these things.

"You heavens above, rain down my righteousness;
let the clouds shower it down.

Let the earth open wide,
let salvation spring up,

let righteousness flourish with it;
I, the Lord, have created it.

"Woe to those who quarrel with their Maker,
those who are nothing but potsherds
among the potsherds on the ground.

Does the clay say to the potter,
'What are you making?'

Does your work say,
'The potter has no hands'?

Woe to the one who says to a father,
'What have you begotten?'

or to a mother,
'What have you brought to birth?'

"This is what the LORD says—
the Holy One of Israel, and its Maker:

Concerning things to come,
do you question me about my children,
or give me orders about the work of my hands?

It is I who made the earth
and created mankind on it.

My own hands stretched out the heavens;
I marshaled their starry hosts.

I will raise up Cyrus in my righteousness:
I will make all his ways straight.

He will rebuild my city
and set my exiles free,

but not for a price or reward,
says the LORD Almighty."

This is what the LORD says:

"The products of Egypt and the merchandise of Cush,
and those tall Sabeans—

they will come over to you
and will be yours;

they will trudge behind you,
coming over to you in chains.

They will bow down before you
and plead with you, saying,

'Surely God is with you, and there is no other;
there is no other god.'"

Truly you are a God who has been hiding himself,
the God and Savior of Israel.

All the makers of idols will be put to shame and
        disgraced;
they will go off into disgrace together.

But Israel will be saved by the LORD
with an everlasting salvation;

you will never be put to shame or disgraced,
to ages everlasting.

For this is what the LORD says—

he who created the heavens,
he is God;

he who fashioned and made the earth,
he founded it;

he did not create it to be empty,
but formed it to be inhabited—

he says:

"I am the LORD,
and there is no other.

I have not spoken in secret,
from somewhere in a land of darkness;

I have not said to Jacob's descendants,
'Seek me in vain.'

I, the LORD, speak the truth;
I declare what is right.

"Gather together and come;
assemble, you fugitives from the nations.

Ignorant are those who carry about idols
of wood,
who pray to gods that cannot save.

Declare what is to be, present it—
let them take counsel together.

Who foretold this long ago,
who declared it from the distant past?

Was it not I, the LORD?
And there is no God apart from me,

a righteous God and a Savior;
there is none but me.

"Turn to me and be saved,
all you ends of the earth;
for I am God, and there is no other.

By myself I have sworn,
my mouth has uttered in all integrity
a word that will not be revoked:

Before me every knee will bow;
by me every tongue will swear.

They will say of me, 'In the LORD alone
are deliverance and strength.' "

All who have raged against him
will come to him and be put to shame.

But all the descendants of Israel
will find deliverance in the LORD
and will make their boast in him.

Bel bows down, Nebo stoops low;
their idols are borne by beasts of burden.
The images that are carried about are burdensome,
a burden for the weary.
They stoop and bow down together;
unable to rescue the burden,
they themselves go off into captivity.

"Listen to me, you descendants of Jacob,
all the remnant of the people of Israel,
you whom I have upheld since your birth,
and have carried since you were born.
Even to your old age and gray hairs
I am he, I am he who will sustain you.
I have made you and I will carry you;
I will sustain you and I will rescue you.

"With whom will you compare me or count me equal?
To whom will you liken me that we may be compared?
Some pour out gold from their bags
and weigh out silver on the scales;
they hire a goldsmith to make it into a god,
and they bow down and worship it.
They lift it to their shoulders and carry it;
they set it up in its place, and there it stands.
From that spot it cannot move.
Even though someone cries out to it, it cannot answer;
it cannot save them from their troubles.

"Remember this, keep it in mind,
take it to heart, you rebels.
Remember the former things, those of long ago;
I am God, and there is no other;
I am God, and there is none like me.
I make known the end from the beginning,
from ancient times, what is still to come.

I say, 'My purpose will stand,
and I will do all that I please.'

From the east I summon a bird of prey;
from a far-off land, a man to fulfill my purpose.

What I have said, that I will bring about;
what I have planned, that I will do.

Listen to me, you stubborn-hearted,
you who are now far from my righteousness.

I am bringing my righteousness near,
it is not far away;
and my salvation will not be delayed.

I will grant salvation to Zion,
my splendor to Israel.

"Go down, sit in the dust,
Virgin Daughter Babylon;

sit on the ground without a throne,
queen city of the Babylonians.

No more will you be called
tender or delicate.

Take millstones and grind flour;
take off your veil.

Lift up your skirts, bare your legs,
and wade through the streams.

Your nakedness will be exposed
and your shame uncovered.

I will take vengeance;
I will spare no one."

Our Redeemer — the Lord Almighty is
his name —
is the Holy One of Israel.

"Sit in silence, go into darkness,
queen city of the Babylonians;

no more will you be called
queen of kingdoms.

I was angry with my people
and desecrated my inheritance;

I gave them into your hand,
and you showed them no mercy.

Even on the aged
you laid a very heavy yoke.

You said, 'I am forever—
the eternal queen!'

But you did not consider these things
or reflect on what might happen.

"Now then, listen, you lover of pleasure,
lounging in your security

and saying to yourself,
'I am, and there is none besides me.

I will never be a widow
or suffer the loss of children.'

Both of these will overtake you
in a moment, on a single day:
loss of children and widowhood.

They will come upon you in full measure,
in spite of your many sorceries
and all your potent spells.

You have trusted in your wickedness
and have said, 'No one sees me.'

Your wisdom and knowledge mislead you
when you say to yourself,
'I am, and there is none besides me.'

Disaster will come upon you,
and you will not know how to conjure it away.

A calamity will fall upon you
that you cannot ward off with a ransom;

a catastrophe you cannot foresee
will suddenly come upon you.

"Keep on, then, with your magic spells
and with your many sorceries,
which you have labored at since childhood.

Perhaps you will succeed,
perhaps you will cause terror.

All the counsel you have received has only
worn you out!
Let your astrologers come forward,

those stargazers who make predictions month by
    month,
let them save you from what is coming upon you.

Surely they are like stubble;
the fire will burn them up.

They cannot even save themselves
from the power of the flame.

These are not coals for warmth;
this is not a fire to sit by.

That is all they are to you—
these you have dealt with
and labored with since childhood.

All of them go on in their error;
there is not one that can save you.

"Listen to this, you descendants of Jacob,
you who are called by the name of Israel
and come from the line of Judah,

you who take oaths in the name of the LORD
and invoke the God of Israel—
but not in truth or righteousness—

you who call yourselves citizens of the holy city
and claim to rely on the God of Israel—
the LORD Almighty is his name:

I foretold the former things long ago,
my mouth announced them and I made
    them known;
then suddenly I acted, and they came to pass.

For I knew how stubborn you were;
your neck muscles were iron,
your forehead was bronze.

Therefore I told you these things long ago;
before they happened I announced them to you
so that you could not say,
'My images brought them about;
my wooden image and metal god ordained them.'

You have heard these things; look at them all.
Will you not admit them?

"From now on I will tell you of new things,
of hidden things unknown to you.

They are created now, and not long ago;
you have not heard of them before today.

So you cannot say,
'Yes, I knew of them.'

You have neither heard nor understood;
from of old your ears have not been open.

Well do I know how treacherous you are;
you were called a rebel from birth.

For my own name's sake I delay my wrath;
for the sake of my praise I hold it back
    from you,
so as not to destroy you completely.

See, I have refined you, though not as silver;
I have tested you in the furnace of affliction.

For my own sake, for my own sake, I do this.
How can I let myself be defamed?
I will not yield my glory to another.

"Listen to me, Jacob,
Israel, whom I have called:

I am he;
I am the first and I am the last.

My own hand laid the foundations
    of the earth,
and my right hand spread out the heavens;

when I summon them,
they all stand up together.

"Come together, all of you, and listen:
Which of the idols has foretold these
    things?

The LORD's chosen ally
will carry out his purpose against Babylon;
his arm will be against the Babylonians.

I, even I, have spoken;
yes, I have called him.

I will bring him,
and he will succeed in his mission.

"Come near me and listen to this:

"From the first announcement I have not spoken
　　in secret;
at the time it happens, I am there."

And now the Sovereign Lord has sent me,
endowed with his Spirit.

This is what the Lord says—
your Redeemer, the Holy One of Israel:
"I am the Lord your God,
who teaches you what is best for you,
who directs you in the way you should go.

If only you had paid attention to my commands,
your peace would have been like a river,
your well-being like the waves of the sea.

Your descendants would have been like the sand,
your children like its numberless grains;
their name would never be blotted out
nor destroyed from before me."

Leave Babylon,
flee from the Babylonians!
Announce this with shouts of joy
and proclaim it.
Send it out to the ends of the earth;
say, "The Lord has redeemed his servant Jacob."

They did not thirst when he led them through the
　　deserts;
he made water flow for them from the rock;
he split the rock
and water gushed out.

"There is no peace," says the Lord, "for the wicked."

Listen to me, you islands;
hear this, you distant nations:
Before I was born the Lord called me;
from my mother's womb he has spoken my name.

He made my mouth like a sharpened sword,
in the shadow of his hand he hid me;

he made me into a polished arrow
and concealed me in his quiver.

He said to me, "You are my servant,
Israel, in whom I will display my splendor."

But I said, "I have labored in vain;
I have spent my strength for nothing at all.

Yet what is due me is in the LORD's hand,
and my reward is with my God."

And now the LORD says—
he who formed me in the womb to be his servant

to bring Jacob back to him
and gather Israel to himself,

for I am honored in the eyes of the LORD
and my God has been my strength—

he says:

"It is too small a thing for you to be my servant
to restore the tribes of Jacob
and bring back those of Israel I have kept.

I will also make you a light for the Gentiles,
that my salvation may reach to the ends of the earth."

This is what the LORD says—
the Redeemer and Holy One of Israel—

to him who was despised and abhorred by the nation,
to the servant of rulers:

"Kings will see you and stand up,
princes will see and bow down,

because of the LORD, who is faithful,
the Holy One of Israel, who has chosen you."

This is what the LORD says:

"In the time of my favor I will answer you,
and in the day of salvation I will help you;

I will keep you and will make you
to be a covenant for the people,

to restore the land
and to reassign its desolate inheritances,

to say to the captives, 'Come out,'
and to those in darkness, 'Be free!'

"They will feed beside the roads
and find pasture on every barren hill.

They will neither hunger nor thirst,
nor will the desert heat or the sun beat down on them.

He who has compassion on them will guide them
and lead them beside springs of water.

I will turn all my mountains into roads,
and my highways will be raised up.

See, they will come from afar —
some from the north, some from the west,
some from the region of Aswan."

Shout for joy, you heavens;
rejoice, you earth;
burst into song, you mountains!

For the Lord comforts his people
and will have compassion on his afflicted ones.

But Zion said, "The Lord has forsaken me,
the Lord has forgotten me."

"Can a mother forget the baby at her breast
and have no compassion on the child she has borne?

Though she may forget,
I will not forget you!

See, I have engraved you on the palms of my hands;
your walls are ever before me.

Your children hasten back,
and those who laid you waste depart from you.

Lift up your eyes and look around;
all your children gather and come to you.

As surely as I live," declares the Lord,
"you will wear them all as ornaments;
you will put them on, like a bride.

"Though you were ruined and made desolate
and your land laid waste,

now you will be too small for your people,
and those who devoured you will be far away.

The children born during your bereavement
will yet say in your hearing,

'This place is too small for us;
give us more space to live in.'

Then you will say in your heart,
'Who bore me these?
I was bereaved and barren;
I was exiled and rejected.
Who brought these up?

I was left all alone,
but these — where have they come from?' "

This is what the Sovereign Lord says:

"See, I will beckon to the nations,
I will lift up my banner to the peoples;

they will bring your sons in their arms
and carry your daughters on their hips.

Kings will be your foster fathers,
and their queens your nursing mothers.

They will bow down before you with their faces
    to the ground;
they will lick the dust at your feet.

Then you will know that I am the Lord;
those who hope in me will not be disappointed."

Can plunder be taken from warriors,
or captives be rescued from the fierce?

But this is what the Lord says:

"Yes, captives will be taken from warriors,
and plunder retrieved from the fierce;

I will contend with those who contend with you,
and your children I will save.

I will make your oppressors eat their own flesh;
they will be drunk on their own blood, as with wine.

Then all mankind will know
that I, the Lord, am your Savior,
your Redeemer, the Mighty One of Jacob."

This is what the LORD says:

"Where is your mother's certificate of divorce
with which I sent her away?
Or to which of my creditors
did I sell you?
Because of your sins you were sold;
because of your transgressions your mother
      was sent away.
When I came, why was there no one?
When I called, why was there no one to answer?
Was my arm too short to deliver you?
Do I lack the strength to rescue you?
By a mere rebuke I dry up the sea,
I turn rivers into a desert;
their fish rot for lack of water
and die of thirst.
I clothe the heavens with darkness
and make sackcloth its covering."

The Sovereign LORD has given me a well-instructed
      tongue,
to know the word that sustains the weary.
He wakens me morning by morning,
wakens my ear to listen like one being instructed.
The Sovereign LORD has opened my ears;
I have not been rebellious,
I have not turned away.
I offered my back to those who beat me,
my cheeks to those who pulled out my beard;
I did not hide my face
from mocking and spitting.
Because the Sovereign LORD helps me,
I will not be disgraced.
Therefore have I set my face like flint,
and I know I will not be put to shame.
He who vindicates me is near.
Who then will bring charges against me?
Let us face each other!

Who is my accuser?
Let him confront me!

It is the Sovereign Lord who helps me.
Who will condemn me?

They will all wear out like a garment;
the moths will eat them up.

Who among you fears the Lord
and obeys the word of his servant?

Let the one who walks in the dark,
who has no light,

trust in the name of the Lord
and rely on their God.

But now, all you who light fires
and provide yourselves with flaming torches,

go, walk in the light of your fires
and of the torches you have set ablaze.

This is what you shall receive from my hand:
You will lie down in torment.

"Listen to me, you who pursue righteousness
and who seek the Lord:

Look to the rock from which you were cut
and to the quarry from which you were hewn;

look to Abraham, your father,
and to Sarah, who gave you birth.

When I called him he was only one man,
and I blessed him and made him many.

The Lord will surely comfort Zion
and will look with compassion on all her ruins;

he will make her deserts like Eden,
her wastelands like the garden of the Lord.

Joy and gladness will be found in her,
thanksgiving and the sound of singing.

"Listen to me, my people;
hear me, my nation:

Instruction will go out from me;
my justice will become a light to the nations.

My righteousness draws near speedily,
my salvation is on the way,
and my arm will bring justice to the nations.

The islands will look to me
and wait in hope for my arm.

Lift up your eyes to the heavens,
look at the earth beneath;

the heavens will vanish like smoke,
the earth will wear out like a garment
and its inhabitants die like flies.

But my salvation will last forever,
my righteousness will never fail.

"Hear me, you who know what is right,
you people who have taken my instruction to heart:

Do not fear the reproach of mere mortals
or be terrified by their insults.

For the moth will eat them up like a garment;
the worm will devour them like wool.

But my righteousness will last forever,
my salvation through all generations."

Awake, awake, arm of the Lord,
clothe yourself with strength!

Awake, as in days gone by,
as in generations of old.

Was it not you who cut Rahab to pieces,
who pierced that monster through?

Was it not you who dried up the sea,
the waters of the great deep,

who made a road in the depths of the sea
so that the redeemed might cross over?

Those the Lord has rescued will return.
They will enter Zion with singing;
everlasting joy will crown their heads.

Gladness and joy will overtake them,
and sorrow and sighing will flee away.

"I, even I, am he who comforts you.
Who are you that you fear mere mortals,
human beings who are but grass,

that you forget the LORD your Maker,
who stretches out the heavens
and who lays the foundations of the earth,

that you live in constant terror every day
because of the wrath of the oppressor,
who is bent on destruction?

For where is the wrath of the oppressor?
The cowering prisoners will soon be set free;

they will not die in their dungeon,
nor will they lack bread.

For I am the LORD your God,
who stirs up the sea so that its waves roar —
the LORD Almighty is his name.

I have put my words in your mouth
and covered you with the shadow of my hand —

I who set the heavens in place,
who laid the foundations of the earth,
and who say to Zion, 'You are my people.'"

Awake, awake!
Rise up, Jerusalem,

you who have drunk from the hand of the LORD
the cup of his wrath,

you who have drained to its dregs
the goblet that makes people stagger.

Among all the children she bore
there was none to guide her;

among all the children she reared
there was none to take her by the hand.

These double calamities have come upon you —
who can comfort you? —

ruin and destruction, famine and sword —
who can console you?

Your children have fainted;
they lie at every street corner,
like antelope caught in a net.

They are filled with the wrath of the LORD,
with the rebuke of your God.

Therefore hear this, you afflicted one,
made drunk, but not with wine.

This is what your Sovereign Lord says,
your God, who defends his people:

"See, I have taken out of your hand
the cup that made you stagger;

from that cup, the goblet of my wrath,
you will never drink again.

I will put it into the hands of your tormentors,
who said to you,
'Fall prostrate that we may walk on you.'

And you made your back like the ground,
like a street to be walked on."

Awake, awake, Zion,
clothe yourself with strength!

Put on your garments of splendor,
Jerusalem, the holy city.

The uncircumcised and defiled
will not enter you again.

Shake off your dust;
rise up, sit enthroned, Jerusalem.

Free yourself from the chains on your neck,
Daughter Zion, now a captive.

For this is what the Lord says:

"You were sold for nothing,
and without money you will be redeemed."

For this is what the Sovereign Lord says:

"At first my people went down to Egypt to live;
lately, Assyria has oppressed them.

"And now what do I have here?" declares the Lord.

"For my people have been taken away for nothing,
and those who rule them mock,"
declares the Lord.

"And all day long
my name is constantly blasphemed.

Therefore my people will know my name;
therefore in that day they will know

that it is I who foretold it.
Yes, it is I."

How beautiful on the mountains
are the feet of those who bring good news,

who proclaim peace,
who bring good tidings,
who proclaim salvation,

who say to Zion,
"Your God reigns!"

Listen! Your watchmen lift up their voices;
together they shout for joy.

When the Lord returns to Zion,
they will see it with their own eyes.

Burst into songs of joy together,
you ruins of Jerusalem,

for the Lord has comforted his people,
he has redeemed Jerusalem.

The Lord will lay bare his holy arm
in the sight of all the nations,

and all the ends of the earth will see
the salvation of our God.

Depart, depart, go out from there!
Touch no unclean thing!

Come out from it and be pure,
you who carry the articles of the Lord's house.

But you will not leave in haste
or go in flight;

for the Lord will go before you,
the God of Israel will be your rear guard.

See, my servant will act wisely;
he will be raised and lifted up and
highly exalted.

Just as there were many who were appalled at him —
his appearance was so disfigured beyond that of any
human being
and his form marred beyond human likeness —

so he will sprinkle many nations,
and kings will shut their mouths because of him.

For what they were not told, they will see,
and what they have not heard, they will understand.

Who has believed our message
and to whom has the arm of the LORD been
  revealed?

He grew up before him like a tender shoot,
and like a root out of dry ground.

He had no beauty or majesty to attract us to him,
nothing in his appearance that we should desire him.

He was despised and rejected by mankind,
a man of suffering, and familiar with pain.

Like one from whom people hide their faces
he was despised, and we held him in low esteem.

Surely he took up our pain
and bore our suffering,

yet we considered him punished by God,
stricken by him, and afflicted.

But he was pierced for our transgressions,
he was crushed for our iniquities;

the punishment that brought us peace was on him,
and by his wounds we are healed.

We all, like sheep, have gone astray,
each of us has turned to our own way;

and the LORD has laid on him
the iniquity of us all.

He was oppressed and afflicted,
yet he did not open his mouth;

he was led like a lamb to the slaughter,
and as a sheep before its shearers is silent,
so he did not open his mouth.

By oppression and judgment he was taken away.
Yet who of his generation protested?

For he was cut off from the land of the living;
for the transgression of my people he was punished.

He was assigned a grave with the wicked,
and with the rich in his death,

though he had done no violence,
nor was any deceit in his mouth.

Yet it was the LORD's will to crush him and cause him
to suffer,
and though the LORD makes his life an offering for sin,
he will see his offspring and prolong his days,
and the will of the LORD will prosper in his hand.
After he has suffered,
he will see the light of life and be satisfied;
by his knowledge my righteous servant will justify
many,
and he will bear their iniquities.
Therefore I will give him a portion among the great,
and he will divide the spoils with the strong,
because he poured out his life unto death,
and was numbered with the transgressors.
For he bore the sin of many,
and made intercession for the transgressors.

"Sing, barren woman,
you who never bore a child;
burst into song, shout for joy,
you who were never in labor;
because more are the children of the desolate woman
than of her who has a husband,"
says the LORD.

"Enlarge the place of your tent,
stretch your tent curtains wide,
do not hold back;
lengthen your cords,
strengthen your stakes.
For you will spread out to the right and to the left;
your descendants will dispossess nations
and settle in their desolate cities.

"Do not be afraid; you will not be put to shame.
Do not fear disgrace; you will not be humiliated.
You will forget the shame of your youth
and remember no more the reproach of your widowhood.

For your Maker is your husband—
the Lord Almighty is his name—

the Holy One of Israel is your Redeemer;
he is called the God of all the earth.

The Lord will call you back
as if you were a wife deserted and distressed in spirit—
a wife who married young,
only to be rejected," says your God.

"For a brief moment I abandoned you,
but with deep compassion I will bring you back.

In a surge of anger
I hid my face from you for a moment,

but with everlasting kindness
I will have compassion on you,"
says the Lord your Redeemer.

"To me this is like the days of Noah,
when I swore that the waters of Noah would never
      again cover the earth.

So now I have sworn not to be angry with you,
never to rebuke you again.

Though the mountains be shaken
and the hills be removed,

yet my unfailing love for you will not be shaken
nor my covenant of peace be removed,"
says the Lord, who has compassion on you.

"Afflicted city, lashed by storms and
      not comforted,
I will rebuild you with stones of turquoise,
your foundations with lapis lazuli.

I will make your battlements of rubies,
your gates of sparkling jewels,
and all your walls of precious stones.

All your children will be taught by the Lord,
and great will be their peace.

In righteousness you will be established:

Tyranny will be far from you;
you will have nothing to fear.

Terror will be far removed;
it will not come near you.

If anyone does attack you, it will not be my doing;
whoever attacks you will surrender to you.

"See, it is I who created the blacksmith
who fans the coals into flame
and forges a weapon fit for its work.
And it is I who have created the destroyer to wreak
havoc;
no weapon forged against you will prevail,
and you will refute every tongue that accuses you.
This is the heritage of the servants of the LORD,
and this is their vindication from me,"
declares the LORD.

"Come, all you who are thirsty,
come to the waters;
and you who have no money,
come, buy and eat!
Come, buy wine and milk
without money and without cost.
Why spend money on what is not bread,
and your labor on what does not satisfy?
Listen, listen to me, and eat what is good,
and you will delight in the richest of fare.
Give ear and come to me;
listen, that you may live.
I will make an everlasting covenant with you,
my faithful love promised to David.
See, I have made him a witness to the peoples,
a ruler and commander of the peoples.
Surely you will summon nations you know not,
and nations you do not know will come
running to you,
because of the LORD your God,
the Holy One of Israel,
for he has endowed you with splendor."

Seek the LORD while he may be found;
call on him while he is near.
Let the wicked forsake their ways
and the unrighteous their thoughts.

Let them turn to the Lord, and he will have mercy
    on them,
and to our God, for he will freely pardon.

"For my thoughts are not your thoughts,
neither are your ways my ways,"
                    declares the Lord.
"As the heavens are higher than the earth,
so are my ways higher than your ways
and my thoughts than your thoughts.

As the rain and the snow
come down from heaven,

and do not return to it
without watering the earth

and making it bud and flourish,
so that it yields seed for the sower and bread
    for the eater,

so is my word that goes out from my mouth:
It will not return to me empty,

but will accomplish what I desire
and achieve the purpose for which I sent it.

You will go out in joy
and be led forth in peace;

the mountains and hills
will burst into song before you,

and all the trees of the field
will clap their hands.

Instead of the thornbush will grow
    the juniper,
and instead of briers the myrtle will grow.

This will be for the Lord's renown,
for an everlasting sign,
that will endure forever."

This is what the Lord says:

"Maintain justice
and do what is right,

for my salvation is close at hand
and my righteousness will soon be revealed.

Blessed is the one who does this —
the person who holds it fast,

who keeps the Sabbath without desecrating it,
and keeps their hands from doing any evil."

Let no foreigner who is bound to the LORD say,
"The LORD will surely exclude me from his people."

And let no eunuch complain,
"I am only a dry tree."

For this is what the LORD says:

"To the eunuchs who keep my Sabbaths,
who choose what pleases me
and hold fast to my covenant —

to them I will give within my temple and its walls
a memorial and a name
better than sons and daughters;

I will give them an everlasting name
that will endure forever.

And foreigners who bind themselves to the LORD
to minister to him,

to love the name of the LORD,
and to be his servants,

all who keep the Sabbath without desecrating it
and who hold fast to my covenant —

these I will bring to my holy mountain
and give them joy in my house of prayer.

Their burnt offerings and sacrifices
will be accepted on my altar;

for my house will be called
a house of prayer for all nations."

The Sovereign LORD declares —
he who gathers the exiles of Israel:

"I will gather still others to them
besides those already gathered."

Come, all you beasts of the field,
come and devour, all you beasts of the forest!

Israel's watchmen are blind,
they all lack knowledge;

they are all mute dogs,
they cannot bark;

they lie around and dream,
they love to sleep.

They are dogs with mighty appetites;
they never have enough.

They are shepherds who lack understanding;
they all turn to their own way,
they seek their own gain.

"Come," each one cries, "let me get wine!
Let us drink our fill of beer!

And tomorrow will be like today,
or even far better."

The righteous perish,
and no one takes it to heart;

the devout are taken away,
and no one understands

that the righteous are taken away
to be spared from evil.

Those who walk uprightly
enter into peace;
they find rest as they lie in death.

"But you — come here, you children of a sorceress,
you offspring of adulterers and prostitutes!

Who are you mocking?
At whom do you sneer
and stick out your tongue?

Are you not a brood of rebels,
the offspring of liars?

You burn with lust among the oaks
and under every spreading tree;

you sacrifice your children in the ravines
and under the overhanging crags.

The idols among the smooth stones of the ravines are
your portion;
indeed, they are your lot.

Yes, to them you have poured out drink offerings
and offered grain offerings.
In view of all this, should I relent?

You have made your bed on a high and lofty hill;
there you went up to offer your sacrifices.

Behind your doors and your doorposts
you have put your pagan symbols.

Forsaking me, you uncovered your bed,
you climbed into it and opened it wide;

you made a pact with those whose beds you love,
and you looked with lust on their naked bodies.

You went to Molek with olive oil
and increased your perfumes.

You sent your ambassadors far away;
you descended to the very realm of the dead!

You wearied yourself by such going about,
but you would not say, 'It is hopeless.'

You found renewal of your strength,
and so you did not faint.

"Whom have you so dreaded and feared
that you have not been true to me,

and have neither remembered me
nor taken this to heart?

Is it not because I have long been silent
that you do not fear me?

I will expose your righteousness and
your works,
and they will not benefit you.

When you cry out for help,
let your collection of idols save you!

The wind will carry all of them off,
a mere breath will blow them away.

But whoever takes refuge in me
will inherit the land
and possess my holy mountain."

And it will be said:

"Build up, build up, prepare the road!
Remove the obstacles out of the way of my people."

For this is what the high and exalted One says —
he who lives forever, whose name is holy:

"I live in a high and holy place,
but also with the one who is contrite and lowly
    in spirit,
to revive the spirit of the lowly
and to revive the heart of the contrite.

I will not accuse them forever,
nor will I always be angry,
for then they would faint away because of me —
the very people I have created.

I was enraged by their sinful greed;
I punished them, and hid my face in anger,
yet they kept on in their willful ways.

I have seen their ways, but I will heal them;
I will guide them and restore comfort to Israel's
    mourners,
creating praise on their lips.

Peace, peace, to those far and near,"
says the LORD. "And I will heal them."

But the wicked are like the tossing sea,
which cannot rest,
whose waves cast up mire and mud.

"There is no peace," says my God, "for the wicked."

"Shout it aloud, do not hold back.
Raise your voice like a trumpet.

Declare to my people their rebellion
and to the descendants of Jacob their sins.

For day after day they seek me out;
they seem eager to know my ways,
as if they were a nation that does what is right
and has not forsaken the commands of its God.

They ask me for just decisions
and seem eager for God to come near them.

'Why have we fasted,' they say,
'and you have not seen it?

Why have we humbled ourselves,
and you have not noticed?'

"Yet on the day of your fasting, you do as you please
and exploit all your workers.

Your fasting ends in quarreling and strife,
and in striking each other with wicked fists.

You cannot fast as you do today
and expect your voice to be heard on high.

Is this the kind of fast I have chosen,
only a day for people to humble themselves?

Is it only for bowing one's head like a reed
and for lying in sackcloth and ashes?

Is that what you call a fast,
a day acceptable to the Lord?

"Is not this the kind of fasting I have chosen:

to loose the chains of injustice
and untie the cords of the yoke,

to set the oppressed free
and break every yoke?

Is it not to share your food with the hungry
and to provide the poor wanderer with shelter —

when you see the naked, to clothe them,
and not to turn away from your own flesh and blood?

Then your light will break forth like the dawn,
and your healing will quickly appear;

then your righteousness will go before you,
and the glory of the Lord will be your rear guard.

Then you will call, and the Lord will answer;
you will cry for help, and he will say: Here am I.

"If you do away with the yoke of oppression,
with the pointing finger and malicious talk,

and if you spend yourselves in behalf of the hungry
and satisfy the needs of the oppressed,

then your light will rise in the darkness,
and your night will become like the noonday.

The Lord will guide you always;
he will satisfy your needs in a sun-scorched land
and will strengthen your frame.

You will be like a well-watered garden,
like a spring whose waters never fail.

Your people will rebuild the ancient ruins
and will raise up the age-old foundations;

you will be called Repairer of Broken Walls,
Restorer of Streets with Dwellings.

"If you keep your feet from breaking the Sabbath
and from doing as you please on my holy day,

if you call the Sabbath a delight
and the LORD's holy day honorable,

and if you honor it by not going your own way
and not doing as you please or speaking idle words,

then you will find your joy in the LORD,
and I will cause you to ride in triumph on the heights
    of the land
and to feast on the inheritance of your father Jacob."

For the mouth of the LORD has spoken.

Surely the arm of the LORD is not too short to save,
nor his ear too dull to hear.

But your iniquities have separated
you from your God;

your sins have hidden his face from you,
so that he will not hear.

For your hands are stained with blood,
your fingers with guilt.

Your lips have spoken falsely,
and your tongue mutters wicked things.

No one calls for justice;
no one pleads a case with integrity.

They rely on empty arguments, they utter lies;
they conceive trouble and give birth to evil.

They hatch the eggs of vipers
and spin a spider's web.

Whoever eats their eggs will die,
and when one is broken, an adder is hatched.

Their cobwebs are useless for clothing;
they cannot cover themselves with what they make.

Their deeds are evil deeds,
and acts of violence are in their hands.

Their feet rush into sin;
they are swift to shed innocent blood.

They pursue evil schemes;
acts of violence mark their ways.

The way of peace they do not know;
there is no justice in their paths.

They have turned them into crooked roads;
no one who walks along them will know peace.

So justice is far from us,
and righteousness does not reach us.

We look for light, but all is darkness;
for brightness, but we walk in deep shadows.

Like the blind we grope along the wall,
feeling our way like people without eyes.

At midday we stumble as if it were twilight;
among the strong, we are like the dead.

We all growl like bears;
we moan mournfully like doves.

We look for justice, but find none;
for deliverance, but it is far away.

For our offenses are many in your sight,
and our sins testify against us.

Our offenses are ever with us,
and we acknowledge our iniquities:

rebellion and treachery against the Lord,
turning our backs on our God,

inciting revolt and oppression,
uttering lies our hearts have conceived.

So justice is driven back,
and righteousness stands at a distance;

truth has stumbled in the streets,
honesty cannot enter.

Truth is nowhere to be found,
and whoever shuns evil becomes a prey.

The Lord looked and was displeased
that there was no justice.

He saw that there was no one,
he was appalled that there was no one to intervene;

so his own arm achieved salvation for him,
and his own righteousness sustained him.

He put on righteousness as his breastplate,
and the helmet of salvation on his head;

he put on the garments of vengeance
and wrapped himself in zeal as in a cloak.

According to what they have done,
so will he repay

wrath to his enemies
and retribution to his foes;
he will repay the islands their due.

From the west, people will fear the name of the Lord,
and from the rising of the sun, they will revere his glory.

For he will come like a pent-up flood
that the breath of the Lord drives along.

"The Redeemer will come to Zion,
to those in Jacob who repent of their sins,"
                              declares the Lord.

"As for me, this is my covenant with them," says the Lord. "My Spirit, who is on you, will not depart from you, and my words that I have put in your mouth will always be on your lips, on the lips of your children and on the lips of their descendants — from this time on and forever," says the Lord.

"Arise, shine, for your light has come,
and the glory of the Lord rises upon you.

See, darkness covers the earth
and thick darkness is over the peoples,

but the Lord rises upon you
and his glory appears over you.

Nations will come to your light,
and kings to the brightness of your dawn.

"Lift up your eyes and look about you:
All assemble and come to you;

your sons come from afar,
and your daughters are carried on the hip.

Then you will look and be radiant,
your heart will throb and swell with joy;

the wealth on the seas will be brought to you,
to you the riches of the nations will come.

Herds of camels will cover your land,
young camels of Midian and Ephah.

And all from Sheba will come,
bearing gold and incense
and proclaiming the praise of the Lord.

All Kedar's flocks will be gathered to you,
the rams of Nebaioth will serve you;

they will be accepted as offerings on my altar,
and I will adorn my glorious temple.

"Who are these that fly along like clouds,
like doves to their nests?

Surely the islands look to me;
in the lead are the ships of Tarshish,

bringing your children from afar,
with their silver and gold,

to the honor of the Lord your God,
the Holy One of Israel,
for he has endowed you with splendor.

"Foreigners will rebuild your walls,
and their kings will serve you.

Though in anger I struck you,
in favor I will show you compassion.

Your gates will always stand open,
they will never be shut, day or night,

so that people may bring you the wealth
of the nations—
their kings led in triumphal procession.

For the nation or kingdom that will not serve you
will perish;
it will be utterly ruined.

"The glory of Lebanon will come to you,
the juniper, the fir and the cypress together,

to adorn my sanctuary;
and I will glorify the place for my feet.

The children of your oppressors will come bowing
before you;
all who despise you will bow down at your feet
and will call you the City of the Lord,
Zion of the Holy One of Israel.

"Although you have been forsaken and hated,
with no one traveling through,
I will make you the everlasting pride
and the joy of all generations.

You will drink the milk of nations
and be nursed at royal breasts.

Then you will know that I, the LORD, am your Savior,
your Redeemer, the Mighty One of Jacob.

Instead of bronze I will bring you gold,
and silver in place of iron.

Instead of wood I will bring you bronze,
and iron in place of stones.

I will make peace your governor
and well-being your ruler.

No longer will violence be heard in your land,
nor ruin or destruction within your borders,

but you will call your walls Salvation
and your gates Praise.

The sun will no more be your light by day,
nor will the brightness of the moon shine on you,

for the LORD will be your everlasting light,
and your God will be your glory.

Your sun will never set again,
and your moon will wane no more;

the LORD will be your everlasting light,
and your days of sorrow will end.

Then all your people will be righteous
and they will possess the land forever.

They are the shoot I have planted,
the work of my hands,
for the display of my splendor.

The least of you will become a thousand,
the smallest a mighty nation.

I am the LORD;
in its time I will do this swiftly."

The Spirit of the Sovereign LORD is on me,
because the LORD has anointed me
to proclaim good news to the poor.

He has sent me to bind up the brokenhearted,
to proclaim freedom for the captives
and release from darkness for the prisoners,

to proclaim the year of the LORD's favor
and the day of vengeance of our God,

to comfort all who mourn,
and provide for those who grieve in Zion—

to bestow on them a crown of beauty
instead of ashes,

the oil of joy
instead of mourning,

and a garment of praise
instead of a spirit of despair.

They will be called oaks of righteousness,
a planting of the LORD
for the display of his splendor.

They will rebuild the ancient ruins
and restore the places long devastated;

they will renew the ruined cities
that have been devastated for generations.

Strangers will shepherd your flocks;
foreigners will work your fields and vineyards.

And you will be called priests of the LORD,
you will be named ministers of our God.

You will feed on the wealth of nations,
and in their riches you will boast.

Instead of your shame
you will receive a double portion,

and instead of disgrace
you will rejoice in your inheritance.

And so you will inherit a double portion in your land,
and everlasting joy will be yours.

"For I, the LORD, love justice;
I hate robbery and wrongdoing.

In my faithfulness I will reward my people
and make an everlasting covenant with them.

Their descendants will be known among the nations
and their offspring among the peoples.

All who see them will acknowledge
that they are a people the Lord has blessed."

I delight greatly in the Lord;
my soul rejoices in my God.

For he has clothed me with garments of salvation
and arrayed me in a robe of his righteousness,

as a bridegroom adorns his head like a priest,
and as a bride adorns herself with her jewels.

For as the soil makes the sprout come up
and a garden causes seeds to grow,

so the Sovereign Lord will make righteousness
and praise spring up before all nations.

For Zion's sake I will not keep silent,
for Jerusalem's sake I will not remain quiet,

till her vindication shines out like the dawn,
her salvation like a blazing torch.

The nations will see your vindication,
and all kings your glory;

you will be called by a new name
that the mouth of the Lord will bestow.

You will be a crown of splendor in the Lord's hand,
a royal diadem in the hand of your God.

No longer will they call you Deserted,
or name your land Desolate.

But you will be called Hephzibah,
and your land Beulah;

for the Lord will take delight in you,
and your land will be married.

As a young man marries a young woman,
so will your Builder marry you;

as a bridegroom rejoices over his bride,
so will your God rejoice over you.

I have posted watchmen on your walls, Jerusalem;
they will never be silent day or night.

You who call on the Lord,
give yourselves no rest,

and give him no rest till he establishes Jerusalem
and makes her the praise of the earth.

The Lord has sworn by his right hand
and by his mighty arm:
"Never again will I give your grain
as food for your enemies,
and never again will foreigners drink the new wine
for which you have toiled;
but those who harvest it will eat it
and praise the Lord,
and those who gather the grapes will drink it
in the courts of my sanctuary."

Pass through, pass through the gates!
Prepare the way for the people.
Build up, build up the highway!
Remove the stones.
Raise a banner for the nations.

The Lord has made proclamation
to the ends of the earth:
"Say to Daughter Zion,
'See, your Savior comes!
See, his reward is with him,
and his recompense accompanies him.'"
They will be called the Holy People,
the Redeemed of the Lord;
and you will be called Sought After,
the City No Longer Deserted.

Who is this coming from Edom,
from Bozrah, with his garments stained crimson?
Who is this, robed in splendor,
striding forward in the greatness of his strength?

"It is I, proclaiming victory,
mighty to save."

Why are your garments red,
like those of one treading the winepress?

"I have trodden the winepress alone;
from the nations no one was with me.

I trampled them in my anger
and trod them down in my wrath;

their blood spattered my garments,
and I stained all my clothing.

It was for me the day of vengeance;
the year for me to redeem had come.

I looked, but there was no one to help,
I was appalled that no one gave support;

so my own arm achieved salvation for me,
and my own wrath sustained me.

I trampled the nations in my anger;
in my wrath I made them drunk
and poured their blood on the ground."

I will tell of the kindnesses of the LORD,
the deeds for which he is to be praised,
according to all the LORD has done for us—

yes, the many good things
he has done for Israel,
according to his compassion and many
kindnesses.

He said, "Surely they are my people,
children who will be true to me";
and so he became their Savior.

In all their distress he too was distressed,
and the angel of his presence saved them.

In his love and mercy he redeemed them;
he lifted them up and carried them
all the days of old.

Yet they rebelled
and grieved his Holy Spirit.

So he turned and became their enemy
and he himself fought against them.

Then his people recalled the days of old,
the days of Moses and his people—

where is he who brought them through the sea,
with the shepherd of his flock?

Where is he who set
his Holy Spirit among them,

who sent his glorious arm of power
to be at Moses' right hand,

who divided the waters before them,
to gain for himself everlasting renown,

who led them through the depths?

Like a horse in open country,
they did not stumble;

like cattle that go down to the plain,
they were given rest by the Spirit of the Lord.

This is how you guided your people
to make for yourself a glorious name.

Look down from heaven and see,
from your lofty throne, holy and glorious.

Where are your zeal and your might?
Your tenderness and compassion are withheld from us.

But you are our Father,
though Abraham does not know us
or Israel acknowledge us;

you, Lord, are our Father,
our Redeemer from of old is your name.

Why, Lord, do you make us wander from your ways
and harden our hearts so we do not revere you?

Return for the sake of your servants,
the tribes that are your inheritance.

For a little while your people possessed your
holy place,

but now our enemies have trampled down your
sanctuary.

We are yours from of old;
but you have not ruled over them,
they have not been called by your name.

Oh, that you would rend the heavens and come down,
that the mountains would tremble before you!

As when fire sets twigs ablaze
and causes water to boil,

come down to make your name known to your enemies
and cause the nations to quake before you!

For when you did awesome things that we did not
        expect,
you came down, and the mountains trembled before
        you.

Since ancient times no one has heard,
no ear has perceived,

no eye has seen any God besides you,
who acts on behalf of those who wait for him.

You come to the help of those who gladly do right,
who remember your ways.

But when we continued to sin against them,
you were angry.
How then can we be saved?

All of us have become like one who is unclean,
and all our righteous acts are like filthy rags;

we all shrivel up like a leaf,
and like the wind our sins sweep us away.

No one calls on your name
or strives to lay hold of you;

for you have hidden your face from us
and have given us over to our sins.

Yet you, Lord, are our Father.
We are the clay, you are the potter;
we are all the work of your hand.

Do not be angry beyond measure, Lord;
do not remember our sins forever.

Oh, look on us, we pray,
for we are all your people.

Your sacred cities have become a wasteland;
even Zion is a wasteland, Jerusalem a desolation.

Our holy and glorious temple, where our ancestors
        praised you,
has been burned with fire,
and all that we treasured lies in ruins.

After all this, Lord, will you hold yourself back?
Will you keep silent and punish us beyond measure?

"I revealed myself to those who did not ask for me;
I was found by those who did not seek me.

To a nation that did not call on my name,
I said, 'Here am I, here am I.'

All day long I have held out my hands
to an obstinate people,

who walk in ways not good,
pursuing their own imaginations—

a people who continually provoke me
to my very face,

offering sacrifices in gardens
and burning incense on altars of brick;

who sit among the graves
and spend their nights keeping secret vigil;

who eat the flesh of pigs,
and whose pots hold broth of impure meat;

who say, 'Keep away; don't come near me,
for I am too sacred for you!'

Such people are smoke in my nostrils,
a fire that keeps burning all day.

"See, it stands written before me:
I will not keep silent but will pay back in full;
I will pay it back into their laps—

both your sins and the sins of your ancestors,"
says the Lord.

"Because they burned sacrifices on the mountains
and defied me on the hills,

I will measure into their laps
the full payment for their former deeds."

This is what the Lord says:

"As when juice is still found in a cluster of grapes
and people say, 'Don't destroy it,
there is still a blessing in it,'

so will I do in behalf of my servants;
I will not destroy them all.

I will bring forth descendants from Jacob,
and from Judah those who will possess
my mountains;

my chosen people will inherit them,
and there will my servants live.

Sharon will become a pasture for flocks,
and the Valley of Achor a resting place for herds,
for my people who seek me.

"But as for you who forsake the LORD
and forget my holy mountain,
who spread a table for Fortune
and fill bowls of mixed wine for Destiny,
I will destine you for the sword,
and all of you will fall in the slaughter;
for I called but you did not answer,
I spoke but you did not listen.
You did evil in my sight
and chose what displeases me."

Therefore this is what the Sovereign LORD says:

"My servants will eat,
but you will go hungry;
my servants will drink,
but you will go thirsty;
my servants will rejoice,
but you will be put to shame.
My servants will sing
out of the joy of their hearts,
but you will cry out
from anguish of heart
and wail in brokenness of spirit.
You will leave your name
for my chosen ones to use in their curses;
the Sovereign LORD will put you to death,
but to his servants he will give another name.
Whoever invokes a blessing in the land
will do so by the one true God;
whoever takes an oath in the land
will swear by the one true God.
For the past troubles will be forgotten
and hidden from my eyes.

"See, I will create
new heavens and a new earth.

The former things will not be remembered,
nor will they come to mind.

But be glad and rejoice forever
in what I will create,
for I will create Jerusalem to be a delight
and its people a joy.

I will rejoice over Jerusalem
and take delight in my people;
the sound of weeping and of crying
will be heard in it no more.

"Never again will there be in it
an infant who lives but a few days,
or an old man who does not live out his years;
the one who dies at a hundred
will be thought a mere child;
the one who fails to reach a hundred
will be considered accursed.

They will build houses and dwell in them;
they will plant vineyards and eat their fruit.

No longer will they build houses and others
live in them,
or plant and others eat.

For as the days of a tree,
so will be the days of my people;
my chosen ones will long enjoy
the work of their hands.

They will not labor in vain,
nor will they bear children doomed
to misfortune;
for they will be a people blessed by the LORD,
they and their descendants with them.

Before they call I will answer;
while they are still speaking I will hear.

The wolf and the lamb will feed together,
and the lion will eat straw like the ox,
and dust will be the serpent's food.

They will neither harm nor destroy
on all my holy mountain,"

says the LORD.

This is what the LORD says:

> "Heaven is my throne,
> and the earth is my footstool.
> Where is the house you will build for me?
> Where will my resting place be?
> Has not my hand made all these things,
> and so they came into being?"
> declares the LORD.

> "These are the ones I look on with favor:
> those who are humble and contrite in spirit,
> and who tremble at my word.
> But whoever sacrifices a bull
> is like one who kills a person,
> and whoever offers a lamb
> is like one who breaks a dog's neck;
> whoever makes a grain offering
> is like one who presents pig's blood,
> and whoever burns memorial incense
> is like one who worships an idol.
> They have chosen their own ways,
> and they delight in their abominations;
> so I also will choose harsh treatment for them
> and will bring on them what they dread.
> For when I called, no one answered,
> when I spoke, no one listened.
> They did evil in my sight
> and chose what displeases me."

> Hear the word of the LORD,
> you who tremble at his word:
> "Your own people who hate you,
> and exclude you because of my name, have said,
> 'Let the LORD be glorified,
> that we may see your joy!'
> Yet they will be put to shame.
> Hear that uproar from the city,
> hear that noise from the temple!

It is the sound of the LORD
repaying his enemies all they deserve.

"Before she goes into labor,
she gives birth;

before the pains come upon her,
she delivers a son.

Who has ever heard of such things?
Who has ever seen things like this?

Can a country be born in a day
or a nation be brought forth in a moment?

Yet no sooner is Zion in labor
than she gives birth to her children.

Do I bring to the moment of birth
and not give delivery?" says the LORD.

"Do I close up the womb
when I bring to delivery?" says your God.

"Rejoice with Jerusalem and be glad for her,
all you who love her;

rejoice greatly with her,
all you who mourn over her.

For you will nurse and be satisfied
at her comforting breasts;

you will drink deeply
and delight in her overflowing abundance."

For this is what the LORD says:

"I will extend peace to her like a river,
and the wealth of nations like a flooding
stream;

you will nurse and be carried on her arm
and dandled on her knees.

As a mother comforts her child,
so will I comfort you;
and you will be comforted over Jerusalem."

When you see this, your heart will rejoice
and you will flourish like grass;

the hand of the LORD will be made known to his
servants,
but his fury will be shown to his foes.

See, the Lord is coming with fire,
and his chariots are like a whirlwind;

he will bring down his anger with fury,
and his rebuke with flames of fire.

For with fire and with his sword
the Lord will execute judgment on all people,
and many will be those slain by the Lord.

"Those who consecrate and purify themselves to go into the gardens, following one who is among those who eat the flesh of pigs, rats and other unclean things—they will meet their end together with the one they follow," declares the Lord.

"And I, because of what they have planned and done, am about to come and gather the people of all nations and languages, and they will come and see my glory.

"I will set a sign among them, and I will send some of those who survive to the nations—to Tarshish, to the Libyans and Lydians (famous as archers), to Tubal and Greece, and to the distant islands that have not heard of my fame or seen my glory. They will proclaim my glory among the nations. And they will bring all your people, from all the nations, to my holy mountain in Jerusalem as an offering to the Lord—on horses, in chariots and wagons, and on mules and camels," says the Lord. "They will bring them, as the Israelites bring their grain offerings, to the temple of the Lord in ceremonially clean vessels. And I will select some of them also to be priests and Levites," says the Lord.

"As the new heavens and the new earth that I make will endure before me," declares the Lord, "so will your name and descendants endure. From one New Moon to another and from one Sabbath to another, all mankind will come and bow down before me," says the Lord. "And they will go out and look on the dead bodies of those who rebelled against me; the worms that eat them will not die, the fire that burns them will not be quenched, and they will be loathsome to all mankind."

INVITATION TO ZEPHANIAH

INVITATION TO
ZEPHANIAH

King Hezekiah of Judah was delivered from both a deadly illness and an Assyrian invasion because he trusted in God. But his son Manasseh returned to a policy of appeasing the Assyrian Empire by paying tribute money and promoting Assyrian-style religious practices throughout the kingdom. Manasseh's reign of fifty-five years coincided with the height of Assyria's power and influence. It was also the time of greatest corruption, injustice and paganism in Judah's history. Manasseh was succeeded by his son Amon, who continued his policies. But Amon was assassinated after only two years. He was succeeded by his young son Josiah. The Assyrian Empire had begun to crumble by this time and after Ashurbanipal, its last strong king, died around 627 BC, its decline accelerated. Josiah was then just old enough to start ruling effectively in his own right. He seized the opportunity and reasserted Judah's independence and traditional faith. He did this, for one thing, because a member of his court stood up and warned, in God's name, that the ways of his father and grandfather had brought his kingdom to the brink of destruction. The person who offered this warning was the prophet Zephaniah.

In the prologue to the book of his prophecies, Zephaniah is described as the great-great-grandson of a man named Hezekiah. This probably means the great reforming king of Judah. No other prophet's ancestry is traced back four generations, so this prologue is likely intended to associate Zephaniah with the reforming spirit of his ancestor. Zephaniah appears to have been of royal blood, since his oracles show he was familiar with particular districts in Jerusalem and with specific activities in the capital, as a member of the royal court would have been. But unlike other members of the court who were saying, *The Lord will do nothing, either good or bad*, Zephaniah wasn't complacent about the future. Instead, he warned that the *day of the Lord* was approaching and that God would soon judge the nations, including both Judah and the formerly invincible Assyria. Zephaniah's warning seems to have helped inspire national and religious renewal under King Josiah.

The collection of Zephaniah's prophecies has three main parts. The first is a description of *the day of the Lord* that will come against Judah and Jerusalem. The next section begins with a call for national repentance and then includes oracles of destruction against the Philistines, Moabites, Cushites (Ethiopians), Assyrians and Jerusalem itself. But in the final section, Zephaniah promises, as Isaiah had, that God will restore a humble remnant from among his people when he returns as *the Mighty Warrior who saves*. As a result, all the nations will *call on the name of the Lord and serve him shoulder to shoulder*.

ZEPHANIAH

T he word of the Lord that came to Zephaniah son of Cushi, the
son of Gedaliah, the son of Amariah, the son of Hezekiah, during the reign of Josiah son of Amon king of Judah:

" I will sweep away everything
from the face of the earth,"
                                    declares the Lord.
"I will sweep away both man and beast;
I will sweep away the birds in the sky
and the fish in the sea —
and the idols that cause the wicked to stumble."

"When I destroy all mankind
on the face of the earth,"
                                    declares the Lord,
"I will stretch out my hand against Judah
and against all who live in Jerusalem.
I will destroy every remnant of Baal worship in this
        place,
the very names of the idolatrous priests —

those who bow down on the roofs
to worship the starry host,

those who bow down and swear by the Lord
and who also swear by Molek,

those who turn back from following the Lord
and neither seek the Lord nor inquire of him."

Be silent before the Sovereign Lord,
for the day of the Lord is near.

The Lord has prepared a sacrifice;
he has consecrated those he has invited.

"On the day of the Lord's sacrifice
I will punish the officials
and the king's sons

and all those clad
in foreign clothes.

On that day I will punish
all who avoid stepping on the threshold,

who fill the temple of their gods
with violence and deceit.

"On that day,"
declares the Lord,

"a cry will go up from the Fish Gate,
wailing from the New Quarter,
and a loud crash from the hills.

Wail, you who live in the market district;
all your merchants will be wiped out,
all who trade with silver will be destroyed.

At that time I will search Jerusalem with lamps
and punish those who are complacent,
who are like wine left on its dregs,
who think, 'The Lord will do nothing,
either good or bad.'

Their wealth will be plundered,
their houses demolished.

Though they build houses,
they will not live in them;

though they plant vineyards,
they will not drink the wine."

The great day of the Lord is near —
near and coming quickly.

The cry on the day of the Lord is bitter;
the Mighty Warrior shouts his battle cry.

That day will be a day of wrath —
a day of distress and anguish,
a day of trouble and ruin,
a day of darkness and gloom,
a day of clouds and blackness —
a day of trumpet and battle cry

against the fortified cities
and against the corner towers.

"I will bring such distress on all people
that they will grope about like those who are blind,
because they have sinned against the LORD.
Their blood will be poured out like dust
and their entrails like dung.

Neither their silver nor their gold
will be able to save them
on the day of the LORD's wrath."

In the fire of his jealousy
the whole earth will be consumed,
for he will make a sudden end
of all who live on the earth.

G ather together, gather yourselves together,
you shameful nation,

before the decree takes effect
and that day passes like windblown chaff,
before the LORD's fierce anger
comes upon you,
before the day of the LORD's wrath
comes upon you.
Seek the LORD, all you humble of the land,
you who do what he commands.

Seek righteousness, seek humility;
perhaps you will be sheltered
on the day of the LORD's anger.

Gaza will be abandoned
and Ashkelon left in ruins.
At midday Ashdod will be emptied
and Ekron uprooted.

Woe to you who live by the sea,
you Kerethite people;
the word of the LORD is against you,
Canaan, land of the Philistines.

He says, "I will destroy you,
and none will be left."

The land by the sea will become pastures
having wells for shepherds
and pens for flocks.

That land will belong
to the remnant of the people of Judah;
there they will find pasture.

In the evening they will lie down
in the houses of Ashkelon.

The Lord their God will care for them;
he will restore their fortunes.

"I have heard the insults of Moab
and the taunts of the Ammonites,

who insulted my people
and made threats against their land.

Therefore, as surely as I live,"
declares the Lord Almighty,
the God of Israel,

"surely Moab will become like Sodom,
the Ammonites like Gomorrah—

a place of weeds and salt pits,
a wasteland forever.

The remnant of my people will plunder them;
the survivors of my nation will inherit
their land."

This is what they will get in return for
their pride,
for insulting and mocking
the people of the Lord Almighty.

The Lord will be awesome to them
when he destroys all the gods of the earth.

Distant nations will bow down to him,
all of them in their own lands.

"You Cushites, too,
will be slain by my sword."

He will stretch out his hand against
the north
and destroy Assyria,

leaving Nineveh utterly desolate
and dry as the desert.

Flocks and herds will lie down there,
creatures of every kind.

The desert owl and the screech owl
will roost on her columns.

Their hooting will echo through the windows,
rubble will fill the doorways,
the beams of cedar will be exposed.

This is the city of revelry
that lived in safety.

She said to herself,
"I am the one! And there is none besides me."

What a ruin she has become,
a lair for wild beasts!

All who pass by her scoff
and shake their fists.

Woe to the city of oppressors,
rebellious and defiled!

She obeys no one,
she accepts no correction.

She does not trust in the Lord,
she does not draw near to her God.

Her officials within her
are roaring lions;

her rulers are evening wolves,
who leave nothing for the morning.

Her prophets are unprincipled;
they are treacherous people.

Her priests profane the sanctuary
and do violence to the law.

The Lord within her is righteous;
he does no wrong.

Morning by morning he dispenses his justice,
and every new day he does not fail,
yet the unrighteous know no shame.

"I have destroyed nations;
their strongholds are demolished.
I have left their streets deserted,
with no one passing through.
Their cities are laid waste;
they are deserted and empty.
Of Jerusalem I thought,
'Surely you will fear me
and accept correction!'
Then her place of refuge would not be destroyed,
nor all my punishments come upon her.
But they were still eager
to act corruptly in all they did.
Therefore wait for me,"
declares the LORD,
"for the day I will stand up to testify.
I have decided to assemble the nations,
to gather the kingdoms
and to pour out my wrath on them —
all my fierce anger.
The whole world will be consumed
by the fire of my jealous anger.

" **T**hen I will purify the lips of the peoples,
that all of them may call on the name of the LORD
and serve him shoulder to shoulder.
From beyond the rivers of Cush
my worshipers, my scattered people,
will bring me offerings.
On that day you, Jerusalem, will not be put to shame
for all the wrongs you have done to me,
because I will remove from you
your arrogant boasters.
Never again will you be haughty
on my holy hill.

But I will leave within you
the meek and humble.

The remnant of Israel
will trust in the name of the Lord.

They will do no wrong;
they will tell no lies.

A deceitful tongue
will not be found in their mouths.

They will eat and lie down
and no one will make them afraid."

Sing, Daughter Zion;
shout aloud, Israel!

Be glad and rejoice with all your heart,
Daughter Jerusalem!

The Lord has taken away your punishment,
he has turned back your enemy.

The Lord, the King of Israel, is with you;
never again will you fear any harm.

On that day
they will say to Jerusalem,

"Do not fear, Zion;
do not let your hands hang limp.

The Lord your God is with you,
the Mighty Warrior who saves.

He will take great delight in you;
in his love he will no longer rebuke you,
but will rejoice over you with singing."

"I will remove from you
all who mourn over the loss of your appointed
        festivals,
which is a burden and reproach for you.

At that time I will deal
with all who oppressed you.

I will rescue the lame;
I will gather the exiles.

I will give them praise and honor
in every land where they have suffered
        shame.

At that time I will gather you;
at that time I will bring you home.
I will give you honor and praise
among all the peoples of the earth

when I restore your fortunes
before your very eyes,"
says the LORD.

INVITATION TO
NAHUM

In 612 BC the Assyrian Empire was nearing collapse. Its capital of Nineveh was about to fall to a combined invasion of Babylonian, Median and Scythian forces. The people this empire had cruelly oppressed felt little pity for it. In their view, the Assyrians were simply getting a long-overdue taste of their own medicine. The prophet Nahum put these feelings into words on behalf of the people of Judah. He situated the destruction of Nineveh within the larger context of God's rule over all the kingdoms of the earth. Isaiah had warned that God would judge the Assyrians, even though he'd used them as instruments of his purposes, because they'd been excessively destructive and proud (see p. 91). In the same way, Nahum says that Assyria will fall because of its *endless cruelty*. God is *slow to anger but great in power; the* LORD *will not leave the guilty unpunished.*

The book of Nahum consists of the oracle this prophet delivered just before the fall of Nineveh. It first describes God's character and power, and announces that God intends to judge Assyria. It then alternately speaks words of comfort to Judah and of doom to Nineveh. A vivid description follows of how the defense of the Assyrian capital will prove futile, and of how the city will be plundered. The book then describes the reasons for God's judgment. Finally, it warns the people of Nineveh not to feel secure behind their city's defenses, but rather to remember how their own army had once captured the seemingly impregnable Egyptian city of Thebes. The need for this comparison shows that even to the very end, the Assyrians persisted in the arrogance for which they were finally judged.

NAHUM

A prophecy concerning Nineveh. The book of the vision of Nahum the Elkoshite.

The LORD is a jealous and avenging God;
the LORD takes vengeance and is filled with wrath.
The LORD takes vengeance on his foes
and vents his wrath against his enemies.
The LORD is slow to anger but great in power;
the LORD will not leave the guilty unpunished.
His way is in the whirlwind and the storm,
and clouds are the dust of his feet.
He rebukes the sea and dries it up;
he makes all the rivers run dry.
Bashan and Carmel wither
and the blossoms of Lebanon fade.
The mountains quake before him
and the hills melt away.
The earth trembles at his presence,
the world and all who live in it.
Who can withstand his indignation?
Who can endure his fierce anger?
His wrath is poured out like fire;
the rocks are shattered before him.

The LORD is good,
a refuge in times of trouble.
He cares for those who trust in him,
but with an overwhelming flood
he will make an end of Nineveh;
he will pursue his foes into the realm of darkness.

Whatever they plot against the LORD
he will bring to an end;
trouble will not come a second time.

They will be entangled among thorns
and drunk from their wine;
they will be consumed like dry stubble.

From you, Nineveh, has one come forth
who plots evil against the LORD
and devises wicked plans.

This is what the LORD says:

"Although they have allies and are numerous,
they will be destroyed and pass away.
Although I have afflicted you, Judah,
I will afflict you no more.
Now I will break their yoke from your neck
and tear your shackles away."

The LORD has given a command concerning you,
    Nineveh:
"You will have no descendants to bear your name.
I will destroy the images and idols
that are in the temple of your gods.
I will prepare your grave,
for you are vile."

Look, there on the mountains,
the feet of one who brings good news,
who proclaims peace!
Celebrate your festivals, Judah,
and fulfill your vows.
No more will the wicked invade you;
they will be completely destroyed.

An attacker advances against you, Nineveh.
Guard the fortress,
watch the road,
brace yourselves,
marshal all your strength!

The LORD will restore the splendor of Jacob
like the splendor of Israel,

though destroyers have laid them waste
and have ruined their vines.

The shields of the soldiers are red;
the warriors are clad in scarlet.

The metal on the chariots flashes
on the day they are made ready;
the spears of juniper are brandished.

The chariots storm through the streets,
rushing back and forth through the squares.

They look like flaming torches;
they dart about like lightning.

Nineveh summons her picked troops,
yet they stumble on their way.

They dash to the city wall;
the protective shield is put in place.

The river gates are thrown open
and the palace collapses.

It is decreed that Nineveh
be exiled and carried away.

Her female slaves moan like doves
and beat on their breasts.

Nineveh is like a pool
whose water is draining away.

"Stop! Stop!" they cry,
but no one turns back.

Plunder the silver!
Plunder the gold!

The supply is endless,
the wealth from all its treasures!

She is pillaged, plundered, stripped!
Hearts melt, knees give way,
bodies tremble, every face grows pale.

Where now is the lions' den,
the place where they fed their young,

where the lion and lioness went,
and the cubs, with nothing to fear?

The lion killed enough for his cubs
and strangled the prey for his mate,

filling his lairs with the kill
and his dens with the prey.

"I am against you,"
declares the Lord Almighty.

"I will burn up your chariots in smoke,
and the sword will devour your young lions.
I will leave you no prey on the earth.

The voices of your messengers
will no longer be heard."

Woe to the city of blood,
full of lies,

full of plunder,
never without victims!

The crack of whips,
the clatter of wheels,

galloping horses
and jolting chariots!

Charging cavalry,
flashing swords
and glittering spears!

Many casualties,
piles of dead,

bodies without number,
people stumbling over the corpses—

all because of the wanton lust of a prostitute,
alluring, the mistress of sorceries,

who enslaved nations by her prostitution
and peoples by her witchcraft.

"I am against you," declares the Lord Almighty.
"I will lift your skirts over your face.
I will show the nations your nakedness
and the kingdoms your shame.

I will pelt you with filth,
I will treat you with contempt
and make you a spectacle.

All who see you will flee from you and say,
'Nineveh is in ruins — who will mourn for her?'
Where can I find anyone to comfort you?"

Are you better than Thebes,
situated on the Nile,
with water around her?
The river was her defense,
the waters her wall.

Cush and Egypt were her boundless strength;
Put and Libya were among her allies.

Yet she was taken captive
and went into exile.
Her infants were dashed to pieces
at every street corner.
Lots were cast for her nobles,
and all her great men were put in chains.

You too will become drunk;
you will go into hiding
and seek refuge from the enemy.

All your fortresses are like fig trees
with their first ripe fruit;
when they are shaken,
the figs fall into the mouth of the eater.

Look at your troops —
they are all weaklings.
The gates of your land
are wide open to your enemies;
fire has consumed the bars of your gates.

Draw water for the siege,
strengthen your defenses!
Work the clay,
tread the mortar,
repair the brickwork!

There the fire will consume you;
the sword will cut you down —
they will devour you like a swarm of locusts.
Multiply like grasshoppers,
multiply like locusts!

You have increased the number of your merchants
till they are more numerous than the stars in the sky,

but like locusts they strip the land
and then fly away.

Your guards are like locusts,
your officials like swarms of locusts
that settle in the walls on a cold day—

but when the sun appears they fly away,
and no one knows where.

King of Assyria, your shepherds slumber;
your nobles lie down to rest.

Your people are scattered on the mountains
with no one to gather them.

Nothing can heal you;
your wound is fatal.

All who hear the news about you
clap their hands at your fall,

for who has not felt
your endless cruelty?

INVITATION TO
HABAKKUK

The book of Habakkuk begins with a dialogue between the prophet and God. Habakkuk is writing around the time that Nineveh fell. He complains to God that violence and injustice persist in Judah, despite the chastening experience of Assyrian oppression. God responds that he will deal with the Judeans by a means *that you would not believe*. He will raise up the Babylonians to oppress the people just as the Assyrians did.

God has answered Habakkuk's first question, but his response leads to a further challenge from Habakkuk. The people of Judah were just now coming up for breath after a century of oppression. Would God really plunge them right back under? Why would God allow the wicked to *swallow up those more righteous than themselves*? (Whatever the Judeans have done, he feels, it doesn't compare with the ruthlessness the Babylonians are already showing.) God replies again, explaining that in due time the Babylonians will be judged just like the Assyrians, and that the righteous must await this outcome in faith and patience. To emphasize the inevitability of Babylon's doom, God then pronounces a series of five woes against its rising empire. In each case, the oppressor gets a taste of its own medicine (for example: *because you have plundered many nations, the peoples who are left will plunder you*). Babylon is replacing Assyria more surely than it knows.

After the dialogue between Habakkuk and God, the book concludes with what is described as "A prayer of Habakkuk the prophet." This closing section is clearly intended to be sung, because it bears musical notations. In his song Habakkuk celebrates God's past victories and prays that God will do similar deeds in his own time. Habakkuk articulates the urgent prayer of many readers of the biblical drama: *I stand in awe of your deeds, LORD. Repeat them in our day.* In the meantime, however, Habakkuk determines to wait patiently, saying *I will be joyful in God my Savior*.

HABAKKUK

T he prophecy that Habakkuk the prophet received.

> H ow long, LORD, must I call for help,
>   but you do not listen?
> Or cry out to you, "Violence!"
>   but you do not save?
> Why do you make me look at injustice?
>   Why do you tolerate wrongdoing?
> Destruction and violence are before me;
>   there is strife, and conflict abounds.
> Therefore the law is paralyzed,
>   and justice never prevails.
> The wicked hem in the righteous,
>   so that justice is perverted.

> "Look at the nations and watch—
>   and be utterly amazed.
> For I am going to do something in your days
>   that you would not believe,
>   even if you were told.
> I am raising up the Babylonians,
>   that ruthless and impetuous people,
> who sweep across the whole earth
>   to seize dwellings not their own.
> They are a feared and dreaded people;
>   they are a law to themselves
>   and promote their own honor.
> Their horses are swifter than leopards,
>   fiercer than wolves at dusk.

Their cavalry gallops headlong;
their horsemen come from afar.

They fly like an eagle swooping to devour;
they all come intent on violence.

Their hordes advance like a desert wind
and gather prisoners like sand.

They mock kings
and scoff at rulers.

They laugh at all fortified cities;
by building earthen ramps they capture them.

Then they sweep past like the wind and go on —
guilty people, whose own strength is their god."

Lord, are you not from everlasting?
My God, my Holy One, you will never die.

You, Lord, have appointed them to execute judgment;
you, my Rock, have ordained them to punish.

Your eyes are too pure to look on evil;
you cannot tolerate wrongdoing.

Why then do you tolerate the treacherous?
Why are you silent while the wicked
swallow up those more righteous than themselves?

You have made people like the fish in the sea,
like the sea creatures that have no ruler.

The wicked foe pulls all of them up with hooks,
he catches them in his net,

he gathers them up in his dragnet;
and so he rejoices and is glad.

Therefore he sacrifices to his net
and burns incense to his dragnet,

for by his net he lives in luxury
and enjoys the choicest food.

Is he to keep on emptying his net,
destroying nations without mercy?

I will stand at my watch
and station myself on the ramparts;

I will look to see what he will say to me,
and what answer I am to give to this complaint.

Then the LORD replied:

> "Write down the revelation
> and make it plain on tablets
> so that a herald may run with it.

> For the revelation awaits an appointed time;
> it speaks of the end
> and will not prove false.

> Though it linger, wait for it;
> it will certainly come
> and will not delay.

> "See, the enemy is puffed up;
> his desires are not upright—
> but the righteous person will live by his
>   faithfulness—

> indeed, wine betrays him;
> he is arrogant and never at rest.

> Because he is as greedy as the grave
> and like death is never satisfied,

> he gathers to himself all the nations
> and takes captive all the peoples.

"Will not all of them taunt him with ridicule and scorn, saying,

> " 'Woe to him who piles up stolen goods
> and makes himself wealthy by extortion!
> How long must this go on?'

> Will not your creditors suddenly arise?
> Will they not wake up and make you tremble?
> Then you will become their prey.

> Because you have plundered many nations,
> the peoples who are left will plunder you.

> For you have shed human blood;
> you have destroyed lands and cities and everyone
>   in them.

> "Woe to him who builds his house by unjust gain,
> setting his nest on high
> to escape the clutches of ruin!

You have plotted the ruin of many peoples,
shaming your own house and forfeiting your life.

The stones of the wall will cry out,
and the beams of the woodwork will echo it.

"Woe to him who builds a city with bloodshed
and establishes a town by injustice!

Has not the Lord Almighty determined
that the people's labor is only fuel for the fire,
that the nations exhaust themselves for nothing?

For the earth will be filled with the knowledge of the
glory of the Lord
as the waters cover the sea.

"Woe to him who gives drink to his neighbors,
pouring it from the wineskin till they are drunk,
so that he can gaze on their naked bodies!

You will be filled with shame instead of glory.
Now it is your turn! Drink and let your nakedness be
exposed!

The cup from the Lord's right hand is coming
around to you,
and disgrace will cover your glory.

The violence you have done to Lebanon will
overwhelm you,
and your destruction of animals will terrify you.

For you have shed human blood;
you have destroyed lands and cities and everyone in
them.

"Of what value is an idol carved by a craftsman?
Or an image that teaches lies?

For the one who makes it trusts in his own creation;
he makes idols that cannot speak.

Woe to him who says to wood, 'Come to life!'
Or to lifeless stone, 'Wake up!'

Can it give guidance?
It is covered with gold and silver;
there is no breath in it."

The Lord is in his holy temple;
let all the earth be silent before him.

A prayer of Habakkuk the prophet. On *shigionoth*.

Lord, I have heard of your fame;
  I stand in awe of your deeds, Lord.
Repeat them in our day,
  in our time make them known;
  in wrath remember mercy.

God came from Teman,
  the Holy One from Mount Paran.
His glory covered the heavens
  and his praise filled the earth.
His splendor was like the sunrise;
  rays flashed from his hand,
  where his power was hidden.
Plague went before him;
  pestilence followed his steps.
He stood, and shook the earth;
  he looked, and made the nations
      tremble.
The ancient mountains crumbled
  and the age-old hills collapsed —
  but he marches on forever.
I saw the tents of Cushan in distress,
  the dwellings of Midian in anguish.

Were you angry with the rivers, Lord?
  Was your wrath against the streams?
Did you rage against the sea
  when you rode your horses
  and your chariots to victory?
You uncovered your bow,
  you called for many arrows.
You split the earth with rivers;
  the mountains saw you and writhed.
Torrents of water swept by;
  the deep roared
  and lifted its waves on high.

Sun and moon stood still in the heavens
at the glint of your flying arrows,
at the lightning of your flashing spear.

In wrath you strode through the earth
and in anger you threshed the nations.

You came out to deliver your people,
to save your anointed one.

You crushed the leader of the land of wickedness,
you stripped him from head to foot.

With his own spear you pierced his head
when his warriors stormed out to scatter us,

gloating as though about to devour
the wretched who were in hiding.

You trampled the sea with your horses,
churning the great waters.

I heard and my heart pounded,
my lips quivered at the sound;

decay crept into my bones,
and my legs trembled.

Yet I will wait patiently for the day of calamity
to come on the nation invading us.

Though the fig tree does not bud
and there are no grapes on the vines,

though the olive crop fails
and the fields produce no food,

though there are no sheep in the pen
and no cattle in the stalls,

yet I will rejoice in the Lord,
I will be joyful in God my Savior.

The Sovereign Lord is my strength;
he makes my feet like the feet of a deer,
he enables me to tread on the heights.

For the director of music. On my stringed instruments.

INVITATION TO
JEREMIAH

The prophet Jeremiah began to speak to the kingdom of Judah around the time that Ashurbanipal, the last great king of Assyria, died. Jeremiah continued to bring *the word of the LORD* to the kingdom of Judah for the next forty years. As the Assyrian Empire crumbled, Judah experienced a revival of its fortunes and national character under Josiah. But it then fell back into spiritual and moral decline under kings Jehoiakim and Zedekiah. It was eventually destroyed by Babylon. The book that preserves Jeremiah's prophecies chronicles these events from his eyewitness perspective.

This book contains many of his sermons and prophetic oracles, as well as biographical narratives of his experiences during the last years of the Judean kingdom. These materials are not ordered chronologically or thematically. Instead, they're intricately arranged based on matching words and phrases.

For example, in one episode, Jeremiah visits a potter, and then shortly afterwards he smashes a pottery jar. Pashhur the son of Immer arrests Jeremiah, and then a different Pashhur, the son of Malkijah, comes from the king to ask his advice. Prayers of Jeremiah that express his inner anguish are placed inside each of these pairs of episodes. In this way, the very form of the book illustrates how Jeremiah experienced external conflict with those who resisted his message and internal conflict as he struggled to bring that message in the face of their opposition. This entire section is bracketed by oracles that Jeremiah delivered at the city gates to the kings and people of Judah who went through them. So the arrangement is:

Gates				Gates
	Potter	Potter	Pashhur	Pashhur
		Prayer	Prayer	

Arrangements like this represent the smallest level of organization in the book. There are also larger principles of organization. The book begins with a historical heading and ends with a historical narrative that describes the fall of Jerusalem, the event Jeremiah was best known for predicting. In between, the book is built out of basic units that are marked with a reference to *the word of the LORD* coming to the prophet under particular circumstances. Jeremiah's trip to the potter and his visit from Pashhur son of Malkijah are examples of these individual units. All of them are gathered into four large groups, so that the book as a whole has four main parts:

: The first part consists mostly of poetic oracles, with relatively brief prose sermons and narratives interspersed. Most of this material is not dated. The few indications that are given show that it comes from a variety of periods, from the reign of Josiah right down to the time of Zedekiah, the last king of Judah (pp. 237–292).

: The second part of the book is mostly narrative. The episodes it contains typically are dated, but they're not in chronological order. They come from the reigns of Jehoiakim and Zedekiah (pp. 294–315).

: The third part of the book consists of narrative episodes that are in chronological order. These describe the last days of the Judean kingdom (pp. 315–326).

: The fourth and final large part of the book contains poetic oracles that Jeremiah spoke against surrounding nations over a period of many years. This section culminates in an oracle against Babylon (pp. 326–352).

There's another large organizing principle in the book of Jeremiah as well. Even though the oracles against the nations are now the fourth part of the book, the introduction to these oracles (pp. 292–293) comes right after the first part, so this is where they may originally have been placed. (This is where they're found in the Septuagint, an early Greek translation of the First Testament.) In addition, a long poetic oracle (pp. 300–306) has been inserted in the middle of the second part of the book, which is otherwise mostly narrative. The result of this further arranging is a book in which Jeremiah's poetic oracles appear at the beginning, middle and end. This highlights their importance. The middle oracle, which promises a new covenant to heal the hearts of God's people, and which also begins with a description of Jeremiah's words being written down, is shown to be the most important of all.

While the book of Jeremiah carries us back and forth in place and time, its themes nevertheless remain constant. Like his predecessors, Jeremiah declares that there will be judgment for wrongdoing, but that it will be followed by forgiveness and new life. God calls him both *to uproot and tear down* and *to build and to plant*. In particular, the promise in the center of the book, that the Lord *will make a new covenant with the people of Israel,* that God will *put [his] law in their minds and write it on their hearts,* demonstrates God's power and plan to do more than simply punish evil. He will overcome it with good. In spite of everything that has happened to seemingly derail God's plan—for Israel and for the world—God will find a way to bring those plans to fruition.

Unlike his predecessors, however, Jeremiah also gives us an intimate look into his own heart and into his relationship with God as his fellow Judeans reject him and even conspire to kill him for speaking the word of the Lord. His questions, his protests and his anguish pour forth—and God frequently replies—as he faithfully carries out his mission.

JEREMIAH

T he words of Jeremiah son of Hilkiah, one of the priests at Anathoth in the territory of Benjamin. The word of the LORD came
to him in the thirteenth year of the reign of Josiah son of Amon king
of Judah, and through the reign of Jehoiakim son of Josiah king of
Judah, down to the fifth month of the eleventh year of Zedekiah
son of Josiah king of Judah, when the people of Jerusalem went into
exile.

T he word of the LORD came to me, saying,

> "Before I formed you in the womb I knew you,
>   before you were born I set you apart;
>   I appointed you as a prophet to the nations."

"Alas, Sovereign LORD," I said, "I do not know how to speak; I
am too young."

But the LORD said to me, "Do not say, 'I am too young.' You must
go to everyone I send you to and say whatever I command you. Do
not be afraid of them, for I am with you and will rescue you," declares the LORD.

Then the LORD reached out his hand and touched my mouth
and said to me, "I have put my words in your mouth. See, today I
appoint you over nations and kingdoms to uproot and tear down,
to destroy and overthrow, to build and to plant."

The word of the LORD came to me: "What do you see, Jeremiah?"

"I see the branch of an almond tree," I replied.

The LORD said to me, "You have seen correctly, for I am watching to see that my word is fulfilled."

The word of the LORD came to me again: "What do you see?"

"I see a pot that is boiling," I answered. "It is tilting toward us
from the north."

The LORD said to me, "From the north disaster will be poured out on all who live in the land. I am about to summon all the peoples of the northern kingdoms," declares the Lord.

> "Their kings will come and set up their thrones
> in the entrance of the gates of Jerusalem;
> they will come against all her surrounding walls
> and against all the towns of Judah.
> I will pronounce my judgments on my people
> because of their wickedness in forsaking me,
> in burning incense to other gods
> and in worshiping what their hands have made.

"Get yourself ready! Stand up and say to them whatever I command you. Do not be terrified by them, or I will terrify you before them. Today I have made you a fortified city, an iron pillar and a bronze wall to stand against the whole land — against the kings of Judah, its officials, its priests and the people of the land. They will fight against you but will not overcome you, for I am with you and will rescue you," declares the Lord.

The word of the Lord came to me: "Go and proclaim in the hearing of Jerusalem:

"This is what the Lord says:

> "'I remember the devotion of your youth,
> how as a bride you loved me
> and followed me through the wilderness,
> through a land not sown.
> Israel was holy to the Lord,
> the firstfruits of his harvest;
> all who devoured her were held guilty,
> and disaster overtook them,'"
>
> declares the Lord.

> Hear the word of the Lord, you descendants of Jacob,
> all you clans of Israel.

This is what the Lord says:

> "What fault did your ancestors find in me,
> that they strayed so far from me?

They followed worthless idols
and became worthless themselves.

They did not ask, 'Where is the LORD,
who brought us up out of Egypt

and led us through the barren wilderness,
through a land of deserts and ravines,

a land of drought and utter darkness,
a land where no one travels and no one lives?'

I brought you into a fertile land
to eat its fruit and rich produce.

But you came and defiled my land
and made my inheritance detestable.

The priests did not ask,
'Where is the LORD?'

Those who deal with the law did not know me;
the leaders rebelled against me.

The prophets prophesied by Baal,
following worthless idols.

"Therefore I bring charges against you again,"
declares the LORD.
"And I will bring charges against your children's
children.

Cross over to the coasts of Cyprus and look,
send to Kedar and observe closely;
see if there has ever been anything like this:

Has a nation ever changed its gods?
(Yet they are not gods at all.)

But my people have exchanged their glorious God
for worthless idols.

Be appalled at this, you heavens,
and shudder with great horror,"
declares the LORD.

"My people have committed two sins:

They have forsaken me,
the spring of living water,

and have dug their own cisterns,
broken cisterns that cannot hold water.

Is Israel a servant, a slave by birth?
Why then has he become plunder?

Lions have roared;
they have growled at him.

They have laid waste his land;
his towns are burned and deserted.

Also, the men of Memphis and Tahpanhes
have cracked your skull.

Have you not brought this on yourselves
by forsaking the LORD your God
when he led you in the way?

Now why go to Egypt
to drink water from the Nile?

And why go to Assyria
to drink water from the Euphrates?

Your wickedness will punish you;
your backsliding will rebuke you.

Consider then and realize
how evil and bitter it is for you

when you forsake the LORD your God
and have no awe of me,"
declares the Lord, the LORD Almighty.

"Long ago you broke off your yoke
and tore off your bonds;
you said, 'I will not serve you!'

Indeed, on every high hill
and under every spreading tree
you lay down as a prostitute.

I had planted you like a choice vine
of sound and reliable stock.

How then did you turn against me
into a corrupt, wild vine?

Although you wash yourself with soap
and use an abundance of cleansing powder,
the stain of your guilt is still before me,"
declares the Sovereign LORD.

"How can you say, 'I am not defiled;
I have not run after the Baals'?

See how you behaved in the valley;
consider what you have done.

You are a swift she-camel
running here and there,

a wild donkey accustomed to the desert,
sniffing the wind in her craving —
in her heat who can restrain her?

Any males that pursue her need not tire
themselves;
at mating time they will find her.

Do not run until your feet are bare
and your throat is dry.

But you said, 'It's no use!
I love foreign gods,
and I must go after them.'

"As a thief is disgraced when he is caught,
so the people of Israel are disgraced —

they, their kings and their officials,
their priests and their prophets.

They say to wood, 'You are my father,'
and to stone, 'You gave me birth.'

They have turned their backs to me
and not their faces;

yet when they are in trouble, they say,
'Come and save us!'

Where then are the gods you made for yourselves?
Let them come if they can save you
when you are in trouble!

For you, Judah, have as many gods
as you have towns.

"Why do you bring charges against me?
You have all rebelled against me,"

                                        declares the LORD.

"In vain I punished your people;
they did not respond to correction.

Your sword has devoured your prophets
like a ravenous lion.

"You of this generation, consider the word of the LORD:

"Have I been a desert to Israel
or a land of great darkness?

Why do my people say, 'We are free to roam;
we will come to you no more'?

Does a young woman forget her jewelry,
a bride her wedding ornaments?
Yet my people have forgotten me,
days without number.

How skilled you are at pursuing love!
Even the worst of women can learn from your ways.

On your clothes is found
the lifeblood of the innocent poor,
though you did not catch them breaking in.

Yet in spite of all this
you say, 'I am innocent;
he is not angry with me.'
But I will pass judgment on you
because you say, 'I have not sinned.'

Why do you go about so much,
changing your ways?
You will be disappointed by Egypt
as you were by Assyria.

You will also leave that place
with your hands on your head,
for the LORD has rejected those you trust;
you will not be helped by them.

"If a man divorces his wife
and she leaves him and marries another man,
should he return to her again?
Would not the land be completely defiled?
But you have lived as a prostitute with many lovers —
would you now return to me?"

declares the LORD.

"Look up to the barren heights and see.
Is there any place where you have not been ravished?
By the roadside you sat waiting for lovers,
sat like a nomad in the desert.
You have defiled the land
with your prostitution and wickedness.
Therefore the showers have been withheld,
and no spring rains have fallen.
Yet you have the brazen look of a prostitute;
you refuse to blush with shame.

Have you not just called to me:
'My Father, my friend from my youth,

will you always be angry?
Will your wrath continue forever?'

This is how you talk,
but you do all the evil you can."

During the reign of King Josiah, the LORD said to me, "Have you seen what faithless Israel has done? She has gone up on every high hill and under every spreading tree and has committed adultery there. I thought that after she had done all this she would return to me but she did not, and her unfaithful sister Judah saw it. I gave faithless Israel her certificate of divorce and sent her away because of all her adulteries. Yet I saw that her unfaithful sister Judah had no fear; she also went out and committed adultery. Because Israel's immorality mattered so little to her, she defiled the land and committed adultery with stone and wood. In spite of all this, her unfaithful sister Judah did not return to me with all her heart, but only in pretense," declares the LORD.

The LORD said to me, "Faithless Israel is more righteous than unfaithful Judah. Go, proclaim this message toward the north:

" 'Return, faithless Israel,' declares the LORD,
'I will frown on you no longer,

for I am faithful,' declares the LORD,
'I will not be angry forever.

Only acknowledge your guilt —
you have rebelled against the LORD your God,

you have scattered your favors to foreign gods
under every spreading tree,
and have not obeyed me,' "

declares the LORD.

"Return, faithless people," declares the LORD, "for I am your husband. I will choose you — one from a town and two from a clan — and bring you to Zion. Then I will give you shepherds after my own heart, who will lead you with knowledge and understanding. In those days, when your numbers have increased greatly in the land," declares the LORD, "people will no longer say, 'The ark of the covenant of the LORD.' It will never enter their minds or be remembered; it will not be missed, nor will another one be made. At that time they will call Jerusalem The Throne of the LORD, and

all nations will gather in Jerusalem to honor the name of the LORD.
No longer will they follow the stubbornness of their evil hearts. In
those days the people of Judah will join the people of Israel, and together they will come from a northern land to the land I gave your
ancestors as an inheritance.

"I myself said,

> " 'How gladly would I treat you like my children
> and give you a pleasant land,
> the most beautiful inheritance of any nation.'
> I thought you would call me 'Father'
> and not turn away from following me.
> But like a woman unfaithful to her husband,
> so you, Israel, have been unfaithful to me,"
>
> declares the LORD.

> A cry is heard on the barren heights,
> the weeping and pleading of the people
> of Israel,
> because they have perverted their ways
> and have forgotten the LORD their God.

> "Return, faithless people;
> I will cure you of backsliding."

> "Yes, we will come to you,
> for you are the LORD our God.

> Surely the idolatrous commotion on the hills
> and mountains is a deception;
> surely in the LORD our God
> is the salvation of Israel.

> From our youth shameful gods have
> consumed
> the fruits of our ancestors' labor —

> their flocks and herds,
> their sons and daughters.

> Let us lie down in our shame,
> and let our disgrace cover us.

> We have sinned against the LORD our God,
> both we and our ancestors;

> from our youth till this day
> we have not obeyed the LORD our God."

"If you, Israel, will return,
then return to me,"

declares the LORD.

"If you put your detestable idols out of my sight
and no longer go astray,
and if in a truthful, just and righteous way
you swear, 'As surely as the LORD lives,'
then the nations will invoke blessings by him
and in him they will boast."

This is what the LORD says to the people of Judah and to Jerusalem:

"Break up your unplowed ground
and do not sow among thorns.

Circumcise yourselves to the LORD,
circumcise your hearts,
you people of Judah and inhabitants of Jerusalem,
or my wrath will flare up and burn like fire
because of the evil you have done—
burn with no one to quench it.

"Announce in Judah and proclaim in Jerusalem and say:
'Sound the trumpet throughout the land!'

Cry aloud and say:
'Gather together!
Let us flee to the fortified cities!'

Raise the signal to go to Zion!
Flee for safety without delay!

For I am bringing disaster from the north,
even terrible destruction."

A lion has come out of his lair;
a destroyer of nations has set out.

He has left his place
to lay waste your land.

Your towns will lie in ruins
without inhabitant.

So put on sackcloth,
lament and wail,
for the fierce anger of the LORD
has not turned away from us.

"In that day," declares the Lord,
"the king and the officials will lose heart,

the priests will be horrified,
and the prophets will be appalled."

Then I said, "Alas, Sovereign Lord! How completely you have deceived this people and Jerusalem by saying, 'You will have peace,' when the sword is at our throats!"

At that time this people and Jerusalem will be told, "A scorching wind from the barren heights in the desert blows toward my people, but not to winnow or cleanse; a wind too strong for that comes from me. Now I pronounce my judgments against them."

Look! He advances like the clouds,
his chariots come like a whirlwind,

his horses are swifter than eagles.
Woe to us! We are ruined!
Jerusalem, wash the evil from your heart
and be saved.
How long will you harbor wicked thoughts?

A voice is announcing from Dan,
proclaiming disaster from the hills of Ephraim.

"Tell this to the nations,
proclaim concerning Jerusalem:

'A besieging army is coming from a distant land,
raising a war cry against the cities of Judah.

They surround her like men guarding a field,
because she has rebelled against me,'"
declares the Lord.

"Your own conduct and actions
have brought this on you.

This is your punishment.
How bitter it is!
How it pierces to the heart!"

Oh, my anguish, my anguish!
I writhe in pain.

Oh, the agony of my heart!
My heart pounds within me,
I cannot keep silent.
For I have heard the sound of the trumpet;
I have heard the battle cry.

Disaster follows disaster;
the whole land lies in ruins.

In an instant my tents are destroyed,
my shelter in a moment.

How long must I see the battle standard
and hear the sound of the trumpet?

"My people are fools;
they do not know me.

They are senseless children;
they have no understanding.

They are skilled in doing evil;
they know not how to do good."

I looked at the earth,
and it was formless and empty;

and at the heavens,
and their light was gone.

I looked at the mountains,
and they were quaking;
all the hills were swaying.

I looked, and there were no people;
every bird in the sky had flown away.

I looked, and the fruitful land was a desert;
all its towns lay in ruins
before the Lord, before his fierce anger.

This is what the Lord says:

"The whole land will be ruined,
though I will not destroy it completely.

Therefore the earth will mourn
and the heavens above grow dark,

because I have spoken and will not relent,
I have decided and will not turn back."

At the sound of horsemen and archers
every town takes to flight.

Some go into the thickets;
some climb up among the rocks.

All the towns are deserted;
no one lives in them.

What are you doing, you devastated one?
Why dress yourself in scarlet
and put on jewels of gold?

Why highlight your eyes with makeup?
You adorn yourself in vain.

Your lovers despise you;
they want to kill you.

I hear a cry as of a woman in labor,
a groan as of one bearing her first child —

the cry of Daughter Zion gasping for breath,
stretching out her hands and saying,

"Alas! I am fainting;
my life is given over to murderers."

"Go up and down the streets of Jerusalem,
look around and consider,
search through her squares.

If you can find but one person
who deals honestly and seeks the truth,
I will forgive this city.

Although they say, 'As surely as the Lord lives,'
still they are swearing falsely."

Lord, do not your eyes look for truth?
You struck them, but they felt no pain;
you crushed them, but they refused correction.

They made their faces harder than stone
and refused to repent.

I thought, "These are only the poor;
they are foolish,

for they do not know the way of the Lord,
the requirements of their God.

So I will go to the leaders
and speak to them;

surely they know the way of the Lord,
the requirements of their God."

But with one accord they too had broken
off the yoke
and torn off the bonds.

Therefore a lion from the forest will attack them,
a wolf from the desert will ravage them,

a leopard will lie in wait near their towns
to tear to pieces any who venture out,

for their rebellion is great
and their backslidings many.

"Why should I forgive you?
Your children have forsaken me
and sworn by gods that are not gods.

I supplied all their needs,
yet they committed adultery
and thronged to the houses of prostitutes.

They are well-fed, lusty stallions,
each neighing for another man's wife.

Should I not punish them for this?"
declares the Lord.

"Should I not avenge myself
on such a nation as this?

"Go through her vineyards and ravage them,
but do not destroy them completely.

Strip off her branches,
for these people do not belong to the Lord.

The people of Israel and the people of Judah
have been utterly unfaithful to me,"
declares the Lord.

They have lied about the Lord;
they said, "He will do nothing!

No harm will come to us;
we will never see sword or famine.

The prophets are but wind
and the word is not in them;
so let what they say be done to them."

Therefore this is what the Lord God Almighty says:

"Because the people have spoken these words,
I will make my words in your mouth a fire
and these people the wood it consumes.

People of Israel," declares the Lord,
"I am bringing a distant nation against you —

an ancient and enduring nation,
a people whose language you do not know,
whose speech you do not understand.

Their quivers are like an open grave;
all of them are mighty warriors.

They will devour your harvests and food,
devour your sons and daughters;

they will devour your flocks and herds,
devour your vines and fig trees.

With the sword they will destroy
the fortified cities in which you trust.

"Yet even in those days," declares the Lord, "I will not destroy you completely. And when the people ask, 'Why has the Lord our God done all this to us?' you will tell them, 'As you have forsaken me and served foreign gods in your own land, so now you will serve foreigners in a land not your own.'

"Announce this to the descendants of Jacob
and proclaim it in Judah:

Hear this, you foolish and senseless people,
who have eyes but do not see,
who have ears but do not hear:

Should you not fear me?" declares the Lord.
"Should you not tremble in my presence?

I made the sand a boundary for the sea,
an everlasting barrier it cannot cross.

The waves may roll, but they cannot prevail;
they may roar, but they cannot cross it.

But these people have stubborn and
rebellious hearts;
they have turned aside and gone away.

They do not say to themselves,
'Let us fear the Lord our God,

who gives autumn and spring rains in season,
who assures us of the regular weeks of harvest.'

Your wrongdoings have kept these away;
your sins have deprived you of good.

"Among my people are the wicked
who lie in wait like men who snare birds
and like those who set traps to catch people.

Like cages full of birds,
their houses are full of deceit;

they have become rich and powerful
and have grown fat and sleek.

Their evil deeds have no limit;
they do not seek justice.

They do not promote the case of the fatherless;
they do not defend the just cause
of the poor.

Should I not punish them for this?"
declares the LORD.

"Should I not avenge myself
on such a nation as this?

"A horrible and shocking thing
has happened in the land:

The prophets prophesy lies,
the priests rule by their own authority,

and my people love it this way.
But what will you do in the end?

"Flee for safety, people of Benjamin!
Flee from Jerusalem!

Sound the trumpet in Tekoa!
Raise the signal over Beth Hakkerem!

For disaster looms out of the north,
even terrible destruction.

I will destroy Daughter Zion,
so beautiful and delicate.

Shepherds with their flocks will come
against her;
they will pitch their tents around her,
each tending his own portion."

"Prepare for battle against her!
Arise, let us attack at noon!

But, alas, the daylight is fading,
and the shadows of evening grow long.

So arise, let us attack at night
and destroy her fortresses!"

This is what the LORD Almighty says:

> "Cut down the trees
> and build siege ramps against Jerusalem.
> This city must be punished;
> it is filled with oppression.
> As a well pours out its water,
> so she pours out her wickedness.
> Violence and destruction resound in her;
> her sickness and wounds are ever before me.
> Take warning, Jerusalem,
> or I will turn away from you
> and make your land desolate
> so no one can live in it."

This is what the LORD Almighty says:

> "Let them glean the remnant of Israel
> as thoroughly as a vine;
> pass your hand over the branches again,
> like one gathering grapes."

> To whom can I speak and give warning?
> Who will listen to me?
> Their ears are closed
> so they cannot hear.
> The word of the LORD is offensive to them;
> they find no pleasure in it.
> But I am full of the wrath of the LORD,
> and I cannot hold it in.

> "Pour it out on the children in the street
> and on the young men gathered together;
> both husband and wife will be caught in it,
> and the old, those weighed down with years.
> Their houses will be turned over to others,
> together with their fields and their wives,
> when I stretch out my hand
> against those who live in the land,"
>
> > declares the LORD.

> "From the least to the greatest,
> all are greedy for gain;

prophets and priests alike,
all practice deceit.

They dress the wound of my people
as though it were not serious.

'Peace, peace,' they say,
when there is no peace.

Are they ashamed of their detestable conduct?
No, they have no shame at all;
they do not even know how to blush.

So they will fall among the fallen;
they will be brought down when I punish them,"
                                    says the LORD.

This is what the LORD says:

"Stand at the crossroads and look;
ask for the ancient paths,

ask where the good way is, and walk in it,
and you will find rest for your souls.
But you said, 'We will not walk in it.'

I appointed watchmen over you and said,
'Listen to the sound of the trumpet!'
But you said, 'We will not listen.'

Therefore hear, you nations;
you who are witnesses,
observe what will happen to them.

Hear, you earth:
I am bringing disaster on this people,
the fruit of their schemes,

because they have not listened to my words
and have rejected my law.

What do I care about incense from Sheba
or sweet calamus from a distant land?

Your burnt offerings are not acceptable;
your sacrifices do not please me."

Therefore this is what the LORD says:

"I will put obstacles before this people.
Parents and children alike will stumble
        over them;
neighbors and friends will perish."

This is what the LORD says:

"Look, an army is coming
from the land of the north;
a great nation is being stirred up
from the ends of the earth.
They are armed with bow and spear;
they are cruel and show no mercy.
They sound like the roaring sea
as they ride on their horses;
they come like men in battle formation
to attack you, Daughter Zion."

We have heard reports about them,
and our hands hang limp.
Anguish has gripped us,
pain like that of a woman in labor.
Do not go out to the fields
or walk on the roads,
for the enemy has a sword,
and there is terror on every side.
Put on sackcloth, my people,
and roll in ashes;
mourn with bitter wailing
as for an only son,
for suddenly the destroyer
will come upon us.

"I have made you a tester of metals
and my people the ore,
that you may observe
and test their ways.
They are all hardened rebels,
going about to slander.
They are bronze and iron;
they all act corruptly.
The bellows blow fiercely
to burn away the lead with fire,
but the refining goes on in vain;
the wicked are not purged out.

> They are called rejected silver,
> because the Lord has rejected them."

This is the word that came to Jeremiah from the Lord: "Stand at the gate of the Lord's house and there proclaim this message:

"'Hear the word of the Lord, all you people of Judah who come through these gates to worship the Lord. This is what the Lord Almighty, the God of Israel, says: Reform your ways and your actions, and I will let you live in this place. Do not trust in deceptive words and say, "This is the temple of the Lord, the temple of the Lord, the temple of the Lord!" If you really change your ways and your actions and deal with each other justly, if you do not oppress the foreigner, the fatherless or the widow and do not shed innocent blood in this place, and if you do not follow other gods to your own harm, then I will let you live in this place, in the land I gave your ancestors for ever and ever. But look, you are trusting in deceptive words that are worthless.

"'Will you steal and murder, commit adultery and perjury, burn incense to Baal and follow other gods you have not known, and then come and stand before me in this house, which bears my Name, and say, "We are safe"—safe to do all these detestable things? Has this house, which bears my Name, become a den of robbers to you? But I have been watching! declares the Lord.

"'Go now to the place in Shiloh where I first made a dwelling for my Name, and see what I did to it because of the wickedness of my people Israel. While you were doing all these things, declares the Lord, I spoke to you again and again, but you did not listen; I called you, but you did not answer. Therefore, what I did to Shiloh I will now do to the house that bears my Name, the temple you trust in, the place I gave to you and your ancestors. I will thrust you from my presence, just as I did all your fellow Israelites, the people of Ephraim.'

"So do not pray for this people nor offer any plea or petition for them; do not plead with me, for I will not listen to you. Do you not see what they are doing in the towns of Judah and in the streets of Jerusalem? The children gather wood, the fathers light the fire, and the women knead the dough and make cakes to offer to the Queen of Heaven. They pour out drink offerings to other gods to arouse my anger. But am I the one they are provoking? declares the Lord. Are they not rather harming themselves, to their own shame?

"'Therefore this is what the Sovereign Lord says: My anger and my wrath will be poured out on this place—on man and beast, on the trees of the field and on the crops of your land — and it will burn and not be quenched.

"'This is what the Lord Almighty, the God of Israel, says: Go ahead, add your burnt offerings to your other sacrifices and eat the meat yourselves! For when I brought your ancestors out of Egypt and spoke to them, I did not just give them commands about burnt offerings and sacrifices, but I gave them this command: Obey me, and I will be your God and you will be my people. Walk in obedience to all I command you, that it may go well with you. But they did not listen or pay attention; instead, they followed the stubborn inclinations of their evil hearts. They went backward and not forward. From the time your ancestors left Egypt until now, day after day, again and again I sent you my servants the prophets. But they did not listen to me or pay attention. They were stiff-necked and did more evil than their ancestors.'

"When you tell them all this, they will not listen to you; when you call to them, they will not answer. Therefore say to them, 'This is the nation that has not obeyed the Lord its God or responded to correction. Truth has perished; it has vanished from their lips.

"'Cut off your hair and throw it away; take up a lament on the barren heights, for the Lord has rejected and abandoned this generation that is under his wrath.

"'The people of Judah have done evil in my eyes, declares the Lord. They have set up their detestable idols in the house that bears my Name and have defiled it. They have built the high places of Topheth in the Valley of Ben Hinnom to burn their sons and daughters in the fire — something I did not command, nor did it enter my mind. So beware, the days are coming, declares the Lord, when people will no longer call it Topheth or the Valley of Ben Hinnom, but the Valley of Slaughter, for they will bury the dead in Topheth until there is no more room. Then the carcasses of this people will become food for the birds and the wild animals, and there will be no one to frighten them away. I will bring an end to the sounds of joy and gladness and to the voices of bride and bridegroom in the towns of Judah and the streets of Jerusalem, for the land will become desolate.

"'At that time, declares the Lord, the bones of the kings and officials of Judah, the bones of the priests and prophets, and the bones of the people of Jerusalem will be removed from their graves. They will be exposed to the sun and the moon and all the stars of the heavens, which they have loved and served and which they have followed and consulted and worshiped. They will not be gathered up or buried, but will be like dung lying on the ground. Wherever I banish them, all the survivors of this evil nation will prefer death to life, declares the Lord Almighty.'

"Say to them, 'This is what the LORD says:

> "'When people fall down, do they not get up?
> When someone turns away, do they not return?
>
> Why then have these people turned away?
> Why does Jerusalem always turn away?
>
> They cling to deceit;
> they refuse to return.
>
> I have listened attentively,
> but they do not say what is right.
>
> None of them repent of their wickedness,
> saying, "What have I done?"
>
> Each pursues their own course
> like a horse charging into battle.
>
> Even the stork in the sky
> knows her appointed seasons,
>
> and the dove, the swift and the thrush
> observe the time of their migration.
>
> But my people do not know
> the requirements of the LORD.
>
> "'How can you say, "We are wise,
> for we have the law of the LORD,"
>
> when actually the lying pen of the scribes
> has handled it falsely?
>
> The wise will be put to shame;
> they will be dismayed and trapped.
>
> Since they have rejected the word of the LORD,
> what kind of wisdom do they have?
>
> Therefore I will give their wives to other men
> and their fields to new owners.
>
> From the least to the greatest,
> all are greedy for gain;
>
> prophets and priests alike,
> all practice deceit.
>
> They dress the wound of my people
> as though it were not serious.
>
> "Peace, peace," they say,
> when there is no peace.

Are they ashamed of their detestable conduct?
No, they have no shame at all;
they do not even know how to blush.

So they will fall among the fallen;
they will be brought down when they are punished,
says the LORD.

" 'I will take away their harvest,
declares the LORD.
There will be no grapes on the vine.

There will be no figs on the tree,
and their leaves will wither.

What I have given them
will be taken from them.' "

Why are we sitting here?
Gather together!

Let us flee to the fortified cities
and perish there!

For the LORD our God has doomed us to perish
and given us poisoned water to drink,
because we have sinned against him.

We hoped for peace
but no good has come,

for a time of healing
but there is only terror.

The snorting of the enemy's horses
is heard from Dan;

at the neighing of their stallions
the whole land trembles.

They have come to devour
the land and everything in it,
the city and all who live there.

"See, I will send venomous snakes among you,
vipers that cannot be charmed,
and they will bite you,"
declares the LORD.

You who are my Comforter in sorrow,
my heart is faint within me.

Listen to the cry of my people
from a land far away:

"Is the Lord not in Zion?
Is her King no longer there?"

"Why have they aroused my anger with their images,
with their worthless foreign idols?"

"The harvest is past,
the summer has ended,
and we are not saved."

Since my people are crushed, I am crushed;
I mourn, and horror grips me.
Is there no balm in Gilead?
Is there no physician there?
Why then is there no healing
for the wound of my people?

Oh, that my head were a spring of water
and my eyes a fountain of tears!
I would weep day and night
for the slain of my people.
Oh, that I had in the desert
a lodging place for travelers,
so that I might leave my people
and go away from them;
for they are all adulterers,
a crowd of unfaithful people.

"They make ready their tongue
like a bow, to shoot lies;
it is not by truth
that they triumph in the land.
They go from one sin to another;
they do not acknowledge me,"
                    declares the Lord.

"Beware of your friends;
do not trust anyone in your clan.
For every one of them is a deceiver,
and every friend a slanderer.
Friend deceives friend,
and no one speaks the truth.
They have taught their tongues to lie;
they weary themselves with sinning.

You live in the midst of deception;
in their deceit they refuse to acknowledge me,"
declares the LORD.

Therefore this is what the LORD Almighty says:

"See, I will refine and test them,
for what else can I do
because of the sin of my people?

Their tongue is a deadly arrow;
it speaks deceitfully.

With their mouths they all speak cordially to their
neighbors,
but in their hearts they set traps for them.

Should I not punish them for this?"
declares the LORD.

"Should I not avenge myself
on such a nation as this?"

I will weep and wail for the mountains
and take up a lament concerning the wilderness
grasslands.

They are desolate and untraveled,
and the lowing of cattle is not heard.

The birds have all fled
and the animals are gone.

"I will make Jerusalem a heap of ruins,
a haunt of jackals;

and I will lay waste the towns of Judah
so no one can live there."

Who is wise enough to understand this? Who has been instructed by the LORD and can explain it? Why has the land been
ruined and laid waste like a desert that no one can cross?

The LORD said, "It is because they have forsaken my law, which
I set before them; they have not obeyed me or followed my law. Instead, they have followed the stubbornness of their hearts; they
have followed the Baals, as their ancestors taught them." Therefore
this is what the LORD Almighty, the God of Israel, says: "See, I will
make this people eat bitter food and drink poisoned water. I will
scatter them among nations that neither they nor their ancestors
have known, and I will pursue them with the sword until I have
made an end of them."

This is what the Lord Almighty says:

> "Consider now! Call for the wailing women to come;
> send for the most skillful of them.

> Let them come quickly
> and wail over us

> till our eyes overflow with tears
> and water streams from our eyelids.

> The sound of wailing is heard from Zion:
> 'How ruined we are!
> How great is our shame!

> We must leave our land
> because our houses are in ruins.'"

> Now, you women, hear the word of the Lord;
> open your ears to the words of his mouth.

> Teach your daughters how to wail;
> teach one another a lament.

> Death has climbed in through our windows
> and has entered our fortresses;

> it has removed the children from the streets
> and the young men from the public squares.

Say, "This is what the Lord declares:

> "'Dead bodies will lie
> like dung on the open field,

> like cut grain behind the reaper,
> with no one to gather them.'"

This is what the Lord says:

> "Let not the wise boast of their wisdom
> or the strong boast of their strength
> or the rich boast of their riches,

> but let the one who boasts boast about this:
> that they have the understanding to know me,

> that I am the Lord, who exercises kindness,
> justice and righteousness on earth,
> for in these I delight,"

> > declares the Lord.

"The days are coming," declares the Lord, "when I will punish all who are circumcised only in the flesh — Egypt, Judah, Edom,

Ammon, Moab and all who live in the wilderness in distant places. For all these nations are really uncircumcised, and even the whole house of Israel is uncircumcised in heart."

Hear what the LORD says to you, people of Israel. This is what the LORD says:

> "Do not learn the ways of the nations
> or be terrified by signs in the heavens,
> though the nations are terrified by them.

> For the practices of the peoples are worthless;
> they cut a tree out of the forest,
> and a craftsman shapes it with his chisel.

> They adorn it with silver and gold;
> they fasten it with hammer and nails
> so it will not totter.

> Like a scarecrow in a cucumber field,
> their idols cannot speak;
> they must be carried
> because they cannot walk.

> Do not fear them;
> they can do no harm
> nor can they do any good."

> No one is like you, LORD;
> you are great,
> and your name is mighty in power.

> Who should not fear you,
> King of the nations?
> This is your due.

> Among all the wise leaders of the nations
> and in all their kingdoms,
> there is no one like you.

> They are all senseless and foolish;
> they are taught by worthless wooden idols.

> Hammered silver is brought from Tarshish
> and gold from Uphaz.

> What the craftsman and goldsmith
> have made
> is then dressed in blue and purple —
> all made by skilled workers.

But the Lord is the true God;
he is the living God, the eternal King.

When he is angry, the earth trembles;
the nations cannot endure his wrath.

"Tell them this: 'These gods, who did not make the heavens and the earth, will perish from the earth and from under the heavens.'"

But God made the earth by his power;
he founded the world by his wisdom
and stretched out the heavens by his understanding.

When he thunders, the waters in the heavens roar;
he makes clouds rise from the ends of the earth.

He sends lightning with the rain
and brings out the wind from his storehouses.

Everyone is senseless and without knowledge;
every goldsmith is shamed by his idols.

The images he makes are a fraud;
they have no breath in them.

They are worthless, the objects of mockery;
when their judgment comes, they will perish.

He who is the Portion of Jacob is not like these,
for he is the Maker of all things,

including Israel, the people of his inheritance —
the Lord Almighty is his name.

Gather up your belongings to leave the land,
you who live under siege.

For this is what the Lord says:
"At this time I will hurl out
those who live in this land;
I will bring distress on them
so that they may be captured."

Woe to me because of my injury!
My wound is incurable!

Yet I said to myself,
"This is my sickness, and I must endure it."

My tent is destroyed;
all its ropes are snapped.

My children are gone from me and are no more;
no one is left now to pitch my tent
or to set up my shelter.

The shepherds are senseless
and do not inquire of the LORD;
so they do not prosper
and all their flock is scattered.

Listen! The report is coming—
a great commotion from the land of the north!
It will make the towns of Judah desolate,
a haunt of jackals.

LORD, I know that people's lives are not their own;
it is not for them to direct their steps.

Discipline me, LORD, but only in due measure—
not in your anger,
or you will reduce me to nothing.

Pour out your wrath on the nations
that do not acknowledge you,
on the peoples who do not call on your name.

For they have devoured Jacob;
they have devoured him completely
and destroyed his homeland.

This is the word that came to Jeremiah from the LORD: "Listen to the terms of this covenant and tell them to the people of Judah and to those who live in Jerusalem. Tell them that this is what the LORD, the God of Israel, says: 'Cursed is the one who does not obey the terms of this covenant—the terms I commanded your ancestors when I brought them out of Egypt, out of the iron-smelting furnace.' I said, 'Obey me and do everything I command you, and you will be my people, and I will be your God. Then I will fulfill the oath I swore to your ancestors, to give them a land flowing with milk and honey'—the land you possess today."

I answered, "Amen, LORD."

The LORD said to me, "Proclaim all these words in the towns of Judah and in the streets of Jerusalem: 'Listen to the terms of this covenant and follow them. From the time I brought your ancestors up from Egypt until today, I warned them again and again, saying, "Obey me." But they did not listen or pay attention; instead, they followed the stubbornness of their evil hearts. So I brought on them all the curses of the covenant I had commanded them to follow but that they did not keep.'"

Then the LORD said to me, "There is a conspiracy among the people of Judah and those who live in Jerusalem. They have returned to the sins of their ancestors, who refused to listen to my words. They have followed other gods to serve them. Both Israel and Judah have broken the covenant I made with their ancestors. Therefore this is what the LORD says: 'I will bring on them a disaster they cannot escape. Although they cry out to me, I will not listen to them. The towns of Judah and the people of Jerusalem will go and cry out to the gods to whom they burn incense, but they will not help them at all when disaster strikes. You, Judah, have as many gods as you have towns; and the altars you have set up to burn incense to that shameful god Baal are as many as the streets of Jerusalem.'

"Do not pray for this people or offer any plea or petition for them, because I will not listen when they call to me in the time of their distress.

> "What is my beloved doing in my temple
> as she, with many others, works out her evil schemes?
> Can consecrated meat avert your punishment?

> When you engage in your wickedness,
> then you rejoice."

> The LORD called you a thriving olive tree
> with fruit beautiful in form.
> But with the roar of a mighty storm
> he will set it on fire,
> and its branches will be broken.

The LORD Almighty, who planted you, has decreed disaster for you, because the people of both Israel and Judah have done evil and aroused my anger by burning incense to Baal.

Because the LORD revealed their plot to me, I knew it, for at that time he showed me what they were doing. I had been like a gentle lamb led to the slaughter; I did not realize that they had plotted against me, saying,

> "Let us destroy the tree and its fruit;
> let us cut him off from the land of the living,
> that his name be remembered no more."

But you, LORD Almighty, who judge righteously
and test the heart and mind,

let me see your vengeance on them,
for to you I have committed my cause.

Therefore this is what the LORD says about the people of Anathoth who are threatening to kill you, saying, "Do not prophesy in
the name of the LORD or you will die by our hands"—therefore this
is what the LORD Almighty says: "I will punish them. Their young
men will die by the sword, their sons and daughters by famine. Not
even a remnant will be left to them, because I will bring disaster on
the people of Anathoth in the year of their punishment."

You are always righteous, LORD,
when I bring a case before you.

Yet I would speak with you about your justice:
Why does the way of the wicked prosper?
Why do all the faithless live at ease?

You have planted them, and they have taken root;
they grow and bear fruit.

You are always on their lips
but far from their hearts.

Yet you know me, LORD;
you see me and test my thoughts about you.

Drag them off like sheep to be butchered!
Set them apart for the day of slaughter!

How long will the land lie parched
and the grass in every field be withered?

Because those who live in it are wicked,
the animals and birds have perished.

Moreover, the people are saying,
"He will not see what happens to us."

"If you have raced with men on foot
and they have worn you out,
how can you compete with horses?

If you stumble in safe country,
how will you manage in the thickets by the Jordan?

Your relatives, members of your own family—
even they have betrayed you;
they have raised a loud cry against you.

Do not trust them,
though they speak well of you.

"I will forsake my house,
abandon my inheritance;

I will give the one I love
into the hands of her enemies.

My inheritance has become to me
like a lion in the forest.

She roars at me;
therefore I hate her.

Has not my inheritance become to me
like a speckled bird of prey
that other birds of prey surround and attack?

Go and gather all the wild beasts;
bring them to devour.

Many shepherds will ruin my vineyard
and trample down my field;

they will turn my pleasant field
into a desolate wasteland.

It will be made a wasteland,
parched and desolate before me;

the whole land will be laid waste
because there is no one who cares.

Over all the barren heights in the desert
destroyers will swarm,

for the sword of the Lord will devour
from one end of the land to the other;
no one will be safe.

They will sow wheat but reap thorns;
they will wear themselves out but gain nothing.

They will bear the shame of their harvest
because of the Lord's fierce anger."

This is what the Lord says: "As for all my wicked neighbors who seize the inheritance I gave my people Israel, I will uproot them from their lands and I will uproot the people of Judah from among them. But after I uproot them, I will again have compassion and will bring each of them back to their own inheritance and their own country. And if they learn well the ways of my people and swear by my name, saying, 'As surely as the Lord lives'—even as they once taught my people to swear by Baal—then they will be established among my people. But if any nation does not listen, I will completely uproot and destroy it," declares the LORD.

This is what the LORD said to me: "Go and buy a linen belt and put it around your waist, but do not let it touch water." So I bought a belt, as the LORD directed, and put it around my waist.

Then the word of the LORD came to me a second time: "Take the belt you bought and are wearing around your waist, and go now to Perath and hide it there in a crevice in the rocks." So I went and hid it at Perath, as the LORD told me.

Many days later the LORD said to me, "Go now to Perath and get the belt I told you to hide there." So I went to Perath and dug up the belt and took it from the place where I had hidden it, but now it was ruined and completely useless.

Then the word of the LORD came to me: "This is what the LORD says: 'In the same way I will ruin the pride of Judah and the great pride of Jerusalem. These wicked people, who refuse to listen to my words, who follow the stubbornness of their hearts and go after other gods to serve and worship them, will be like this belt — completely useless! For as a belt is bound around the waist, so I bound all the people of Israel and all the people of Judah to me,' declares the LORD, 'to be my people for my renown and praise and honor. But they have not listened.'

"Say to them: 'This is what the LORD, the God of Israel, says: Every wineskin should be filled with wine.' And if they say to you, 'Don't we know that every wineskin should be filled with wine?' then tell them, 'This is what the LORD says: I am going to fill with drunkenness all who live in this land, including the kings who sit on David's throne, the priests, the prophets and all those living in Jerusalem. I will smash them one against the other, parents and children alike, declares the LORD. I will allow no pity or mercy or compassion to keep me from destroying them.'"

Hear and pay attention,
do not be arrogant,
for the LORD has spoken.
Give glory to the LORD your God
before he brings the darkness,
before your feet stumble
on the darkening hills.

You hope for light,
but he will turn it to utter darkness
and change it to deep gloom.

If you do not listen,
I will weep in secret
because of your pride;

my eyes will weep bitterly,
overflowing with tears,
because the Lord's flock will be taken captive.

Say to the king and to the queen mother,
"Come down from your thrones,

for your glorious crowns
will fall from your heads."

The cities in the Negev will be shut up,
and there will be no one to open them.

All Judah will be carried into exile,
carried completely away.

Look up and see
those who are coming from the north.

Where is the flock that was entrusted to you,
the sheep of which you boasted?

What will you say when the Lord sets over you
those you cultivated as your special allies?

Will not pain grip you
like that of a woman in labor?

And if you ask yourself,
"Why has this happened to me?"—

it is because of your many sins
that your skirts have been torn off
and your body mistreated.

Can an Ethiopian change his skin
or a leopard its spots?

Neither can you do good
who are accustomed to doing evil.

"I will scatter you like chaff
driven by the desert wind.

This is your lot,
the portion I have decreed for you,"

declares the Lord,

"because you have forgotten me
and trusted in false gods.

I will pull up your skirts over your face
that your shame may be seen—

your adulteries and lustful neighings,
your shameless prostitution!

I have seen your detestable acts
on the hills and in the fields.

Woe to you, Jerusalem!
How long will you be unclean?"

This is the word of the LORD that came to Jeremiah concerning the drought:

"Judah mourns,
her cities languish;

they wail for the land,
and a cry goes up from Jerusalem.

The nobles send their servants for water;
they go to the cisterns
but find no water.

They return with their jars unfilled;
dismayed and despairing,
they cover their heads.

The ground is cracked
because there is no rain in the land;

the farmers are dismayed
and cover their heads.

Even the doe in the field
deserts her newborn fawn
because there is no grass.

Wild donkeys stand on the barren heights
and pant like jackals;

their eyes fail
for lack of food."

Although our sins testify against us,
do something, LORD, for the sake of your name.

For we have often rebelled;
we have sinned against you.

You who are the hope of Israel,
its Savior in times of distress,

why are you like a stranger in the land,
like a traveler who stays only a night?

Why are you like a man taken by surprise,
like a warrior powerless to save?

You are among us, Lord,
and we bear your name;
do not forsake us!

This is what the Lord says about this people:

"They greatly love to wander;
they do not restrain their feet.

So the Lord does not accept them;
he will now remember their wickedness
and punish them for their sins."

Then the Lord said to me, "Do not pray for the well-being of this people. Although they fast, I will not listen to their cry; though they offer burnt offerings and grain offerings, I will not accept them. Instead, I will destroy them with the sword, famine and plague."

But I said, "Alas, Sovereign Lord! The prophets keep telling them, 'You will not see the sword or suffer famine. Indeed, I will give you lasting peace in this place.'"

Then the Lord said to me, "The prophets are prophesying lies in my name. I have not sent them or appointed them or spoken to them. They are prophesying to you false visions, divinations, idolatries and the delusions of their own minds. Therefore this is what the Lord says about the prophets who are prophesying in my name: I did not send them, yet they are saying, 'No sword or famine will touch this land.' Those same prophets will perish by sword and famine. And the people they are prophesying to will be thrown out into the streets of Jerusalem because of the famine and sword. There will be no one to bury them, their wives, their sons and their daughters. I will pour out on them the calamity they deserve.

"Speak this word to them:

"'Let my eyes overflow with tears
night and day without ceasing;
for the Virgin Daughter, my people,
has suffered a grievous wound,
a crushing blow.

If I go into the country,
I see those slain by the sword;

if I go into the city,
I see the ravages of famine.

Both prophet and priest
have gone to a land they know not.' "

Have you rejected Judah completely?
Do you despise Zion?

Why have you afflicted us
so that we cannot be healed?

We hoped for peace
but no good has come,

for a time of healing
but there is only terror.

We acknowledge our wickedness, Lord,
and the guilt of our ancestors;
we have indeed sinned against you.

For the sake of your name do not despise us;
do not dishonor your glorious throne.

Remember your covenant with us
and do not break it.

Do any of the worthless idols of the nations
bring rain?
Do the skies themselves send down showers?

No, it is you, Lord our God.
Therefore our hope is in you,
for you are the one who does all this.

Then the Lord said to me: "Even if Moses and Samuel were to stand before me, my heart would not go out to this people. Send them away from my presence! Let them go! And if they ask you, 'Where shall we go?' tell them, 'This is what the Lord says:

" 'Those destined for death, to death;

those for the sword, to the sword;

those for starvation, to starvation;

those for captivity, to captivity.'

"I will send four kinds of destroyers against them," declares the Lord, "the sword to kill and the dogs to drag away and the birds and the wild animals to devour and destroy. I will make them abhorrent

to all the kingdoms of the earth because of what Manasseh son of
Hezekiah king of Judah did in Jerusalem.

"Who will have pity on you, Jerusalem?
Who will mourn for you?
Who will stop to ask how you are?

You have rejected me," declares the LORD.
"You keep on backsliding.

So I will reach out and destroy you;
I am tired of holding back.

I will winnow them with a winnowing fork
at the city gates of the land.

I will bring bereavement and destruction on my people,
for they have not changed their ways.

I will make their widows more numerous
than the sand of the sea.

At midday I will bring a destroyer
against the mothers of their young men;

suddenly I will bring down on them
anguish and terror.

The mother of seven will grow faint
and breathe her last.

Her sun will set while it is still day;
she will be disgraced and humiliated.

I will put the survivors to the sword
before their enemies,"

declares the LORD.

Alas, my mother, that you gave me birth,
a man with whom the whole land strives and contends!

I have neither lent nor borrowed,
yet everyone curses me.

The LORD said,

"Surely I will deliver you for a good purpose;
surely I will make your enemies plead with you
in times of disaster and times of distress.

"Can a man break iron —
iron from the north — or bronze?

"Your wealth and your treasures
I will give as plunder, without charge,

because of all your sins
throughout your country.

I will enslave you to your enemies
in a land you do not know,

for my anger will kindle a fire
that will burn against you."

Lord, you understand;
remember me and care for me.
Avenge me on my persecutors.

You are long-suffering—do not take me away;
think of how I suffer reproach for your sake.

When your words came, I ate them;
they were my joy and my heart's delight,

for I bear your name,
Lord God Almighty.

I never sat in the company of revelers,
never made merry with them;

I sat alone because your hand was on me
and you had filled me with indignation.

Why is my pain unending
and my wound grievous and incurable?

You are to me like a deceptive brook,
like a spring that fails.

Therefore this is what the Lord says:

"If you repent, I will restore you
that you may serve me;

if you utter worthy, not worthless, words,
you will be my spokesman.

Let this people turn to you,
but you must not turn to them.

I will make you a wall to this people,
a fortified wall of bronze;

they will fight against you
but will not overcome you,

for I am with you
to rescue and save you,"

declares the Lord.

"I will save you from the hands of the wicked
and deliver you from the grasp of the cruel."

Then the word of the LORD came to me: "You must not marry and have sons or daughters in this place." For this is what the LORD says about the sons and daughters born in this land and about the women who are their mothers and the men who are their fathers: "They will die of deadly diseases. They will not be mourned or buried but will be like dung lying on the ground. They will perish by sword and famine, and their dead bodies will become food for the birds and the wild animals."

For this is what the LORD says: "Do not enter a house where there is a funeral meal; do not go to mourn or show sympathy, because I have withdrawn my blessing, my love and my pity from this people," declares the LORD. "Both high and low will die in this land. They will not be buried or mourned, and no one will cut themselves or shave their head for the dead. No one will offer food to comfort those who mourn for the dead — not even for a father or a mother — nor will anyone give them a drink to console them.

"And do not enter a house where there is feasting and sit down to eat and drink. For this is what the LORD Almighty, the God of Israel, says: Before your eyes and in your days I will bring an end to the sounds of joy and gladness and to the voices of bride and bridegroom in this place.

"When you tell these people all this and they ask you, 'Why has the LORD decreed such a great disaster against us? What wrong have we done? What sin have we committed against the LORD our God?' then say to them, 'It is because your ancestors forsook me,' declares the LORD, 'and followed other gods and served and worshiped them. They forsook me and did not keep my law. But you have behaved more wickedly than your ancestors. See how all of you are following the stubbornness of your evil hearts instead of obeying me. So I will throw you out of this land into a land neither you nor your ancestors have known, and there you will serve other gods day and night, for I will show you no favor.'

"However, the days are coming," declares the LORD, "when it will no longer be said, 'As surely as the LORD lives, who brought the Israelites up out of Egypt,' but it will be said, 'As surely as the LORD lives, who brought the Israelites up out of the land of the north and out of all the countries where he had banished them.' For I will restore them to the land I gave their ancestors.

"But now I will send for many fishermen," declares the LORD, "and they will catch them. After that I will send for many hunters, and they will hunt them down on every mountain and hill and from the crevices of the rocks. My eyes are on all their ways; they are not hidden from me, nor is their sin concealed from my eyes. I will repay them double for their wickedness and their sin, because they have defiled my land with the lifeless forms of their vile images and have filled my inheritance with their detestable idols."

LORD, my strength and my fortress,
my refuge in time of distress,

to you the nations will come
from the ends of the earth and say,

"Our ancestors possessed nothing
but false gods,
worthless idols that did them no good.

Do people make their own gods?
Yes, but they are not gods!"

"Therefore I will teach them—
this time I will teach them
my power and might.

Then they will know
that my name is the LORD.

"Judah's sin is engraved with
an iron tool,
inscribed with a flint point,

on the tablets of their hearts
and on the horns of their altars.

Even their children remember
their altars and Asherah poles

beside the spreading trees
and on the high hills.

My mountain in the land
and your wealth and all your treasures

I will give away as plunder,
together with your high places,
because of sin throughout your country.

Through your own fault you will lose
the inheritance I gave you.

I will enslave you to your enemies
in a land you do not know,

for you have kindled my anger,
and it will burn forever."

This is what the LORD says:

"Cursed is the one who trusts in man,
who draws strength from mere flesh
and whose heart turns away from the LORD.

That person will be like a bush in the wastelands;
they will not see prosperity when it comes.

They will dwell in the parched places
        of the desert,
in a salt land where no one lives.

"But blessed is the one who trusts in the LORD,
whose confidence is in him.

They will be like a tree planted by the water
that sends out its roots by the stream.

It does not fear when heat comes;
its leaves are always green.

It has no worries in a year of drought
and never fails to bear fruit."

The heart is deceitful above all things
and beyond cure.
Who can understand it?

"I the LORD search the heart
and examine the mind,

to reward each person according to their conduct,
according to what their deeds deserve."

Like a partridge that hatches eggs it did not lay
are those who gain riches by unjust means.

When their lives are half gone, their riches
        will desert them,
and in the end they will prove to be fools.

A glorious throne, exalted from the beginning,
is the place of our sanctuary.

LORD, you are the hope of Israel;
all who forsake you will be put to shame.

Those who turn away from you will be written
        in the dust
because they have forsaken the LORD,
the spring of living water.

Heal me, Lord, and I will be healed;
save me and I will be saved,
for you are the one I praise.

They keep saying to me,
"Where is the word of the Lord?
Let it now be fulfilled!"

I have not run away from being your shepherd;
you know I have not desired the day of despair.
What passes my lips is open before you.

Do not be a terror to me;
you are my refuge in the day of disaster.

Let my persecutors be put to shame,
but keep me from shame;

let them be terrified,
but keep me from terror.

Bring on them the day of disaster;
destroy them with double destruction.

This is what the Lord said to me: "Go and stand at the Gate of the People, through which the kings of Judah go in and out; stand also at all the other gates of Jerusalem. Say to them, 'Hear the word of the Lord, you kings of Judah and all people of Judah and everyone living in Jerusalem who come through these gates. This is what the Lord says: Be careful not to carry a load on the Sabbath day or bring it through the gates of Jerusalem. Do not bring a load out of your houses or do any work on the Sabbath, but keep the Sabbath day holy, as I commanded your ancestors. Yet they did not listen or pay attention; they were stiff-necked and would not listen or respond to discipline. But if you are careful to obey me, declares the Lord, and bring no load through the gates of this city on the Sabbath, but keep the Sabbath day holy by not doing any work on it, then kings who sit on David's throne will come through the gates of this city with their officials. They and their officials will come riding in chariots and on horses, accompanied by the men of Judah and those living in Jerusalem, and this city will be inhabited forever. People will come from the towns of Judah and the villages around Jerusalem, from the territory of Benjamin and the western foothills, from the hill country and the Negev, bringing burnt offerings and sacrifices, grain offerings and incense, and bringing thank offerings to the house of the Lord. But if you do not obey me to keep the Sabbath day holy by not carrying any load as you come through the gates of

Jerusalem on the Sabbath day, then I will kindle an unquenchable fire in the gates of Jerusalem that will consume her fortresses.' "

This is the word that came to Jeremiah from the LORD: "Go down to the potter's house, and there I will give you my message." So I went down to the potter's house, and I saw him working at the wheel. But the pot he was shaping from the clay was marred in his hands; so the potter formed it into another pot, shaping it as seemed best to him.

Then the word of the LORD came to me. He said, "Can I not do with you, Israel, as this potter does?" declares the LORD. "Like clay in the hand of the potter, so are you in my hand, Israel. If at any time I announce that a nation or kingdom is to be uprooted, torn down and destroyed, and if that nation I warned repents of its evil, then I will relent and not inflict on it the disaster I had planned. And if at another time I announce that a nation or kingdom is to be built up and planted, and if it does evil in my sight and does not obey me, then I will reconsider the good I had intended to do for it.

"Now therefore say to the people of Judah and those living in Jerusalem, 'This is what the LORD says: Look! I am preparing a disaster for you and devising a plan against you. So turn from your evil ways, each one of you, and reform your ways and your actions.' But they will reply, 'It's no use. We will continue with our own plans; we will all follow the stubbornness of our evil hearts.' "

Therefore this is what the LORD says:

> "Inquire among the nations:
> Who has ever heard anything like this?
>
> A most horrible thing has been done
> by Virgin Israel.
>
> Does the snow of Lebanon
> ever vanish from its rocky slopes?
>
> Do its cool waters from distant sources
> ever stop flowing?
>
> Yet my people have forgotten me;
> they burn incense to worthless idols,
>
> which made them stumble in their ways,
> in the ancient paths.
>
> They made them walk in byways,
> on roads not built up.

> Their land will be an object of horror
> and of lasting scorn;
>
> all who pass by will be appalled
> and will shake their heads.
>
> Like a wind from the east,
> I will scatter them before their enemies;
>
> I will show them my back and not my face
> in the day of their disaster."

They said, "Come, let's make plans against Jeremiah; for the teaching of the law by the priest will not cease, nor will counsel from the wise, nor the word from the prophets. So come, let's attack him with our tongues and pay no attention to anything he says."

> Listen to me, LORD;
> hear what my accusers are saying!
>
> Should good be repaid with evil?
> Yet they have dug a pit for me.
>
> Remember that I stood before you
> and spoke in their behalf
> to turn your wrath away from them.
>
> So give their children over to famine;
> hand them over to the power of the sword.
>
> Let their wives be made childless and widows;
> let their men be put to death,
> their young men slain by the sword in battle.
>
> Let a cry be heard from their houses
> when you suddenly bring invaders against them,
>
> for they have dug a pit to capture me
> and have hidden snares for my feet.
>
> But you, LORD, know
> all their plots to kill me.
>
> Do not forgive their crimes
> or blot out their sins from your sight.
>
> Let them be overthrown before you;
> deal with them in the time of your anger.

This is what the LORD says: "Go and buy a clay jar from a potter. Take along some of the elders of the people and of the priests and go out to the Valley of Ben Hinnom, near the entrance of the Potsherd Gate. There proclaim the words I tell you, and say, 'Hear the word of the LORD, you kings of Judah and people of Jerusalem. This is what the LORD Almighty, the God of Israel, says: Listen! I am going to bring a disaster on this place that will make the ears of everyone who hears of it tingle. For they have forsaken me and made this a place of foreign gods; they have burned incense in it to gods that neither they nor their ancestors nor the kings of Judah ever knew, and they have filled this place with the blood of the innocent. They have built the high places of Baal to burn their children in the fire as offerings to Baal—something I did not command or mention, nor did it enter my mind. So beware, the days are coming, declares the LORD, when people will no longer call this place Topheth or the Valley of Ben Hinnom, but the Valley of Slaughter.

" 'In this place I will ruin the plans of Judah and Jerusalem. I will make them fall by the sword before their enemies, at the hands of those who want to kill them, and I will give their carcasses as food to the birds and the wild animals. I will devastate this city and make it an object of horror and scorn; all who pass by will be appalled and will scoff because of all its wounds. I will make them eat the flesh of their sons and daughters, and they will eat one another's flesh because their enemies will press the siege so hard against them to destroy them.'

"Then break the jar while those who go with you are watching, and say to them, 'This is what the LORD Almighty says: I will smash this nation and this city just as this potter's jar is smashed and cannot be repaired. They will bury the dead in Topheth until there is no more room. This is what I will do to this place and to those who live here, declares the LORD. I will make this city like Topheth. The houses in Jerusalem and those of the kings of Judah will be defiled like this place, Topheth—all the houses where they burned incense on the roofs to all the starry hosts and poured out drink offerings to other gods.' "

Jeremiah then returned from Topheth, where the LORD had sent him to prophesy, and stood in the court of the LORD's temple and said to all the people, "This is what the LORD Almighty, the God of Israel, says: 'Listen! I am going to bring on this city and all the villages around it every disaster I pronounced against them, because they were stiff-necked and would not listen to my words.' "

When the priest Pashhur son of Immer, the official in charge of the temple of the LORD, heard Jeremiah prophesying these things, he had Jeremiah the prophet beaten and put in the stocks at the Upper Gate of Benjamin at the LORD's temple. The next day, when Pashhur released him from the stocks, Jeremiah said to him, "The LORD's name for you is not Pashhur, but Terror on Every Side. For this is what the Lord says: 'I will make you a terror to yourself and to all your friends; with your own eyes you will see them fall by the sword of their enemies. I will give all Judah into the hands of the king of Babylon, who will carry them away to Babylon or put them to the sword. I will deliver all the wealth of this city into the hands of their enemies — all its products, all its valuables and all the treasures of the kings of Judah. They will take it away as plunder and carry it off to Babylon. And you, Pashhur, and all who live in your house will go into exile to Babylon. There you will die and be buried, you and all your friends to whom you have prophesied lies.'"

You deceived me, Lord, and I was deceived;
  you overpowered me and prevailed.
I am ridiculed all day long;
  everyone mocks me.
Whenever I speak, I cry out
  proclaiming violence and destruction.
So the word of the Lord has brought me
  insult and reproach all day long.
But if I say, "I will not mention his word
  or speak anymore in his name,"
his word is in my heart like a fire,
  a fire shut up in my bones.
I am weary of holding it in;
  indeed, I cannot.
I hear many whispering,
  "Terror on every side!
  Denounce him! Let's denounce him!"
All my friends
  are waiting for me to slip, saying,
"Perhaps he will be deceived;
  then we will prevail over him
  and take our revenge on him."

But the Lord is with me like a mighty warrior;
  so my persecutors will stumble and not prevail.
They will fail and be thoroughly disgraced;
  their dishonor will never be forgotten.
Lord Almighty, you who examine the righteous
  and probe the heart and mind,

> let me see your vengeance on them,
> for to you I have committed my cause.

> Sing to the LORD!
> Give praise to the LORD!

> He rescues the life of the needy
> from the hands of the wicked.

> Cursed be the day I was born!
> May the day my mother bore me not be blessed!

> Cursed be the man who brought my father the news,
> who made him very glad, saying,
> "A child is born to you—a son!"

> May that man be like the towns
> the LORD overthrew without pity.

> May he hear wailing in the morning,
> a battle cry at noon.

> For he did not kill me in the womb,
> with my mother as my grave,
> her womb enlarged forever.

> Why did I ever come out of the womb
> to see trouble and sorrow
> and to end my days in shame?

The word came to Jeremiah from the LORD when King Zedekiah sent to him Pashhur son of Malkijah and the priest Zephaniah son of Maaseiah. They said: "Inquire now of the LORD for us because Nebuchadnezzar king of Babylon is attacking us. Perhaps the LORD will perform wonders for us as in times past so that he will withdraw from us."

But Jeremiah answered them, "Tell Zedekiah, 'This is what the LORD, the God of Israel, says: I am about to turn against you the weapons of war that are in your hands, which you are using to fight the king of Babylon and the Babylonians who are outside the wall besieging you. And I will gather them inside this city. I myself will fight against you with an outstretched hand and a mighty arm in furious anger and in great wrath. I will strike down those who live in this city—both man and beast—and they will die of a terrible plague. After that, declares the LORD, I will give Zedekiah king of Judah, his officials and the people in this city who survive the plague, sword and famine, into the hands of Nebuchadnezzar king of Babylon and to their enemies who want to kill them. He will put them to the sword; he will show them no mercy or pity or compassion.'

"Furthermore, tell the people, 'This is what the LORD says: See, I am setting before you the way of life and the way of death. Whoever stays in this city will die by the sword, famine or plague. But whoever goes out and surrenders to the Babylonians who are besieging you will live; they will escape with their lives. I have determined to do this city harm and not good, declares the LORD. It will be given into the hands of the king of Babylon, and he will destroy it with fire.'

"Moreover, say to the royal house of Judah, 'Hear the word of the LORD. This is what the LORD says to you, house of David:

> " 'Administer justice every morning;
> rescue from the hand of the oppressor
> the one who has been robbed,
>
> or my wrath will break out and burn like fire
> because of the evil you have done—
> burn with no one to quench it.
>
> I am against you, Jerusalem,
> you who live above this valley
> on the rocky plateau, declares the LORD—
>
> you who say, "Who can come against us?
> Who can enter our refuge?"
>
> I will punish you as your deeds deserve,
> declares the LORD.
>
> I will kindle a fire in your forests
> that will consume everything around you.' "

This is what the LORD says: "Go down to the palace of the king of Judah and proclaim this message there: 'Hear the word of the LORD to you, king of Judah, you who sit on David's throne—you, your officials and your people who come through these gates. This is what the LORD says: Do what is just and right. Rescue from the hand of the oppressor the one who has been robbed. Do no wrong or violence to the foreigner, the fatherless or the widow, and do not shed innocent blood in this place. For if you are careful to carry out these commands, then kings who sit on David's throne will come through the gates of this palace, riding in chariots and on horses, accompanied by their officials and their people. But if you do not obey these commands, declares the LORD, I swear by myself that this palace will become a ruin.' "

For this is what the LORD says about the palace of the king of Judah:

> "Though you are like Gilead to me,
>   like the summit of Lebanon,
>
> I will surely make you like a wasteland,
>   like towns not inhabited.
>
> I will send destroyers against you,
>   each man with his weapons,
>
> and they will cut up your fine cedar beams
>   and throw them into the fire.

"People from many nations will pass by this city and will ask one another, 'Why has the LORD done such a thing to this great city?' And the answer will be: 'Because they have forsaken the covenant of the LORD their God and have worshiped and served other gods.'"

> Do not weep for the dead king or mourn his loss;
>   rather, weep bitterly for him who is exiled,
>
> because he will never return
>   nor see his native land again.

For this is what the LORD says about Shallum son of Josiah, who succeeded his father as king of Judah but has gone from this place: "He will never return. He will die in the place where they have led him captive; he will not see this land again."

> "Woe to him who builds his palace by unrighteousness,
>   his upper rooms by injustice,
>
> making his own people work for nothing,
>   not paying them for their labor.
>
> He says, 'I will build myself a great palace
>   with spacious upper rooms.'
>
> So he makes large windows in it,
>   panels it with cedar
>   and decorates it in red.
>
> "Does it make you a king
>   to have more and more cedar?
>
> Did not your father have food and drink?
>   He did what was right and just,
>   so all went well with him.
>
> He defended the cause of the poor and needy,
>   and so all went well.

Is that not what it means to know me?"
declares the LORD.

"But your eyes and your heart
are set only on dishonest gain,

on shedding innocent blood
and on oppression and extortion."

Therefore this is what the LORD says about Jehoiakim son of Josiah king of Judah:

"They will not mourn for him:
'Alas, my brother! Alas, my sister!'

They will not mourn for him:
'Alas, my master! Alas, his splendor!'

He will have the burial of a donkey—
dragged away and thrown
outside the gates of Jerusalem."

"Go up to Lebanon and cry out,
let your voice be heard in Bashan,

cry out from Abarim,
for all your allies are crushed.

I warned you when you felt secure,
but you said, 'I will not listen!'

This has been your way from your youth;
you have not obeyed me.

The wind will drive all your shepherds away,
and your allies will go into exile.

Then you will be ashamed and disgraced
because of all your wickedness.

You who live in 'Lebanon,'
who are nestled in cedar buildings,

how you will groan when pangs come upon you,
pain like that of a woman in labor!

"As surely as I live," declares the LORD, "even if you, Jehoiachin son of Jehoiakim king of Judah, were a signet ring on my right hand, I would still pull you off. I will deliver you into the hands of those who want to kill you, those you fear—Nebuchadnezzar king of Babylon and the Babylonians. I will hurl you and the mother who gave you birth into another country, where neither of you was born, and there you both will die. You will never come back to the land you long to return to."

Is this man Jehoiachin a despised, broken pot,
an object no one wants?

Why will he and his children be hurled out,
cast into a land they do not know?

O land, land, land,
hear the word of the Lord!

This is what the Lord says:

"Record this man as if childless,
a man who will not prosper in his lifetime,

for none of his offspring will prosper,
none will sit on the throne of David
or rule anymore in Judah."

"Woe to the shepherds who are destroying and scattering the sheep of my pasture!" declares the Lord. Therefore this is what the Lord, the God of Israel, says to the shepherds who tend my people: "Because you have scattered my flock and driven them away and have not bestowed care on them, I will bestow punishment on you for the evil you have done," declares the Lord. "I myself will gather the remnant of my flock out of all the countries where I have driven them and will bring them back to their pasture, where they will be fruitful and increase in number. I will place shepherds over them who will tend them, and they will no longer be afraid or terrified, nor will any be missing," declares the Lord.

"The days are coming," declares the Lord,
"when I will raise up for David a righteous
Branch,

a King who will reign wisely
and do what is just and right in the land.

In his days Judah will be saved
and Israel will live in safety.

This is the name by which he will be called:
The Lord Our Righteous Savior.

"So then, the days are coming," declares the Lord, "when people will no longer say, 'As surely as the Lord lives, who brought the Israelites up out of Egypt,' but they will say, 'As surely as the Lord lives, who brought the descendants of Israel up out of the land of the north and out of all the countries where he had banished them.' Then they will live in their own land."

Concerning the prophets:

> My heart is broken within me;
>> all my bones tremble.
> I am like a drunken man,
>> like a strong man overcome by wine,
> because of the Lᴏʀᴅ
>> and his holy words.
> The land is full of adulterers;
>> because of the curse the land lies parched
>> and the pastures in the wilderness are withered.
> The prophets follow an evil course
>> and use their power unjustly.

> "Both prophet and priest are godless;
>> even in my temple I find their wickedness,"
>>>> declares the Lᴏʀᴅ.
> "Therefore their path will become slippery;
>> they will be banished to darkness
>> and there they will fall.
> I will bring disaster on them
>> in the year they are punished,"
>>>> declares the Lᴏʀᴅ.

> "Among the prophets of Samaria
>> I saw this repulsive thing:
> They prophesied by Baal
>> and led my people Israel astray.
> And among the prophets of Jerusalem
>> I have seen something horrible:
> They commit adultery and live a lie.
> They strengthen the hands of evildoers,
>> so that not one of them turns from their wickedness.
> They are all like Sodom to me;
>> the people of Jerusalem are like Gomorrah."

Therefore this is what the Lᴏʀᴅ Almighty says concerning the prophets:

> "I will make them eat bitter food
>> and drink poisoned water,

because from the prophets of Jerusalem
ungodliness has spread throughout
    the land."

This is what the LORD Almighty says:

"Do not listen to what the prophets are
    prophesying to you;
they fill you with false hopes.

They speak visions from their own minds,
not from the mouth of the LORD.

They keep saying to those who despise me,
'The LORD says: You will have peace.'

And to all who follow the stubbornness
    of their hearts
they say, 'No harm will come to you.'

But which of them has stood in the council
    of the LORD
to see or to hear his word?
Who has listened and heard his word?

See, the storm of the LORD
will burst out in wrath,

a whirlwind swirling down
on the heads of the wicked.

The anger of the LORD will not turn back
until he fully accomplishes
the purposes of his heart.

In days to come
you will understand it clearly.

I did not send these prophets,
yet they have run with their message;

I did not speak to them,
yet they have prophesied.

But if they had stood in my council,
they would have proclaimed my words
    to my people

and would have turned them from their
    evil ways
and from their evil deeds.

"Am I only a God nearby,"
                        declares the LORD,

"and not a God far away?
Who can hide in secret places
so that I cannot see them?"

declares the LORD.

"Do not I fill heaven and earth?"

declares the LORD.

"I have heard what the prophets say who prophesy lies in my name. They say, 'I had a dream! I had a dream!' How long will this continue in the hearts of these lying prophets, who prophesy the delusions of their own minds? They think the dreams they tell one another will make my people forget my name, just as their ancestors forgot my name through Baal worship. Let the prophet who has a dream recount the dream, but let the one who has my word speak it faithfully. For what has straw to do with grain?" declares the LORD. "Is not my word like fire," declares the LORD, "and like a hammer that breaks a rock in pieces?

"Therefore," declares the LORD, "I am against the prophets who steal from one another words supposedly from me. Yes," declares the LORD, "I am against the prophets who wag their own tongues and yet declare, 'The LORD declares.' Indeed, I am against those who prophesy false dreams," declares the LORD. "They tell them and lead my people astray with their reckless lies, yet I did not send or appoint them. They do not benefit these people in the least," declares the LORD.

"When these people, or a prophet or a priest, ask you, 'What is the message from the LORD?' say to them, 'What message? I will forsake you, declares the LORD.' If a prophet or a priest or anyone else claims, 'This is a message from the LORD,' I will punish them and their household. This is what each of you keeps saying to your friends and other Israelites: 'What is the LORD's answer?' or 'What has the LORD spoken?' But you must not mention 'a message from the LORD' again, because each one's word becomes their own message. So you distort the words of the living God, the LORD Almighty, our God. This is what you keep saying to a prophet: 'What is the LORD's answer to you?' or 'What has the LORD spoken?' Although you claim, 'This is a message from the LORD,' this is what the LORD says: You used the words, 'This is a message from the LORD,' even though I told you that you must not claim, 'This is a message from the LORD.' Therefore, I will surely forget you and cast you out of my presence along with the city I gave to you and your ancestors. I will bring on you everlasting disgrace — everlasting shame that will not be forgotten."

After Jehoiachin son of Jehoiakim king of Judah and the officials, the skilled workers and the artisans of Judah were carried into exile from Jerusalem to Babylon by Nebuchadnezzar king of Babylon, the LORD showed me two baskets of figs placed in front of the temple of the LORD. One basket had very good figs, like those that ripen early; the other basket had very bad figs, so bad they could not be eaten.

Then the LORD asked me, "What do you see, Jeremiah?"

"Figs," I answered. "The good ones are very good, but the bad ones are so bad they cannot be eaten."

Then the word of the LORD came to me: "This is what the LORD, the God of Israel, says: 'Like these good figs, I regard as good the exiles from Judah, whom I sent away from this place to the land of the Babylonians. My eyes will watch over them for their good, and I will bring them back to this land. I will build them up and not tear them down; I will plant them and not uproot them. I will give them a heart to know me, that I am the LORD. They will be my people, and I will be their God, for they will return to me with all their heart.

" 'But like the bad figs, which are so bad they cannot be eaten,' says the LORD, 'so will I deal with Zedekiah king of Judah, his officials and the survivors from Jerusalem, whether they remain in this land or live in Egypt. I will make them abhorrent and an offense to all the kingdoms of the earth, a reproach and a byword, a curse and an object of ridicule, wherever I banish them. I will send the sword, famine and plague against them until they are destroyed from the land I gave to them and their ancestors.' "

The word came to Jeremiah concerning all the people of Judah in the fourth year of Jehoiakim son of Josiah king of Judah, which was the first year of Nebuchadnezzar king of Babylon. So Jeremiah the prophet said to all the people of Judah and to all those living in Jerusalem: For twenty-three years — from the thirteenth year of Josiah son of Amon king of Judah until this very day — the word of the LORD has come to me and I have spoken to you again and again, but you have not listened.

And though the LORD has sent all his servants the prophets to you again and again, you have not listened or paid any attention. They said, "Turn now, each of you, from your evil ways and your evil practices, and you can stay in the land the LORD gave to you and your ancestors for ever and ever. Do not follow other gods to serve and worship them; do not arouse my anger with what your hands have made. Then I will not harm you."

"But you did not listen to me," declares the LORD, "and you have aroused my anger with what your hands have made, and you have brought harm to yourselves."

Therefore the LORD Almighty says this: "Because you have not listened to my words, I will summon all the peoples of the north and my servant Nebuchadnezzar king of Babylon," declares the LORD, "and I will bring them against this land and its inhabitants and against all the surrounding nations. I will completely destroy them and make them an object of horror and scorn, and an everlasting ruin. I will banish from them the sounds of joy and gladness, the voices of bride and bridegroom, the sound of millstones and the light of the lamp. This whole country will become a desolate wasteland, and these nations will serve the king of Babylon seventy years.

"But when the seventy years are fulfilled, I will punish the king of Babylon and his nation, the land of the Babylonians, for their guilt," declares the LORD, "and will make it desolate forever. I will bring on that land all the things I have spoken against it, all that are written in this book and prophesied by Jeremiah against all the nations. They themselves will be enslaved by many nations and great kings; I will repay them according to their deeds and the work of their hands."

This is what the LORD, the God of Israel, said to me: "Take from my hand this cup filled with the wine of my wrath and make all the nations to whom I send you drink it. When they drink it, they will stagger and go mad because of the sword I will send among them."

So I took the cup from the LORD's hand and made all the nations to whom he sent me drink it: Jerusalem and the towns of Judah, its kings and officials, to make them a ruin and an object of horror and scorn, a curse — as they are today; Pharaoh king of Egypt, his attendants, his officials and all his people, and all the foreign people there; all the kings of Uz; all the kings of the Philistines (those of Ashkelon, Gaza, Ekron, and the people left at Ashdod); Edom, Moab and Ammon; all the kings of Tyre and Sidon; the kings of the coastlands across the sea; Dedan, Tema, Buz and all who are in distant places; all the kings of Arabia and all the kings of the foreign people who live in the wilderness; all the kings of Zimri, Elam and Media; and all the kings of the north, near and far, one after the other—all the kingdoms on the face of the earth. And after all of them, the king of Sheshak will drink it too.

"Then tell them, 'This is what the Lord Almighty, the God of Israel, says: Drink, get drunk and vomit, and fall to rise no more because of the sword I will send among you.' But if they refuse to take the cup from your hand and drink, tell them, 'This is what the Lord Almighty says: You must drink it! See, I am beginning to bring disaster on the city that bears my Name, and will you indeed go unpunished? You will not go unpunished, for I am calling down a sword on all who live on the earth, declares the Lord Almighty.'

"Now prophesy all these words against them and say to them:

> " 'The Lord will roar from on high;
> he will thunder from his holy dwelling
> and roar mightily against his land.
>
> He will shout like those who tread the grapes,
> shout against all who live on the earth.
>
> The tumult will resound to the ends of the earth,
> for the Lord will bring charges against the nations;
>
> he will bring judgment on all mankind
> and put the wicked to the sword,' "

declares the Lord.

This is what the Lord Almighty says:

> "Look! Disaster is spreading
> from nation to nation;
>
> a mighty storm is rising
> from the ends of the earth."

At that time those slain by the Lord will be everywhere—from one end of the earth to the other. They will not be mourned or gathered up or buried, but will be like dung lying on the ground.

> Weep and wail, you shepherds;
> roll in the dust, you leaders of the flock.
>
> For your time to be slaughtered has come;
> you will fall like the best of the rams.
>
> The shepherds will have nowhere to flee,
> the leaders of the flock no place to escape.
>
> Hear the cry of the shepherds,
> the wailing of the leaders of the flock,
> for the Lord is destroying their pasture.

The peaceful meadows will be laid waste
because of the fierce anger of the LORD.

Like a lion he will leave his lair,
and their land will become desolate

because of the sword of the oppressor
and because of the LORD's fierce anger.

Early in the reign of Jehoiakim son of Josiah king of Judah, this word came from the LORD: "This is what the LORD says: Stand in the courtyard of the LORD's house and speak to all the people of the towns of Judah who come to worship in the house of the LORD. Tell them everything I command you; do not omit a word. Perhaps they will listen and each will turn from their evil ways. Then I will relent and not inflict on them the disaster I was planning because of the evil they have done. Say to them, 'This is what the LORD says: If you do not listen to me and follow my law, which I have set before you, and if you do not listen to the words of my servants the prophets, whom I have sent to you again and again (though you have not listened), then I will make this house like Shiloh and this city a curse among all the nations of the earth.'"

The priests, the prophets and all the people heard Jeremiah speak these words in the house of the LORD. But as soon as Jeremiah finished telling all the people everything the LORD had commanded him to say, the priests, the prophets and all the people seized him and said, "You must die! Why do you prophesy in the LORD's name that this house will be like Shiloh and this city will be desolate and deserted?" And all the people crowded around Jeremiah in the house of the LORD.

When the officials of Judah heard about these things, they went up from the royal palace to the house of the LORD and took their places at the entrance of the New Gate of the LORD's house. Then the priests and the prophets said to the officials and all the people, "This man should be sentenced to death because he has prophesied against this city. You have heard it with your own ears!"

Then Jeremiah said to all the officials and all the people: "The LORD sent me to prophesy against this house and this city all the things you have heard. Now reform your ways and your actions and obey the LORD your God. Then the LORD will relent and not bring the disaster he has pronounced against you. As for me, I am in your hands; do with me whatever you think is good and right. Be assured, however, that if you put me to death, you will bring the guilt of innocent blood on yourselves and on this city and on those who live in it, for in truth the LORD has sent me to you to speak all these words in your hearing."

Then the officials and all the people said to the priests and the prophets, "This man should not be sentenced to death! He has spoken to us in the name of the LORD our God."

Some of the elders of the land stepped forward and said to the entire assembly of people, "Micah of Moresheth prophesied in the days of Hezekiah king of Judah. He told all the people of Judah, 'This is what the LORD Almighty says:

> " 'Zion will be plowed like a field,
> Jerusalem will become a heap of rubble,
> the temple hill a mound overgrown with thickets.'

"Did Hezekiah king of Judah or anyone else in Judah put him to death? Did not Hezekiah fear the LORD and seek his favor? And did not the LORD relent, so that he did not bring the disaster he pronounced against them? We are about to bring a terrible disaster on ourselves!"

(Now Uriah son of Shemaiah from Kiriath Jearim was another man who prophesied in the name of the LORD; he prophesied the same things against this city and this land as Jeremiah did. When King Jehoiakim and all his officers and officials heard his words, the king was determined to put him to death. But Uriah heard of it and fled in fear to Egypt. King Jehoiakim, however, sent Elnathan son of Akbor to Egypt, along with some other men. They brought Uriah out of Egypt and took him to King Jehoiakim, who had him struck down with a sword and his body thrown into the burial place of the common people.)

Furthermore, Ahikam son of Shaphan supported Jeremiah, and so he was not handed over to the people to be put to death.

Early in the reign of Zedekiah son of Josiah king of Judah, this word came to Jeremiah from the LORD: This is what the LORD said to me: "Make a yoke out of straps and crossbars and put it on your neck. Then send word to the kings of Edom, Moab, Ammon, Tyre and Sidon through the envoys who have come to Jerusalem to Zedekiah king of Judah. Give them a message for their masters and say, 'This is what the LORD Almighty, the God of Israel, says: "Tell this to your masters: With my great power and outstretched arm I made the earth and its people and the animals that are on it, and I give it to anyone I please. Now I will give all your countries into the hands of my servant Nebuchadnezzar king of Babylon; I will make even the wild animals subject to him. All nations will serve him and his son and his grandson until the time for his land comes; then many nations and great kings will subjugate him.

" ' "If, however, any nation or kingdom will not serve Nebuchadnezzar king of Babylon or bow its neck under his yoke, I will punish that nation with the sword, famine and plague, declares the LORD, until I destroy it by his hand. So do not listen to your prophets, your diviners, your interpreters of dreams, your mediums or your sorcerers who tell you, 'You will not serve the king of Babylon.' They prophesy lies to you that will only serve to remove you far from your lands; I will banish you and you will perish. But if any nation will bow its neck under the yoke of the king of Babylon and serve him, I will let that nation remain in its own land to till it and to live there, declares the LORD." ' "

I gave the same message to Zedekiah king of Judah. I said, "Bow your neck under the yoke of the king of Babylon; serve him and his people, and you will live. Why will you and your people die by the sword, famine and plague with which the LORD has threatened any nation that will not serve the king of Babylon? Do not listen to the words of the prophets who say to you, 'You will not serve the king of Babylon,' for they are prophesying lies to you. 'I have not sent them,' declares the LORD. 'They are prophesying lies in my name. Therefore, I will banish you and you will perish, both you and the prophets who prophesy to you.' "

Then I said to the priests and all these people, "This is what the LORD says: Do not listen to the prophets who say, 'Very soon now the articles from the LORD's house will be brought back from Babylon.' They are prophesying lies to you. Do not listen to them. Serve the king of Babylon, and you will live. Why should this city become a ruin? If they are prophets and have the word of the LORD, let them plead with the LORD Almighty that the articles remaining in the house of the LORD and in the palace of the king of Judah and in Jerusalem not be taken to Babylon. For this is what the LORD Almighty says about the pillars, the bronze Sea, the movable stands and the other articles that are left in this city, which Nebuchadnezzar king of Babylon did not take away when he carried Jehoiachin son of Jehoiakim king of Judah into exile from Jerusalem to Babylon, along with all the nobles of Judah and Jerusalem — yes, this is what the LORD Almighty, the God of Israel, says about the things that are left in the house of the LORD and in the palace of the king of Judah and in Jerusalem: 'They will be taken to Babylon and there they will remain until the day I come for them,' declares the LORD. 'Then I will bring them back and restore them to this place.' "

In the fifth month of that same year, the fourth year, early in the reign of Zedekiah king of Judah, the prophet Hananiah son of Azzur, who was from Gibeon, said to me in the house of the Lord in the presence of the priests and all the people: "This is what the Lord Almighty, the God of Israel, says: 'I will break the yoke of the king of Babylon. Within two years I will bring back to this place all the articles of the Lord's house that Nebuchadnezzar king of Babylon removed from here and took to Babylon. I will also bring back to this place Jehoiachin son of Jehoiakim king of Judah and all the other exiles from Judah who went to Babylon,' declares the Lord, 'for I will break the yoke of the king of Babylon.'"

Then the prophet Jeremiah replied to the prophet Hananiah before the priests and all the people who were standing in the house of the Lord. He said, "Amen! May the Lord do so! May the Lord fulfill the words you have prophesied by bringing the articles of the Lord's house and all the exiles back to this place from Babylon. Nevertheless, listen to what I have to say in your hearing and in the hearing of all the people: From early times the prophets who preceded you and me have prophesied war, disaster and plague against many countries and great kingdoms. But the prophet who prophesies peace will be recognized as one truly sent by the Lord only if his prediction comes true."

Then the prophet Hananiah took the yoke off the neck of the prophet Jeremiah and broke it, and he said before all the people, "This is what the Lord says: 'In the same way I will break the yoke of Nebuchadnezzar king of Babylon off the neck of all the nations within two years.'" At this, the prophet Jeremiah went on his way.

After the prophet Hananiah had broken the yoke off the neck of the prophet Jeremiah, the word of the Lord came to Jeremiah: "Go and tell Hananiah, 'This is what the Lord says: You have broken a wooden yoke, but in its place you will get a yoke of iron. This is what the Lord Almighty, the God of Israel, says: I will put an iron yoke on the necks of all these nations to make them serve Nebuchadnezzar king of Babylon, and they will serve him. I will even give him control over the wild animals.'"

Then the prophet Jeremiah said to Hananiah the prophet, "Listen, Hananiah! The Lord has not sent you, yet you have persuaded this nation to trust in lies. Therefore this is what the Lord says: 'I am about to remove you from the face of the earth. This very year you are going to die, because you have preached rebellion against the Lord.'"

In the seventh month of that same year, Hananiah the prophet died.

This is the text of the letter that the prophet Jeremiah sent from Jerusalem to the surviving elders among the exiles and to the priests, the prophets and all the other people Nebuchadnezzar had carried into exile from Jerusalem to Babylon. (This was after King Jehoiachin and the queen mother, the court officials and the leaders of Judah and Jerusalem, the skilled workers and the artisans had gone into exile from Jerusalem.) He entrusted the letter to Elasah son of Shaphan and to Gemariah son of Hilkiah, whom Zedekiah king of Judah sent to King Nebuchadnezzar in Babylon. It said:

This is what the LORD Almighty, the God of Israel, says to all those I carried into exile from Jerusalem to Babylon: "Build houses and settle down; plant gardens and eat what they produce. Marry and have sons and daughters; find wives for your sons and give your daughters in marriage, so that they too may have sons and daughters. Increase in number there; do not decrease. Also, seek the peace and prosperity of the city to which I have carried you into exile. Pray to the LORD for it, because if it prospers, you too will prosper." Yes, this is what the LORD Almighty, the God of Israel, says: "Do not let the prophets and diviners among you deceive you. Do not listen to the dreams you encourage them to have. They are prophesying lies to you in my name. I have not sent them," declares the LORD.

This is what the LORD says: "When seventy years are completed for Babylon, I will come to you and fulfill my good promise to bring you back to this place. For I know the plans I have for you," declares the LORD, "plans to prosper you and not to harm you, plans to give you hope and a future. Then you will call on me and come and pray to me, and I will listen to you. You will seek me and find me when you seek me with all your heart. I will be found by you," declares the LORD, "and will bring you back from captivity. I will gather you from all the nations and places where I have banished you," declares the LORD, "and will bring you back to the place from which I carried you into exile."

You may say, "The LORD has raised up prophets for us in Babylon," but this is what the LORD says about the king who sits on David's throne and all the people who remain in this city, your fellow citizens who did not go with you into exile—yes, this is what the LORD Almighty says: "I will send the sword, famine and plague against them and I will make them like figs that are so bad they cannot be eaten. I will pursue them with the sword, famine and plague and will make them abhorrent to all the kingdoms of the earth, a curse and an object of horror, of scorn and reproach, among all the nations where I drive them. For they have not listened to my words," declares the LORD, "words that I sent to them again and again by my servants the prophets. And you exiles have not listened either," declares the LORD.

Therefore, hear the word of the LORD, all you exiles whom I have sent away from Jerusalem to Babylon. This is what the LORD Almighty, the God of Israel, says about Ahab son of Kolaiah and Zedekiah son of Maaseiah, who are prophesying lies to you in my name: "I will deliver them into the hands of Nebuchadnezzar king of Babylon, and he will put them to death before your very eyes. Because of them, all the exiles from Judah who are in Babylon will use this curse: 'May the LORD treat you like Zedekiah and Ahab, whom the king of Babylon burned in the fire.' For they have done outrageous things in Israel; they have committed adultery with their neighbors' wives, and in my name they have uttered lies — which I did not authorize. I know it and am a witness to it," declares the LORD.

Tell Shemaiah the Nehelamite, "This is what the LORD Almighty, the God of Israel, says: You sent letters in your own name to all the people in Jerusalem, to the priest Zephaniah son of Maaseiah, and to all the other priests. You said to Zephaniah, 'The LORD has appointed you priest in place of Jehoiada to be in charge of the house of the LORD; you should put any maniac who acts like a prophet into the stocks and neck-irons. So why have you not reprimanded Jeremiah from Anathoth, who poses as a prophet among you? He has sent this message to us in Babylon: It will be a long time. Therefore build houses and settle down; plant gardens and eat what they produce.' "

Zephaniah the priest, however, read the letter to Jeremiah the prophet. Then the word of the LORD came to Jeremiah: "Send this message to all the exiles: 'This is what the LORD says about Shemaiah the Nehelamite: Because Shemaiah has prophesied to you, even though I did not send him, and has persuaded you to trust in lies, this is what the LORD says: I will surely punish Shemaiah the Nehelamite and his descendants. He will have no one left among this people, nor will he see the good things I will do for my people, declares the LORD, because he has preached rebellion against me.' "

This is the word that came to Jeremiah from the Lord: "This is what the Lord, the God of Israel, says: 'Write in a book all the words I have spoken to you. The days are coming,' declares the Lord, 'when I will bring my people Israel and Judah back from captivity and restore them to the land I gave their ancestors to possess,' says the Lord."

These are the words the Lord spoke concerning Israel and Judah: "This is what the Lord says:

> " 'Cries of fear are heard —
> terror, not peace.

> Ask and see:
> Can a man bear children?

> Then why do I see every strong man
> with his hands on his stomach like a woman in labor,
> every face turned deathly pale?

> How awful that day will be!
> No other will be like it.

> It will be a time of trouble for Jacob,
> but he will be saved out of it.

> " 'In that day,' declares the Lord Almighty,
> 'I will break the yoke off their necks

> and will tear off their bonds;
> no longer will foreigners enslave them.

> Instead, they will serve the Lord their God
> and David their king,
> whom I will raise up for them.

> " 'So do not be afraid, Jacob my servant;
> do not be dismayed, Israel,'
>   declares the Lord.

> 'I will surely save you out of a distant place,
> your descendants from the land of their exile.

> Jacob will again have peace and security,
> and no one will make him afraid.

> I am with you and will save you,'
> declares the Lord.

> 'Though I completely destroy all the nations
> among which I scatter you,
> I will not completely destroy you.

I will discipline you but only in due measure;
I will not let you go entirely unpunished.'

"This is what the LORD says:

"'Your wound is incurable,
your injury beyond healing.

There is no one to plead your cause,
no remedy for your sore,
no healing for you.

All your allies have forgotten you;
they care nothing for you.

I have struck you as an enemy would
and punished you as would the cruel,

because your guilt is so great
and your sins so many.

Why do you cry out over your wound,
your pain that has no cure?

Because of your great guilt and many sins
I have done these things to you.

"'But all who devour you will be devoured;
all your enemies will go into exile.

Those who plunder you will be plundered;
all who make spoil of you I will despoil.

But I will restore you to health
and heal your wounds,'

declares the LORD,

'because you are called an outcast,
Zion for whom no one cares.'

"This is what the LORD says:

"'I will restore the fortunes of Jacob's tents
and have compassion on his dwellings;

the city will be rebuilt on her ruins,
and the palace will stand in its proper place.

From them will come songs of thanksgiving
and the sound of rejoicing.

I will add to their numbers,
and they will not be decreased;

I will bring them honor,
and they will not be disdained.

Their children will be as in days of old,
and their community will be established before me;
I will punish all who oppress them.

Their leader will be one of their own;
their ruler will arise from among them.

I will bring him near and he will come close to me—
for who is he who will devote himself
to be close to me?'
declares the LORD.

"'So you will be my people,
and I will be your God.'"

See, the storm of the LORD
will burst out in wrath,

a driving wind swirling down
on the heads of the wicked.

The fierce anger of the LORD will not turn back
until he fully accomplishes
the purposes of his heart.

In days to come
you will understand this.

"At that time," declares the LORD, "I will be the God of all the
families of Israel, and they will be my people."
This is what the LORD says:

"The people who survive the sword
will find favor in the wilderness;
I will come to give rest to Israel."

The LORD appeared to us in the past, saying:

"I have loved you with an everlasting love;
I have drawn you with unfailing kindness.

I will build you up again,
and you, Virgin Israel, will be rebuilt.

Again you will take up your timbrels
and go out to dance with the joyful.

Again you will plant vineyards
on the hills of Samaria;

the farmers will plant them
and enjoy their fruit.

There will be a day when watchmen cry out
on the hills of Ephraim,

'Come, let us go up to Zion,
to the Lord our God.'"

This is what the Lord says:

"Sing with joy for Jacob;
shout for the foremost of the nations.

Make your praises heard, and say,
'Lord, save your people,
the remnant of Israel.'

See, I will bring them from the land of the north
and gather them from the ends of the earth.

Among them will be the blind and the lame,
expectant mothers and women in labor;
a great throng will return.

They will come with weeping;
they will pray as I bring them back.

I will lead them beside streams of water
on a level path where they will not stumble,

because I am Israel's father,
and Ephraim is my firstborn son.

"Hear the word of the Lord, you nations;
proclaim it in distant coastlands:

'He who scattered Israel will gather them
and will watch over his flock like a shepherd.'

For the Lord will deliver Jacob
and redeem them from the hand of those stronger than
    they.

They will come and shout for joy on the heights of Zion;
they will rejoice in the bounty of the Lord—

the grain, the new wine and the olive oil,
the young of the flocks and herds.

They will be like a well-watered garden,
and they will sorrow no more.

Then young women will dance and be glad,
young men and old as well.

I will turn their mourning into gladness;
I will give them comfort and joy instead of sorrow.

I will satisfy the priests with abundance,
and my people will be filled with my bounty,"
declares the LORD.

This is what the LORD says:

"A voice is heard in Ramah,
mourning and great weeping,

Rachel weeping for her children
and refusing to be comforted,
because they are no more."

This is what the LORD says:

"Restrain your voice from weeping
and your eyes from tears,

for your work will be rewarded,"
declares the LORD.
"They will return from the land of the enemy.

So there is hope for your descendants,"
declares the LORD.
"Your children will return to their own land.

"I have surely heard Ephraim's moaning:
'You disciplined me like an unruly calf,
and I have been disciplined.

Restore me, and I will return,
because you are the LORD my God.

After I strayed,
I repented;

after I came to understand,
I beat my breast.

I was ashamed and humiliated
because I bore the disgrace of my youth.'

Is not Ephraim my dear son,
the child in whom I delight?

Though I often speak against him,
I still remember him.

Therefore my heart yearns for him;
I have great compassion for him,"
declares the LORD.

"Set up road signs;
put up guideposts.

> Take note of the highway,
> the road that you take.

> Return, Virgin Israel,
> return to your towns.

> How long will you wander,
> unfaithful Daughter Israel?

> The Lord will create a new thing on earth—
> the woman will return to the man."

This is what the Lord Almighty, the God of Israel, says: "When I bring them back from captivity, the people in the land of Judah and in its towns will once again use these words: 'The Lord bless you, you prosperous city, you sacred mountain.' People will live together in Judah and all its towns—farmers and those who move about with their flocks. I will refresh the weary and satisfy the faint."

At this I awoke and looked around. My sleep had been pleasant to me.

"The days are coming," declares the Lord, "when I will plant the kingdoms of Israel and Judah with the offspring of people and of animals. Just as I watched over them to uproot and tear down, and to overthrow, destroy and bring disaster, so I will watch over them to build and to plant," declares the Lord. "In those days people will no longer say,

> 'The parents have eaten sour grapes,
> and the children's teeth are set on edge.'

Instead, everyone will die for their own sin; whoever eats sour grapes—their own teeth will be set on edge.

> "The days are coming," declares the Lord,
> "when I will make a new covenant

> with the people of Israel
> and with the people of Judah.

> It will not be like the covenant
> I made with their ancestors

> when I took them by the hand
> to lead them out of Egypt,

> because they broke my covenant,
> though I was a husband to them,"
>   declares the Lord.

> "This is the covenant I will make with the people
>   of Israel
> after that time," declares the Lord.

"I will put my law in their minds
and write it on their hearts.
I will be their God,
and they will be my people.
No longer will they teach their neighbor,
or say to one another, 'Know the LORD,'
because they will all know me,
from the least of them to the greatest,"
declares the LORD.
"For I will forgive their wickedness
and will remember their sins no more."

This is what the LORD says,

he who appoints the sun
to shine by day,
who decrees the moon and stars
to shine by night,
who stirs up the sea
so that its waves roar —
the LORD Almighty is his name:
"Only if these decrees vanish from
my sight,"
declares the LORD,
"will Israel ever cease
being a nation before me."

This is what the LORD says:

"Only if the heavens above can be measured
and the foundations of the earth below
be searched out
will I reject all the descendants of Israel
because of all they have done,"
declares the LORD.

"The days are coming," declares the LORD, "when this city will be rebuilt for me from the Tower of Hananel to the Corner Gate. The measuring line will stretch from there straight to the hill of Gareb and then turn to Goah. The whole valley where dead bodies and ashes are thrown, and all the terraces out to the Kidron Valley on the east as far as the corner of the Horse Gate, will be holy to the LORD. The city will never again be uprooted or demolished."

This is the word that came to Jeremiah from the LORD in the tenth year of Zedekiah king of Judah, which was the eighteenth year of Nebuchadnezzar. The army of the king of Babylon was then besieging Jerusalem, and Jeremiah the prophet was confined in the courtyard of the guard in the royal palace of Judah.

Now Zedekiah king of Judah had imprisoned him there, saying, "Why do you prophesy as you do? You say, 'This is what the LORD says: I am about to give this city into the hands of the king of Babylon, and he will capture it. Zedekiah king of Judah will not escape the Babylonians but will certainly be given into the hands of the king of Babylon, and will speak with him face to face and see him with his own eyes. He will take Zedekiah to Babylon, where he will remain until I deal with him, declares the LORD. If you fight against the Babylonians, you will not succeed.' "

Jeremiah said, "The word of the LORD came to me: Hanamel son of Shallum your uncle is going to come to you and say, 'Buy my field at Anathoth, because as nearest relative it is your right and duty to buy it.'

"Then, just as the LORD had said, my cousin Hanamel came to me in the courtyard of the guard and said, 'Buy my field at Anathoth in the territory of Benjamin. Since it is your right to redeem it and possess it, buy it for yourself.'

"I knew that this was the word of the LORD; so I bought the field at Anathoth from my cousin Hanamel and weighed out for him seventeen shekels of silver. I signed and sealed the deed, had it witnessed, and weighed out the silver on the scales. I took the deed of purchase — the sealed copy containing the terms and conditions, as well as the unsealed copy — and I gave this deed to Baruch son of Neriah, the son of Mahseiah, in the presence of my cousin Hanamel and of the witnesses who had signed the deed and of all the Jews sitting in the courtyard of the guard.

"In their presence I gave Baruch these instructions: 'This is what the LORD Almighty, the God of Israel, says: Take these documents, both the sealed and unsealed copies of the deed of purchase, and put them in a clay jar so they will last a long time. For this is what the LORD Almighty, the God of Israel, says: Houses, fields and vineyards will again be bought in this land.'

"After I had given the deed of purchase to Baruch son of Neriah, I prayed to the LORD:

"Ah, Sovereign LORD, you have made the heavens and the earth
by your great power and outstretched arm. Nothing is too hard

for you. You show love to thousands but bring the punishment for the parents' sins into the laps of their children after them. Great and mighty God, whose name is the LORD Almighty, great are your purposes and mighty are your deeds. Your eyes are open to the ways of all mankind; you reward each person according to their conduct and as their deeds deserve. You performed signs and wonders in Egypt and have continued them to this day, in Israel and among all mankind, and have gained the renown that is still yours. You brought your people Israel out of Egypt with signs and wonders, by a mighty hand and an outstretched arm and with great terror. You gave them this land you had sworn to give their ancestors, a land flowing with milk and honey. They came in and took possession of it, but they did not obey you or follow your law; they did not do what you commanded them to do. So you brought all this disaster on them.

"See how the siege ramps are built up to take the city. Because of the sword, famine and plague, the city will be given into the hands of the Babylonians who are attacking it. What you said has happened, as you now see. And though the city will be given into the hands of the Babylonians, you, Sovereign LORD, say to me, 'Buy the field with silver and have the transaction witnessed.'"

Then the word of the LORD came to Jeremiah: "I am the LORD, the God of all mankind. Is anything too hard for me? Therefore this is what the LORD says: I am about to give this city into the hands of the Babylonians and to Nebuchadnezzar king of Babylon, who will capture it. The Babylonians who are attacking this city will come in and set it on fire; they will burn it down, along with the houses where the people aroused my anger by burning incense on the roofs to Baal and by pouring out drink offerings to other gods.

"The people of Israel and Judah have done nothing but evil in my sight from their youth; indeed, the people of Israel have done nothing but arouse my anger with what their hands have made, declares the LORD. From the day it was built until now, this city has so aroused my anger and wrath that I must remove it from my sight. The people of Israel and Judah have provoked me by all the evil they have done — they, their kings and officials, their priests and prophets, the people of Judah and those living in Jerusalem. They turned their backs to me and not their faces; though I taught them again and again, they would not listen or respond to discipline. They set up their vile images in the house that bears my Name and defiled it. They built high places for Baal in the Valley of Ben Hinnom to sacrifice their sons and daughters to Molek, though I never commanded — nor did it enter my mind — that they should do such a detestable thing and so make Judah sin.

"You are saying about this city, 'By the sword, famine and plague it will be given into the hands of the king of Babylon'; but this is what the LORD, the God of Israel, says: I will surely gather them from all the lands where I banish them in my furious anger and great wrath; I will bring them back to this place and let them live in safety. They will be my people, and I will be their God. I will give them singleness of heart and action, so that they will always fear me and that all will then go well for them and for their children after them. I will make an everlasting covenant with them: I will never stop doing good to them, and I will inspire them to fear me, so that they will never turn away from me. I will rejoice in doing them good and will assuredly plant them in this land with all my heart and soul.

"This is what the LORD says: As I have brought all this great calamity on this people, so I will give them all the prosperity I have promised them. Once more fields will be bought in this land of which you say, 'It is a desolate waste, without people or animals, for it has been given into the hands of the Babylonians.' Fields will be bought for silver, and deeds will be signed, sealed and witnessed in the territory of Benjamin, in the villages around Jerusalem, in the towns of Judah and in the towns of the hill country, of the western foothills and of the Negev, because I will restore their fortunes, declares the LORD."

While Jeremiah was still confined in the courtyard of the guard, the word of the LORD came to him a second time: "This is what the LORD says, he who made the earth, the LORD who formed it and established it — the LORD is his name: 'Call to me and I will answer you and tell you great and unsearchable things you do not know.' For this is what the LORD, the God of Israel, says about the houses in this city and the royal palaces of Judah that have been torn down to be used against the siege ramps and the sword in the fight with the Babylonians: 'They will be filled with the dead bodies of the people I will slay in my anger and wrath. I will hide my face from this city because of all its wickedness.

" 'Nevertheless, I will bring health and healing to it; I will heal my people and will let them enjoy abundant peace and security. I will bring Judah and Israel back from captivity and will rebuild them as they were before. I will cleanse them from all the sin they have committed against me and will forgive all their sins of rebellion against me. Then this city will bring me renown, joy, praise and honor before all nations on earth that hear of all the good things I do for it; and they will be in awe and will tremble at the abundant prosperity and peace I provide for it.'

"This is what the Lord says: 'You say about this place, "It is a desolate waste, without people or animals." Yet in the towns of Judah and the streets of Jerusalem that are deserted, inhabited by neither people nor animals, there will be heard once more the sounds of joy and gladness, the voices of bride and bridegroom, and the voices of those who bring thank offerings to the house of the Lord, saying,

> "Give thanks to the Lord Almighty,
>   for the Lord is good;
>   his love endures forever."

For I will restore the fortunes of the land as they were before,' says the Lord.

"This is what the Lord Almighty says: 'In this place, desolate and without people or animals — in all its towns there will again be pastures for shepherds to rest their flocks. In the towns of the hill country, of the western foothills and of the Negev, in the territory of Benjamin, in the villages around Jerusalem and in the towns of Judah, flocks will again pass under the hand of the one who counts them,' says the Lord.

" 'The days are coming,' declares the Lord, 'when I will fulfill the good promise I made to the people of Israel and Judah.

> " 'In those days and at that time
>   I will make a righteous Branch sprout from David's line;
>   he will do what is just and right in the land.
>
> In those days Judah will be saved
>   and Jerusalem will live in safety.
>
> This is the name by which it will be called:
>   The Lord Our Righteous Savior.'

For this is what the Lord says: 'David will never fail to have a man to sit on the throne of Israel, nor will the Levitical priests ever fail to have a man to stand before me continually to offer burnt offerings, to burn grain offerings and to present sacrifices.' "

The word of the Lord came to Jeremiah: "This is what the Lord says: 'If you can break my covenant with the day and my covenant with the night, so that day and night no longer come at their appointed time, then my covenant with David my servant — and my covenant with the Levites who are priests ministering before me — can be broken and David will no longer have a descendant to reign on his throne. I will make the descendants of David my servant and the Levites who minister before me as countless as the stars in the sky and as measureless as the sand on the seashore.'"

The word of the LORD came to Jeremiah: "Have you not noticed that these people are saying, 'The LORD has rejected the two kingdoms he chose'? So they despise my people and no longer regard them as a nation. This is what the LORD says: 'If I have not made my covenant with day and night and established the laws of heaven and earth, then I will reject the descendants of Jacob and David my servant and will not choose one of his sons to rule over the descendants of Abraham, Isaac and Jacob. For I will restore their fortunes and have compassion on them.'"

While Nebuchadnezzar king of Babylon and all his army and all the kingdoms and peoples in the empire he ruled were fighting against Jerusalem and all its surrounding towns, this word came to Jeremiah from the LORD: "This is what the LORD, the God of Israel, says: Go to Zedekiah king of Judah and tell him, 'This is what the LORD says: I am about to give this city into the hands of the king of Babylon, and he will burn it down. You will not escape from his grasp but will surely be captured and given into his hands. You will see the king of Babylon with your own eyes, and he will speak with you face to face. And you will go to Babylon.

"'Yet hear the LORD's promise to you, Zedekiah king of Judah. This is what the LORD says concerning you: You will not die by the sword; you will die peacefully. As people made a funeral fire in honor of your predecessors, the kings who ruled before you, so they will make a fire in your honor and lament, "Alas, master!" I myself make this promise, declares the LORD.'"

Then Jeremiah the prophet told all this to Zedekiah king of Judah, in Jerusalem, while the army of the king of Babylon was fighting against Jerusalem and the other cities of Judah that were still holding out—Lachish and Azekah. These were the only fortified cities left in Judah.

The word came to Jeremiah from the LORD after King Zedekiah had made a covenant with all the people in Jerusalem to proclaim freedom for the slaves. Everyone was to free their Hebrew slaves, both male and female; no one was to hold a fellow Hebrew in bondage. So all the officials and people who entered into this covenant agreed that they would free their male and female slaves and no longer hold them in bondage. They agreed, and set them free. But afterward they changed their minds and took back the slaves they had freed and enslaved them again.

Then the word of the LORD came to Jeremiah: "This is what the LORD, the God of Israel, says: I made a covenant with your ancestors when I brought them out of Egypt, out of the land of slavery. I said, 'Every seventh year each of you must free any fellow Hebrews who have sold themselves to you. After they have served you six years, you must let them go free.' Your ancestors, however, did not listen to me or pay attention to me. Recently you repented and did what is right in my sight: Each of you proclaimed freedom to your own people. You even made a covenant before me in the house that bears my Name. But now you have turned around and profaned my name; each of you has taken back the male and female slaves you had set free to go where they wished. You have forced them to become your slaves again.

"Therefore this is what the LORD says: You have not obeyed me; you have not proclaimed freedom to your own people. So I now proclaim 'freedom' for you, declares the LORD — 'freedom' to fall by the sword, plague and famine. I will make you abhorrent to all the kingdoms of the earth. Those who have violated my covenant and have not fulfilled the terms of the covenant they made before me, I will treat like the calf they cut in two and then walked between its pieces. The leaders of Judah and Jerusalem, the court officials, the priests and all the people of the land who walked between the pieces of the calf, I will deliver into the hands of their enemies who want to kill them. Their dead bodies will become food for the birds and the wild animals.

"I will deliver Zedekiah king of Judah and his officials into the hands of their enemies who want to kill them, to the army of the king of Babylon, which has withdrawn from you. I am going to give the order, declares the LORD, and I will bring them back to this city. They will fight against it, take it and burn it down. And I will lay waste the towns of Judah so no one can live there."

This is the word that came to Jeremiah from the LORD during the reign of Jehoiakim son of Josiah king of Judah: "Go to the Rekabite family and invite them to come to one of the side rooms of the house of the LORD and give them wine to drink."

So I went to get Jaazaniah son of Jeremiah, the son of Habazziniah, and his brothers and all his sons — the whole family of the Rekabites. I brought them into the house of the LORD, into the room of the sons of Hanan son of Igdaliah the man of God. It was next to the room of the officials, which was over that of Maaseiah son of Shallum the doorkeeper. Then I set bowls full of wine and some cups before the Rekabites and said to them, "Drink some wine."

But they replied, "We do not drink wine, because our forefather Jehonadab son of Rekab gave us this command: 'Neither you nor your descendants must ever drink wine. Also you must never build houses, sow seed or plant vineyards; you must never have any of these things, but must always live in tents. Then you will live a long time in the land where you are nomads.' We have obeyed everything our forefather Jehonadab son of Rekab commanded us. Neither we nor our wives nor our sons and daughters have ever drunk wine or built houses to live in or had vineyards, fields or crops. We have lived in tents and have fully obeyed everything our forefather Jehonadab commanded us. But when Nebuchadnezzar king of Babylon invaded this land, we said, 'Come, we must go to Jerusalem to escape the Babylonian and Aramean armies.' So we have remained in Jerusalem."

Then the word of the LORD came to Jeremiah, saying: "This is what the LORD Almighty, the God of Israel, says: Go and tell the people of Judah and those living in Jerusalem, 'Will you not learn a lesson and obey my words?' declares the LORD. 'Jehonadab son of Rekab ordered his descendants not to drink wine and this command has been kept. To this day they do not drink wine, because they obey their forefather's command. But I have spoken to you again and again, yet you have not obeyed me. Again and again I sent all my servants the prophets to you. They said, "Each of you must turn from your wicked ways and reform your actions; do not follow other gods to serve them. Then you will live in the land I have given to you and your ancestors." But you have not paid attention or listened to me. The descendants of Jehonadab son of Rekab have carried out the command their forefather gave them, but these people have not obeyed me.'

"Therefore this is what the LORD God Almighty, the God of Israel, says: 'Listen! I am going to bring on Judah and on everyone living in Jerusalem every disaster I pronounced against them. I spoke to them, but they did not listen; I called to them, but they did not answer.'"

Then Jeremiah said to the family of the Rekabites, "This is what the LORD Almighty, the God of Israel, says: 'You have obeyed the command of your forefather Jehonadab and have followed all his instructions and have done everything he ordered.' Therefore this is what the LORD Almighty, the God of Israel, says: 'Jehonadab son of Rekab will never fail to have a descendant to serve me.'"

In the fourth year of Jehoiakim son of Josiah king of Judah, this word came to Jeremiah from the LORD: "Take a scroll and write on it all the words I have spoken to you concerning Israel, Judah and all the other nations from the time I began speaking to you in the reign of Josiah till now. Perhaps when the people of Judah hear about every disaster I plan to inflict on them, they will each turn from their wicked ways; then I will forgive their wickedness and their sin."

So Jeremiah called Baruch son of Neriah, and while Jeremiah dictated all the words the LORD had spoken to him, Baruch wrote them on the scroll. Then Jeremiah told Baruch, "I am restricted; I am not allowed to go to the LORD's temple. So you go to the house of the LORD on a day of fasting and read to the people from the scroll the words of the LORD that you wrote as I dictated. Read them to all the people of Judah who come in from their towns. Perhaps they will bring their petition before the LORD and will each turn from their wicked ways, for the anger and wrath pronounced against this people by the LORD are great."

Baruch son of Neriah did everything Jeremiah the prophet told him to do; at the LORD's temple he read the words of the LORD from the scroll. In the ninth month of the fifth year of Jehoiakim son of Josiah king of Judah, a time of fasting before the LORD was proclaimed for all the people in Jerusalem and those who had come from the towns of Judah. From the room of Gemariah son of Shaphan the secretary, which was in the upper courtyard at the entrance of the New Gate of the temple, Baruch read to all the people at the LORD's temple the words of Jeremiah from the scroll.

When Micaiah son of Gemariah, the son of Shaphan, heard all the words of the LORD from the scroll, he went down to the secretary's room in the royal palace, where all the officials were sitting: Elishama the secretary, Delaiah son of Shemaiah, Elnathan son of Akbor, Gemariah son of Shaphan, Zedekiah son of Hananiah, and all the other officials. After Micaiah told them everything he had heard Baruch read to the people from the scroll, all the officials sent Jehudi son of Nethaniah, the son of Shelemiah, the son of Cushi, to say to Baruch, "Bring the scroll from which you have read to the people and come." So Baruch son of Neriah went to them with the scroll in his hand. They said to him, "Sit down, please, and read it to us."

So Baruch read it to them. When they heard all these words, they looked at each other in fear and said to Baruch, "We must report all these words to the king." Then they asked Baruch, "Tell us, how did you come to write all this? Did Jeremiah dictate it?"

"Yes," Baruch replied, "he dictated all these words to me, and I wrote them in ink on the scroll."

Then the officials said to Baruch, "You and Jeremiah, go and hide. Don't let anyone know where you are."

After they put the scroll in the room of Elishama the secretary, they went to the king in the courtyard and reported everything to him. The king sent Jehudi to get the scroll, and Jehudi brought it from the room of Elishama the secretary and read it to the king and all the officials standing beside him. It was the ninth month and the king was sitting in the winter apartment, with a fire burning in the firepot in front of him. Whenever Jehudi had read three or four columns of the scroll, the king cut them off with a scribe's knife and threw them into the firepot, until the entire scroll was burned in the fire. The king and all his attendants who heard all these words showed no fear, nor did they tear their clothes. Even though Elnathan, Delaiah and Gemariah urged the king not to burn the scroll, he would not listen to them. Instead, the king commanded Jerahmeel, a son of the king, Seraiah son of Azriel and Shelemiah son of Abdeel to arrest Baruch the scribe and Jeremiah the prophet. But the LORD had hidden them.

After the king burned the scroll containing the words that Baruch had written at Jeremiah's dictation, the word of the LORD came to Jeremiah: "Take another scroll and write on it all the words that were on the first scroll, which Jehoiakim king of Judah burned up. Also tell Jehoiakim king of Judah, 'This is what the LORD says: You burned that scroll and said, "Why did you write on it that the king of Babylon would certainly come and destroy this land and wipe from it both man and beast?" Therefore this is what the LORD says about Jehoiakim king of Judah: He will have no one to sit on the throne of David; his body will be thrown out and exposed to the heat by day and the frost by night. I will punish him and his children and his attendants for their wickedness; I will bring on them and those living in Jerusalem and the people of Judah every disaster I pronounced against them, because they have not listened.' "

So Jeremiah took another scroll and gave it to the scribe Baruch son of Neriah, and as Jeremiah dictated, Baruch wrote on it all the words of the scroll that Jehoiakim king of Judah had burned in the fire. And many similar words were added to them.

Z edekiah son of Josiah was made king of Judah by Nebuchadnezzar king of Babylon; he reigned in place of Jehoiachin son of Jehoiakim. Neither he nor his attendants nor the people of the land paid any attention to the words the Lord had spoken through Jeremiah the prophet.

King Zedekiah, however, sent Jehukal son of Shelemiah with the priest Zephaniah son of Maaseiah to Jeremiah the prophet with this message: "Please pray to the Lord our God for us."

Now Jeremiah was free to come and go among the people, for he had not yet been put in prison. Pharaoh's army had marched out of Egypt, and when the Babylonians who were besieging Jerusalem heard the report about them, they withdrew from Jerusalem.

Then the word of the Lord came to Jeremiah the prophet: "This is what the Lord, the God of Israel, says: Tell the king of Judah, who sent you to inquire of me, 'Pharaoh's army, which has marched out to support you, will go back to its own land, to Egypt. Then the Babylonians will return and attack this city; they will capture it and burn it down.'

"This is what the Lord says: Do not deceive yourselves, thinking, 'The Babylonians will surely leave us.' They will not! Even if you were to defeat the entire Babylonian army that is attacking you and only wounded men were left in their tents, they would come out and burn this city down."

After the Babylonian army had withdrawn from Jerusalem because of Pharaoh's army, Jeremiah started to leave the city to go to the territory of Benjamin to get his share of the property among the people there. But when he reached the Benjamin Gate, the captain of the guard, whose name was Irijah son of Shelemiah, the son of Hananiah, arrested him and said, "You are deserting to the Babylonians!"

"That's not true!" Jeremiah said. "I am not deserting to the Babylonians." But Irijah would not listen to him; instead, he arrested Jeremiah and brought him to the officials. They were angry with Jeremiah and had him beaten and imprisoned in the house of Jonathan the secretary, which they had made into a prison.

Jeremiah was put into a vaulted cell in a dungeon, where he remained a long time. Then King Zedekiah sent for him and had him brought to the palace, where he asked him privately, "Is there any word from the Lord?"

"Yes," Jeremiah replied, "you will be delivered into the hands of the king of Babylon."

Then Jeremiah said to King Zedekiah, "What crime have I committed against you or your attendants or this people, that you have put me in prison? Where are your prophets who prophesied to you, 'The king of Babylon will not attack you or this land'? But now, my lord the king, please listen. Let me bring my petition before you: Do not send me back to the house of Jonathan the secretary, or I will die there."

King Zedekiah then gave orders for Jeremiah to be placed in the courtyard of the guard and given a loaf of bread from the street of the bakers each day until all the bread in the city was gone. So Jeremiah remained in the courtyard of the guard.

Shephatiah son of Mattan, Gedaliah son of Pashhur, Jehukal son of Shelemiah, and Pashhur son of Malkijah heard what Jeremiah was telling all the people when he said, "This is what the Lord says: 'Whoever stays in this city will die by the sword, famine or plague, but whoever goes over to the Babylonians will live. They will escape with their lives; they will live.' And this is what the Lord says: 'This city will certainly be given into the hands of the army of the king of Babylon, who will capture it.'"

Then the officials said to the king, "This man should be put to death. He is discouraging the soldiers who are left in this city, as well as all the people, by the things he is saying to them. This man is not seeking the good of these people but their ruin."

"He is in your hands," King Zedekiah answered. "The king can do nothing to oppose you."

So they took Jeremiah and put him into the cistern of Malkijah, the king's son, which was in the courtyard of the guard. They lowered Jeremiah by ropes into the cistern; it had no water in it, only mud, and Jeremiah sank down into the mud.

But Ebed-Melek, a Cushite, an official in the royal palace, heard that they had put Jeremiah into the cistern. While the king was sitting in the Benjamin Gate, Ebed-Melek went out of the palace and said to him, "My lord the king, these men have acted wickedly in all they have done to Jeremiah the prophet. They have thrown him into a cistern, where he will starve to death when there is no longer any bread in the city."

Then the king commanded Ebed-Melek the Cushite, "Take thirty men from here with you and lift Jeremiah the prophet out of the cistern before he dies."

So Ebed-Melek took the men with him and went to a room under the treasury in the palace. He took some old rags and worn-out clothes from there and let them down with ropes to Jeremiah in the cistern. Ebed-Melek the Cushite said to Jeremiah, "Put these old rags and worn-out clothes under your arms to pad the ropes." Jeremiah did so, and they pulled him up with the ropes and lifted him out of the cistern. And Jeremiah remained in the courtyard of the guard.

Then King Zedekiah sent for Jeremiah the prophet and had him brought to the third entrance to the temple of the Lord. "I am going to ask you something," the king said to Jeremiah. "Do not hide anything from me."

Jeremiah said to Zedekiah, "If I give you an answer, will you not kill me? Even if I did give you counsel, you would not listen to me."

But King Zedekiah swore this oath secretly to Jeremiah: "As surely as the LORD lives, who has given us breath, I will neither kill you nor hand you over to those who want to kill you."

Then Jeremiah said to Zedekiah, "This is what the LORD God Almighty, the God of Israel, says: 'If you surrender to the officers of the king of Babylon, your life will be spared and this city will not be burned down; you and your family will live. But if you will not surrender to the officers of the king of Babylon, this city will be given into the hands of the Babylonians and they will burn it down; you yourself will not escape from them.'"

King Zedekiah said to Jeremiah, "I am afraid of the Jews who have gone over to the Babylonians, for the Babylonians may hand me over to them and they will mistreat me."

"They will not hand you over," Jeremiah replied. "Obey the LORD by doing what I tell you. Then it will go well with you, and your life will be spared. But if you refuse to surrender, this is what the LORD has revealed to me: All the women left in the palace of the king of Judah will be brought out to the officials of the king of Babylon. Those women will say to you:

> "'They misled you and overcame you—
> those trusted friends of yours.
>
> Your feet are sunk in the mud;
> your friends have deserted you.'

"All your wives and children will be brought out to the Babylonians. You yourself will not escape from their hands but will be captured by the king of Babylon; and this city will be burned down."

Then Zedekiah said to Jeremiah, "Do not let anyone know about this conversation, or you may die. If the officials hear that I talked with you, and they come to you and say, 'Tell us what you said to the king and what the king said to you; do not hide it from us or we will kill you,' then tell them, 'I was pleading with the king not to send me back to Jonathan's house to die there.'"

All the officials did come to Jeremiah and question him, and he told them everything the king had ordered him to say. So they said no more to him, for no one had heard his conversation with the king.

And Jeremiah remained in the courtyard of the guard until the day Jerusalem was captured.

This is how Jerusalem was taken: In the ninth year of Zedekiah king of Judah, in the tenth month, Nebuchadnezzar king of Babylon marched against Jerusalem with his whole army and laid siege to it. And on the ninth day of the fourth month of Zedekiah's eleventh year, the city wall was broken through. Then all the officials of the king of Babylon came and took seats in the Middle Gate: Nergal-Sharezer of Samgar, Nebo-Sarsekim a chief officer, Nergal-Sharezer a high official and all the other officials of the king of Babylon. When Zedekiah king of Judah and all the soldiers saw them, they fled; they left the city at night by way of the king's garden, through the gate between the two walls, and headed toward the Arabah.

But the Babylonian army pursued them and overtook Zedekiah in the plains of Jericho. They captured him and took him to Nebuchadnezzar king of Babylon at Riblah in the land of Hamath, where he pronounced sentence on him. There at Riblah the king of Babylon slaughtered the sons of Zedekiah before his eyes and also killed all the nobles of Judah. Then he put out Zedekiah's eyes and bound him with bronze shackles to take him to Babylon.

The Babylonians set fire to the royal palace and the houses of the people and broke down the walls of Jerusalem. Nebuzaradan commander of the imperial guard carried into exile to Babylon the people who remained in the city, along with those who had gone over to him, and the rest of the people. But Nebuzaradan the commander of the guard left behind in the land of Judah some of the poor people, who owned nothing; and at that time he gave them vineyards and fields.

Now Nebuchadnezzar king of Babylon had given these orders about Jeremiah through Nebuzaradan commander of the imperial guard: "Take him and look after him; don't harm him but do for him whatever he asks." So Nebuzaradan the commander of the guard, Nebushazban a chief officer, Nergal-Sharezer a high official and all the other officers of the king of Babylon sent and had Jeremiah taken out of the courtyard of the guard. They turned him over to Gedaliah son of Ahikam, the son of Shaphan, to take him back to his home. So he remained among his own people.

While Jeremiah had been confined in the courtyard of the guard, the word of the LORD came to him: "Go and tell Ebed-Melek the Cushite, 'This is what the LORD Almighty, the God of Israel, says: I am about to fulfill my words against this city — words concerning disaster, not prosperity. At that time they will be fulfilled before your eyes. But I will rescue you on that day, declares the LORD; you will not be given into the hands of those you fear. I will save you; you will not fall by the sword but will escape with your life, because you trust in me, declares the LORD.'"

The word came to Jeremiah from the LORD after Nebuzaradan commander of the imperial guard had released him at Ramah. He had found Jeremiah bound in chains among all the captives from Jerusalem and Judah who were being carried into exile to Babylon. When the commander of the guard found Jeremiah, he said to him, "The LORD your God decreed this disaster for this place. And now the LORD has brought it about; he has done just as he said he would. All this happened because you people sinned against the LORD and did not obey him. But today I am freeing you from the chains on your wrists. Come with me to Babylon, if you like, and I will look after you; but if you do not want to, then don't come. Look, the whole country lies before you; go wherever you please." However, before Jeremiah turned to go, Nebuzaradan added, "Go back to Gedaliah son of Ahikam, the son of Shaphan, whom the king of Babylon has appointed over the towns of Judah, and live with him among the people, or go anywhere else you please."

Then the commander gave him provisions and a present and let him go. So Jeremiah went to Gedaliah son of Ahikam at Mizpah and stayed with him among the people who were left behind in the land.

When all the army officers and their men who were still in the open country heard that the king of Babylon had appointed Gedaliah son of Ahikam as governor over the land and had put him in charge of the men, women and children who were the poorest in the land and who had not been carried into exile to Babylon, they came to Gedaliah at Mizpah — Ishmael son of Nethaniah, Johanan and Jonathan the sons of Kareah, Seraiah son of Tanhumeth, the sons of Ephai the Netophathite, and Jaazaniah the son of the Maakathite, and their men. Gedaliah son of Ahikam, the son of Shaphan, took an oath to reassure them and their men. "Do not be afraid to serve the Babylonians," he said. "Settle down in the land and serve the king of Babylon, and it will go well with you. I myself will stay at Mizpah to represent you before the Babylonians who come to us, but you are to harvest the wine, summer fruit and olive oil, and put them in your storage jars, and live in the towns you have taken over."

When all the Jews in Moab, Ammon, Edom and all the other

countries heard that the king of Babylon had left a remnant in Judah and had appointed Gedaliah son of Ahikam, the son of Shaphan, as governor over them, they all came back to the land of Judah, to Gedaliah at Mizpah, from all the countries where they had been scattered. And they harvested an abundance of wine and summer fruit.

Johanan son of Kareah and all the army officers still in the open country came to Gedaliah at Mizpah and said to him, "Don't you know that Baalis king of the Ammonites has sent Ishmael son of Nethaniah to take your life?" But Gedaliah son of Ahikam did not believe them.

Then Johanan son of Kareah said privately to Gedaliah in Mizpah, "Let me go and kill Ishmael son of Nethaniah, and no one will know it. Why should he take your life and cause all the Jews who are gathered around you to be scattered and the remnant of Judah to perish?"

But Gedaliah son of Ahikam said to Johanan son of Kareah, "Don't do such a thing! What you are saying about Ishmael is not true."

In the seventh month Ishmael son of Nethaniah, the son of Elishama, who was of royal blood and had been one of the king's officers, came with ten men to Gedaliah son of Ahikam at Mizpah. While they were eating together there, Ishmael son of Nethaniah and the ten men who were with him got up and struck down Gedaliah son of Ahikam, the son of Shaphan, with the sword, killing the one whom the king of Babylon had appointed as governor over the land. Ishmael also killed all the men of Judah who were with Gedaliah at Mizpah, as well as the Babylonian soldiers who were there.

The day after Gedaliah's assassination, before anyone knew about it, eighty men who had shaved off their beards, torn their clothes and cut themselves came from Shechem, Shiloh and Samaria, bringing grain offerings and incense with them to the house of the LORD. Ishmael son of Nethaniah went out from Mizpah to meet them, weeping as he went. When he met them, he said, "Come to Gedaliah son of Ahikam." When they went into the city, Ishmael son of Nethaniah and the men who were with him slaughtered them and threw them into a cistern. But ten of them said to Ishmael, "Don't kill us! We have wheat and barley, olive oil and honey, hidden in a field." So he let them alone and did not kill them with the others. Now the cistern where he threw all the bodies of the men he had killed along with Gedaliah was the one King Asa had made as part of his defense against Baasha king of Israel. Ishmael son of Nethaniah filled it with the dead.

Ishmael made captives of all the rest of the people who were in Mizpah—the king's daughters along with all the others who were left there, over whom Nebuzaradan commander of the imperial guard had appointed Gedaliah son of Ahikam. Ishmael son of Nethaniah took them captive and set out to cross over to the Ammonites.

When Johanan son of Kareah and all the army officers who were with him heard about all the crimes Ishmael son of Nethaniah had committed, they took all their men and went to fight Ishmael son of Nethaniah. They caught up with him near the great pool in Gibeon. When all the people Ishmael had with him saw Johanan son of Kareah and the army officers who were with him, they were glad. All the people Ishmael had taken captive at Mizpah turned and went over to Johanan son of Kareah. But Ishmael son of Nethaniah and eight of his men escaped from Johanan and fled to the Ammonites.

Then Johanan son of Kareah and all the army officers who were with him led away all the people of Mizpah who had survived, whom Johanan had recovered from Ishmael son of Nethaniah after Ishmael had assassinated Gedaliah son of Ahikam—the soldiers, women, children and court officials he had recovered from Gibeon. And they went on, stopping at Geruth Kimham near Bethlehem on their way to Egypt to escape the Babylonians. They were afraid of them because Ishmael son of Nethaniah had killed Gedaliah son of Ahikam, whom the king of Babylon had appointed as governor over the land.

Then all the army officers, including Johanan son of Kareah and Jezaniah son of Hoshaiah, and all the people from the least to the greatest approached Jeremiah the prophet and said to him, "Please hear our petition and pray to the Lord your God for this entire remnant. For as you now see, though we were once many, now only a few are left. Pray that the Lord your God will tell us where we should go and what we should do."

"I have heard you," replied Jeremiah the prophet. "I will certainly pray to the Lord your God as you have requested; I will tell you everything the Lord says and will keep nothing back from you."

Then they said to Jeremiah, "May the Lord be a true and faithful witness against us if we do not act in accordance with everything the Lord your God sends you to tell us. Whether it is favorable or unfavorable, we will obey the Lord our God, to whom we are sending you, so that it will go well with us, for we will obey the Lord our God."

Ten days later the word of the Lord came to Jeremiah. So he called together Johanan son of Kareah and all the army officers who were with him and all the people from the least to the greatest. He said to them, "This is what the LORD, the God of Israel, to whom you sent me to present your petition, says: 'If you stay in this land, I will build you up and not tear you down; I will plant you and not uproot you, for I have relented concerning the disaster I have inflicted on you. Do not be afraid of the king of Babylon, whom you now fear. Do not be afraid of him, declares the LORD, for I am with you and will save you and deliver you from his hands. I will show you compassion so that he will have compassion on you and restore you to your land.'

"However, if you say, 'We will not stay in this land,' and so disobey the LORD your God, and if you say, 'No, we will go and live in Egypt, where we will not see war or hear the trumpet or be hungry for bread,' then hear the word of the LORD, you remnant of Judah. This is what the LORD Almighty, the God of Israel, says: 'If you are determined to go to Egypt and you do go to settle there, then the sword you fear will overtake you there, and the famine you dread will follow you into Egypt, and there you will die. Indeed, all who are determined to go to Egypt to settle there will die by the sword, famine and plague; not one of them will survive or escape the disaster I will bring on them.' This is what the LORD Almighty, the God of Israel, says: 'As my anger and wrath have been poured out on those who lived in Jerusalem, so will my wrath be poured out on you when you go to Egypt. You will be a curse and an object of horror, a curse and an object of reproach; you will never see this place again.'

"Remnant of Judah, the LORD has told you, 'Do not go to Egypt.' Be sure of this: I warn you today that you made a fatal mistake when you sent me to the LORD your God and said, 'Pray to the LORD our God for us; tell us everything he says and we will do it.' I have told you today, but you still have not obeyed the LORD your God in all he sent me to tell you. So now, be sure of this: You will die by the sword, famine and plague in the place where you want to go to settle."

When Jeremiah had finished telling the people all the words of the LORD their God—everything the LORD had sent him to tell them—Azariah son of Hoshaiah and Johanan son of Kareah and all the arrogant men said to Jeremiah, "You are lying! The LORD our God has not sent you to say, 'You must not go to Egypt to settle there.' But Baruch son of Neriah is inciting you against us to hand us over to the Babylonians, so they may kill us or carry us into exile to Babylon."

So Johanan son of Kareah and all the army officers and all the people disobeyed the LORD's command to stay in the land of Judah. Instead, Johanan son of Kareah and all the army officers led away all the remnant of Judah who had come back to live in the land of Judah from all the nations where they had been scattered. They also led away all those whom Nebuzaradan commander of the imperial guard had left with Gedaliah son of Ahikam, the son of Shaphan—the men, the women, the children and the king's daughters. And they took Jeremiah the prophet and Baruch son of Neriah along with them. So they entered Egypt in disobedience to the LORD and went as far as Tahpanhes.

In Tahpanhes the word of the LORD came to Jeremiah: "While the Jews are watching, take some large stones with you and bury them in clay in the brick pavement at the entrance to Pharaoh's palace in Tahpanhes. Then say to them, 'This is what the LORD Almighty, the God of Israel, says: I will send for my servant Nebuchadnezzar king of Babylon, and I will set his throne over these stones I have buried here; he will spread his royal canopy above them. He will come and attack Egypt, bringing death to those destined for death, captivity to those destined for captivity, and the sword to those destined for the sword. He will set fire to the temples of the gods of Egypt; he will burn their temples and take their gods captive. As a shepherd picks his garment clean of lice, so he will pick Egypt clean and depart. There in the temple of the sun in Egypt he will demolish the sacred pillars and will burn down the temples of the gods of Egypt.'"

This word came to Jeremiah concerning all the Jews living in Lower Egypt—in Migdol, Tahpanhes and Memphis—and in Upper Egypt: "This is what the LORD Almighty, the God of Israel, says: You saw the great disaster I brought on Jerusalem and on all the towns of Judah. Today they lie deserted and in ruins because of the evil they have done. They aroused my anger by burning incense to and worshiping other gods that neither they nor you nor your ancestors ever knew. Again and again I sent my servants the prophets, who said, 'Do not do this detestable thing that I hate!' But they did not listen or pay attention; they did not turn from their wickedness or stop burning incense to other gods. Therefore, my fierce anger was poured out; it raged against the towns of Judah and the streets of Jerusalem and made them the desolate ruins they are today.

"Now this is what the LORD God Almighty, the God of Israel, says: Why bring such great disaster on yourselves by cutting off from Judah the men and women, the children and infants, and so leave yourselves without a remnant? Why arouse my anger with what your hands have made, burning incense to other gods in

Egypt, where you have come to live? You will destroy yourselves and make yourselves a curse and an object of reproach among all the nations on earth. Have you forgotten the wickedness committed by your ancestors and by the kings and queens of Judah and the wickedness committed by you and your wives in the land of Judah and the streets of Jerusalem? To this day they have not humbled themselves or shown reverence, nor have they followed my law and the decrees I set before you and your ancestors.

"Therefore this is what the Lord Almighty, the God of Israel, says: I am determined to bring disaster on you and to destroy all Judah. I will take away the remnant of Judah who were determined to go to Egypt to settle there. They will all perish in Egypt; they will fall by the sword or die from famine. From the least to the greatest, they will die by sword or famine. They will become a curse and an object of horror, a curse and an object of reproach. I will punish those who live in Egypt with the sword, famine and plague, as I punished Jerusalem. None of the remnant of Judah who have gone to live in Egypt will escape or survive to return to the land of Judah, to which they long to return and live; none will return except a few fugitives."

Then all the men who knew that their wives were burning incense to other gods, along with all the women who were present—a large assembly—and all the people living in Lower and Upper Egypt, said to Jeremiah, "We will not listen to the message you have spoken to us in the name of the Lord! We will certainly do everything we said we would: We will burn incense to the Queen of Heaven and will pour out drink offerings to her just as we and our ancestors, our kings and our officials did in the towns of Judah and in the streets of Jerusalem. At that time we had plenty of food and were well off and suffered no harm. But ever since we stopped burning incense to the Queen of Heaven and pouring out drink offerings to her, we have had nothing and have been perishing by sword and famine."

The women added, "When we burned incense to the Queen of Heaven and poured out drink offerings to her, did not our husbands know that we were making cakes impressed with her image and pouring out drink offerings to her?"

Then Jeremiah said to all the people, both men and women, who were answering him, "Did not the Lord remember and call to mind the incense burned in the towns of Judah and the streets of Jerusalem by you and your ancestors, your kings and your officials and the people of the land? When the Lord could no longer endure your wicked actions and the detestable things you did, your land became a curse and a desolate waste without inhabitants, as it is today. Because you have burned incense and have sinned against the LORD and have not obeyed him or followed his law or his decrees or his stipulations, this disaster has come upon you, as you now see."

Then Jeremiah said to all the people, including the women, "Hear the word of the LORD, all you people of Judah in Egypt. This is what the LORD Almighty, the God of Israel, says: You and your wives have done what you said you would do when you promised, 'We will certainly carry out the vows we made to burn incense and pour out drink offerings to the Queen of Heaven.'

"Go ahead then, do what you promised! Keep your vows! But hear the word of the LORD, all you Jews living in Egypt: 'I swear by my great name,' says the LORD, 'that no one from Judah living anywhere in Egypt will ever again invoke my name or swear, "As surely as the Sovereign LORD lives." For I am watching over them for harm, not for good; the Jews in Egypt will perish by sword and famine until they are all destroyed. Those who escape the sword and return to the land of Judah from Egypt will be very few. Then the whole remnant of Judah who came to live in Egypt will know whose word will stand—mine or theirs.

" 'This will be the sign to you that I will punish you in this place,' declares the LORD, 'so that you will know that my threats of harm against you will surely stand.' This is what the LORD says: 'I am going to deliver Pharaoh Hophra king of Egypt into the hands of his enemies who want to kill him, just as I gave Zedekiah king of Judah into the hands of Nebuchadnezzar king of Babylon, the enemy who wanted to kill him.' "

When Baruch son of Neriah wrote on a scroll the words Jeremiah the prophet dictated in the fourth year of Jehoiakim son of Josiah king of Judah, Jeremiah said this to Baruch: "This is what the LORD, the God of Israel, says to you, Baruch: You said, 'Woe to me! The LORD has added sorrow to my pain; I am worn out with groaning and find no rest.' But the LORD has told me to say to you, 'This is what the LORD says: I will overthrow what I have built and uproot what I have planted, throughout the earth. Should you then seek great things for yourself? Do not seek them. For I will bring disaster on all people, declares the LORD, but wherever you go I will let you escape with your life.' "

T his is the word of the LORD that came to Jeremiah the prophet concerning the nations:

Concerning Egypt:

This is the message against the army of Pharaoh Necho king of Egypt, which was defeated at Carchemish on the Euphrates River by Nebuchadnezzar king of Babylon in the fourth year of Jehoiakim son of Josiah king of Judah:

> "Prepare your shields, both large and small,
> and march out for battle!
>
> Harness the horses,
> mount the steeds!
>
> Take your positions
> with helmets on!
>
> Polish your spears,
> put on your armor!
>
> What do I see?
> They are terrified,
>
> they are retreating,
> their warriors are defeated.
>
> They flee in haste
> without looking back,
> and there is terror on every side,"

declares the LORD.

> "The swift cannot flee
> nor the strong escape.
>
> In the north by the River Euphrates
> they stumble and fall.
>
> "Who is this that rises like the Nile,
> like rivers of surging waters?
>
> Egypt rises like the Nile,
> like rivers of surging waters.
>
> She says, 'I will rise and cover the earth;
> I will destroy cities and their people.'
>
> Charge, you horses!
> Drive furiously, you charioteers!
>
> March on, you warriors — men of Cush and Put who
>   carry shields,
> men of Lydia who draw the bow.
>
> But that day belongs to the Lord, the LORD Almighty —
> a day of vengeance, for vengeance on his foes.

The sword will devour till it is satisfied,
till it has quenched its thirst with blood.

For the Lord, the LORD Almighty, will offer sacrifice
in the land of the north by the River Euphrates.

"Go up to Gilead and get balm,
Virgin Daughter Egypt.

But you try many medicines in vain;
there is no healing for you.

The nations will hear of your shame;
your cries will fill the earth.

One warrior will stumble over another;
both will fall down together."

This is the message the LORD spoke to Jeremiah the prophet about the coming of Nebuchadnezzar king of Babylon to attack Egypt:

"Announce this in Egypt, and proclaim it in Migdol;
proclaim it also in Memphis and Tahpanhes:

'Take your positions and get ready,
for the sword devours those around you.'

Why will your warriors be laid low?
They cannot stand, for the LORD will push them down.

They will stumble repeatedly;
they will fall over each other.

They will say, 'Get up, let us go back
to our own people and our native lands,
away from the sword of the oppressor.'

There they will exclaim,
'Pharaoh king of Egypt is only a loud noise;
he has missed his opportunity.'

"As surely as I live," declares the King,
whose name is the LORD Almighty,

"one will come who is like Tabor among the mountains,
like Carmel by the sea.

Pack your belongings for exile,
you who live in Egypt,

for Memphis will be laid waste
and lie in ruins without inhabitant.

"Egypt is a beautiful heifer,
but a gadfly is coming
against her from the north.

The mercenaries in her ranks
are like fattened calves.

They too will turn and flee together,
they will not stand their ground,

for the day of disaster is coming upon them,
the time for them to be punished.

Egypt will hiss like a fleeing serpent
as the enemy advances in force;

they will come against her with axes,
like men who cut down trees.

They will chop down her forest,"
declares the LORD,
"dense though it be.

They are more numerous than locusts,
they cannot be counted.

Daughter Egypt will be put to shame,
given into the hands of the people of the north."

The LORD Almighty, the God of Israel, says: "I am about to
bring punishment on Amon god of Thebes, on Pharaoh, on Egypt
and her gods and her kings, and on those who rely on Pharaoh. I will
give them into the hands of those who want to kill them — Nebuchadnezzar king of Babylon and his officers. Later, however, Egypt
will be inhabited as in times past," declares the LORD.

"Do not be afraid, Jacob my servant;
do not be dismayed, Israel.

I will surely save you out of a distant place,
your descendants from the land of their exile.

Jacob will again have peace and security,
and no one will make him afraid.

Do not be afraid, Jacob my servant,
for I am with you," declares the LORD.

"Though I completely destroy all the nations
among which I scatter you,
I will not completely destroy you.

I will discipline you but only in due measure;
I will not let you go entirely unpunished."

This is the word of the Lord that came to Jeremiah the prophet concerning the Philistines before Pharaoh attacked Gaza:

This is what the Lord says:

"See how the waters are rising in the north;
they will become an overflowing torrent.

They will overflow the land and
everything in it,
the towns and those who live in them.

The people will cry out;
all who dwell in the land will wail

at the sound of the hooves of galloping
steeds,
at the noise of enemy chariots
and the rumble of their wheels.

Parents will not turn to help their children;
their hands will hang limp.

For the day has come
to destroy all the Philistines

and to remove all survivors
who could help Tyre and Sidon.

The Lord is about to destroy
the Philistines,
the remnant from the coasts
of Caphtor.

Gaza will shave her head in mourning;
Ashkelon will be silenced.

You remnant on the plain,
how long will you cut yourselves?

"'Alas, sword of the Lord,
how long till you rest?

Return to your sheath;
cease and be still.'

But how can it rest
when the Lord has commanded it,
when he has ordered it
to attack Ashkelon and the coast?"

Concerning Moab:

This is what the LORD Almighty, the God of Israel, says:

"Woe to Nebo, for it will be ruined.
Kiriathaim will be disgraced and captured;
the stronghold will be disgraced and shattered.

Moab will be praised no more;
in Heshbon people will plot her downfall:
'Come, let us put an end to that nation.'

You, the people of Madmen, will also be silenced;
the sword will pursue you.

Cries of anguish arise from Horonaim,
cries of great havoc and destruction.

Moab will be broken;
her little ones will cry out.

They go up the hill to Luhith,
weeping bitterly as they go;

on the road down to Horonaim
anguished cries over the destruction are heard.

Flee! Run for your lives;
become like a bush in the desert.

Since you trust in your deeds and riches,
you too will be taken captive,

and Chemosh will go into exile,
together with his priests and officials.

The destroyer will come against every town,
and not a town will escape.

The valley will be ruined
and the plateau destroyed,
because the LORD has spoken.

Put salt on Moab,
for she will be laid waste;

her towns will become desolate,
with no one to live in them.

"A curse on anyone who is lax in doing the LORD's work!
A curse on anyone who keeps their sword from
    bloodshed!

"Moab has been at rest from youth,
like wine left on its dregs,

not poured from one jar to another —
she has not gone into exile.

So she tastes as she did,
and her aroma is unchanged.

But days are coming,"
declares the LORD,
"when I will send men who pour from
          pitchers,
and they will pour her out;

they will empty her pitchers
and smash her jars.

Then Moab will be ashamed of Chemosh,
as Israel was ashamed
when they trusted in Bethel.

"How can you say, 'We are warriors,
men valiant in battle'?

Moab will be destroyed and her towns invaded;
her finest young men will go down in the slaughter,"
declares the King, whose name is the LORD Almighty.

"The fall of Moab is at hand;
her calamity will come quickly.

Mourn for her, all who live around her,
all who know her fame;

say, 'How broken is the mighty scepter,
how broken the glorious staff!'

"Come down from your glory
and sit on the parched ground,
you inhabitants of Daughter Dibon,

for the one who destroys Moab
will come up against you
and ruin your fortified cities.

Stand by the road and watch,
you who live in Aroer.

Ask the man fleeing and the woman escaping,
ask them, 'What has happened?'

Moab is disgraced, for she is shattered.
Wail and cry out!

Announce by the Arnon
that Moab is destroyed.

Judgment has come to the plateau—
to Holon, Jahzah and Mephaath,
to Dibon, Nebo and Beth Diblathaim,
to Kiriathaim, Beth Gamul and Beth Meon,
to Kerioth and Bozrah—
to all the towns of Moab, far and near.

Moab's horn is cut off;
her arm is broken,"

> declares the Lord.

"Make her drunk,
for she has defied the Lord.

Let Moab wallow in her vomit;
let her be an object of ridicule.

Was not Israel the object of your ridicule?
Was she caught among thieves,

that you shake your head in scorn
whenever you speak of her?

Abandon your towns and dwell among the rocks,
you who live in Moab.

Be like a dove that makes its nest
at the mouth of a cave.

"We have heard of Moab's pride—
how great is her arrogance!—
of her insolence, her pride, her conceit
and the haughtiness of her heart.

I know her insolence but it is futile,"

> declares the Lord,

"and her boasts accomplish nothing.

Therefore I wail over Moab,
for all Moab I cry out,
I moan for the people of Kir Hareseth.

I weep for you, as Jazer weeps,
you vines of Sibmah.

Your branches spread as far as the sea;
they reached as far as Jazer.

The destroyer has fallen
on your ripened fruit and grapes.

Joy and gladness are gone
from the orchards and fields of Moab.

I have stopped the flow of wine from the presses;
no one treads them with shouts of joy.

Although there are shouts,
they are not shouts of joy.

"The sound of their cry rises
from Heshbon to Elealeh and Jahaz,

from Zoar as far as Horonaim and Eglath Shelishiyah,
for even the waters of Nimrim are dried up.

In Moab I will put an end
to those who make offerings on the high places
and burn incense to their gods,"

declares the Lord.

"So my heart laments for Moab like the music of a pipe;
it laments like a pipe for the people of Kir Hareseth.
The wealth they acquired is gone.

Every head is shaved
and every beard cut off;

every hand is slashed
and every waist is covered with sackcloth.

On all the roofs in Moab
and in the public squares

there is nothing but mourning,
for I have broken Moab
like a jar that no one wants,"

declares the Lord.

"How shattered she is! How they wail!
How Moab turns her back in shame!

Moab has become an object of ridicule,
an object of horror to all those around her."

This is what the Lord says:

"Look! An eagle is swooping down,
spreading its wings over Moab.

Kerioth will be captured
and the strongholds taken.

In that day the hearts of Moab's warriors
will be like the heart of a woman in labor.

Moab will be destroyed as a nation
because she defied the LORD.

Terror and pit and snare await you,
you people of Moab,"

declares the LORD.

"Whoever flees from the terror
will fall into a pit,

whoever climbs out of the pit
will be caught in a snare;

for I will bring on Moab
the year of her punishment,"

declares the LORD.

"In the shadow of Heshbon
the fugitives stand helpless,

for a fire has gone out from Heshbon,
a blaze from the midst of Sihon;

it burns the foreheads of Moab,
the skulls of the noisy boasters.

Woe to you, Moab!
The people of Chemosh are destroyed;

your sons are taken into exile
and your daughters into captivity.

"Yet I will restore the fortunes of Moab
in days to come,"

declares the LORD.

Here ends the judgment on Moab.

Concerning the Ammonites:

This is what the LORD says:

"Has Israel no sons?
Has Israel no heir?

Why then has Molek taken possession of Gad?
Why do his people live in its towns?

But the days are coming,"
declares the LORD,

"when I will sound the battle cry
against Rabbah of the Ammonites;

it will become a mound of ruins,
and its surrounding villages will be set on fire.

Then Israel will drive out
those who drove her out,"

says the Lord.

"Wail, Heshbon, for Ai is destroyed!
Cry out, you inhabitants of Rabbah!

Put on sackcloth and mourn;
rush here and there inside the walls,

for Molek will go into exile,
together with his priests and officials.

Why do you boast of your valleys,
boast of your valleys so fruitful?

Unfaithful Daughter Ammon,
you trust in your riches and say,
'Who will attack me?'

I will bring terror on you
from all those around you,"

declares the Lord, the Lord Almighty.

"Every one of you will be driven away,
and no one will gather the fugitives.

"Yet afterward, I will restore the fortunes
of the Ammonites,"

declares the Lord.

Concerning Edom:

This is what the Lord Almighty says:

"Is there no longer wisdom in Teman?
Has counsel perished from the prudent?
Has their wisdom decayed?

Turn and flee, hide in deep caves,
you who live in Dedan,

for I will bring disaster on Esau
at the time when I punish him.

If grape pickers came to you,
would they not leave a few grapes?

If thieves came during the night,
would they not steal only as much as they wanted?

But I will strip Esau bare;
I will uncover his hiding places,
so that he cannot conceal himself.

His armed men are destroyed,
also his allies and neighbors,
so there is no one to say,

'Leave your fatherless children; I will keep them alive.
Your widows too can depend on me.'"

This is what the LORD says: "If those who do not deserve to drink the cup must drink it, why should you go unpunished? You will not go unpunished, but must drink it. I swear by myself," declares the LORD, "that Bozrah will become a ruin and a curse, an object of horror and reproach; and all its towns will be in ruins forever."

I have heard a message from the LORD;
an envoy was sent to the nations to say,

"Assemble yourselves to attack it!
Rise up for battle!"

"Now I will make you small among the nations,
despised by mankind.

The terror you inspire
and the pride of your heart have deceived you,

you who live in the clefts of the rocks,
who occupy the heights of the hill.

Though you build your nest as high as the eagle's,
from there I will bring you down,"
declares the LORD.

"Edom will become an object of horror;
all who pass by will be appalled and will scoff
because of all its wounds.

As Sodom and Gomorrah were overthrown,
along with their neighboring towns,"
says the LORD,

"so no one will live there;
no people will dwell in it.

"Like a lion coming up from Jordan's thickets
to a rich pastureland,

I will chase Edom from its land in an instant.
Who is the chosen one I will appoint for this?

Who is like me and who can challenge me?
And what shepherd can stand against me?"

Therefore, hear what the LORD has planned against
    Edom,
what he has purposed against those who live in Teman:

The young of the flock will be dragged away;
their pasture will be appalled at their fate.

At the sound of their fall the earth will tremble;
their cry will resound to the Red Sea.

Look! An eagle will soar and swoop down,
spreading its wings over Bozrah.

In that day the hearts of Edom's warriors
will be like the heart of a woman in labor.

Concerning Damascus:

"Hamath and Arpad are dismayed,
for they have heard bad news.

They are disheartened,
troubled like the restless sea.

Damascus has become feeble,
she has turned to flee
and panic has gripped her;

anguish and pain have seized her,
pain like that of a woman in labor.

Why has the city of renown not been abandoned,
the town in which I delight?

Surely, her young men will fall in the streets;
all her soldiers will be silenced in that day,"
                            declares the LORD Almighty.

"I will set fire to the walls of Damascus;
it will consume the fortresses of Ben-Hadad."

Concerning Kedar and the kingdoms of Hazor, which Nebuchadnezzar king of Babylon attacked:

This is what the LORD says:

> "Arise, and attack Kedar
> and destroy the people of the East.

> Their tents and their flocks will be taken;
> their shelters will be carried off
> with all their goods and camels.

> People will shout to them,
> 'Terror on every side!'

> "Flee quickly away!
> Stay in deep caves, you who live in Hazor,"
>> declares the LORD.

> "Nebuchadnezzar king of Babylon has plotted against
>> you;
> he has devised a plan against you.

> "Arise and attack a nation at ease,
> which lives in confidence,"
>> declares the LORD,

> "a nation that has neither gates nor bars;
> its people live far from danger.

> Their camels will become plunder,
> and their large herds will be spoils of war.

> I will scatter to the winds those who are in distant places
> and will bring disaster on them from every side,"
>> declares the LORD.

> "Hazor will become a haunt of jackals,
> a desolate place forever.

> No one will live there;
> no people will dwell in it."

This is the word of the LORD that came to Jeremiah the prophet concerning Elam, early in the reign of Zedekiah king of Judah:

This is what the LORD Almighty says:

> "See, I will break the bow of Elam,
> the mainstay of their might.

> I will bring against Elam the four winds
> from the four quarters of heaven;

I will scatter them to the four winds,
and there will not be a nation
where Elam's exiles do not go.

I will shatter Elam before their foes,
before those who want to kill them;

I will bring disaster on them,
even my fierce anger,"

declares the LORD.

"I will pursue them with the sword
until I have made an end of them.

I will set my throne in Elam
and destroy her king and officials,"

declares the LORD.

"Yet I will restore the fortunes of Elam
in days to come,"

declares the LORD.

This is the word the LORD spoke through Jeremiah the prophet concerning Babylon and the land of the Babylonians:

"Announce and proclaim among the nations,
lift up a banner and proclaim it;
keep nothing back, but say,

'Babylon will be captured;
Bel will be put to shame,
Marduk filled with terror.

Her images will be put to shame
and her idols filled with terror.'

A nation from the north will attack her
and lay waste her land.

No one will live in it;
both people and animals will flee away.

"In those days, at that time,"
declares the LORD,

"the people of Israel and the people of Judah together
will go in tears to seek the LORD their God.

They will ask the way to Zion
and turn their faces toward it.

They will come and bind themselves to the LORD
in an everlasting covenant
that will not be forgotten.

"My people have been lost sheep;
their shepherds have led them astray
and caused them to roam on the mountains.

They wandered over mountain and hill
and forgot their own resting place.

Whoever found them devoured them;
their enemies said, 'We are not guilty,

for they sinned against the LORD, their verdant pasture,
the LORD, the hope of their ancestors.'

"Flee out of Babylon;
leave the land of the Babylonians,
and be like the goats that lead the flock.

For I will stir up and bring against Babylon
an alliance of great nations from the land of the north.

They will take up their positions against her,
and from the north she will be captured.

Their arrows will be like skilled warriors
who do not return empty-handed.

So Babylonia will be plundered;
all who plunder her will have their fill,"
declares the LORD.

"Because you rejoice and are glad,
you who pillage my inheritance,

because you frolic like a heifer threshing grain
and neigh like stallions,

your mother will be greatly ashamed;
she who gave you birth will be disgraced.

She will be the least of the nations—
a wilderness, a dry land, a desert.

Because of the LORD's anger she will not be inhabited
but will be completely desolate.

All who pass Babylon will be appalled;
they will scoff because of all her wounds.

"Take up your positions around Babylon,
all you who draw the bow.

Shoot at her! Spare no arrows,
for she has sinned against the Lord.

Shout against her on every side!
She surrenders, her towers fall,
her walls are torn down.

Since this is the vengeance of the Lord,
take vengeance on her;
do to her as she has done to others.

Cut off from Babylon the sower,
and the reaper with his sickle at harvest.

Because of the sword of the oppressor
let everyone return to their own people,
let everyone flee to their own land.

"Israel is a scattered flock
that lions have chased away.

The first to devour them
was the king of Assyria;

the last to crush their bones
was Nebuchadnezzar king of Babylon."

Therefore this is what the Lord Almighty, the God of Israel,
says:

"I will punish the king of Babylon and his land
as I punished the king of Assyria.

But I will bring Israel back to their own pasture,
and they will graze on Carmel and Bashan;

their appetite will be satisfied
on the hills of Ephraim and Gilead.

In those days, at that time,"
declares the Lord,

"search will be made for Israel's guilt,
but there will be none,

and for the sins of Judah,
but none will be found,
for I will forgive the remnant I spare.

"Attack the land of Merathaim
and those who live in Pekod.

Pursue, kill and completely destroy them,"
declares the Lord.

"Do everything I have commanded you.

The noise of battle is in the land,
the noise of great destruction!

How broken and shattered
is the hammer of the whole earth!

How desolate is Babylon
among the nations!

I set a trap for you, Babylon,
and you were caught before you knew it;

you were found and captured
because you opposed the LORD.

The LORD has opened his arsenal
and brought out the weapons of his wrath,

for the Sovereign LORD Almighty has work to do
in the land of the Babylonians.

Come against her from afar.
Break open her granaries;
pile her up like heaps of grain.

Completely destroy her
and leave her no remnant.

Kill all her young bulls;
let them go down to the slaughter!

Woe to them! For their day has come,
the time for them to be punished.

Listen to the fugitives and refugees from Babylon
declaring in Zion

how the LORD our God has taken vengeance,
vengeance for his temple.

"Summon archers against Babylon,
all those who draw the bow.

Encamp all around her;
let no one escape.

Repay her for her deeds;
do to her as she has done.

For she has defied the LORD,
the Holy One of Israel.

Therefore, her young men will fall in the streets;
all her soldiers will be silenced in that day,"
                                        declares the LORD.

"See, I am against you, you arrogant one,"
declares the Lord, the LORD Almighty,

"for your day has come,
the time for you to be punished.

The arrogant one will stumble and fall
and no one will help her up;

I will kindle a fire in her towns
that will consume all who are around her."

This is what the LORD Almighty says:

"The people of Israel are oppressed,
and the people of Judah as well.

All their captors hold them fast,
refusing to let them go.

Yet their Redeemer is strong;
the LORD Almighty is his name.

He will vigorously defend their cause
so that he may bring rest to their land,
but unrest to those who live in Babylon.

"A sword against the Babylonians!"
declares the LORD—

"against those who live in Babylon
and against her officials and wise men!

A sword against her false prophets!
They will become fools.

A sword against her warriors!
They will be filled with terror.

A sword against her horses and chariots
and all the foreigners in her ranks!
They will become weaklings.

A sword against her treasures!
They will be plundered.

A drought on her waters!
They will dry up.

For it is a land of idols,
idols that will go mad with terror.

"So desert creatures and hyenas will live there,
and there the owl will dwell.

It will never again be inhabited
or lived in from generation to generation.

As I overthrew Sodom and Gomorrah
along with their neighboring towns,"
                              declares the Lord,

"so no one will live there;
no people will dwell in it.

"Look! An army is coming from the north;
a great nation and many kings
are being stirred up from the ends of the earth.

They are armed with bows and spears;
they are cruel and without mercy.

They sound like the roaring sea
as they ride on their horses;

they come like men in battle formation
to attack you, Daughter Babylon.

The king of Babylon has heard reports about them,
and his hands hang limp.

Anguish has gripped him,
pain like that of a woman in labor.

Like a lion coming up from Jordan's thickets
to a rich pastureland,

I will chase Babylon from its land in an instant.
Who is the chosen one I will appoint for this?

Who is like me and who can challenge me?
And what shepherd can stand against me?"

Therefore, hear what the Lord has planned against
         Babylon,
what he has purposed against the land of the
         Babylonians:

The young of the flock will be dragged away;
their pasture will be appalled at their fate.

At the sound of Babylon's capture the earth will tremble;
its cry will resound among the nations.

This is what the Lord says:

"See, I will stir up the spirit of a destroyer
against Babylon and the people of Leb Kamai.

I will send foreigners to Babylon
to winnow her and to devastate her land;

they will oppose her on every side
in the day of her disaster.

Let not the archer string his bow,
nor let him put on his armor.
Do not spare her young men;
completely destroy her army.
They will fall down slain in Babylon,
fatally wounded in her streets.
For Israel and Judah have not been forsaken
by their God, the LORD Almighty,
though their land is full of guilt
before the Holy One of Israel.

"Flee from Babylon!
Run for your lives!
Do not be destroyed because of her sins.
It is time for the LORD's vengeance;
he will repay her what she deserves.
Babylon was a gold cup in the LORD's hand;
she made the whole earth drunk.
The nations drank her wine;
therefore they have now gone mad.
Babylon will suddenly fall and be broken.
Wail over her!
Get balm for her pain;
perhaps she can be healed.

" 'We would have healed Babylon,
but she cannot be healed;
let us leave her and each go to our own land,
for her judgment reaches to the skies,
it rises as high as the heavens.'

" 'The LORD has vindicated us;
come, let us tell in Zion
what the LORD our God has done.'

"Sharpen the arrows,
take up the shields!
The LORD has stirred up the kings of the Medes,
because his purpose is to destroy Babylon.
The LORD will take vengeance,
vengeance for his temple.
Lift up a banner against the walls of Babylon!
Reinforce the guard,

station the watchmen,
prepare an ambush!

The Lord will carry out his purpose,
his decree against the people of Babylon.

You who live by many waters
and are rich in treasures,

your end has come,
the time for you to be destroyed.

The Lord Almighty has sworn by himself:
I will surely fill you with troops, as with a swarm
    of locusts,
and they will shout in triumph over you.

"He made the earth by his power;
he founded the world by his wisdom
and stretched out the heavens by his
    understanding.

When he thunders, the waters in the heavens roar;
he makes clouds rise from the ends of the earth.

He sends lightning with the rain
and brings out the wind from his storehouses.

"Everyone is senseless and without knowledge;
every goldsmith is shamed by his idols.

The images he makes are a fraud;
they have no breath in them.

They are worthless, the objects of mockery;
when their judgment comes, they will perish.

He who is the Portion of Jacob is not like these,
for he is the Maker of all things,

including the people of his inheritance—
the Lord Almighty is his name.

"You are my war club,
my weapon for battle—

with you I shatter nations,
with you I destroy kingdoms,

with you I shatter horse and rider,
with you I shatter chariot and driver,

with you I shatter man and woman,
with you I shatter old man and youth,
with you I shatter young man and young woman,

with you I shatter shepherd and flock,
with you I shatter farmer and oxen,
with you I shatter governors and officials.

"Before your eyes I will repay Babylon and all who live in Babylonia for all the wrong they have done in Zion," declares the LORD.

"I am against you, you destroying mountain,
you who destroy the whole earth,"
declares the LORD.
"I will stretch out my hand against you,
roll you off the cliffs,
and make you a burned-out mountain.

No rock will be taken from you for a cornerstone,
nor any stone for a foundation,
for you will be desolate forever,"
declares the LORD.

"Lift up a banner in the land!
Blow the trumpet among the nations!

Prepare the nations for battle against her;
summon against her these kingdoms:
Ararat, Minni and Ashkenaz.

Appoint a commander against her;
send up horses like a swarm of locusts.

Prepare the nations for battle against her —
the kings of the Medes,

their governors and all their officials,
and all the countries they rule.

The land trembles and writhes,
for the LORD's purposes against Babylon stand —

to lay waste the land of Babylon
so that no one will live there.

Babylon's warriors have stopped fighting;
they remain in their strongholds.

Their strength is exhausted;
they have become weaklings.

Her dwellings are set on fire;
the bars of her gates are broken.

One courier follows another
and messenger follows messenger

to announce to the king of Babylon
that his entire city is captured,

the river crossings seized,
the marshes set on fire,
and the soldiers terrified."

This is what the Lord Almighty, the God of Israel, says:

"Daughter Babylon is like a threshing floor
at the time it is trampled;
the time to harvest her will soon come."

"Nebuchadnezzar king of Babylon has devoured us,
he has thrown us into confusion,
he has made us an empty jar.
Like a serpent he has swallowed us
and filled his stomach with our delicacies,
and then has spewed us out.
May the violence done to our flesh be on Babylon,"
say the inhabitants of Zion.
"May our blood be on those who live in Babylonia,"
says Jerusalem.

Therefore this is what the Lord says:

"See, I will defend your cause
and avenge you;
I will dry up her sea
and make her springs dry.
Babylon will be a heap of ruins,
a haunt of jackals,
an object of horror and scorn,
a place where no one lives.
Her people all roar like young lions,
they growl like lion cubs.
But while they are aroused,
I will set out a feast for them
and make them drunk,
so that they shout with laughter—
then sleep forever and not awake,"
declares the Lord.
"I will bring them down
like lambs to the slaughter,
like rams and goats.

"How Sheshak will be captured,
the boast of the whole earth seized!

How desolate Babylon will be
among the nations!

The sea will rise over Babylon;
its roaring waves will cover her.

Her towns will be desolate,
a dry and desert land,

a land where no one lives,
through which no one travels.

I will punish Bel in Babylon
and make him spew out what he has swallowed.

The nations will no longer stream to him.
And the wall of Babylon will fall.

"Come out of her, my people!
Run for your lives!
Run from the fierce anger of the LORD.

Do not lose heart or be afraid
when rumors are heard in the land;

one rumor comes this year, another the next,
rumors of violence in the land
and of ruler against ruler.

For the time will surely come
when I will punish the idols of Babylon;

her whole land will be disgraced
and her slain will all lie fallen within her.

Then heaven and earth and all that is in them
will shout for joy over Babylon,

for out of the north
destroyers will attack her,"

declares the LORD.

"Babylon must fall because of Israel's slain,
just as the slain in all the earth
have fallen because of Babylon.

You who have escaped the sword,
leave and do not linger!

Remember the LORD in a distant land,
and call to mind Jerusalem."

"We are disgraced,
for we have been insulted
and shame covers our faces,

because foreigners have entered
the holy places of the Lord's house."

"But days are coming," declares the Lord,
"when I will punish her idols,

and throughout her land
the wounded will groan.

Even if Babylon ascends to the heavens
and fortifies her lofty stronghold,
I will send destroyers against her,"
declares the Lord.

"The sound of a cry comes from Babylon,
the sound of great destruction
from the land of the Babylonians.

The Lord will destroy Babylon;
he will silence her noisy din.

Waves of enemies will rage like great waters;
the roar of their voices will resound.

A destroyer will come against Babylon;
her warriors will be captured,
and their bows will be broken.

For the Lord is a God of retribution;
he will repay in full.

I will make her officials and wise men drunk,
her governors, officers and warriors as well;

they will sleep forever and not awake,"
declares the King, whose name is the Lord Almighty.

This is what the Lord Almighty says:

"Babylon's thick wall will be leveled
and her high gates set on fire;

the peoples exhaust themselves for nothing,
the nations' labor is only fuel for the flames."

This is the message Jeremiah the prophet gave to the staff officer Seraiah son of Neriah, the son of Mahseiah, when he went to Babylon with Zedekiah king of Judah in the fourth year of his reign. Jeremiah had written on a scroll about all the disasters that would come upon Babylon — all that had been recorded concerning Babylon. He said to Seraiah, "When you get to Babylon, see that you read all these words aloud. Then say, 'LORD, you have said you will destroy this place, so that neither people nor animals will live in it; it will be desolate forever.' When you finish reading this scroll, tie a stone to it and throw it into the Euphrates. Then say, 'So will Babylon sink to rise no more because of the disaster I will bring on her. And her people will fall.' "

The words of Jeremiah end here.

Zedekiah was twenty-one years old when he became king, and he reigned in Jerusalem eleven years. His mother's name was Hamutal daughter of Jeremiah; she was from Libnah. He did evil in the eyes of the LORD, just as Jehoiakim had done. It was because of the LORD's anger that all this happened to Jerusalem and Judah, and in the end he thrust them from his presence.

Now Zedekiah rebelled against the king of Babylon.

So in the ninth year of Zedekiah's reign, on the tenth day of the tenth month, Nebuchadnezzar king of Babylon marched against Jerusalem with his whole army. They encamped outside the city and built siege works all around it. The city was kept under siege until the eleventh year of King Zedekiah.

By the ninth day of the fourth month the famine in the city had become so severe that there was no food for the people to eat. Then the city wall was broken through, and the whole army fled. They left the city at night through the gate between the two walls near the king's garden, though the Babylonians were surrounding the city. They fled toward the Arabah, but the Babylonian army pursued King Zedekiah and overtook him in the plains of Jericho. All his soldiers were separated from him and scattered, and he was captured.

He was taken to the king of Babylon at Riblah in the land of Hamath, where he pronounced sentence on him. There at Riblah the king of Babylon killed the sons of Zedekiah before his eyes; he also killed all the officials of Judah. Then he put out Zedekiah's eyes, bound him with bronze shackles and took him to Babylon, where he put him in prison till the day of his death.

On the tenth day of the fifth month, in the nineteenth year of Nebuchadnezzar king of Babylon, Nebuzaradan commander of the imperial guard, who served the king of Babylon, came to Jerusalem. He set fire to the temple of the LORD, the royal palace and all the houses of Jerusalem. Every important building he burned down. The whole Babylonian army, under the commander of the imperial guard, broke down all the walls around Jerusalem. Nebuzaradan the commander of the guard carried into exile some of the poorest people and those who remained in the city, along with the rest of the craftsmen and those who had deserted to the king of Babylon. But Nebuzaradan left behind the rest of the poorest people of the land to work the vineyards and fields.

The Babylonians broke up the bronze pillars, the movable stands and the bronze Sea that were at the temple of the LORD and they carried all the bronze to Babylon. They also took away the pots, shovels, wick trimmers, sprinkling bowls, dishes and all the bronze articles used in the temple service. The commander of the imperial guard took away the basins, censers, sprinkling bowls, pots, lampstands, dishes and bowls used for drink offerings—all that were made of pure gold or silver.

The bronze from the two pillars, the Sea and the twelve bronze bulls under it, and the movable stands, which King Solomon had made for the temple of the LORD, was more than could be weighed. Each pillar was eighteen cubits high and twelve cubits in circumference; each was four fingers thick, and hollow. The bronze capital on top of one pillar was five cubits high and was decorated with a network and pomegranates of bronze all around. The other pillar, with its pomegranates, was similar. There were ninety-six pomegranates on the sides; the total number of pomegranates above the surrounding network was a hundred.

The commander of the guard took as prisoners Seraiah the chief priest, Zephaniah the priest next in rank and the three doorkeepers. Of those still in the city, he took the officer in charge of the fighting men, and seven royal advisers. He also took the secretary who was chief officer in charge of conscripting the people of the land, sixty of whom were found in the city. Nebuzaradan the commander took them all and brought them to the king of Babylon at Riblah. There at Riblah, in the land of Hamath, the king had them executed.

So Judah went into captivity, away from her land. This is the number of the people Nebuchadnezzar carried into exile:

in the seventh year, 3,023 Jews;
in Nebuchadnezzar's eighteenth year,
    832 people from Jerusalem;
in his twenty-third year,
    745 Jews taken into exile by Nebuzaradan the commander of
        the imperial guard.
There were 4,600 people in all.

In the thirty-seventh year of the exile of Jehoiachin king of Judah, in the year Awel-Marduk became king of Babylon, on the twenty-fifth day of the twelfth month, he released Jehoiachin king of Judah and freed him from prison. He spoke kindly to him and gave him a seat of honor higher than those of the other kings who were with him in Babylon. So Jehoiachin put aside his prison clothes and for the rest of his life ate regularly at the king's table. Day by day the king of Babylon gave Jehoiachin a regular allowance as long as he lived, till the day of his death.

INVITATION TO
OBADIAH

When Jerusalem, Judah's capital, fell to the Babylonian army in 587 or 586 BC, the people of the neighboring kingdom of Edom joined in looting the city. They even intercepted fleeing Judeans and turned them over to the Babylonians to be executed or enslaved. The Edomites showed no compassion to the Judeans even though they were related to them. Edom was descended from Esau and Judah was descended from Jacob, his brother.

The Edomites' ruthless treatment of their helpless neighbors drew rebukes from the prophets Jeremiah (see p. 338) and Ezekiel (p. 404). The prophet Obadiah, who seems to have been among those who remained behind when many Judeans were taken into exile, added an oracle of his own. He assured the people of his community that God would repay Edom for its treachery but restore their own fortunes. Obadiah may have begun with a well-known oracle by Jeremiah against Edom and developed it to speak to his own situation, since there are many similarities between his oracle and Jeremiah's.

Obadiah first rebukes the kingdom of Edom for its pride. He foretells its destruction and describes the crimes, specifically against Judah, for which Edom will suffer this fate. Finally, he promises restoration to Israel and assures them that in the end, *the kingdom will be the LORD's*.

OBADIAH

The vision of Obadiah.

This is what the Sovereign Lord says about Edom —

> We have heard a message from the Lord:
> An envoy was sent to the nations to say,
>
> "Rise, let us go against her for battle" —
>
> "See, I will make you small among the nations;
> you will be utterly despised.
>
> The pride of your heart has deceived you,
> you who live in the clefts of the rocks
> and make your home on the heights,
>
> you who say to yourself,
> 'Who can bring me down to the ground?'
>
> Though you soar like the eagle
> and make your nest among the stars,
> from there I will bring you down,"
> > declares the Lord.
>
> "If thieves came to you,
> if robbers in the night —
>
> oh, what a disaster awaits you! —
> would they not steal only as much as
> they wanted?
>
> If grape pickers came to you,
> would they not leave a few grapes?
>
> But how Esau will be ransacked,
> his hidden treasures pillaged!
>
> All your allies will force you to the border;
> your friends will deceive and overpower you;
>
> those who eat your bread will set a trap for you,
> but you will not detect it.

"In that day," declares the LORD,
"will I not destroy the wise men of Edom,
those of understanding in the mountains of Esau?

Your warriors, Teman, will be terrified,
and everyone in Esau's mountains
will be cut down in the slaughter.

Because of the violence against your brother Jacob,
you will be covered with shame;
you will be destroyed forever.

On the day you stood aloof
while strangers carried off his wealth
and foreigners entered his gates
and cast lots for Jerusalem,
you were like one of them.

You should not gloat over your brother
in the day of his misfortune,

nor rejoice over the people of Judah
in the day of their destruction,

nor boast so much
in the day of their trouble.

You should not march through the gates
          of my people
in the day of their disaster,

nor gloat over them in their calamity
in the day of their disaster,

nor seize their wealth
in the day of their disaster.

You should not wait at the crossroads
to cut down their fugitives,

nor hand over their survivors
in the day of their trouble.

"The day of the LORD is near
for all nations.
As you have done, it will be done to you;
your deeds will return upon your own head.

Just as you drank on my holy hill,
so all the nations will drink continually;

they will drink and drink
and be as if they had never been.

But on Mount Zion will be deliverance;
it will be holy,
and Jacob will possess his inheritance.

Jacob will be a fire
and Joseph a flame;

Esau will be stubble,
and they will set him on fire and destroy him.

There will be no survivors
from Esau."

The Lord has spoken.

People from the Negev will occupy
the mountains of Esau,

and people from the foothills will possess
the land of the Philistines.

They will occupy the fields of Ephraim and Samaria,
and Benjamin will possess Gilead.

This company of Israelite exiles who are in Canaan
will possess the land as far as Zarephath;

the exiles from Jerusalem who are in Sepharad
will possess the towns of the Negev.

Deliverers will go up on Mount Zion
to govern the mountains of Esau.
And the kingdom will be the Lord's.

INVITATION TO
EZEKIEL

The priest Ezekiel was among the Judeans that Nebuchadnezzar brought to Babylon in 597 BC. Five years into this exile, God told Ezekiel to *go now to the house of Israel*, meaning both those in Babylon and those back in Judea, *and speak my words to them*. Like the prophets who came before him, Ezekiel often brought God's messages by composing finely polished poetic oracles and speaking (or perhaps singing) them in public. But he also used many other forms of communication. At God's instructions, he told stories that had symbolic meanings, he performed and interpreted symbolic actions, and he described extraordinary visions that he'd received.

The book of Ezekiel records these messages. It has three main parts. The first contains oracles of judgment against Israel; the second contains oracles of judgment against other nations; and the third contains promises of Israel's restoration. These three parts of the book, which are already distinct in content, are also marked off by references to a unique situation in the prophet's life. Near the beginning of the first part, God tells Ezekiel he'll be unable to speak except when God has to say something through him. From then on, Ezekiel can only speak when, as he puts it, *the word of the LORD came to me* or *the hand of the LORD was on me*. At the end of the first part of the book, God tells Ezekiel that someone will soon bring news of the destruction of Jerusalem, and at that point he'll be able to speak freely again. Early in the third part of the book, this happens. These references to the prophet becoming unable or able to speak help mark the divisions between the thematic groups that Ezekiel's messages have been organized into.

: The first part of the book (pp. 365–403) contains the warnings that Ezekiel delivered in the years leading up to the destruction of Jerusalem. Its opening episode describes Ezekiel's call to prophesy. It relates a vision he had in Babylon of God's glorious presence attended by *cherubim*. Sculptures of these angelic beings were in the holiest part of the Jerusalem temple, symbolically supporting God's presence there. But, this vision showed, God's presence had now moved to Babylon. In a vision shortly after this one, Ezekiel sees the glory of God actually departing from the Jerusalem temple. The relocation of God's presence to Babylon signifies that God will watch over the exiled community, but judge those who remain behind. The rest of this part of the book documents Judah and Jerusalem's offenses against God and describes the symbolic messages Ezekiel delivered to call for their repentance.

: The oracles in the second part of the book (pp. 403–419) are spoken against many nations, but they address Tyre and Egypt at length. These two countries were determined holdouts against the Babylonians, God's chosen agent of judgment. In these oracles Ezekiel, like the other prophets before him, proclaims God's sovereignty over all the kingdoms of the earth. No one should take the destruction of the temple in Jerusalem to mean that God doesn't still control the nations of the world and their destinies.

: In part three of the book (pp. 419–445), Ezekiel offers hopeful prophecies of Israel's restoration. One of the most important prophecies in this section takes up a theme that's already been struck twice in the book: the people's need for *a new heart and a new spirit*. God promises, *I will remove from you your heart of stone and give you a heart of flesh. And I will put my Spirit in you and move you to follow my decrees and be careful to keep my laws*. This coming spiritual transformation is then illustrated in a dramatic vision of a valley of dry bones. The bones come together to form skeletons, which are clothed with sinews and flesh and brought to life by the breath of God. This is, first of all, a promise to the people in exile: *I will bring you back to the land of Israel*. But this vision ultimately looks forward to the new life that God will bring to people of all nations.

Continuing in this part of the book Ezekiel next delivers a long oracle against Magog. He prophesies that when this country leads a coalition against the restored Israel, its invading army will be obliterated. This oracle may refer on one level to Babylon. Since Ezekiel was living in that country, he had to speak about it carefully. He doesn't predict the downfall of Babylon openly. But he may do this in a coded way. The name "Magog" may come from reversing the root consonants of "Babylon" (L-B-B) and replacing them with the following letters of the Hebrew alphabet (M-G-G). In this way Ezekiel may be describing the same event that Jeremiah predicted: the ultimate destruction of the destroyer of God's temple. On another level, this oracle looks to the more distant future, to God's final triumph over all those who oppose him.

This third part, and the entire book, concludes with an extended vision of a newly rebuilt temple, the return of God's glory to the midst of his people, a restored priesthood, and the regifting of the land to Israel's tribes. Significantly, a river flows out of the new temple and *where the river flows everything will live*. There are trees growing along both banks of the river, and *their fruit will serve for food and their leaves for healing*. When God's presence returns to dwell among his people, new life will flourish in the land. Ezekiel's promising visions of the future can be clearly situated within the ongoing drama of the Bible. The pain and brokenness of sin will be healed, and the LORD will come to live with his people in a land that has become like the garden of Eden.

EZEKIEL

I n my thirtieth year, in the fourth month on the fifth day, while I was among the exiles by the Kebar River, the heavens were opened and I saw visions of God.

On the fifth of the month—it was the fifth year of the exile of King Jehoiachin—the word of the LORD came to Ezekiel the priest, the son of Buzi, by the Kebar River in the land of the Babylonians. There the hand of the LORD was on him.

I looked, and I saw a windstorm coming out of the north—an immense cloud with flashing lightning and surrounded by brilliant light. The center of the fire looked like glowing metal, and in the fire was what looked like four living creatures. In appearance their form was human, but each of them had four faces and four wings. Their legs were straight; their feet were like those of a calf and gleamed like burnished bronze. Under their wings on their four sides they had human hands. All four of them had faces and wings, and the wings of one touched the wings of another. Each one went straight ahead; they did not turn as they moved.

Their faces looked like this: Each of the four had the face of a human being, and on the right side each had the face of a lion, and on the left the face of an ox; each also had the face of an eagle. Such were their faces. They each had two wings spreading out upward, each wing touching that of the creature on either side; and each had two other wings covering its body. Each one went straight ahead. Wherever the spirit would go, they would go, without turning as they went. The appearance of the living creatures was like burning coals of fire or like torches. Fire moved back and forth among the creatures; it was bright, and lightning flashed out of it. The creatures sped back and forth like flashes of lightning.

As I looked at the living creatures, I saw a wheel on the ground beside each creature with its four faces. This was the appearance and structure of the wheels: They sparkled like topaz, and all four looked alike. Each appeared to be made like a wheel intersecting a wheel. As they moved, they would go in any one of the four directions the creatures faced; the wheels did not change direction as the creatures went. Their rims were high and awesome, and all four rims were full of eyes all around.

When the living creatures moved, the wheels beside them moved; and when the living creatures rose from the ground, the wheels also rose. Wherever the spirit would go, they would go, and the wheels would rise along with them, because the spirit of the living creatures was in the wheels. When the creatures moved, they also moved; when the creatures stood still, they also stood still; and when the creatures rose from the ground, the wheels rose along with them, because the spirit of the living creatures was in the wheels.

Spread out above the heads of the living creatures was what looked something like a vault, sparkling like crystal, and awesome. Under the vault their wings were stretched out one toward the other, and each had two wings covering its body. When the creatures moved, I heard the sound of their wings, like the roar of rushing waters, like the voice of the Almighty, like the tumult of an army. When they stood still, they lowered their wings.

Then there came a voice from above the vault over their heads as they stood with lowered wings. Above the vault over their heads was what looked like a throne of lapis lazuli, and high above on the throne was a figure like that of a man. I saw that from what appeared to be his waist up he looked like glowing metal, as if full of fire, and that from there down he looked like fire; and brilliant light surrounded him. Like the appearance of a rainbow in the clouds on a rainy day, so was the radiance around him.

This was the appearance of the likeness of the glory of the LORD. When I saw it, I fell facedown, and I heard the voice of one speaking.

He said to me, "Son of man, stand up on your feet and I will speak to you." As he spoke, the Spirit came into me and raised me to my feet, and I heard him speaking to me.

He said: "Son of man, I am sending you to the Israelites, to a rebellious nation that has rebelled against me; they and their ancestors have been in revolt against me to this very day. The people to whom I am sending you are obstinate and stubborn. Say to them, 'This is what the Sovereign LORD says.' And whether they listen or fail to listen — for they are a rebellious people — they will know that a prophet has been among them. And you, son of man, do not be afraid of them or their words. Do not be afraid, though briers and thorns are all around you and you live among scorpions. Do not be afraid of what they say or be terrified by them, though they are a rebellious people. You must speak my words to them, whether they listen or fail to listen, for they are rebellious. But you, son of man, listen to what I say to you. Do not rebel like that rebellious people; open your mouth and eat what I give you."

Then I looked, and I saw a hand stretched out to me. In it was a scroll, which he unrolled before me. On both sides of it were written words of lament and mourning and woe.

And he said to me, "Son of man, eat what is before you, eat this scroll; then go and speak to the people of Israel." So I opened my mouth, and he gave me the scroll to eat.

Then he said to me, "Son of man, eat this scroll I am giving you and fill your stomach with it." So I ate it, and it tasted as sweet as honey in my mouth.

He then said to me: "Son of man, go now to the people of Israel and speak my words to them. You are not being sent to a people of obscure speech and strange language, but to the people of Israel—not to many peoples of obscure speech and strange language, whose words you cannot understand. Surely if I had sent you to them, they would have listened to you. But the people of Israel are not willing to listen to you because they are not willing to listen to me, for all the Israelites are hardened and obstinate. But I will make you as unyielding and hardened as they are. I will make your forehead like the hardest stone, harder than flint. Do not be afraid of them or terrified by them, though they are a rebellious people."

And he said to me, "Son of man, listen carefully and take to heart all the words I speak to you. Go now to your people in exile and speak to them. Say to them, 'This is what the Sovereign LORD says,' whether they listen or fail to listen."

Then the Spirit lifted me up, and I heard behind me a loud rumbling sound as the glory of the LORD rose from the place where it was standing. It was the sound of the wings of the living creatures brushing against each other and the sound of the wheels beside them, a loud rumbling sound. The Spirit then lifted me up and took me away, and I went in bitterness and in the anger of my spirit, with the strong hand of the LORD on me. I came to the exiles who lived at Tel Aviv near the Kebar River. And there, where they were living, I sat among them for seven days—deeply distressed.

At the end of seven days the word of the LORD came to me: "Son of man, I have made you a watchman for the people of Israel; so hear the word I speak and give them warning from me. When I say to a wicked person, 'You will surely die,' and you do not warn them or speak out to dissuade them from their evil ways in order to save their life, that wicked person will die for their sin, and I will hold you accountable for their blood. But if you do warn the wicked person and they do not turn from their wickedness or from their evil ways, they will die for their sin; but you will have saved yourself.

"Again, when a righteous person turns from their righteousness and does evil, and I put a stumbling block before them, they will die. Since you did not warn them, they will die for their sin. The righteous things that person did will not be remembered, and I will hold you accountable for their blood. But if you do warn the righteous person not to sin and they do not sin, they will surely live because they took warning, and you will have saved yourself."

The hand of the LORD was on me there, and he said to me, "Get up and go out to the plain, and there I will speak to you." So I got up and went out to the plain. And the glory of the LORD was standing there, like the glory I had seen by the Kebar River, and I fell facedown.

Then the Spirit came into me and raised me to my feet. He spoke to me and said: "Go, shut yourself inside your house. And you, son of man, they will tie with ropes; you will be bound so that you cannot go out among the people. I will make your tongue stick to the roof of your mouth so that you will be silent and unable to rebuke them, for they are a rebellious people. But when I speak to you, I will open your mouth and you shall say to them, 'This is what the Sovereign LORD says.' Whoever will listen let them listen, and whoever will refuse let them refuse; for they are a rebellious people.

"Now, son of man, take a block of clay, put it in front of you and draw the city of Jerusalem on it. Then lay siege to it: Erect siege works against it, build a ramp up to it, set up camps against it and put battering rams around it. Then take an iron pan, place it as an iron wall between you and the city and turn your face toward it. It will be under siege, and you shall besiege it. This will be a sign to the people of Israel.

"Then lie on your left side and put the sin of the people of Israel upon yourself. You are to bear their sin for the number of days you lie on your side. I have assigned you the same number of days as the years of their sin. So for 390 days you will bear the sin of the people of Israel.

"After you have finished this, lie down again, this time on your right side, and bear the sin of the people of Judah. I have assigned you 40 days, a day for each year. Turn your face toward the siege of Jerusalem and with bared arm prophesy against her. I will tie you up with ropes so that you cannot turn from one side to the other until you have finished the days of your siege.

"Take wheat and barley, beans and lentils, millet and spelt; put them in a storage jar and use them to make bread for yourself. You are to eat it during the 390 days you lie on your side. Weigh out twenty shekels of food to eat each day and eat it at set times. Also measure out a sixth of a hin of water and drink it at set times. Eat the food as you would a loaf of barley bread; bake it in the sight of the people, using human excrement for fuel." The Lord said, "In this way the people of Israel will eat defiled food among the nations where I will drive them."

Then I said, "Not so, Sovereign Lord! I have never defiled myself. From my youth until now I have never eaten anything found dead or torn by wild animals. No impure meat has ever entered my mouth."

"Very well," he said, "I will let you bake your bread over cow dung instead of human excrement."

He then said to me: "Son of man, I am about to cut off the food supply in Jerusalem. The people will eat rationed food in anxiety and drink rationed water in despair, for food and water will be scarce. They will be appalled at the sight of each other and will waste away because of their sin.

"Now, son of man, take a sharp sword and use it as a barber's razor to shave your head and your beard. Then take a set of scales and divide up the hair. When the days of your siege come to an end, burn a third of the hair inside the city. Take a third and strike it with the sword all around the city. And scatter a third to the wind. For I will pursue them with drawn sword. But take a few hairs and tuck them away in the folds of your garment. Again, take a few of these and throw them into the fire and burn them up. A fire will spread from there to all Israel.

"This is what the Sovereign Lord says: This is Jerusalem, which I have set in the center of the nations, with countries all around her. Yet in her wickedness she has rebelled against my laws and decrees more than the nations and countries around her. She has rejected my laws and has not followed my decrees.

"Therefore this is what the Sovereign Lord says: You have been more unruly than the nations around you and have not followed my decrees or kept my laws. You have not even conformed to the standards of the nations around you.

"Therefore this is what the Sovereign Lord says: I myself am against you, Jerusalem, and I will inflict punishment on you in the sight of the nations. Because of all your detestable idols, I will do to you what I have never done before and will never do again. Therefore in your midst parents will eat their children, and children will eat their parents. I will inflict punishment on you and will scatter all your survivors to the winds. Therefore as surely as I live, declares the Sovereign Lord, because you have defiled my sanctuary with all your vile images and detestable practices, I myself will shave you; I will not look on you with pity or spare you. A third of your people will die of the plague or perish by famine inside you; a third will fall by the sword outside your walls; and a third I will scatter to the winds and pursue with drawn sword.

"Then my anger will cease and my wrath against them will subside, and I will be avenged. And when I have spent my wrath on them, they will know that I the LORD have spoken in my zeal.

"I will make you a ruin and a reproach among the nations around you, in the sight of all who pass by. You will be a reproach and a taunt, a warning and an object of horror to the nations around you when I inflict punishment on you in anger and in wrath and with stinging rebuke. I the LORD have spoken. When I shoot at you with my deadly and destructive arrows of famine, I will shoot to destroy you. I will bring more and more famine upon you and cut off your supply of food. I will send famine and wild beasts against you, and they will leave you childless. Plague and bloodshed will sweep through you, and I will bring the sword against you. I the LORD have spoken."

The word of the LORD came to me: "Son of man, set your face against the mountains of Israel; prophesy against them and say: 'You mountains of Israel, hear the word of the Sovereign LORD. This is what the Sovereign LORD says to the mountains and hills, to the ravines and valleys: I am about to bring a sword against you, and I will destroy your high places. Your altars will be demolished and your incense altars will be smashed; and I will slay your people in front of your idols. I will lay the dead bodies of the Israelites in front of their idols, and I will scatter your bones around your altars. Wherever you live, the towns will be laid waste and the high places demolished, so that your altars will be laid waste and devastated, your idols smashed and ruined, your incense altars broken down, and what you have made wiped out. Your people will fall slain among you, and you will know that I am the LORD.

" 'But I will spare some, for some of you will escape the sword when you are scattered among the lands and nations. Then in the nations where they have been carried captive, those who escape will remember me — how I have been grieved by their adulterous hearts, which have turned away from me, and by their eyes, which have lusted after their idols. They will loathe themselves for the evil they have done and for all their detestable practices. And they will know that I am the LORD; I did not threaten in vain to bring this calamity on them.

" 'This is what the Sovereign LORD says: Strike your hands together and stamp your feet and cry out "Alas!" because of all the wicked and detestable practices of the people of Israel, for they will fall by the sword, famine and plague. One who is far away will die of the plague, and one who is near will fall by the sword, and anyone who survives and is spared will die of famine. So will I pour out my wrath on them. And they will know that I am the Lord, when their people lie slain among their idols around their altars, on every high hill and on all the mountaintops, under every spreading tree and every leafy oak — places where they offered fragrant incense to all their idols. And I will stretch out my hand against them and make the land a desolate waste from the desert to Diblah — wherever they live. Then they will know that I am the Lord.' "

The word of the Lord came to me: "Son of man, this is what the Sovereign Lord says to the land of Israel:

> " 'The end! The end has come
> upon the four corners of the land!

> The end is now upon you,
> and I will unleash my anger against you.

> I will judge you according to your conduct
> and repay you for all your detestable practices.

> I will not look on you with pity;
> I will not spare you.

> I will surely repay you for your conduct
> and for the detestable practices among you.

" 'Then you will know that I am the Lord.'

"This is what the Sovereign Lord says:

> " 'Disaster! Unheard-of disaster!
> See, it comes!

> The end has come!
> The end has come!

> It has roused itself against you.
> See, it comes!

> Doom has come upon you,
> upon you who dwell in the land.

> The time has come! The day is near!
> There is panic, not joy, on the mountains.

> I am about to pour out my wrath on you
> and spend my anger against you.

I will judge you according to your conduct
and repay you for all your detestable practices.

I will not look on you with pity;
I will not spare you.

I will repay you for your conduct
and for the detestable practices among you.

" 'Then you will know that it is I the LORD who strikes you.

" 'See, the day!
See, it comes!

Doom has burst forth,
the rod has budded,
arrogance has blossomed!

Violence has arisen,
a rod to punish the wicked.

None of the people will be left,
none of that crowd—

none of their wealth,
nothing of value.

The time has come!
The day has arrived!

Let not the buyer rejoice
nor the seller grieve,
for my wrath is on the whole crowd.

The seller will not recover
the property that was sold—
as long as both buyer and seller live.

For the vision concerning the whole crowd
will not be reversed.

Because of their sins, not one of them
will preserve their life.

" 'They have blown the trumpet,
they have made all things ready,

but no one will go into battle,
for my wrath is on the whole crowd.

Outside is the sword;
inside are plague and famine.

Those in the country
will die by the sword;

those in the city
will be devoured by famine and plague.

The fugitives who escape
will flee to the mountains.

Like doves of the valleys,
they will all moan,
each for their own sins.

Every hand will go limp;
every leg will be wet with urine.

They will put on sackcloth
and be clothed with terror.

Every face will be covered with shame,
and every head will be shaved.

" 'They will throw their silver into the streets,
and their gold will be treated as a thing unclean.

Their silver and gold
will not be able to deliver them
in the day of the LORD's wrath.

It will not satisfy their hunger
or fill their stomachs,
for it has caused them to stumble into sin.

They took pride in their beautiful jewelry
and used it to make their detestable idols.

They made it into vile images;
therefore I will make it a thing unclean for them.

I will give their wealth as plunder to foreigners
and as loot to the wicked of the earth,
who will defile it.

I will turn my face away from the people,
and robbers will desecrate the place I treasure.

They will enter it
and will defile it.

" 'Prepare chains!
For the land is full of bloodshed,
and the city is full of violence.

I will bring the most wicked of nations
to take possession of their houses.

I will put an end to the pride of the mighty,
and their sanctuaries will be desecrated.

> When terror comes,
> they will seek peace in vain.

> Calamity upon calamity will come,
> and rumor upon rumor.

> They will go searching for a vision from the prophet,
> priestly instruction in the law will cease,
> the counsel of the elders will come to an end.

> The king will mourn,
> the prince will be clothed with despair,
> and the hands of the people of the land will tremble.

> I will deal with them according to their conduct,
> and by their own standards I will judge them.

" 'Then they will know that I am the Lord.' "

In the sixth year, in the sixth month on the fifth day, while I was sitting in my house and the elders of Judah were sitting before me, the hand of the Sovereign Lord came on me there. I looked, and I saw a figure like that of a man. From what appeared to be his waist down he was like fire, and from there up his appearance was as bright as glowing metal. He stretched out what looked like a hand and took me by the hair of my head. The Spirit lifted me up between earth and heaven and in visions of God he took me to Jerusalem, to the entrance of the north gate of the inner court, where the idol that provokes to jealousy stood. And there before me was the glory of the God of Israel, as in the vision I had seen in the plain.

Then he said to me, "Son of man, look toward the north." So I looked, and in the entrance north of the gate of the altar I saw this idol of jealousy.

And he said to me, "Son of man, do you see what they are doing—the utterly detestable things the Israelites are doing here, things that will drive me far from my sanctuary? But you will see things that are even more detestable."

Then he brought me to the entrance to the court. I looked, and I saw a hole in the wall. He said to me, "Son of man, now dig into the wall." So I dug into the wall and saw a doorway there.

And he said to me, "Go in and see the wicked and detestable things they are doing here." So I went in and looked, and I saw portrayed all over the walls all kinds of crawling things and unclean animals and all the idols of Israel. In front of them stood seventy elders of Israel, and Jaazaniah son of Shaphan was standing among them. Each had a censer in his hand, and a fragrant cloud of incense was rising.

He said to me, "Son of man, have you seen what the elders of Israel are doing in the darkness, each at the shrine of his own idol? They say, 'The LORD does not see us; the LORD has forsaken the land.'" Again, he said, "You will see them doing things that are even more detestable."

Then he brought me to the entrance of the north gate of the house of the LORD, and I saw women sitting there, mourning the god Tammuz. He said to me, "Do you see this, son of man? You will see things that are even more detestable than this."

He then brought me into the inner court of the house of the LORD, and there at the entrance to the temple, between the portico and the altar, were about twenty-five men. With their backs toward the temple of the LORD and their faces toward the east, they were bowing down to the sun in the east.

He said to me, "Have you seen this, son of man? Is it a trivial matter for the people of Judah to do the detestable things they are doing here? Must they also fill the land with violence and continually arouse my anger? Look at them putting the branch to their nose! Therefore I will deal with them in anger; I will not look on them with pity or spare them. Although they shout in my ears, I will not listen to them."

Then I heard him call out in a loud voice, "Bring near those who are appointed to execute judgment on the city, each with a weapon in his hand." And I saw six men coming from the direction of the upper gate, which faces north, each with a deadly weapon in his hand. With them was a man clothed in linen who had a writing kit at his side. They came in and stood beside the bronze altar.

Now the glory of the God of Israel went up from above the cherubim, where it had been, and moved to the threshold of the temple. Then the LORD called to the man clothed in linen who had the writing kit at his side and said to him, "Go throughout the city of Jerusalem and put a mark on the foreheads of those who grieve and lament over all the detestable things that are done in it."

As I listened, he said to the others, "Follow him through the city and kill, without showing pity or compassion. Slaughter the old men, the young men and women, the mothers and children, but do not touch anyone who has the mark. Begin at my sanctuary." So they began with the old men who were in front of the temple.

Then he said to them, "Defile the temple and fill the courts with the slain. Go!" So they went out and began killing throughout the city. While they were killing and I was left alone, I fell facedown, crying out, "Alas, Sovereign LORD! Are you going to destroy the entire remnant of Israel in this outpouring of your wrath on Jerusalem?"

He answered me, "The sin of the people of Israel and Judah is exceedingly great; the land is full of bloodshed and the city is full of injustice. They say, 'The LORD has forsaken the land; the LORD does not see.' So I will not look on them with pity or spare them, but I will bring down on their own heads what they have done."

Then the man in linen with the writing kit at his side brought back word, saying, "I have done as you commanded."

I looked, and I saw the likeness of a throne of lapis lazuli above the vault that was over the heads of the cherubim. The LORD said to the man clothed in linen, "Go in among the wheels beneath the cherubim. Fill your hands with burning coals from among the cherubim and scatter them over the city." And as I watched, he went in.

Now the cherubim were standing on the south side of the temple when the man went in, and a cloud filled the inner court. Then the glory of the LORD rose from above the cherubim and moved to the threshold of the temple. The cloud filled the temple, and the court was full of the radiance of the glory of the LORD. The sound of the wings of the cherubim could be heard as far away as the outer court, like the voice of God Almighty when he speaks.

When the LORD commanded the man in linen, "Take fire from among the wheels, from among the cherubim," the man went in and stood beside a wheel. Then one of the cherubim reached out his hand to the fire that was among them. He took up some of it and put it into the hands of the man in linen, who took it and went out. (Under the wings of the cherubim could be seen what looked like human hands.)

I looked, and I saw beside the cherubim four wheels, one beside each of the cherubim; the wheels sparkled like topaz. As for their appearance, the four of them looked alike; each was like a wheel intersecting a wheel. As they moved, they would go in any one of the four directions the cherubim faced; the wheels did not turn about as the cherubim went. The cherubim went in whatever direction the head faced, without turning as they went. Their entire bodies, including their backs, their hands and their wings, were completely full of eyes, as were their four wheels. I heard the wheels being called "the whirling wheels." Each of the cherubim had four faces: One face was that of a cherub, the second the face of a human being, the third the face of a lion, and the fourth the face of an eagle.

Then the cherubim rose upward. These were the living creatures I had seen by the Kebar River. When the cherubim moved, the wheels beside them moved; and when the cherubim spread their wings to rise from the ground, the wheels did not leave their side. When the cherubim stood still, they also stood still; and when the cherubim rose, they rose with them, because the spirit of the living creatures was in them.

Then the glory of the LORD departed from over the threshold of the temple and stopped above the cherubim. While I watched, the cherubim spread their wings and rose from the ground, and as they went, the wheels went with them. They stopped at the entrance of the east gate of the LORD's house, and the glory of the God of Israel was above them.

These were the living creatures I had seen beneath the God of Israel by the Kebar River, and I realized that they were cherubim. Each had four faces and four wings, and under their wings was what looked like human hands. Their faces had the same appearance as those I had seen by the Kebar River. Each one went straight ahead.

Then the Spirit lifted me up and brought me to the gate of the house of the LORD that faces east. There at the entrance of the gate were twenty-five men, and I saw among them Jaazaniah son of Azzur and Pelatiah son of Benaiah, leaders of the people. The LORD said to me, "Son of man, these are the men who are plotting evil and giving wicked advice in this city. They say, 'Haven't our houses been recently rebuilt? This city is a pot, and we are the meat in it.' Therefore prophesy against them; prophesy, son of man."

Then the Spirit of the LORD came on me, and he told me to say: "This is what the LORD says: That is what you are saying, you leaders in Israel, but I know what is going through your mind. You have killed many people in this city and filled its streets with the dead.

"Therefore this is what the Sovereign LORD says: The bodies you have thrown there are the meat and this city is the pot, but I will drive you out of it. You fear the sword, and the sword is what I will bring against you, declares the Sovereign LORD. I will drive you out of the city and deliver you into the hands of foreigners and inflict punishment on you. You will fall by the sword, and I will execute judgment on you at the borders of Israel. Then you will know that I am the LORD. This city will not be a pot for you, nor will you be the meat in it; I will execute judgment on you at the borders of Israel. And you will know that I am the LORD, for you have not followed my decrees or kept my laws but have conformed to the standards of the nations around you."

Now as I was prophesying, Pelatiah son of Benaiah died. Then I fell facedown and cried out in a loud voice, "Alas, Sovereign LORD! Will you completely destroy the remnant of Israel?"

The word of the LORD came to me: "Son of man, the people of Jerusalem have said of your fellow exiles and all the other Israelites,

'They are far away from the LORD; this land was given to us as our possession.'

"Therefore say: 'This is what the Sovereign LORD says: Although I sent them far away among the nations and scattered them among the countries, yet for a little while I have been a sanctuary for them in the countries where they have gone.'

"Therefore say: 'This is what the Sovereign LORD says: I will gather you from the nations and bring you back from the countries where you have been scattered, and I will give you back the land of Israel again.'

"They will return to it and remove all its vile images and detestable idols. I will give them an undivided heart and put a new spirit in them; I will remove from them their heart of stone and give them a heart of flesh. Then they will follow my decrees and be careful to keep my laws. They will be my people, and I will be their God. But as for those whose hearts are devoted to their vile images and detestable idols, I will bring down on their own heads what they have done, declares the Sovereign LORD."

Then the cherubim, with the wheels beside them, spread their wings, and the glory of the God of Israel was above them. The glory of the LORD went up from within the city and stopped above the mountain east of it. The Spirit lifted me up and brought me to the exiles in Babylonia in the vision given by the Spirit of God.

Then the vision I had seen went up from me, and I told the exiles everything the LORD had shown me.

The word of the LORD came to me: "Son of man, you are living among a rebellious people. They have eyes to see but do not see and ears to hear but do not hear, for they are a rebellious people.

"Therefore, son of man, pack your belongings for exile and in the daytime, as they watch, set out and go from where you are to another place. Perhaps they will understand, though they are a rebellious people. During the daytime, while they watch, bring out your belongings packed for exile. Then in the evening, while they are watching, go out like those who go into exile. While they watch, dig through the wall and take your belongings out through it. Put them on your shoulder as they are watching and carry them out at dusk. Cover your face so that you cannot see the land, for I have made you a sign to the Israelites."

So I did as I was commanded. During the day I brought out my things packed for exile. Then in the evening I dug through the wall with my hands. I took my belongings out at dusk, carrying them on my shoulders while they watched.

In the morning the word of the Lord came to me: "Son of man, did not the Israelites, that rebellious people, ask you, 'What are you doing?'

"Say to them, 'This is what the Sovereign Lord says: This prophecy concerns the prince in Jerusalem and all the Israelites who are there.' Say to them, 'I am a sign to you.'

"As I have done, so it will be done to them. They will go into exile as captives.

"The prince among them will put his things on his shoulder at dusk and leave, and a hole will be dug in the wall for him to go through. He will cover his face so that he cannot see the land. I will spread my net for him, and he will be caught in my snare; I will bring him to Babylonia, the land of the Chaldeans, but he will not see it, and there he will die. I will scatter to the winds all those around him—his staff and all his troops—and I will pursue them with drawn sword.

"They will know that I am the Lord, when I disperse them among the nations and scatter them through the countries. But I will spare a few of them from the sword, famine and plague, so that in the nations where they go they may acknowledge all their detestable practices. Then they will know that I am the Lord."

The word of the Lord came to me: "Son of man, tremble as you eat your food, and shudder in fear as you drink your water. Say to the people of the land: 'This is what the Sovereign Lord says about those living in Jerusalem and in the land of Israel: They will eat their food in anxiety and drink their water in despair, for their land will be stripped of everything in it because of the violence of all who live there. The inhabited towns will be laid waste and the land will be desolate. Then you will know that I am the Lord.' "

The word of the Lord came to me: "Son of man, what is this proverb you have in the land of Israel: 'The days go by and every vision comes to nothing'? Say to them, 'This is what the Sovereign Lord says: I am going to put an end to this proverb, and they will no longer quote it in Israel.' Say to them, 'The days are near when every vision will be fulfilled. For there will be no more false visions or flattering divinations among the people of Israel. But I the Lord will speak what I will, and it shall be fulfilled without delay. For in your days, you rebellious people, I will fulfill whatever I say, declares the Sovereign Lord.' "

The word of the LORD came to me: "Son of man, the Israelites are saying, 'The vision he sees is for many years from now, and he prophesies about the distant future.'

"Therefore say to them, 'This is what the Sovereign LORD says: None of my words will be delayed any longer; whatever I say will be fulfilled, declares the Sovereign LORD.'"

The word of the LORD came to me: "Son of man, prophesy against the prophets of Israel who are now prophesying. Say to those who prophesy out of their own imagination: 'Hear the word of the LORD! This is what the Sovereign LORD says: Woe to the foolish prophets who follow their own spirit and have seen nothing! Your prophets, Israel, are like jackals among ruins. You have not gone up to the breaches in the wall to repair it for the people of Israel so that it will stand firm in the battle on the day of the LORD. Their visions are false and their divinations a lie. Even though the LORD has not sent them, they say, "The LORD declares," and expect him to fulfill their words. Have you not seen false visions and uttered lying divinations when you say, "The LORD declares," though I have not spoken?

"'Therefore this is what the Sovereign LORD says: Because of your false words and lying visions, I am against you, declares the Sovereign LORD. My hand will be against the prophets who see false visions and utter lying divinations. They will not belong to the council of my people or be listed in the records of Israel, nor will they enter the land of Israel. Then you will know that I am the Sovereign LORD.

"'Because they lead my people astray, saying, "Peace," when there is no peace, and because, when a flimsy wall is built, they cover it with whitewash, therefore tell those who cover it with whitewash that it is going to fall. Rain will come in torrents, and I will send hailstones hurtling down, and violent winds will burst forth. When the wall collapses, will people not ask you, "Where is the whitewash you covered it with?"

"'Therefore this is what the Sovereign LORD says: In my wrath I will unleash a violent wind, and in my anger hailstones and torrents of rain will fall with destructive fury. I will tear down the wall you have covered with whitewash and will level it to the ground so that its foundation will be laid bare. When it falls, you will be destroyed in it; and you will know that I am the LORD. So I will pour out my wrath against the wall and against those who covered it with whitewash. I will say to you, "The wall is gone and so are those who whitewashed it, those prophets of Israel who prophesied to Jerusalem and saw visions of peace for her when there was no peace, declares the Sovereign Lord."'

"Now, son of man, set your face against the daughters of your people who prophesy out of their own imagination. Prophesy against them and say, 'This is what the Sovereign Lord says: Woe to the women who sew magic charms on all their wrists and make veils of various lengths for their heads in order to ensnare people. Will you ensnare the lives of my people but preserve your own? You have profaned me among my people for a few handfuls of barley and scraps of bread. By lying to my people, who listen to lies, you have killed those who should not have died and have spared those who should not live.

"'Therefore this is what the Sovereign Lord says: I am against your magic charms with which you ensnare people like birds and I will tear them from your arms; I will set free the people that you ensnare like birds. I will tear off your veils and save my people from your hands, and they will no longer fall prey to your power. Then you will know that I am the Lord. Because you disheartened the righteous with your lies, when I had brought them no grief, and because you encouraged the wicked not to turn from their evil ways and so save their lives, therefore you will no longer see false visions or practice divination. I will save my people from your hands. And then you will know that I am the Lord.'"

Some of the elders of Israel came to me and sat down in front of me. Then the word of the Lord came to me: "Son of man, these men have set up idols in their hearts and put wicked stumbling blocks before their faces. Should I let them inquire of me at all? Therefore speak to them and tell them, 'This is what the Sovereign Lord says: When any of the Israelites set up idols in their hearts and put a wicked stumbling block before their faces and then go to a prophet, I the Lord will answer them myself in keeping with their great idolatry. I will do this to recapture the hearts of the people of Israel, who have all deserted me for their idols.'

"Therefore say to the people of Israel, 'This is what the Sovereign Lord says: Repent! Turn from your idols and renounce all your detestable practices!

"'When any of the Israelites or any foreigner residing in Israel separate themselves from me and set up idols in their hearts and put a wicked stumbling block before their faces and then go to a prophet to inquire of me, I the Lord will answer them myself. I will set my face against them and make them an example and a byword. I will remove them from my people. Then you will know that I am the Lord.

" 'And if the prophet is enticed to utter a prophecy, I the Lᴏʀᴅ have enticed that prophet, and I will stretch out my hand against him and destroy him from among my people Israel. They will bear their guilt—the prophet will be as guilty as the one who consults him. Then the people of Israel will no longer stray from me, nor will they defile themselves anymore with all their sins. They will be my people, and I will be their God, declares the Sovereign Lᴏʀᴅ.' "

The word of the Lᴏʀᴅ came to me: "Son of man, if a country sins against me by being unfaithful and I stretch out my hand against it to cut off its food supply and send famine upon it and kill its people and their animals, even if these three men—Noah, Daniel and Job—were in it, they could save only themselves by their righteousness, declares the Sovereign Lᴏʀᴅ.

"Or if I send wild beasts through that country and they leave it childless and it becomes desolate so that no one can pass through it because of the beasts, as surely as I live, declares the Sovereign Lᴏʀᴅ, even if these three men were in it, they could not save their own sons or daughters. They alone would be saved, but the land would be desolate.

"Or if I bring a sword against that country and say, 'Let the sword pass throughout the land,' and I kill its people and their animals, as surely as I live, declares the Sovereign Lᴏʀᴅ, even if these three men were in it, they could not save their own sons or daughters. They alone would be saved.

"Or if I send a plague into that land and pour out my wrath on it through bloodshed, killing its people and their animals, as surely as I live, declares the Sovereign Lᴏʀᴅ, even if Noah, Daniel and Job were in it, they could save neither son nor daughter. They would save only themselves by their righteousness.

"For this is what the Sovereign Lᴏʀᴅ says: How much worse will it be when I send against Jerusalem my four dreadful judgments—sword and famine and wild beasts and plague—to kill its men and their animals! Yet there will be some survivors—sons and daughters who will be brought out of it. They will come to you, and when you see their conduct and their actions, you will be consoled regarding the disaster I have brought on Jerusalem—every disaster I have brought on it. You will be consoled when you see their conduct and their actions, for you will know that I have done nothing in it without cause, declares the Sovereign Lᴏʀᴅ."

The word of the Lᴏʀᴅ came to me: "Son of man, how is the wood of a vine different from that of a branch from any of the trees in the forest? Is wood ever taken from it to make anything useful? Do they make pegs from it to hang things on? And after it is thrown on the fire as fuel and the fire burns both ends and chars the middle, is it then useful for anything? If it was not useful for anything when it was whole, how much less can it be made into something useful when the fire has burned it and it is charred?

"Therefore this is what the Sovereign Lord says: As I have given the wood of the vine among the trees of the forest as fuel for the fire, so will I treat the people living in Jerusalem. I will set my face against them. Although they have come out of the fire, the fire will yet consume them. And when I set my face against them, you will know that I am the Lord. I will make the land desolate because they have been unfaithful, declares the Sovereign Lord."

The word of the Lord came to me: "Son of man, confront Jerusalem with her detestable practices and say, 'This is what the Sovereign Lord says to Jerusalem: Your ancestry and birth were in the land of the Canaanites; your father was an Amorite and your mother a Hittite. On the day you were born your cord was not cut, nor were you washed with water to make you clean, nor were you rubbed with salt or wrapped in cloths. No one looked on you with pity or had compassion enough to do any of these things for you. Rather, you were thrown out into the open field, for on the day you were born you were despised.

" 'Then I passed by and saw you kicking about in your blood, and as you lay there in your blood I said to you, "Live!" I made you grow like a plant of the field. You grew and developed and entered puberty. Your breasts had formed and your hair had grown, yet you were stark naked.

" 'Later I passed by, and when I looked at you and saw that you were old enough for love, I spread the corner of my garment over you and covered your naked body. I gave you my solemn oath and entered into a covenant with you, declares the Sovereign Lord, and you became mine.

" 'I bathed you with water and washed the blood from you and put ointments on you. I clothed you with an embroidered dress and put sandals of fine leather on you. I dressed you in fine linen and covered you with costly garments. I adorned you with jewelry: I put bracelets on your arms and a necklace around your neck, and I put a ring on your nose, earrings on your ears and a beautiful crown on your head. So you were adorned with gold and silver; your clothes were of fine linen and costly fabric and embroidered cloth. Your food was honey, olive oil and the finest flour. You became very beautiful and rose to be a queen. And your fame spread among the nations on account of your beauty, because the splendor I had given you made your beauty perfect, declares the Sovereign LORD.

"'But you trusted in your beauty and used your fame to become a prostitute. You lavished your favors on anyone who passed by and your beauty became his. You took some of your garments to make gaudy high places, where you carried on your prostitution. You went to him, and he possessed your beauty. You also took the fine jewelry I gave you, the jewelry made of my gold and silver, and you made for yourself male idols and engaged in prostitution with them. And you took your embroidered clothes to put on them, and you offered my oil and incense before them. Also the food I provided for you—the flour, olive oil and honey I gave you to eat—you offered as fragrant incense before them. That is what happened, declares the Sovereign LORD.

"'And you took your sons and daughters whom you bore to me and sacrificed them as food to the idols. Was your prostitution not enough? You slaughtered my children and sacrificed them to the idols. In all your detestable practices and your prostitution you did not remember the days of your youth, when you were naked and bare, kicking about in your blood.

"'Woe! Woe to you, declares the Sovereign LORD. In addition to all your other wickedness, you built a mound for yourself and made a lofty shrine in every public square. At every street corner you built your lofty shrines and degraded your beauty, spreading your legs with increasing promiscuity to anyone who passed by. You engaged in prostitution with the Egyptians, your neighbors with large genitals, and aroused my anger with your increasing promiscuity. So I stretched out my hand against you and reduced your territory; I gave you over to the greed of your enemies, the daughters of the Philistines, who were shocked by your lewd conduct. You engaged in prostitution with the Assyrians too, because you were insatiable; and even after that, you still were not satisfied. Then you increased your promiscuity to include Babylonia, a land of merchants, but even with this you were not satisfied.

"'I am filled with fury against you, declares the Sovereign LORD, when you do all these things, acting like a brazen prostitute! When you built your mounds at every street corner and made your lofty shrines in every public square, you were unlike a prostitute, because you scorned payment.

"'You adulterous wife! You prefer strangers to your own husband! All prostitutes receive gifts, but you give gifts to all your lovers, bribing them to come to you from everywhere for your illicit favors. So in your prostitution you are the opposite of others; no one runs after you for your favors. You are the very opposite, for you give payment and none is given to you.

" 'Therefore, you prostitute, hear the word of the LORD! This is what the Sovereign LORD says: Because you poured out your lust and exposed your naked body in your promiscuity with your lovers, and because of all your detestable idols, and because you gave them your children's blood, therefore I am going to gather all your lovers, with whom you found pleasure, those you loved as well as those you hated. I will gather them against you from all around and will strip you in front of them, and they will see you stark naked. I will sentence you to the punishment of women who commit adultery and who shed blood; I will bring on you the blood vengeance of my wrath and jealous anger. Then I will deliver you into the hands of your lovers, and they will tear down your mounds and destroy your lofty shrines. They will strip you of your clothes and take your fine jewelry and leave you stark naked. They will bring a mob against you, who will stone you and hack you to pieces with their swords. They will burn down your houses and inflict punishment on you in the sight of many women. I will put a stop to your prostitution, and you will no longer pay your lovers. Then my wrath against you will subside and my jealous anger will turn away from you; I will be calm and no longer angry.

" 'Because you did not remember the days of your youth but enraged me with all these things, I will surely bring down on your head what you have done, declares the Sovereign LORD. Did you not add lewdness to all your other detestable practices?

" 'Everyone who quotes proverbs will quote this proverb about you: "Like mother, like daughter." You are a true daughter of your mother, who despised her husband and her children; and you are a true sister of your sisters, who despised their husbands and their children. Your mother was a Hittite and your father an Amorite. Your older sister was Samaria, who lived to the north of you with her daughters; and your younger sister, who lived to the south of you with her daughters, was Sodom. You not only followed their ways and copied their detestable practices, but in all your ways you soon became more depraved than they. As surely as I live, declares the Sovereign LORD, your sister Sodom and her daughters never did what you and your daughters have done.

" 'Now this was the sin of your sister Sodom: She and her daughters were arrogant, overfed and unconcerned; they did not help the poor and needy. They were haughty and did detestable things before me. Therefore I did away with them as you have seen. Samaria did not commit half the sins you did. You have done more detestable things than they, and have made your sisters seem righteous by all these things you have done. Bear your disgrace, for you have furnished some justification for your sisters. Because your sins were more vile than theirs, they appear more righteous than you. So then, be ashamed and bear your disgrace, for you have made your sisters appear righteous.

" 'However, I will restore the fortunes of Sodom and her daughters and of Samaria and her daughters, and your fortunes along with them, so that you may bear your disgrace and be ashamed of all you have done in giving them comfort. And your sisters, Sodom with her daughters and Samaria with her daughters, will return to what they were before; and you and your daughters will return to what you were before. You would not even mention your sister Sodom in the day of your pride, before your wickedness was uncovered. Even so, you are now scorned by the daughters of Edom and all her neighbors and the daughters of the Philistines — all those around you who despise you. You will bear the consequences of your lewdness and your detestable practices, declares the LORD.

" 'This is what the Sovereign LORD says: I will deal with you as you deserve, because you have despised my oath by breaking the covenant. Yet I will remember the covenant I made with you in the days of your youth, and I will establish an everlasting covenant with you. Then you will remember your ways and be ashamed when you receive your sisters, both those who are older than you and those who are younger. I will give them to you as daughters, but not on the basis of my covenant with you. So I will establish my covenant with you, and you will know that I am the LORD. Then, when I make atonement for you for all you have done, you will remember and be ashamed and never again open your mouth because of your humiliation, declares the Sovereign LORD.' "

The word of the LORD came to me: "Son of man, set forth an allegory and tell it to the Israelites as a parable. Say to them, 'This is what the Sovereign LORD says: A great eagle with powerful wings, long feathers and full plumage of varied colors came to Lebanon. Taking hold of the top of a cedar, he broke off its topmost shoot and carried it away to a land of merchants, where he planted it in a city of traders.

" 'He took one of the seedlings of the land and put it in fertile soil. He planted it like a willow by abundant water, and it sprouted and became a low, spreading vine. Its branches turned toward him, but its roots remained under it. So it became a vine and produced branches and put out leafy boughs.

" 'But there was another great eagle with powerful wings and full plumage. The vine now sent out its roots toward him from the plot where it was planted and stretched out its branches to him for water. It had been planted in good soil by abundant water so that it would produce branches, bear fruit and become a splendid vine.'

"Say to them, 'This is what the Sovereign LORD says: Will it thrive? Will it not be uprooted and stripped of its fruit so that it withers? All its new growth will wither. It will not take a strong arm or many people to pull it up by the roots. It has been planted, but will it thrive? Will it not wither completely when the east wind strikes it — wither away in the plot where it grew?' "

Then the word of the LORD came to me: "Say to this rebellious people, 'Do you not know what these things mean?' Say to them: 'The king of Babylon went to Jerusalem and carried off her king and her nobles, bringing them back with him to Babylon. Then he took a member of the royal family and made a treaty with him, putting him under oath. He also carried away the leading men of the land, so that the kingdom would be brought low, unable to rise again, surviving only by keeping his treaty. But the king rebelled against him by sending his envoys to Egypt to get horses and a large army. Will he succeed? Will he who does such things escape? Will he break the treaty and yet escape?

" 'As surely as I live, declares the Sovereign LORD, he shall die in Babylon, in the land of the king who put him on the throne, whose oath he despised and whose treaty he broke. Pharaoh with his mighty army and great horde will be of no help to him in war, when ramps are built and siege works erected to destroy many lives. He despised the oath by breaking the covenant. Because he had given his hand in pledge and yet did all these things, he shall not escape.

" 'Therefore this is what the Sovereign LORD says: As surely as I live, I will repay him for despising my oath and breaking my covenant. I will spread my net for him, and he will be caught in my snare. I will bring him to Babylon and execute judgment on him there because he was unfaithful to me. All his choice troops will fall by the sword, and the survivors will be scattered to the winds. Then you will know that I the LORD have spoken.

" 'This is what the Sovereign LORD says: I myself will take a shoot from the very top of a cedar and plant it; I will break off a tender sprig from its topmost shoots and plant it on a high and lofty mountain. On the mountain heights of Israel I will plant it; it will produce branches and bear fruit and become a splendid cedar. Birds of every kind will nest in it; they will find shelter in the shade of its branches. All the trees of the forest will know that I the LORD bring down the tall tree and make the low tree grow tall. I dry up the green tree and make the dry tree flourish.

" 'I the LORD have spoken, and I will do it.' "

The word of the LORD came to me: "What do you people mean by quoting this proverb about the land of Israel:

" 'The parents eat sour grapes,
        and the children's teeth are set on edge'?

"As surely as I live, declares the Sovereign LORD, you will no longer quote this proverb in Israel. For everyone belongs to me, the parent as well as the child — both alike belong to me. The one who sins is the one who will die.

"Suppose there is a righteous man
who does what is just and right.

He does not eat at the mountain shrines
or look to the idols of Israel.

He does not defile his neighbor's wife
or have sexual relations with a woman during her
period.

He does not oppress anyone,
but returns what he took in pledge for a loan.

He does not commit robbery
but gives his food to the hungry
and provides clothing for the naked.

He does not lend to them at interest
or take a profit from them.

He withholds his hand from doing wrong
and judges fairly between two parties.

He follows my decrees
and faithfully keeps my laws.

That man is righteous;
he will surely live,
declares the Sovereign LORD.

"Suppose he has a violent son, who sheds blood or does any of these other things (though the father has done none of them):

"He eats at the mountain shrines.

He defiles his neighbor's wife.

He oppresses the poor and needy.

He commits robbery.

He does not return what he took in pledge.

He looks to the idols.

He does detestable things.

He lends at interest and takes a profit.

Will such a man live? He will not! Because he has done all these detestable things, he is to be put to death; his blood will be on his own head.

"But suppose this son has a son who sees all the sins his father commits, and though he sees them, he does not do such things:

> "He does not eat at the mountain shrines
> or look to the idols of Israel.
>
> He does not defile his neighbor's wife.
>
> He does not oppress anyone
> or require a pledge for a loan.
>
> He does not commit robbery
> but gives his food to the hungry
> and provides clothing for the naked.
>
> He withholds his hand from mistreating the poor
> and takes no interest or profit from them.
>
> He keeps my laws and follows my decrees.

He will not die for his father's sin; he will surely live. But his father will die for his own sin, because he practiced extortion, robbed his brother and did what was wrong among his people.

"Yet you ask, 'Why does the son not share the guilt of his father?' Since the son has done what is just and right and has been careful to keep all my decrees, he will surely live. The one who sins is the one who will die. The child will not share the guilt of the parent, nor will the parent share the guilt of the child. The righteousness of the righteous will be credited to them, and the wickedness of the wicked will be charged against them.

"But if a wicked person turns away from all the sins they have committed and keeps all my decrees and does what is just and right, that person will surely live; they will not die. None of the offenses they have committed will be remembered against them. Because of the righteous things they have done, they will live. Do I take any pleasure in the death of the wicked? declares the Sovereign LORD. Rather, am I not pleased when they turn from their ways and live?

"But if a righteous person turns from their righteousness and commits sin and does the same detestable things the wicked person does, will they live? None of the righteous things that person has done will be remembered. Because of the unfaithfulness they are guilty of and because of the sins they have committed, they will die.

"Yet you say, 'The way of the Lord is not just.' Hear, you Israelites: Is my way unjust? Is it not your ways that are unjust? If a righteous person turns from their righteousness and commits sin, they will die for it; because of the sin they have committed they will die. But if a wicked person turns away from the wickedness they have committed and does what is just and right, they will save their life. Because they consider all the offenses they have committed and turn away from them, that person will surely live; they will not die. Yet the Israelites say, 'The way of the Lord is not just.' Are my ways unjust, people of Israel? Is it not your ways that are unjust?

"Therefore, you Israelites, I will judge each of you according to your own ways, declares the Sovereign Lord. Repent! Turn away from all your offenses; then sin will not be your downfall. Rid your-selves of all the offenses you have committed, and get a new heart and a new spirit. Why will you die, people of Israel? For I take no pleasure in the death of anyone, declares the Sovereign Lord. Re-pent and live!

"Take up a lament concerning the princes of Israel and say:

> "'What a lioness was your mother
> among the lions!
> She lay down among them
> and reared her cubs.
> She brought up one of her cubs,
> and he became a strong lion.
> He learned to tear the prey
> and he became a man-eater.
> The nations heard about him,
> and he was trapped in their pit.
> They led him with hooks
> to the land of Egypt.
>
> "'When she saw her hope unfulfilled,
> her expectation gone,
> she took another of her cubs
> and made him a strong lion.
> He prowled among the lions,
> for he was now a strong lion.
> He learned to tear the prey
> and he became a man-eater.
> He broke down their strongholds
> and devastated their towns.
> The land and all who were in it
> were terrified by his roaring.
> Then the nations came against him,
> those from regions round about.
> They spread their net for him,
> and he was trapped in their pit.

With hooks they pulled him into a cage
and brought him to the king of Babylon.

They put him in prison,
so his roar was heard no longer
on the mountains of Israel.

" 'Your mother was like a vine in your vineyard
planted by the water;
it was fruitful and full of branches
because of abundant water.

Its branches were strong,
fit for a ruler's scepter.
It towered high
above the thick foliage,
conspicuous for its height
and for its many branches.

But it was uprooted in fury
and thrown to the ground.
The east wind made it shrivel,
it was stripped of its fruit;
its strong branches withered
and fire consumed them.

Now it is planted in the desert,
in a dry and thirsty land.
Fire spread from one of its main branches
and consumed its fruit.

No strong branch is left on it
fit for a ruler's scepter.'

"This is a lament and is to be used as a lament."

In the seventh year, in the fifth month on the tenth day, some of the elders of Israel came to inquire of the Lord, and they sat down in front of me.

Then the word of the Lord came to me: "Son of man, speak to the elders of Israel and say to them, 'This is what the Sovereign Lord says: Have you come to inquire of me? As surely as I live, I will not let you inquire of me, declares the Sovereign Lord.'

"Will you judge them? Will you judge them, son of man? Then confront them with the detestable practices of their ancestors and say to them: 'This is what the Sovereign Lord says: On the day I chose Israel, I swore with uplifted hand to the descendants of Jacob and revealed myself to them in Egypt. With uplifted hand I said to them, "I am the LORD your God." On that day I swore to them that I would bring them out of Egypt into a land I had searched out for them, a land flowing with milk and honey, the most beautiful of all lands. And I said to them, "Each of you, get rid of the vile images you have set your eyes on, and do not defile yourselves with the idols of Egypt. I am the LORD your God."

" 'But they rebelled against me and would not listen to me; they did not get rid of the vile images they had set their eyes on, nor did they forsake the idols of Egypt. So I said I would pour out my wrath on them and spend my anger against them in Egypt. But for the sake of my name, I brought them out of Egypt. I did it to keep my name from being profaned in the eyes of the nations among whom they lived and in whose sight I had revealed myself to the Israelites. Therefore I led them out of Egypt and brought them into the wilderness. I gave them my decrees and made known to them my laws, by which the person who obeys them will live. Also I gave them my Sabbaths as a sign between us, so they would know that I the LORD made them holy.

" 'Yet the people of Israel rebelled against me in the wilderness. They did not follow my decrees but rejected my laws — by which the person who obeys them will live — and they utterly desecrated my Sabbaths. So I said I would pour out my wrath on them and destroy them in the wilderness. But for the sake of my name I did what would keep it from being profaned in the eyes of the nations in whose sight I had brought them out. Also with uplifted hand I swore to them in the wilderness that I would not bring them into the land I had given them — a land flowing with milk and honey, the most beautiful of all lands — because they rejected my laws and did not follow my decrees and desecrated my Sabbaths. For their hearts were devoted to their idols. Yet I looked on them with pity and did not destroy them or put an end to them in the wilderness. I said to their children in the wilderness, "Do not follow the statutes of your parents or keep their laws or defile yourselves with their idols. I am the LORD your God; follow my decrees and be careful to keep my laws. Keep my Sabbaths holy, that they may be a sign between us. Then you will know that I am the LORD your God."

" 'But the children rebelled against me: They did not follow my decrees, they were not careful to keep my laws, of which I said, "The person who obeys them will live by them," and they desecrated my Sabbaths. So I said I would pour out my wrath on them and spend my anger against them in the wilderness. But I withheld my hand, and for the sake of my name I did what would keep it from being profaned in the eyes of the nations in whose sight I had brought them out. Also with uplifted hand I swore to them in the wilderness that I would disperse them among the nations and scatter them through the countries, because they had not obeyed my laws but had rejected my decrees and desecrated my Sabbaths, and their eyes lusted after their parents' idols. So I gave them other statutes that were not good and laws through which they could not live; I defiled them through their gifts — the sacrifice of every firstborn — that I might fill them with horror so they would know that I am the LORD.'

"Therefore, son of man, speak to the people of Israel and say to them, 'This is what the Sovereign LORD says: In this also your ancestors blasphemed me by being unfaithful to me: When I brought them into the land I had sworn to give them and they saw any high hill or any leafy tree, there they offered their sacrifices, made offerings that aroused my anger, presented their fragrant incense and poured out their drink offerings. Then I said to them: What is this high place you go to?' " (It is called Bamah to this day.)

"Therefore say to the Israelites: 'This is what the Sovereign LORD says: Will you defile yourselves the way your ancestors did and lust after their vile images? When you offer your gifts — the sacrifice of your children in the fire — you continue to defile yourselves with all your idols to this day. Am I to let you inquire of me, you Israelites? As surely as I live, declares the Sovereign LORD, I will not let you inquire of me.

" 'You say, "We want to be like the nations, like the peoples of the world, who serve wood and stone." But what you have in mind will never happen. As surely as I live, declares the Sovereign LORD, I will reign over you with a mighty hand and an outstretched arm and with outpoured wrath. I will bring you from the nations and gather you from the countries where you have been scattered — with a mighty hand and an outstretched arm and with outpoured wrath. I will bring you into the wilderness of the nations and there, face to face, I will execute judgment upon you. As I judged your ancestors in the wilderness of the land of Egypt, so I will judge you, declares the Sovereign LORD. I will take note of you as you pass under my rod, and I will bring you into the bond of the covenant. I will purge you of those who revolt and rebel against me. Although I will bring them out of the land where they are living, yet they will not enter the land of Israel. Then you will know that I am the LORD.

" 'As for you, people of Israel, this is what the Sovereign LORD says: Go and serve your idols, every one of you! But afterward you will surely listen to me and no longer profane my holy name with your gifts and idols. For on my holy mountain, the high mountain of Israel, declares the Sovereign LORD, there in the land all the people of Israel will serve me, and there I will accept them. There I will require your offerings and your choice gifts, along with all your holy sacrifices. I will accept you as fragrant incense when I bring you out from the nations and gather you from the countries where you have been scattered, and I will be proved holy through you in the sight of the nations. Then you will know that I am the Lord, when I bring you into the land of Israel, the land I had sworn with uplifted hand to give to your ancestors. There you will remember your conduct and all the actions by which you have defiled yourselves, and you will loathe yourselves for all the evil you have done. You will know that I am the Lord, when I deal with you for my name's sake and not according to your evil ways and your corrupt practices, you people of Israel, declares the Sovereign Lord.'"

The word of the Lord came to me: "Son of man, set your face toward the south; preach against the south and prophesy against the forest of the southland. Say to the southern forest: 'Hear the word of the Lord. This is what the Sovereign Lord says: I am about to set fire to you, and it will consume all your trees, both green and dry. The blazing flame will not be quenched, and every face from south to north will be scorched by it. Everyone will see that I the Lord have kindled it; it will not be quenched.'"

Then I said, "Sovereign Lord, they are saying of me, 'Isn't he just telling parables?'"

The word of the Lord came to me: "Son of man, set your face against Jerusalem and preach against the sanctuary. Prophesy against the land of Israel and say to her: 'This is what the Lord says: I am against you. I will draw my sword from its sheath and cut off from you both the righteous and the wicked. Because I am going to cut off the righteous and the wicked, my sword will be unsheathed against everyone from south to north. Then all people will know that I the Lord have drawn my sword from its sheath; it will not return again.'

"Therefore groan, son of man! Groan before them with broken heart and bitter grief. And when they ask you, 'Why are you groaning?' you shall say, 'Because of the news that is coming. Every heart will melt with fear and every hand go limp; every spirit will become faint and every leg will be wet with urine.' It is coming! It will surely take place, declares the Sovereign Lord."

The word of the Lord came to me: "Son of man, prophesy and say, 'This is what the Lord says:

> " 'A sword, a sword,
>> sharpened and polished—
>
>> sharpened for the slaughter,
>> polished to flash like lightning!

" 'Shall we rejoice in the scepter of my royal son? The sword despises every such stick.

> " 'The sword is appointed to be polished,
>> to be grasped with the hand;
>
>> it is sharpened and polished,
>> made ready for the hand of the slayer.
>
> Cry out and wail, son of man,
>> for it is against my people;
>> it is against all the princes of Israel.
>
> They are thrown to the sword
>> along with my people.
>> Therefore beat your breast.

" 'Testing will surely come. And what if even the scepter, which the sword despises, does not continue? declares the Sovereign LORD.'

> "So then, son of man, prophesy
>> and strike your hands together.
>
> Let the sword strike twice,
>> even three times.
>
> It is a sword for slaughter—
>> a sword for great slaughter,
>> closing in on them from every side.
>
> So that hearts may melt with fear
>> and the fallen be many,
>
> I have stationed the sword for slaughter
>> at all their gates.
>
> Look! It is forged to strike like lightning,
>> it is grasped for slaughter.
>
> Slash to the right, you sword,
>> then to the left,
>> wherever your blade is turned.
>
> I too will strike my hands together,
>> and my wrath will subside.
>> I the LORD have spoken."

The word of the LORD came to me: "Son of man, mark out two roads for the sword of the king of Babylon to take, both starting from the same country. Make a signpost where the road branches off to the city. Mark out one road for the sword to come against Rabbah of the Ammonites and another against Judah and fortified Jerusalem. For the king of Babylon will stop at the fork in the road, at the junction of the two roads, to seek an omen: He will cast lots with arrows, he will consult his idols, he will examine the liver. Into his right hand will come the lot for Jerusalem, where he is to set up battering rams, to give the command to slaughter, to sound the battle cry, to set battering rams against the gates, to build a ramp and to erect siege works. It will seem like a false omen to those who have sworn allegiance to him, but he will remind them of their guilt and take them captive.

"Therefore this is what the Sovereign LORD says: 'Because you people have brought to mind your guilt by your open rebellion, revealing your sins in all that you do—because you have done this, you will be taken captive.

"'You profane and wicked prince of Israel, whose day has come, whose time of punishment has reached its climax, this is what the Sovereign LORD says: Take off the turban, remove the crown. It will not be as it was: The lowly will be exalted and the exalted will be brought low. A ruin! A ruin! I will make it a ruin! The crown will not be restored until he to whom it rightfully belongs shall come; to him I will give it.'

"And you, son of man, prophesy and say, 'This is what the Sovereign LORD says about the Ammonites and their insults:

> "'A sword, a sword,
> drawn for the slaughter,
>
> polished to consume
> and to flash like lightning!
>
> Despite false visions concerning you
> and lying divinations about you,
>
> it will be laid on the necks
> of the wicked who are to be slain,
>
> whose day has come,
> whose time of punishment has reached its climax.
>
> "'Let the sword return to its sheath.
> In the place where you were created,
>
> in the land of your ancestry,
> I will judge you.

I will pour out my wrath on you
and breathe out my fiery anger against you;
I will deliver you into the hands of brutal men,
men skilled in destruction.
You will be fuel for the fire,
your blood will be shed in your land,
you will be remembered no more;
for I the Lord have spoken.'"

The word of the Lord came to me:

"Son of man, will you judge her? Will you judge this city of bloodshed? Then confront her with all her detestable practices and say: 'This is what the Sovereign Lord says: You city that brings on herself doom by shedding blood in her midst and defiles herself by making idols, you have become guilty because of the blood you have shed and have become defiled by the idols you have made. You have brought your days to a close, and the end of your years has come. Therefore I will make you an object of scorn to the nations and a laughingstock to all the countries. Those who are near and those who are far away will mock you, you infamous city, full of turmoil.

" 'See how each of the princes of Israel who are in you uses his power to shed blood. In you they have treated father and mother with contempt; in you they have oppressed the foreigner and mistreated the fatherless and the widow. You have despised my holy things and desecrated my Sabbaths. In you are slanderers who are bent on shedding blood; in you are those who eat at the mountain shrines and commit lewd acts. In you are those who dishonor their father's bed; in you are those who violate women during their period, when they are ceremonially unclean. In you one man commits a detestable offense with his neighbor's wife, another shamefully defiles his daughter-in-law, and another violates his sister, his own father's daughter. In you are people who accept bribes to shed blood; you take interest and make a profit from the poor. You extort unjust gain from your neighbors. And you have forgotten me, declares the Sovereign Lord.

" 'I will surely strike my hands together at the unjust gain you have made and at the blood you have shed in your midst. Will your courage endure or your hands be strong in the day I deal with you? I the Lord have spoken, and I will do it. I will disperse you among the nations and scatter you through the countries; and I will put an end to your uncleanness. When you have been defiled in the eyes of the nations, you will know that I am the Lord.'"

Then the word of the LORD came to me: "Son of man, the people of Israel have become dross to me; all of them are the copper, tin, iron and lead left inside a furnace. They are but the dross of silver. Therefore this is what the Sovereign LORD says: 'Because you have all become dross, I will gather you into Jerusalem. As silver, copper, iron, lead and tin are gathered into a furnace to be melted with a fiery blast, so will I gather you in my anger and my wrath and put you inside the city and melt you. I will gather you and I will blow on you with my fiery wrath, and you will be melted inside her. As silver is melted in a furnace, so you will be melted inside her, and you will know that I the LORD have poured out my wrath on you.'"

Again the word of the LORD came to me: "Son of man, say to the land, 'You are a land that has not been cleansed or rained on in the day of wrath.' There is a conspiracy of her princes within her like a roaring lion tearing its prey; they devour people, take treasures and precious things and make many widows within her. Her priests do violence to my law and profane my holy things; they do not distinguish between the holy and the common; they teach that there is no difference between the unclean and the clean; and they shut their eyes to the keeping of my Sabbaths, so that I am profaned among them. Her officials within her are like wolves tearing their prey; they shed blood and kill people to make unjust gain. Her prophets whitewash these deeds for them by false visions and lying divinations. They say, 'This is what the Sovereign LORD says'—when the LORD has not spoken. The people of the land practice extortion and commit robbery; they oppress the poor and needy and mistreat the foreigner, denying them justice.

"I looked for someone among them who would build up the wall and stand before me in the gap on behalf of the land so I would not have to destroy it, but I found no one. So I will pour out my wrath on them and consume them with my fiery anger, bringing down on their own heads all they have done, declares the Sovereign LORD."

The word of the LORD came to me: "Son of man, there were two women, daughters of the same mother. They became prostitutes in Egypt, engaging in prostitution from their youth. In that land their breasts were fondled and their virgin bosoms caressed. The older was named Oholah, and her sister was Oholibah. They were mine and gave birth to sons and daughters. Oholah is Samaria, and Oholibah is Jerusalem.

"Oholah engaged in prostitution while she was still mine; and she lusted after her lovers, the Assyrians — warriors clothed in blue, governors and commanders, all of them handsome young men, and mounted horsemen. She gave herself as a prostitute to all the elite of the Assyrians and defiled herself with all the idols of everyone she lusted after. She did not give up the prostitution she began in Egypt, when during her youth men slept with her, caressed her virgin bosom and poured out their lust on her.

"Therefore I delivered her into the hands of her lovers, the Assyrians, for whom she lusted. They stripped her naked, took away her sons and daughters and killed her with the sword. She became a byword among women, and punishment was inflicted on her.

"Her sister Oholibah saw this, yet in her lust and prostitution she was more depraved than her sister. She too lusted after the Assyrians — governors and commanders, warriors in full dress, mounted horsemen, all handsome young men. I saw that she too defiled herself; both of them went the same way.

"But she carried her prostitution still further. She saw men portrayed on a wall, figures of Chaldeans portrayed in red, with belts around their waists and flowing turbans on their heads; all of them looked like Babylonian chariot officers, natives of Chaldea. As soon as she saw them, she lusted after them and sent messengers to them in Chaldea. Then the Babylonians came to her, to the bed of love, and in their lust they defiled her. After she had been defiled by them, she turned away from them in disgust. When she carried on her prostitution openly and exposed her naked body, I turned away from her in disgust, just as I had turned away from her sister. Yet she became more and more promiscuous as she recalled the days of her youth, when she was a prostitute in Egypt. There she lusted after her lovers, whose genitals were like those of donkeys and whose emission was like that of horses. So you longed for the lewdness of your youth, when in Egypt your bosom was caressed and your young breasts fondled.

"Therefore, Oholibah, this is what the Sovereign Lord says: I will stir up your lovers against you, those you turned away from in disgust, and I will bring them against you from every side — the Babylonians and all the Chaldeans, the men of Pekod and Shoa and Koa, and all the Assyrians with them, handsome young men, all of them governors and commanders, chariot officers and men of high rank, all mounted on horses. They will come against you with weapons, chariots and wagons and with a throng of people; they will take up positions against you on every side with large and small shields and with helmets. I will turn you over to them for punishment, and they will punish you according to their standards. I will direct my jealous anger against you, and they will deal with you in fury. They will cut off your noses and your ears, and those of you who are left will fall by the sword. They will take away your sons and daughters, and those of you who are left will be consumed by fire. They will also strip you of your clothes and take your fine jewelry. So I will put a stop to the lewdness and prostitution you began in Egypt. You will not look on these things with longing or remember Egypt anymore.

"For this is what the Sovereign Lord says: I am about to deliver you into the hands of those you hate, to those you turned away from in disgust. They will deal with you in hatred and take away everything you have worked for. They will leave you stark naked, and the shame of your prostitution will be exposed. Your lewdness and promiscuity have brought this on you, because you lusted after the nations and defiled yourself with their idols. You have gone the way of your sister; so I will put her cup into your hand.

"This is what the Sovereign Lord says:

> "You will drink your sister's cup,
> a cup large and deep;
> it will bring scorn and derision,
> for it holds so much.
>
> You will be filled with drunkenness and sorrow,
> the cup of ruin and desolation,
> the cup of your sister Samaria.
>
> You will drink it and drain it dry
> and chew on its pieces —
> and you will tear your breasts.

I have spoken, declares the Sovereign Lord.

"Therefore this is what the Sovereign Lord says: Since you have forgotten me and turned your back on me, you must bear the consequences of your lewdness and prostitution."

The Lord said to me: "Son of man, will you judge Oholah and Oholibah? Then confront them with their detestable practices, for they have committed adultery and blood is on their hands. They committed adultery with their idols; they even sacrificed their children, whom they bore to me, as food for them. They have also done this to me: At that same time they defiled my sanctuary and desecrated my Sabbaths. On the very day they sacrificed their children to their idols, they entered my sanctuary and desecrated it. That is what they did in my house.

"They even sent messengers for men who came from far away, and when they arrived you bathed yourself for them, applied eye makeup and put on your jewelry. You sat on an elegant couch, with a table spread before it on which you had placed the incense and olive oil that belonged to me.

"The noise of a carefree crowd was around her; drunkards were brought from the desert along with men from the rabble, and they put bracelets on the wrists of the woman and her sister and beautiful crowns on their heads. Then I said about the one worn out by adultery, 'Now let them use her as a prostitute, for that is all she is.' And they slept with her. As men sleep with a prostitute, so they slept with those lewd women, Oholah and Oholibah. But righteous judges will sentence them to the punishment of women who commit adultery and shed blood, because they are adulterous and blood is on their hands.

"This is what the Sovereign LORD says: Bring a mob against them and give them over to terror and plunder. The mob will stone them and cut them down with their swords; they will kill their sons and daughters and burn down their houses.

"So I will put an end to lewdness in the land, that all women may take warning and not imitate you. You will suffer the penalty for your lewdness and bear the consequences of your sins of idolatry. Then you will know that I am the Sovereign LORD."

In the ninth year, in the tenth month on the tenth day, the word of the LORD came to me: "Son of man, record this date, this very date, because the king of Babylon has laid siege to Jerusalem this very day. Tell this rebellious people a parable and say to them: 'This is what the Sovereign LORD says:

> " 'Put on the cooking pot; put it on
> and pour water into it.
>
> Put into it the pieces of meat,
> all the choice pieces — the leg and the shoulder.
>
> Fill it with the best of these bones;
> take the pick of the flock.
>
> Pile wood beneath it for the bones;
> bring it to a boil
> and cook the bones in it.

" 'For this is what the Sovereign LORD says:

> " 'Woe to the city of bloodshed,
> to the pot now encrusted,
> whose deposit will not go away!
>
> Take the meat out piece by piece
> in whatever order it comes.

" 'For the blood she shed is in her midst:
She poured it on the bare rock;

she did not pour it on the ground,
where the dust would cover it.

To stir up wrath and take revenge
I put her blood on the bare rock,
so that it would not be covered.

" 'Therefore this is what the Sovereign Lord says:

" 'Woe to the city of bloodshed!
I, too, will pile the wood high.

So heap on the wood
and kindle the fire.

Cook the meat well,
mixing in the spices;
and let the bones be charred.

Then set the empty pot on the coals
till it becomes hot and its copper glows,

so that its impurities may be melted
and its deposit burned away.

It has frustrated all efforts;
its heavy deposit has not been removed,
not even by fire.

" 'Now your impurity is lewdness. Because I tried to cleanse you but you would not be cleansed from your impurity, you will not be clean again until my wrath against you has subsided.

" 'I the Lord have spoken. The time has come for me to act. I will not hold back; I will not have pity, nor will I relent. You will be judged according to your conduct and your actions, declares the Sovereign Lord.' "

The word of the Lord came to me: "Son of man, with one blow I am about to take away from you the delight of your eyes. Yet do not lament or weep or shed any tears. Groan quietly; do not mourn for the dead. Keep your turban fastened and your sandals on your feet; do not cover your mustache and beard or eat the customary food of mourners."

So I spoke to the people in the morning, and in the evening my wife died. The next morning I did as I had been commanded.

Then the people asked me, "Won't you tell us what these things have to do with us? Why are you acting like this?"

So I said to them, "The word of the Lord came to me: Say to the people of Israel, 'This is what the Sovereign Lord says: I am about to desecrate my sanctuary—the stronghold in which you take pride, the delight of your eyes, the object of your affection. The sons and daughters you left behind will fall by the sword. And you will do as I have done. You will not cover your mustache and beard or eat the customary food of mourners. You will keep your turbans on your heads and your sandals on your feet. You will not mourn or weep but will waste away because of your sins and groan among yourselves. Ezekiel will be a sign to you; you will do just as he has done. When this happens, you will know that I am the Sovereign Lord.'

"And you, son of man, on the day I take away their stronghold, their joy and glory, the delight of their eyes, their heart's desire, and their sons and daughters as well—on that day a fugitive will come to tell you the news. At that time your mouth will be opened; you will speak with him and will no longer be silent. So you will be a sign to them, and they will know that I am the Lord."

T he word of the Lord came to me: "Son of man, set your face against the Ammonites and prophesy against them. Say to them, 'Hear the word of the Sovereign Lord. This is what the Sovereign Lord says: Because you said "Aha!" over my sanctuary when it was desecrated and over the land of Israel when it was laid waste and over the people of Judah when they went into exile, therefore I am going to give you to the people of the East as a possession. They will set up their camps and pitch their tents among you; they will eat your fruit and drink your milk. I will turn Rabbah into a pasture for camels and Ammon into a resting place for sheep. Then you will know that I am the Lord. For this is what the Sovereign Lord says: Because you have clapped your hands and stamped your feet, rejoicing with all the malice of your heart against the land of Israel, therefore I will stretch out my hand against you and give you as plunder to the nations. I will wipe you out from among the nations and exterminate you from the countries. I will destroy you, and you will know that I am the Lord.'"

"This is what the Sovereign Lord says: 'Because Moab and Seir said, "Look, Judah has become like all the other nations," therefore I will expose the flank of Moab, beginning at its frontier towns—Beth Jeshimoth, Baal Meon and Kiriathaim—the glory of that land. I will give Moab along with the Ammonites to the people of the East as a possession, so that the Ammonites will not be remembered among the nations; and I will inflict punishment on Moab. Then they will know that I am the LORD.'"

"This is what the Sovereign LORD says: 'Because Edom took revenge on Judah and became very guilty by doing so, therefore this is what the Sovereign LORD says: I will stretch out my hand against Edom and kill both man and beast. I will lay it waste, and from Teman to Dedan they will fall by the sword. I will take vengeance on Edom by the hand of my people Israel, and they will deal with Edom in accordance with my anger and my wrath; they will know my vengeance, declares the Sovereign LORD.'"

"This is what the Sovereign LORD says: 'Because the Philistines acted in vengeance and took revenge with malice in their hearts, and with ancient hostility sought to destroy Judah, therefore this is what the Sovereign LORD says: I am about to stretch out my hand against the Philistines, and I will wipe out the Kerethites and destroy those remaining along the coast. I will carry out great vengeance on them and punish them in my wrath. Then they will know that I am the LORD, when I take vengeance on them.'"

In the eleventh month of the twelfth year, on the first day of the month, the word of the LORD came to me: "Son of man, because Tyre has said of Jerusalem, 'Aha! The gate to the nations is broken, and its doors have swung open to me; now that she lies in ruins I will prosper,' therefore this is what the Sovereign LORD says: I am against you, Tyre, and I will bring many nations against you, like the sea casting up its waves. They will destroy the walls of Tyre and pull down her towers; I will scrape away her rubble and make her a bare rock. Out in the sea she will become a place to spread fishnets, for I have spoken, declares the Sovereign LORD. She will become plunder for the nations, and her settlements on the mainland will be ravaged by the sword. Then they will know that I am the LORD.

"For this is what the Sovereign LORD says: From the north I am going to bring against Tyre Nebuchadnezzar king of Babylon, king of kings, with horses and chariots, with horsemen and a great army. He will ravage your settlements on the mainland with the sword; he will set up siege works against you, build a ramp up to your walls and raise his shields against you. He will direct the blows of his battering rams against your walls and demolish your towers with his weapons. His horses will be so many that they will cover you with dust. Your walls will tremble at the noise of the warhorses, wagons and chariots when he enters your gates as men enter a city whose walls have been broken through. The hooves of his horses will trample all your streets; he will kill your people with the sword, and your strong pillars will fall to the ground. They will plunder your wealth and loot your merchandise; they will break down your walls and demolish your fine houses and throw your stones, timber and rubble into the sea. I will put an end to your noisy songs, and the music of your harps will be heard no more. I will make you a bare rock, and you will become a place to spread fishnets. You will never be rebuilt, for I the LORD have spoken, declares the Sovereign LORD.

"This is what the Sovereign LORD says to Tyre: Will not the coastlands tremble at the sound of your fall, when the wounded groan and the slaughter takes place in you? Then all the princes of the coast will step down from their thrones and lay aside their robes and take off their embroidered garments. Clothed with terror, they will sit on the ground, trembling every moment, appalled at you. Then they will take up a lament concerning you and say to you:

> " 'How you are destroyed, city of renown,
>   peopled by men of the sea!
>
> You were a power on the seas,
>   you and your citizens;
>
> you put your terror
>   on all who lived there.
>
> Now the coastlands tremble
>   on the day of your fall;
> the islands in the sea
>   are terrified at your collapse.'

"This is what the Sovereign LORD says: When I make you a desolate city, like cities no longer inhabited, and when I bring the ocean depths over you and its vast waters cover you, then I will bring you down with those who go down to the pit, to the people of long ago. I will make you dwell in the earth below, as in ancient ruins, with those who go down to the pit, and you will not return or take your place in the land of the living. I will bring you to a horrible end and you will be no more. You will be sought, but you will never again be found, declares the Sovereign LORD."

The word of the LORD came to me: "Son of man, take up a lament concerning Tyre. Say to Tyre, situated at the gateway to the sea, merchant of peoples on many coasts, 'This is what the Sovereign LORD says:

> " 'You say, Tyre,
>   "I am perfect in beauty."

Your domain was on the high seas;
your builders brought your beauty to perfection.
They made all your timbers
of juniper from Senir;
they took a cedar from Lebanon
to make a mast for you.
Of oaks from Bashan
they made your oars;
of cypress wood from the coasts of Cyprus
they made your deck, adorned with ivory.
Fine embroidered linen from Egypt was your sail
and served as your banner;
your awnings were of blue and purple
from the coasts of Elishah.
Men of Sidon and Arvad were your oarsmen;
your skilled men, Tyre, were aboard as your sailors.
Veteran craftsmen of Byblos were on board
as shipwrights to caulk your seams.
All the ships of the sea and their sailors
came alongside to trade for your wares.

" 'Men of Persia, Lydia and Put
served as soldiers in your army.
They hung their shields and helmets on your walls,
bringing you splendor.
Men of Arvad and Helek
guarded your walls on every side;
men of Gammad
were in your towers.
They hung their shields around your walls;
they brought your beauty to perfection.

" 'Tarshish did business with you because of your great wealth of goods; they exchanged silver, iron, tin and lead for your merchandise.

" 'Greece, Tubal and Meshek did business with you; they traded human beings and articles of bronze for your wares.

" 'Men of Beth Togarmah exchanged chariot horses, cavalry horses and mules for your merchandise.

" 'The men of Rhodes traded with you, and many coastlands were your customers; they paid you with ivory tusks and ebony.

" 'Aram did business with you because of your many products;

they exchanged turquoise, purple fabric, embroidered work, fine linen, coral and rubies for your merchandise.

"'Judah and Israel traded with you; they exchanged wheat from Minnith and confections, honey, olive oil and balm for your wares.

"'Damascus did business with you because of your many products and great wealth of goods. They offered wine from Helbon, wool from Zahar and casks of wine from Izal in exchange for your wares: wrought iron, cassia and calamus.

"'Dedan traded in saddle blankets with you.

"'Arabia and all the princes of Kedar were your customers; they did business with you in lambs, rams and goats.

"'The merchants of Sheba and Raamah traded with you; for your merchandise they exchanged the finest of all kinds of spices and precious stones, and gold.

"'Harran, Kanneh and Eden and merchants of Sheba, Ashur and Kilmad traded with you. In your marketplace they traded with you beautiful garments, blue fabric, embroidered work and multicolored rugs with cords twisted and tightly knotted.

> "'The ships of Tarshish serve
> as carriers for your wares.
>
> You are filled with heavy cargo
> as you sail the sea.
>
> Your oarsmen take you
> out to the high seas.
>
> But the east wind will break you to pieces
> far out at sea.
>
> Your wealth, merchandise and wares,
> your mariners, sailors and shipwrights,
>
> your merchants and all your soldiers,
> and everyone else on board
>
> will sink into the heart of the sea
> on the day of your shipwreck.
>
> The shorelands will quake
> when your sailors cry out.
>
> All who handle the oars
> will abandon their ships;
>
> the mariners and all the sailors
> will stand on the shore.
>
> They will raise their voice
> and cry bitterly over you;

> they will sprinkle dust on their heads
>   and roll in ashes.

> They will shave their heads because of you
>   and will put on sackcloth.

> They will weep over you with anguish of soul
>   and with bitter mourning.

> As they wail and mourn over you,
>   they will take up a lament concerning you:

> "Who was ever silenced like Tyre,
>   surrounded by the sea?"

> When your merchandise went out on the seas,
>   you satisfied many nations;

> with your great wealth and your wares
>   you enriched the kings of the earth.

> Now you are shattered by the sea
>   in the depths of the waters;

> your wares and all your company
>   have gone down with you.

> All who live in the coastlands
>   are appalled at you;

> their kings shudder with horror
>   and their faces are distorted with fear.

> The merchants among the nations scoff at you;
>   you have come to a horrible end
>   and will be no more.' "

The word of the LORD came to me: "Son of man, say to the ruler of Tyre, 'This is what the Sovereign LORD says:

> " 'In the pride of your heart
>   you say, "I am a god;

> I sit on the throne of a god
>   in the heart of the seas."

> But you are a mere mortal and not a god,
>   though you think you are as wise as a god.

> Are you wiser than Daniel?
>   Is no secret hidden from you?

> By your wisdom and understanding
>   you have gained wealth for yourself

and amassed gold and silver
in your treasuries.

By your great skill in trading
you have increased your wealth,

and because of your wealth
your heart has grown proud.

" 'Therefore this is what the Sovereign LORD says:

" 'Because you think you are wise,
as wise as a god,

I am going to bring foreigners against you,
the most ruthless of nations;

they will draw their swords against your beauty and
wisdom

and pierce your shining splendor.

They will bring you down to the pit,
and you will die a violent death
in the heart of the seas.

Will you then say, "I am a god,"
in the presence of those who kill you?

You will be but a mortal, not a god,
in the hands of those who slay you.

You will die the death of the uncircumcised
at the hands of foreigners.

I have spoken, declares the Sovereign LORD.' "

The word of the LORD came to me: "Son of man, take up a lament
concerning the king of Tyre and say to him: 'This is what the Sovereign LORD says:

" 'You were the seal of perfection,
full of wisdom and perfect in beauty.

You were in Eden,
the garden of God;

every precious stone adorned you:
carnelian, chrysolite and emerald,
topaz, onyx and jasper,
lapis lazuli, turquoise and beryl.

Your settings and mountings were made of gold;
on the day you were created they were prepared.

You were anointed as a guardian cherub,
for so I ordained you.

You were on the holy mount of God;
you walked among the fiery stones.

You were blameless in your ways
from the day you were created
till wickedness was found in you.

Through your widespread trade
you were filled with violence,
and you sinned.

So I drove you in disgrace from the mount
of God,
and I expelled you, guardian cherub,
from among the fiery stones.

Your heart became proud
on account of your beauty,

and you corrupted your wisdom
because of your splendor.

So I threw you to the earth;
I made a spectacle of you before kings.

By your many sins and dishonest trade
you have desecrated your sanctuaries.

So I made a fire come out from you,
and it consumed you,

and I reduced you to ashes on the ground
in the sight of all who were watching.

All the nations who knew you
are appalled at you;

you have come to a horrible end
and will be no more.'"

The word of the LORD came to me: "Son of man, set your face against
Sidon; prophesy against her and say: 'This is what the Sovereign
LORD says:

"'I am against you, Sidon,
and among you I will display my glory.

You will know that I am the LORD,
when I inflict punishment on you
and within you am proved to be holy.

> I will send a plague upon you
> and make blood flow in your streets.

> The slain will fall within you,
> with the sword against you on every side.

> Then you will know that I am the Lord.

" 'No longer will the people of Israel have malicious neighbors who are painful briers and sharp thorns. Then they will know that I am the Sovereign Lord.

" 'This is what the Sovereign Lord says: When I gather the people of Israel from the nations where they have been scattered, I will be proved holy through them in the sight of the nations. Then they will live in their own land, which I gave to my servant Jacob. They will live there in safety and will build houses and plant vineyards; they will live in safety when I inflict punishment on all their neighbors who maligned them. Then they will know that I am the Lord their God.' "

In the tenth year, in the tenth month on the twelfth day, the word of the Lord came to me: "Son of man, set your face against Pharaoh king of Egypt and prophesy against him and against all Egypt. Speak to him and say: 'This is what the Sovereign Lord says:

> " 'I am against you, Pharaoh king of Egypt,
> you great monster lying among your streams.

> You say, "The Nile belongs to me;
> I made it for myself."

> But I will put hooks in your jaws
> and make the fish of your streams stick to your scales.

> I will pull you out from among your streams,
> with all the fish sticking to your scales.

> I will leave you in the desert,
> you and all the fish of your streams.

> You will fall on the open field
> and not be gathered or picked up.

> I will give you as food
> to the beasts of the earth and the birds of the sky.

Then all who live in Egypt will know that I am the Lord.

" 'You have been a staff of reed for the people of Israel. When they grasped you with their hands, you splintered and you tore open their shoulders; when they leaned on you, you broke and their backs were wrenched.

" 'Therefore this is what the Sovereign LORD says: I will bring a sword against you and kill both man and beast. Egypt will become a desolate wasteland. Then they will know that I am the LORD.

" 'Because you said, "The Nile is mine; I made it," therefore I am against you and against your streams, and I will make the land of Egypt a ruin and a desolate waste from Migdol to Aswan, as far as the border of Cush. The foot of neither man nor beast will pass through it; no one will live there for forty years. I will make the land of Egypt desolate among devastated lands, and her cities will lie desolate forty years among ruined cities. And I will disperse the Egyptians among the nations and scatter them through the countries.

" 'Yet this is what the Sovereign LORD says: At the end of forty years I will gather the Egyptians from the nations where they were scattered. I will bring them back from captivity and return them to Upper Egypt, the land of their ancestry. There they will be a lowly kingdom. It will be the lowliest of kingdoms and will never again exalt itself above the other nations. I will make it so weak that it will never again rule over the nations. Egypt will no longer be a source of confidence for the people of Israel but will be a reminder of their sin in turning to her for help. Then they will know that I am the Sovereign LORD.' "

In the twenty-seventh year, in the first month on the first day, the word of the LORD came to me: "Son of man, Nebuchadnezzar king of Babylon drove his army in a hard campaign against Tyre; every head was rubbed bare and every shoulder made raw. Yet he and his army got no reward from the campaign he led against Tyre. Therefore this is what the Sovereign LORD says: I am going to give Egypt to Nebuchadnezzar king of Babylon, and he will carry off its wealth. He will loot and plunder the land as pay for his army. I have given him Egypt as a reward for his efforts because he and his army did it for me, declares the Sovereign LORD.

"On that day I will make a horn grow for the Israelites, and I will open your mouth among them. Then they will know that I am the LORD."

The word of the LORD came to me: "Son of man, prophesy and say: 'This is what the Sovereign LORD says:

" 'Wail and say,
    "Alas for that day!"

For the day is near,
the day of the Lord is near—

a day of clouds,
a time of doom for the nations.

A sword will come against Egypt,
and anguish will come upon Cush.

When the slain fall in Egypt,
her wealth will be carried away
and her foundations torn down.

Cush and Libya, Lydia and all Arabia, Kub and the people of the covenant land will fall by the sword along with Egypt.
" 'This is what the Lord says:

" 'The allies of Egypt will fall
and her proud strength will fail.

From Migdol to Aswan
they will fall by the sword within her,
declares the Sovereign Lord.

" 'They will be desolate
among desolate lands,

and their cities will lie
among ruined cities.

Then they will know that I am the Lord,
when I set fire to Egypt
and all her helpers are crushed.

" 'On that day messengers will go out from me in ships to frighten Cush out of her complacency. Anguish will take hold of them on the day of Egypt's doom, for it is sure to come.

" 'This is what the Sovereign Lord says:

" 'I will put an end to the hordes of Egypt
by the hand of Nebuchadnezzar king of Babylon.

He and his army—the most ruthless of nations—
will be brought in to destroy the land.

They will draw their swords against Egypt
and fill the land with the slain.

I will dry up the waters of the Nile
and sell the land to an evil nation;

by the hand of foreigners
I will lay waste the land and everything in it.

I the Lord have spoken.

"'This is what the Sovereign Lord says:

> "'I will destroy the idols
> and put an end to the images in Memphis.
> No longer will there be a prince in Egypt,
> and I will spread fear throughout the land.
> I will lay waste Upper Egypt,
> set fire to Zoan
> and inflict punishment on Thebes.
> I will pour out my wrath on Pelusium,
> the stronghold of Egypt,
> and wipe out the hordes of Thebes.
> I will set fire to Egypt;
> Pelusium will writhe in agony.
> Thebes will be taken by storm;
> Memphis will be in constant distress.
> The young men of Heliopolis and Bubastis
> will fall by the sword,
> and the cities themselves will go into captivity.
> Dark will be the day at Tahpanhes
> when I break the yoke of Egypt;
> there her proud strength will come to an end.
> She will be covered with clouds,
> and her villages will go into captivity.
> So I will inflict punishment on Egypt,
> and they will know that I am the Lord.'"

In the eleventh year, in the first month on the seventh day, the word of the Lord came to me: "Son of man, I have broken the arm of Pharaoh king of Egypt. It has not been bound up to be healed or put in a splint so that it may become strong enough to hold a sword. Therefore this is what the Sovereign Lord says: I am against Pharaoh king of Egypt. I will break both his arms, the good arm as well as the broken one, and make the sword fall from his hand. I will disperse the Egyptians among the nations and scatter them through the countries. I will strengthen the arms of the king of Babylon and put my sword in his hand, but I will break the arms of Pharaoh, and he will groan before him like a mortally wounded man. I will strengthen the arms of the king of Babylon, but the arms of Pharaoh will fall limp. Then they will know that I am the Lord, when I put my sword into the hand of the king of Babylon and he brandishes it against Egypt. I will disperse the Egyptians among the nations and scatter them through the countries. Then they will know that I am the Lord."

In the eleventh year, in the third month on the first day, the word of the Lord came to me: "Son of man, say to Pharaoh king of Egypt and to his hordes:

> " 'Who can be compared with you in majesty?
>
> Consider Assyria, once a cedar in Lebanon,
> with beautiful branches overshadowing the forest;
>
> it towered on high,
> its top above the thick foliage.
>
> The waters nourished it,
> deep springs made it grow tall;
>
> their streams flowed
> all around its base
>
> and sent their channels
> to all the trees of the field.
>
> So it towered higher
> than all the trees of the field;
>
> its boughs increased
> and its branches grew long,
> spreading because of abundant waters.
>
> All the birds of the sky
> nested in its boughs,
>
> all the animals of the wild
> gave birth under its branches;
>
> all the great nations
> lived in its shade.
>
> It was majestic in beauty,
> with its spreading boughs,
>
> for its roots went down
> to abundant waters.
>
> The cedars in the garden of God
> could not rival it,
>
> nor could the junipers
> equal its boughs,
>
> nor could the plane trees
> compare with its branches—

> no tree in the garden of God
> could match its beauty.
>
> I made it beautiful
> with abundant branches,
>
> the envy of all the trees of Eden
> in the garden of God.

" 'Therefore this is what the Sovereign LORD says: Because the great cedar towered over the thick foliage, and because it was proud of its height, I gave it into the hands of the ruler of the nations, for him to deal with according to its wickedness. I cast it aside, and the most ruthless of foreign nations cut it down and left it. Its boughs fell on the mountains and in all the valleys; its branches lay broken in all the ravines of the land. All the nations of the earth came out from under its shade and left it. All the birds settled on the fallen tree, and all the wild animals lived among its branches. Therefore no other trees by the waters are ever to tower proudly on high, lifting their tops above the thick foliage. No other trees so well-watered are ever to reach such a height; they are all destined for death, for the earth below, among mortals who go down to the realm of the dead.

" 'This is what the Sovereign LORD says: On the day it was brought down to the realm of the dead I covered the deep springs with mourning for it; I held back its streams, and its abundant waters were restrained. Because of it I clothed Lebanon with gloom, and all the trees of the field withered away. I made the nations tremble at the sound of its fall when I brought it down to the realm of the dead to be with those who go down to the pit. Then all the trees of Eden, the choicest and best of Lebanon, the well-watered trees, were consoled in the earth below. They too, like the great cedar, had gone down to the realm of the dead, to those killed by the sword, along with the armed men who lived in its shade among the nations.

" 'Which of the trees of Eden can be compared with you in splendor and majesty? Yet you, too, will be brought down with the trees of Eden to the earth below; you will lie among the uncircumcised, with those killed by the sword.

" 'This is Pharaoh and all his hordes, declares the Sovereign LORD.' "

In the twelfth year, in the twelfth month on the first day, the word of the LORD came to me: "Son of man, take up a lament concerning Pharaoh king of Egypt and say to him:

> " 'You are like a lion among the nations;
> you are like a monster in the seas
>
> thrashing about in your streams,
> churning the water with your feet
> and muddying the streams.

" 'This is what the Sovereign Lord says:

> " 'With a great throng of people
> I will cast my net over you,
> and they will haul you up in my net.
>
> I will throw you on the land
> and hurl you on the open field.
>
> I will let all the birds of the sky settle on you
> and all the animals of the wild gorge themselves on you.
>
> I will spread your flesh on the mountains
> and fill the valleys with your remains.
>
> I will drench the land with your flowing blood
> all the way to the mountains,
> and the ravines will be filled with your flesh.
>
> When I snuff you out, I will cover the heavens
> and darken their stars;
>
> I will cover the sun with a cloud,
> and the moon will not give its light.
>
> All the shining lights in the heavens
> I will darken over you;
> I will bring darkness over your land,
> declares the Sovereign Lord.
>
> I will trouble the hearts of many peoples
> when I bring about your destruction among the nations,
> among lands you have not known.
>
> I will cause many peoples to be appalled at you,
> and their kings will shudder with horror because of you
> when I brandish my sword before them.
>
> On the day of your downfall
> each of them will tremble
> every moment for his life.

" 'For this is what the Sovereign Lord says:

> " 'The sword of the king of Babylon
> will come against you.

I will cause your hordes to fall
by the swords of mighty men—
the most ruthless of all nations.

They will shatter the pride of Egypt,
and all her hordes will be overthrown.

I will destroy all her cattle
from beside abundant waters

no longer to be stirred by the foot of man
or muddied by the hooves of cattle.

Then I will let her waters settle
and make her streams flow like oil,
                    declares the Sovereign LORD.

When I make Egypt desolate
and strip the land of everything in it,

when I strike down all who live there,
then they will know that I am the LORD.'

"This is the lament they will chant for her. The daughters of the nations will chant it; for Egypt and all her hordes they will chant it, declares the Sovereign LORD."

In the twelfth year, on the fifteenth day of the month, the word of the LORD came to me: "Son of man, wail for the hordes of Egypt and consign to the earth below both her and the daughters of mighty nations, along with those who go down to the pit. Say to them, 'Are you more favored than others? Go down and be laid among the uncircumcised.' They will fall among those killed by the sword. The sword is drawn; let her be dragged off with all her hordes. From within the realm of the dead the mighty leaders will say of Egypt and her allies, 'They have come down and they lie with the uncircumcised, with those killed by the sword.'

"Assyria is there with her whole army; she is surrounded by the graves of all her slain, all who have fallen by the sword. Their graves are in the depths of the pit and her army lies around her grave. All who had spread terror in the land of the living are slain, fallen by the sword.

"Elam is there, with all her hordes around her grave. All of them are slain, fallen by the sword. All who had spread terror in the land of the living went down uncircumcised to the earth below. They bear their shame with those who go down to the pit. A bed is made for her among the slain, with all her hordes around her grave. All of them are uncircumcised, killed by the sword. Because their terror had spread in the land of the living, they bear their shame with those who go down to the pit; they are laid among the slain.

"Meshek and Tubal are there, with all their hordes around their graves. All of them are uncircumcised, killed by the sword because they spread their terror in the land of the living. But they do not lie with the fallen warriors of old, who went down to the realm of the dead with their weapons of war — their swords placed under their heads and their shields resting on their bones — though these warriors also had terrorized the land of the living.

"You too, Pharaoh, will be broken and will lie among the uncircumcised, with those killed by the sword.

"Edom is there, her kings and all her princes; despite their power, they are laid with those killed by the sword. They lie with the uncircumcised, with those who go down to the pit.

"All the princes of the north and all the Sidonians are there; they went down with the slain in disgrace despite the terror caused by their power. They lie uncircumcised with those killed by the sword and bear their shame with those who go down to the pit.

"Pharaoh — he and all his army — will see them and he will be consoled for all his hordes that were killed by the sword, declares the Sovereign LORD. Although I had him spread terror in the land of the living, Pharaoh and all his hordes will be laid among the uncircumcised, with those killed by the sword, declares the Sovereign LORD."

T he word of the LORD came to me: "Son of man, speak to your people and say to them: 'When I bring the sword against a land, and the people of the land choose one of their men and make him their watchman, and he sees the sword coming against the land and blows the trumpet to warn the people, then if anyone hears the trumpet but does not heed the warning and the sword comes and takes their life, their blood will be on their own head. Since they heard the sound of the trumpet but did not heed the warning, their blood will be on their own head. If they had heeded the warning, they would have saved themselves. But if the watchman sees the sword coming and does not blow the trumpet to warn the people and the sword comes and takes someone's life, that person's life will be taken because of their sin, but I will hold the watchman accountable for their blood.'

"Son of man, I have made you a watchman for the people of Israel; so hear the word I speak and give them warning from me. When I say to the wicked, 'You wicked person, you will surely die,' and you do not speak out to dissuade them from their ways, that wicked person will die for their sin, and I will hold you accountable for their blood. But if you do warn the wicked person to turn from their ways and they do not do so, they will die for their sin, though you yourself will be saved.

"Son of man, say to the Israelites, 'This is what you are saying: "Our offenses and sins weigh us down, and we are wasting away because of them. How then can we live?"' Say to them, 'As surely as I live, declares the Sovereign LORD, I take no pleasure in the death of the wicked, but rather that they turn from their ways and live. Turn! Turn from your evil ways! Why will you die, people of Israel?'

"Therefore, son of man, say to your people, 'If someone who is righteous disobeys, that person's former righteousness will count for nothing. And if someone who is wicked repents, that person's former wickedness will not bring condemnation. The righteous person who sins will not be allowed to live even though they were formerly righteous.' If I tell a righteous person that they will surely live, but then they trust in their righteousness and do evil, none of the righteous things that person has done will be remembered; they will die for the evil they have done. And if I say to a wicked person, 'You will surely die,' but they then turn away from their sin and do what is just and right — if they give back what they took in pledge for a loan, return what they have stolen, follow the decrees that give life, and do no evil — that person will surely live; they will not die. None of the sins that person has committed will be remembered against them. They have done what is just and right; they will surely live.

"Yet your people say, 'The way of the Lord is not just.' But it is their way that is not just. If a righteous person turns from their righteousness and does evil, they will die for it. And if a wicked person turns away from their wickedness and does what is just and right, they will live by doing so. Yet you Israelites say, 'The way of the Lord is not just.' But I will judge each of you according to your own ways."

In the twelfth year of our exile, in the tenth month on the fifth day, a man who had escaped from Jerusalem came to me and said, "The city has fallen!" Now the evening before the man arrived, the hand of the LORD was on me, and he opened my mouth before the man came to me in the morning. So my mouth was opened and I was no longer silent.

Then the word of the LORD came to me: "Son of man, the people living in those ruins in the land of Israel are saying, 'Abraham was only one man, yet he possessed the land. But we are many; surely the land has been given to us as our possession.' Therefore say to them, 'This is what the Sovereign Lord says: Since you eat meat with the blood still in it and look to your idols and shed blood, should you then possess the land? You rely on your sword, you do detestable things, and each of you defiles his neighbor's wife. Should you then possess the land?'

"Say this to them: 'This is what the Sovereign Lord says: As surely as I live, those who are left in the ruins will fall by the sword, those out in the country I will give to the wild animals to be devoured, and those in strongholds and caves will die of a plague. I will make the land a desolate waste, and her proud strength will come to an end, and the mountains of Israel will become desolate so that no one will cross them. Then they will know that I am the Lord, when I have made the land a desolate waste because of all the detestable things they have done.'

"As for you, son of man, your people are talking together about you by the walls and at the doors of the houses, saying to each other, 'Come and hear the message that has come from the Lord.' My people come to you, as they usually do, and sit before you to hear your words, but they do not put them into practice. Their mouths speak of love, but their hearts are greedy for unjust gain. Indeed, to them you are nothing more than one who sings love songs with a beautiful voice and plays an instrument well, for they hear your words but do not put them into practice.

"When all this comes true—and it surely will—then they will know that a prophet has been among them."

The word of the Lord came to me: "Son of man, prophesy against the shepherds of Israel; prophesy and say to them: 'This is what the Sovereign Lord says: Woe to you shepherds of Israel who only take care of yourselves! Should not shepherds take care of the flock? You eat the curds, clothe yourselves with the wool and slaughter the choice animals, but you do not take care of the flock. You have not strengthened the weak or healed the sick or bound up the injured. You have not brought back the strays or searched for the lost. You have ruled them harshly and brutally. So they were scattered because there was no shepherd, and when they were scattered they became food for all the wild animals. My sheep wandered over all the mountains and on every high hill. They were scattered over the whole earth, and no one searched or looked for them.

" 'Therefore, you shepherds, hear the word of the Lord: As surely as I live, declares the Sovereign Lord, because my flock lacks a shepherd and so has been plundered and has become food for all the wild animals, and because my shepherds did not search for my flock but cared for themselves rather than for my flock, therefore, you shepherds, hear the word of the LORD: This is what the Sovereign LORD says: I am against the shepherds and will hold them accountable for my flock. I will remove them from tending the flock so that the shepherds can no longer feed themselves. I will rescue my flock from their mouths, and it will no longer be food for them.

"'For this is what the Sovereign LORD says: I myself will search for my sheep and look after them. As a shepherd looks after his scattered flock when he is with them, so will I look after my sheep. I will rescue them from all the places where they were scattered on a day of clouds and darkness. I will bring them out from the nations and gather them from the countries, and I will bring them into their own land. I will pasture them on the mountains of Israel, in the ravines and in all the settlements in the land. I will tend them in a good pasture, and the mountain heights of Israel will be their grazing land. There they will lie down in good grazing land, and there they will feed in a rich pasture on the mountains of Israel. I myself will tend my sheep and have them lie down, declares the Sovereign LORD. I will search for the lost and bring back the strays. I will bind up the injured and strengthen the weak, but the sleek and the strong I will destroy. I will shepherd the flock with justice.

"'As for you, my flock, this is what the Sovereign LORD says: I will judge between one sheep and another, and between rams and goats. Is it not enough for you to feed on the good pasture? Must you also trample the rest of your pasture with your feet? Is it not enough for you to drink clear water? Must you also muddy the rest with your feet? Must my flock feed on what you have trampled and drink what you have muddied with your feet?

"'Therefore this is what the Sovereign LORD says to them: See, I myself will judge between the fat sheep and the lean sheep. Because you shove with flank and shoulder, butting all the weak sheep with your horns until you have driven them away, I will save my flock, and they will no longer be plundered. I will judge between one sheep and another. I will place over them one shepherd, my servant David, and he will tend them; he will tend them and be their shepherd. I the LORD will be their God, and my servant David will be prince among them. I the LORD have spoken.

"'I will make a covenant of peace with them and rid the land of savage beasts so that they may live in the wilderness and sleep in the forests in safety. I will make them and the places surrounding my hill a blessing. I will send down showers in season; there will be showers of blessing. The trees will yield their fruit and the ground will yield its crops; the people will be secure in their land. They will know that I am the LORD, when I break the bars of their yoke and rescue them from the hands of those who enslaved them. They will no longer be plundered by the nations, nor will wild animals devour them. They will live in safety, and no one will make them afraid. I will provide for them a land renowned for its crops, and they will no longer be victims of famine in the land or bear the scorn of the nations. Then they will know that I, the LORD their God, am with them and that they, the Israelites, are my people, declares the Sovereign LORD. You are my sheep, the sheep of my pasture, and I am your God, declares the Sovereign LORD.' "

The word of the LORD came to me: "Son of man, set your face against Mount Seir; prophesy against it and say: 'This is what the Sovereign LORD says: I am against you, Mount Seir, and I will stretch out my hand against you and make you a desolate waste. I will turn your towns into ruins and you will be desolate. Then you will know that I am the LORD.

" 'Because you harbored an ancient hostility and delivered the Israelites over to the sword at the time of their calamity, the time their punishment reached its climax, therefore as surely as I live, declares the Sovereign LORD, I will give you over to bloodshed and it will pursue you. Since you did not hate bloodshed, bloodshed will pursue you. I will make Mount Seir a desolate waste and cut off from it all who come and go. I will fill your mountains with the slain; those killed by the sword will fall on your hills and in your valleys and in all your ravines. I will make you desolate forever; your towns will not be inhabited. Then you will know that I am the LORD.

" 'Because you have said, "These two nations and countries will be ours and we will take possession of them," even though I the LORD was there, therefore as surely as I live, declares the Sovereign LORD, I will treat you in accordance with the anger and jealousy you showed in your hatred of them and I will make myself known among them when I judge you. Then you will know that I the LORD have heard all the contemptible things you have said against the mountains of Israel. You said, "They have been laid waste and have been given over to us to devour." You boasted against me and spoke against me without restraint, and I heard it. This is what the Sovereign LORD says: While the whole earth rejoices, I will make you desolate. Because you rejoiced when the inheritance of Israel became desolate, that is how I will treat you. You will be desolate, Mount Seir, you and all of Edom. Then they will know that I am the LORD.' "

"Son of man, prophesy to the mountains of Israel and say, 'Mountains of Israel, hear the word of the LORD. This is what the Sovereign

LORD says: The enemy said of you, "Aha! The ancient heights have become our possession." ' Therefore prophesy and say, 'This is what the Sovereign LORD says: Because they ravaged and crushed you from every side so that you became the possession of the rest of the nations and the object of people's malicious talk and slander, therefore, mountains of Israel, hear the word of the Sovereign LORD: This is what the Sovereign LORD says to the mountains and hills, to the ravines and valleys, to the desolate ruins and the deserted towns that have been plundered and ridiculed by the rest of the nations around you—this is what the Sovereign LORD says: In my burning zeal I have spoken against the rest of the nations, and against all Edom, for with glee and with malice in their hearts they made my land their own possession so that they might plunder its pastureland.' Therefore prophesy concerning the land of Israel and say to the mountains and hills, to the ravines and valleys: 'This is what the Sovereign LORD says: I speak in my jealous wrath because you have suffered the scorn of the nations. Therefore this is what the Sovereign LORD says: I swear with uplifted hand that the nations around you will also suffer scorn.

" 'But you, mountains of Israel, will produce branches and fruit for my people Israel, for they will soon come home. I am concerned for you and will look on you with favor; you will be plowed and sown, and I will cause many people to live on you—yes, all of Israel. The towns will be inhabited and the ruins rebuilt. I will increase the number of people and animals living on you, and they will be fruitful and become numerous. I will settle people on you as in the past and will make you prosper more than before. Then you will know that I am the LORD. I will cause people, my people Israel, to live on you. They will possess you, and you will be their inheritance; you will never again deprive them of their children.

" 'This is what the Sovereign LORD says: Because some say to you, "You devour people and deprive your nation of its children," therefore you will no longer devour people or make your nation childless, declares the Sovereign LORD. No longer will I make you hear the taunts of the nations, and no longer will you suffer the scorn of the peoples or cause your nation to fall, declares the Sovereign LORD.' "

Again the word of the LORD came to me: "Son of man, when the people of Israel were living in their own land, they defiled it by their conduct and their actions. Their conduct was like a woman's monthly uncleanness in my sight. So I poured out my wrath on them because they had shed blood in the land and because they had defiled it with their idols. I dispersed them among the nations, and they were scattered through the countries; I judged them according to their conduct and their actions. And wherever they went among the nations they profaned my holy name, for it was said of them, 'These are the Lord's people, and yet they had to leave his land.' I had concern for my holy name, which the people of Israel profaned among the nations where they had gone.

"Therefore say to the Israelites, 'This is what the Sovereign Lord says: It is not for your sake, people of Israel, that I am going to do these things, but for the sake of my holy name, which you have profaned among the nations where you have gone. I will show the holiness of my great name, which has been profaned among the nations, the name you have profaned among them. Then the nations will know that I am the Lord, declares the Sovereign Lord, when I am proved holy through you before their eyes.

"'For I will take you out of the nations; I will gather you from all the countries and bring you back into your own land. I will sprinkle clean water on you, and you will be clean; I will cleanse you from all your impurities and from all your idols. I will give you a new heart and put a new spirit in you; I will remove from you your heart of stone and give you a heart of flesh. And I will put my Spirit in you and move you to follow my decrees and be careful to keep my laws. Then you will live in the land I gave your ancestors; you will be my people, and I will be your God. I will save you from all your uncleanness. I will call for the grain and make it plentiful and will not bring famine upon you. I will increase the fruit of the trees and the crops of the field, so that you will no longer suffer disgrace among the nations because of famine. Then you will remember your evil ways and wicked deeds, and you will loathe yourselves for your sins and detestable practices. I want you to know that I am not doing this for your sake, declares the Sovereign Lord. Be ashamed and disgraced for your conduct, people of Israel!

"'This is what the Sovereign Lord says: On the day I cleanse you from all your sins, I will resettle your towns, and the ruins will be rebuilt. The desolate land will be cultivated instead of lying desolate in the sight of all who pass through it. They will say, "This land that was laid waste has become like the garden of Eden; the cities that were lying in ruins, desolate and destroyed, are now fortified and inhabited." Then the nations around you that remain will know that I the Lord have rebuilt what was destroyed and have replanted what was desolate. I the Lord have spoken, and I will do it.'

"This is what the Sovereign Lord says: Once again I will yield to Israel's plea and do this for them: I will make their people as numerous as sheep, as numerous as the flocks for offerings at Jerusalem during her appointed festivals. So will the ruined cities be filled with flocks of people. Then they will know that I am the Lord."

The hand of the Lord was on me, and he brought me out by the Spirit of the Lord and set me in the middle of a valley; it was full of bones. He led me back and forth among them, and I saw a great many bones on the floor of the valley, bones that were very dry. He asked me, "Son of man, can these bones live?"

I said, "Sovereign Lord, you alone know."

Then he said to me, "Prophesy to these bones and say to them, 'Dry bones, hear the word of the Lord! This is what the Sovereign Lord says to these bones: I will make breath enter you, and you will come to life. I will attach tendons to you and make flesh come upon you and cover you with skin; I will put breath in you, and you will come to life. Then you will know that I am the Lord.'"

So I prophesied as I was commanded. And as I was prophesying, there was a noise, a rattling sound, and the bones came together, bone to bone. I looked, and tendons and flesh appeared on them and skin covered them, but there was no breath in them.

Then he said to me, "Prophesy to the breath; prophesy, son of man, and say to it, 'This is what the Sovereign Lord says: Come, breath, from the four winds and breathe into these slain, that they may live.'" So I prophesied as he commanded me, and breath entered them; they came to life and stood up on their feet—a vast army.

Then he said to me: "Son of man, these bones are the people of Israel. They say, 'Our bones are dried up and our hope is gone; we are cut off.' Therefore prophesy and say to them: 'This is what the Sovereign Lord says: My people, I am going to open your graves and bring you up from them; I will bring you back to the land of Israel. Then you, my people, will know that I am the Lord, when I open your graves and bring you up from them. I will put my Spirit in you and you will live, and I will settle you in your own land. Then you will know that I the Lord have spoken, and I have done it, declares the Lord.'"

The word of the Lord came to me: "Son of man, take a stick of wood and write on it, 'Belonging to Judah and the Israelites associated with him.' Then take another stick of wood, and write on it, 'Belonging to Joseph (that is, to Ephraim) and all the Israelites associated with him.' Join them together into one stick so that they will become one in your hand.

"When your people ask you, 'Won't you tell us what you mean by this?' say to them, 'This is what the Sovereign Lord says: I am going to take the stick of Joseph—which is in Ephraim's hand—

and of the Israelite tribes associated with him, and join it to Judah's stick. I will make them into a single stick of wood, and they will become one in my hand.' Hold before their eyes the sticks you have written on and say to them, 'This is what the Sovereign Lord says: I will take the Israelites out of the nations where they have gone. I will gather them from all around and bring them back into their own land. I will make them one nation in the land, on the mountains of Israel. There will be one king over all of them and they will never again be two nations or be divided into two kingdoms. They will no longer defile themselves with their idols and vile images or with any of their offenses, for I will save them from all their sinful backsliding, and I will cleanse them. They will be my people, and I will be their God.

"'My servant David will be king over them, and they will all have one shepherd. They will follow my laws and be careful to keep my decrees. They will live in the land I gave to my servant Jacob, the land where your ancestors lived. They and their children and their children's children will live there forever, and David my servant will be their prince forever. I will make a covenant of peace with them; it will be an everlasting covenant. I will establish them and increase their numbers, and I will put my sanctuary among them forever. My dwelling place will be with them; I will be their God, and they will be my people. Then the nations will know that I the Lord make Israel holy, when my sanctuary is among them forever.'"

The word of the Lord came to me: "Son of man, set your face against Gog, of the land of Magog, the chief prince of Meshek and Tubal; prophesy against him and say: 'This is what the Sovereign Lord says: I am against you, Gog, chief prince of Meshek and Tubal. I will turn you around, put hooks in your jaws and bring you out with your whole army—your horses, your horsemen fully armed, and a great horde with large and small shields, all of them brandishing their swords. Persia, Cush and Put will be with them, all with shields and helmets, also Gomer with all its troops, and Beth Togarmah from the far north with all its troops—the many nations with you.

"'Get ready; be prepared, you and all the hordes gathered about you, and take command of them. After many days you will be called to arms. In future years you will invade a land that has recovered from war, whose people were gathered from many nations to the mountains of Israel, which had long been desolate. They had been brought out from the nations, and now all of them live in safety. You and all your troops and the many nations with you will go up, advancing like a storm; you will be like a cloud covering the land.

" 'This is what the Sovereign Lord says: On that day thoughts will come into your mind and you will devise an evil scheme. You will say, "I will invade a land of unwalled villages; I will attack a peaceful and unsuspecting people — all of them living without walls and without gates and bars. I will plunder and loot and turn my hand against the resettled ruins and the people gathered from the nations, rich in livestock and goods, living at the center of the land." Sheba and Dedan and the merchants of Tarshish and all her villages will say to you, "Have you come to plunder? Have you gathered your hordes to loot, to carry off silver and gold, to take away livestock and goods and to seize much plunder?" '

"Therefore, son of man, prophesy and say to Gog: 'This is what the Sovereign Lord says: In that day, when my people Israel are living in safety, will you not take notice of it? You will come from your place in the far north, you and many nations with you, all of them riding on horses, a great horde, a mighty army. You will advance against my people Israel like a cloud that covers the land. In days to come, Gog, I will bring you against my land, so that the nations may know me when I am proved holy through you before their eyes.

" 'This is what the Sovereign Lord says: You are the one I spoke of in former days by my servants the prophets of Israel. At that time they prophesied for years that I would bring you against them. This is what will happen in that day: When Gog attacks the land of Israel, my hot anger will be aroused, declares the Sovereign Lord. In my zeal and fiery wrath I declare that at that time there shall be a great earthquake in the land of Israel. The fish in the sea, the birds in the sky, the beasts of the field, every creature that moves along the ground, and all the people on the face of the earth will tremble at my presence. The mountains will be overturned, the cliffs will crumble and every wall will fall to the ground. I will summon a sword against Gog on all my mountains, declares the Sovereign Lord. Every man's sword will be against his brother. I will execute judgment on him with plague and bloodshed; I will pour down torrents of rain, hailstones and burning sulfur on him and on his troops and on the many nations with him. And so I will show my greatness and my holiness, and I will make myself known in the sight of many nations. Then they will know that I am the Lord.'

"Son of man, prophesy against Gog and say: 'This is what the Sovereign Lord says: I am against you, Gog, chief prince of Meshek and Tubal. I will turn you around and drag you along. I will bring you from the far north and send you against the mountains of Israel. Then I will strike your bow from your left hand and make your arrows drop from your right hand. On the mountains of Israel you will fall, you and all your troops and the nations with you. I will give you as food to all kinds of carrion birds and to the wild animals. You will fall in the open field, for I have spoken, declares the Sovereign Lord. I will send fire on Magog and on those who live in safety in the coastlands, and they will know that I am the Lord.

"'I will make known my holy name among my people Israel. I will no longer let my holy name be profaned, and the nations will know that I the Lord am the Holy One in Israel. It is coming! It will surely take place, declares the Sovereign Lord. This is the day I have spoken of.

"'Then those who live in the towns of Israel will go out and use the weapons for fuel and burn them up—the small and large shields, the bows and arrows, the war clubs and spears. For seven years they will use them for fuel. They will not need to gather wood from the fields or cut it from the forests, because they will use the weapons for fuel. And they will plunder those who plundered them and loot those who looted them, declares the Sovereign Lord.

"'On that day I will give Gog a burial place in Israel, in the valley of those who travel east of the Sea. It will block the way of travelers, because Gog and all his hordes will be buried there. So it will be called the Valley of Hamon Gog.

"'For seven months the Israelites will be burying them in order to cleanse the land. All the people of the land will bury them, and the day I display my glory will be a memorable day for them, declares the Sovereign Lord. People will be continually employed in cleansing the land. They will spread out across the land and, along with others, they will bury any bodies that are lying on the ground.

"'After the seven months they will carry out a more detailed search. As they go through the land, anyone who sees a human bone will leave a marker beside it until the gravediggers bury it in the Valley of Hamon Gog, near a town called Hamonah. And so they will cleanse the land.'

"Son of man, this is what the Sovereign Lord says: Call out to every kind of bird and all the wild animals: 'Assemble and come together from all around to the sacrifice I am preparing for you, the great sacrifice on the mountains of Israel. There you will eat flesh and drink blood. You will eat the flesh of mighty men and drink the blood of the princes of the earth as if they were rams and lambs, goats and bulls—all of them fattened animals from Bashan. At the sacrifice I am preparing for you, you will eat fat till you are glutted and drink blood till you are drunk. At my table you will eat your fill of horses and riders, mighty men and soldiers of every kind,' declares the Sovereign Lord.

"I will display my glory among the nations, and all the nations will see the punishment I inflict and the hand I lay on them. From that day forward the people of Israel will know that I am the Lord their God. And the nations will know that the people of Israel went into exile for their sin, because they were unfaithful to me. So I hid my face from them and handed them over to their enemies, and they all fell by the sword. I dealt with them according to their uncleanness and their offenses, and I hid my face from them.

"Therefore this is what the Sovereign Lord says: I will now restore the fortunes of Jacob and will have compassion on all the people of Israel, and I will be zealous for my holy name. They will forget their shame and all the unfaithfulness they showed toward me when they lived in safety in their land with no one to make them afraid. When I have brought them back from the nations and have gathered them from the countries of their enemies, I will be proved holy through them in the sight of many nations. Then they will know that I am the Lord their God, for though I sent them into exile among the nations, I will gather them to their own land, not leaving any behind. I will no longer hide my face from them, for I will pour out my Spirit on the people of Israel, declares the Sovereign Lord."

In the twenty-fifth year of our exile, at the beginning of the year, on the tenth of the month, in the fourteenth year after the fall of the city—on that very day the hand of the Lord was on me and he took me there. In visions of God he took me to the land of Israel and set me on a very high mountain, on whose south side were some buildings that looked like a city. He took me there, and I saw a man whose appearance was like bronze; he was standing in the gateway with a linen cord and a measuring rod in his hand. The man said to me, "Son of man, look carefully and listen closely and pay attention to everything I am going to show you, for that is why you have been brought here. Tell the people of Israel everything you see."

I saw a wall completely surrounding the temple area. The length of the measuring rod in the man's hand was six long cubits, each of which was a cubit and a handbreadth. He measured the wall; it was one measuring rod thick and one rod high.

Then he went to the east gate. He climbed its steps and measured the threshold of the gate; it was one rod deep. The alcoves for the guards were one rod long and one rod wide, and the projecting walls between the alcoves were five cubits thick. And the threshold of the gate next to the portico facing the temple was one rod deep.

Then he measured the portico of the gateway; it was eight cubits deep and its jambs were two cubits thick. The portico of the gateway faced the temple.

Inside the east gate were three alcoves on each side; the three had the same measurements, and the faces of the projecting walls on each side had the same measurements. Then he measured the width of the entrance of the gateway; it was ten cubits and its length was thirteen cubits. In front of each alcove was a wall one cubit high, and the alcoves were six cubits square. Then he measured the gateway from the top of the rear wall of one alcove to the top of the opposite one; the distance was twenty-five cubits from one parapet opening to the opposite one. He measured along the faces of the projecting walls all around the inside of the gateway — sixty cubits. The measurement was up to the portico facing the courtyard. The distance from the entrance of the gateway to the far end of its portico was fifty cubits. The alcoves and the projecting walls inside the gateway were surmounted by narrow parapet openings all around, as was the portico; the openings all around faced inward. The faces of the projecting walls were decorated with palm trees.

Then he brought me into the outer court. There I saw some rooms and a pavement that had been constructed all around the court; there were thirty rooms along the pavement. It abutted the sides of the gateways and was as wide as they were long; this was the lower pavement. Then he measured the distance from the inside of the lower gateway to the outside of the inner court; it was a hundred cubits on the east side as well as on the north.

Then he measured the length and width of the north gate, leading into the outer court. Its alcoves — three on each side — its projecting walls and its portico had the same measurements as those of the first gateway. It was fifty cubits long and twenty-five cubits wide. Its openings, its portico and its palm tree decorations had the same measurements as those of the gate facing east. Seven steps led up to it, with its portico opposite them. There was a gate to the inner court facing the north gate, just as there was on the east. He measured from one gate to the opposite one; it was a hundred cubits.

Then he led me to the south side and I saw the south gate. He measured its jambs and its portico, and they had the same measurements as the others. The gateway and its portico had narrow openings all around, like the openings of the others. It was fifty cubits long and twenty-five cubits wide. Seven steps led up to it, with its portico opposite them; it had palm tree decorations on the faces of the projecting walls on each side. The inner court also had a gate facing south, and he measured from this gate to the outer gate on the south side; it was a hundred cubits.

Then he brought me into the inner court through the south gate, and he measured the south gate; it had the same measurements as the others. Its alcoves, its projecting walls and its portico had the same measurements as the others. The gateway and its portico had openings all around. It was fifty cubits long and twenty-five cubits wide. (The porticoes of the gateways around the inner court were twenty-five cubits wide and five cubits deep.) Its portico faced the outer court; palm trees decorated its jambs, and eight steps led up to it.

Then he brought me to the inner court on the east side, and he measured the gateway; it had the same measurements as the others. Its alcoves, its projecting walls and its portico had the same measurements as the others. The gateway and its portico had openings all around. It was fifty cubits long and twenty-five cubits wide. Its portico faced the outer court; palm trees decorated the jambs on either side, and eight steps led up to it.

Then he brought me to the north gate and measured it. It had the same measurements as the others, as did its alcoves, its projecting walls and its portico, and it had openings all around. It was fifty cubits long and twenty-five cubits wide. Its portico faced the outer court; palm trees decorated the jambs on either side, and eight steps led up to it.

A room with a doorway was by the portico in each of the inner gateways, where the burnt offerings were washed. In the portico of the gateway were two tables on each side, on which the burnt offerings, sin offerings and guilt offerings were slaughtered. By the outside wall of the portico of the gateway, near the steps at the entrance of the north gateway were two tables, and on the other side of the steps were two tables. So there were four tables on one side of the gateway and four on the other—eight tables in all—on which the sacrifices were slaughtered. There were also four tables of dressed stone for the burnt offerings, each a cubit and a half long, a cubit and a half wide and a cubit high. On them were placed the utensils for slaughtering the burnt offerings and the other sacrifices. And double-pronged hooks, each a handbreadth long, were attached to the wall all around. The tables were for the flesh of the offerings.

Outside the inner gate, within the inner court, were two rooms, one at the side of the north gate and facing south, and another at the side of the south gate and facing north. He said to me, "The room facing south is for the priests who guard the temple, and the room facing north is for the priests who guard the altar. These are the sons of Zadok, who are the only Levites who may draw near to the LORD to minister before him."

Then he measured the court: It was square—a hundred cubits long and a hundred cubits wide. And the altar was in front of the temple.

He brought me to the portico of the temple and measured the jambs of the portico; they were five cubits wide on either side. The width of the entrance was fourteen cubits and its projecting walls were three cubits wide on either side. The portico was twenty cubits wide, and twelve cubits from front to back. It was reached by a flight of stairs, and there were pillars on each side of the jambs.

Then the man brought me to the main hall and measured the jambs; the width of the jambs was six cubits on each side. The entrance was ten cubits wide, and the projecting walls on each side of it were five cubits wide. He also measured the main hall; it was forty cubits long and twenty cubits wide.

Then he went into the inner sanctuary and measured the jambs of the entrance; each was two cubits wide. The entrance was six cubits wide, and the projecting walls on each side of it were seven cubits wide. And he measured the length of the inner sanctuary; it was twenty cubits, and its width was twenty cubits across the end of the main hall. He said to me, "This is the Most Holy Place."

Then he measured the wall of the temple; it was six cubits thick, and each side room around the temple was four cubits wide. The side rooms were on three levels, one above another, thirty on each level. There were ledges all around the wall of the temple to serve as supports for the side rooms, so that the supports were not inserted into the wall of the temple. The side rooms all around the temple were wider at each successive level. The structure surrounding the temple was built in ascending stages, so that the rooms widened as one went upward. A stairway went up from the lowest floor to the top floor through the middle floor.

I saw that the temple had a raised base all around it, forming the foundation of the side rooms. It was the length of the rod, six long cubits. The outer wall of the side rooms was five cubits thick. The open area between the side rooms of the temple and the priests' rooms was twenty cubits wide all around the temple. There were entrances to the side rooms from the open area, one on the north and another on the south; and the base adjoining the open area was five cubits wide all around.

The building facing the temple courtyard on the west side was seventy cubits wide. The wall of the building was five cubits thick all around, and its length was ninety cubits.

Then he measured the temple; it was a hundred cubits long, and the temple courtyard and the building with its walls were also a hundred cubits long. The width of the temple courtyard on the east, including the front of the temple, was a hundred cubits.

Then he measured the length of the building facing the courtyard at the rear of the temple, including its galleries on each side; it was a hundred cubits.

The main hall, the inner sanctuary and the portico facing the court, as well as the thresholds and the narrow windows and galleries around the three of them — everything beyond and including the threshold was covered with wood. The floor, the wall up to the windows, and the windows were covered. In the space above the outside of the entrance to the inner sanctuary and on the walls at regular intervals all around the inner and outer sanctuary were carved cherubim and palm trees. Palm trees alternated with cherubim. Each cherub had two faces: the face of a human being toward the palm tree on one side and the face of a lion toward the palm tree on the other. They were carved all around the whole temple. From the floor to the area above the entrance, cherubim and palm trees were carved on the wall of the main hall.

The main hall had a rectangular doorframe, and the one at the front of the Most Holy Place was similar. There was a wooden altar three cubits high and two cubits square; its corners, its base and its sides were of wood. The man said to me, "This is the table that is before the Lord." Both the main hall and the Most Holy Place had double doors. Each door had two leaves — two hinged leaves for each door. And on the doors of the main hall were carved cherubim and palm trees like those carved on the walls, and there was a wooden overhang on the front of the portico. On the sidewalls of the portico were narrow windows with palm trees carved on each side. The side rooms of the temple also had overhangs.

Then the man led me northward into the outer court and brought me to the rooms opposite the temple courtyard and opposite the outer wall on the north side. The building whose door faced north was a hundred cubits long and fifty cubits wide. Both in the section twenty cubits from the inner court and in the section opposite the pavement of the outer court, gallery faced gallery at the three levels. In front of the rooms was an inner passageway ten cubits wide and a hundred cubits long. Their doors were on the north. Now the upper rooms were narrower, for the galleries took more space from them than from the rooms on the lower and middle floors of the building. The rooms on the top floor had no pillars, as the courts had; so they were smaller in floor space than those on the lower and middle floors. There was an outer wall parallel to the rooms and the outer court; it extended in front of the rooms for fifty cubits. While the row of rooms on the side next to the outer court was fifty cubits long, the row on the side nearest the sanctuary was a hundred cubits long. The lower rooms had an entrance on the east side as one enters them from the outer court.

On the south side along the length of the wall of the outer court, adjoining the temple courtyard and opposite the outer wall, were rooms with a passageway in front of them. These were like the rooms on the north; they had the same length and width, with similar exits and dimensions. Similar to the doorways on the north were the doorways of the rooms on the south. There was a doorway at the beginning of the passageway that was parallel to the corresponding wall extending eastward, by which one enters the rooms.

Then he said to me, "The north and south rooms facing the temple courtyard are the priests' rooms, where the priests who approach the Lord will eat the most holy offerings. There they will put the most holy offerings — the grain offerings, the sin offerings and the guilt offerings—for the place is holy. Once the priests enter the holy precincts, they are not to go into the outer court until they leave behind the garments in which they minister, for these are holy. They are to put on other clothes before they go near the places that are for the people."

When he had finished measuring what was inside the temple area, he led me out by the east gate and measured the area all around: He measured the east side with the measuring rod; it was five hundred cubits. He measured the north side; it was five hundred cubits by the measuring rod. He measured the south side; it was five hundred cubits by the measuring rod. Then he turned to the west side and measured; it was five hundred cubits by the measuring rod. So he measured the area on all four sides. It had a wall around it, five hundred cubits long and five hundred cubits wide, to separate the holy from the common.

Then the man brought me to the gate facing east, and I saw the glory of the God of Israel coming from the east. His voice was like the roar of rushing waters, and the land was radiant with his glory. The vision I saw was like the vision I had seen when he came to destroy the city and like the visions I had seen by the Kebar River, and I fell facedown. The glory of the LORD entered the temple through the gate facing east. Then the Spirit lifted me up and brought me into the inner court, and the glory of the LORD filled the temple.

While the man was standing beside me, I heard someone speaking to me from inside the temple. He said: "Son of man, this is the place of my throne and the place for the soles of my feet. This is where I will live among the Israelites forever. The people of Israel will never again defile my holy name—neither they nor their kings—by their prostitution and the funeral offerings for their kings at their death. When they placed their threshold next to my threshold and their doorposts beside my doorposts, with only a wall between me and them, they defiled my holy name by their detestable practices. So I destroyed them in my anger. Now let them put away from me their prostitution and the funeral offerings for their kings, and I will live among them forever.

"Son of man, describe the temple to the people of Israel, that they may be ashamed of their sins. Let them consider its perfection, and if they are ashamed of all they have done, make known to them the design of the temple—its arrangement, its exits and entrances—its whole design and all its regulations and laws. Write these down before them so that they may be faithful to its design and follow all its regulations.

"This is the law of the temple: All the surrounding area on top of the mountain will be most holy. Such is the law of the temple.

"These are the measurements of the altar in long cubits, that cubit being a cubit and a handbreadth: Its gutter is a cubit deep and a cubit wide, with a rim of one span around the edge. And this is the height of the altar: From the gutter on the ground up to the lower ledge that goes around the altar it is two cubits high, and the ledge is a cubit wide. From this lower ledge to the upper ledge that goes around the altar it is four cubits high, and that ledge is also a cubit wide. Above that, the altar hearth is four cubits high, and four horns project upward from the hearth. The altar hearth is square, twelve cubits long and twelve cubits wide. The upper ledge also is square, fourteen cubits long and fourteen cubits wide. All around the altar is a gutter of one cubit with a rim of half a cubit. The steps of the altar face east."

Then he said to me, "Son of man, this is what the Sovereign LORD says: These will be the regulations for sacrificing burnt offerings and splashing blood against the altar when it is built: You are to give a young bull as a sin offering to the Levitical priests of the family of Zadok, who come near to minister before me, declares the Sovereign LORD. You are to take some of its blood and put it on the four horns of the altar and on the four corners of the upper ledge and all around the rim, and so purify the altar and make atonement for it. You are to take the bull for the sin offering and burn it in the designated part of the temple area outside the sanctuary.

"On the second day you are to offer a male goat without defect for a sin offering, and the altar is to be purified as it was purified with the bull. When you have finished purifying it, you are to offer a young bull and a ram from the flock, both without defect. You are to offer them before the LORD, and the priests are to sprinkle salt on them and sacrifice them as a burnt offering to the LORD.

"For seven days you are to provide a male goat daily for a sin offering; you are also to provide a young bull and a ram from the flock, both without defect. For seven days they are to make atonement for the altar and cleanse it; thus they will dedicate it. At the end of these days, from the eighth day on, the priests are to present your burnt offerings and fellowship offerings on the altar. Then I will accept you, declares the Sovereign LORD."

Then the man brought me back to the outer gate of the sanctuary, the one facing east, and it was shut. The LORD said to me, "This gate is to remain shut. It must not be opened; no one may enter through it. It is to remain shut because the LORD, the God of Israel, has entered through it. The prince himself is the only one who may sit inside the gateway to eat in the presence of the LORD. He is to enter by way of the portico of the gateway and go out the same way."

Then the man brought me by way of the north gate to the front of the temple. I looked and saw the glory of the LORD filling the temple of the LORD, and I fell facedown.

The LORD said to me, "Son of man, look carefully, listen closely and give attention to everything I tell you concerning all the regulations and instructions regarding the temple of the LORD. Give attention to the entrance to the temple and all the exits of the sanctuary. Say to rebellious Israel, 'This is what the Sovereign LORD says: Enough of your detestable practices, people of Israel! In addition to all your other detestable practices, you brought foreigners uncircumcised in heart and flesh into my sanctuary, desecrating my temple while you offered me food, fat and blood, and you broke my covenant. Instead of carrying out your duty in regard to my holy things, you put others in charge of my sanctuary. This is what the Sovereign LORD says: No foreigner uncircumcised in heart and flesh is to enter my sanctuary, not even the foreigners who live among the Israelites.

"'The Levites who went far from me when Israel went astray and who wandered from me after their idols must bear the consequences of their sin. They may serve in my sanctuary, having charge of the gates of the temple and serving in it; they may slaughter the burnt offerings and sacrifices for the people and stand before the people and serve them. But because they served them in the presence of their idols and made the people of Israel fall into sin, therefore I have sworn with uplifted hand that they must bear the consequences of their sin, declares the Sovereign LORD. They are not to come near to serve me as priests or come near any of my holy things or my most holy offerings; they must bear the shame of their detestable practices. And I will appoint them to guard the temple for all the work that is to be done in it.

"'But the Levitical priests, who are descendants of Zadok and who guarded my sanctuary when the Israelites went astray from me, are to come near to minister before me; they are to stand before me to offer sacrifices of fat and blood, declares the Sovereign LORD. They alone are to enter my sanctuary; they alone are to come near my table to minister before me and serve me as guards.

"'When they enter the gates of the inner court, they are to wear linen clothes; they must not wear any woolen garment while ministering at the gates of the inner court or inside the temple. They are to wear linen turbans on their heads and linen undergarments around their waists. They must not wear anything that makes them perspire. When they go out into the outer court where the people are, they are to take off the clothes they have been ministering in and are to leave them in the sacred rooms, and put on other clothes, so that the people are not consecrated through contact with their garments.

"'They must not shave their heads or let their hair grow long, but they are to keep the hair of their heads trimmed. No priest is to drink wine when he enters the inner court. They must not marry widows or divorced women; they may marry only virgins of Israelite descent or widows of priests. They are to teach my people the difference between the holy and the common and show them how to distinguish between the unclean and the clean.

"'In any dispute, the priests are to serve as judges and decide it according to my ordinances. They are to keep my laws and my decrees for all my appointed festivals, and they are to keep my Sabbaths holy.

"'A priest must not defile himself by going near a dead person; however, if the dead person was his father or mother, son or daughter, brother or unmarried sister, then he may defile himself. After he is cleansed, he must wait seven days. On the day he goes into the inner court of the sanctuary to minister in the sanctuary, he is to offer a sin offering for himself, declares the Sovereign LORD.

"'I am to be the only inheritance the priests have. You are to give them no possession in Israel; I will be their possession. They will eat the grain offerings, the sin offerings and the guilt offerings; and everything in Israel devoted to the LORD will belong to them. The best of all the firstfruits and of all your special gifts will belong to the priests. You are to give them the first portion of your ground meal so that a blessing may rest on your household. The priests must not eat anything, whether bird or animal, found dead or torn by wild animals.

"'When you allot the land as an inheritance, you are to present to the LORD a portion of the land as a sacred district, 25,000 cubits long and 20,000 cubits wide; the entire area will be holy. Of this, a section 500 cubits square is to be for the sanctuary, with 50 cubits around it for open land. In the sacred district, measure off a section 25,000 cubits long and 10,000 cubits wide. In it will be the sanctuary, the Most Holy Place. It will be the sacred portion of the land for the priests, who minister in the sanctuary and who draw near to minister before the LORD. It will be a place for their houses as well as a holy place for the sanctuary. An area 25,000 cubits long and 10,000 cubits wide will belong to the Levites, who serve in the temple, as their possession for towns to live in.

"'You are to give the city as its property an area 5,000 cubits wide and 25,000 cubits long, adjoining the sacred portion; it will belong to all Israel.

"'The prince will have the land bordering each side of the area formed by the sacred district and the property of the city. It will extend westward from the west side and eastward from the east side, running lengthwise from the western to the eastern border parallel to one of the tribal portions. This land will be his possession in Israel. And my princes will no longer oppress my people but will allow the people of Israel to possess the land according to their tribes.

"'This is what the Sovereign LORD says: You have gone far enough, princes of Israel! Give up your violence and oppression and do what is just and right. Stop dispossessing my people, declares the Sovereign LORD. You are to use accurate scales, an accurate ephah and an accurate bath. The ephah and the bath are to be the same size, the bath containing a tenth of a homer and the ephah a tenth of a homer; the homer is to be the standard measure for both. The shekel is to consist of twenty gerahs. Twenty shekels plus twenty-five shekels plus fifteen shekels equal one mina.

"'This is the special gift you are to offer: a sixth of an ephah from each homer of wheat and a sixth of an ephah from each homer of barley. The prescribed portion of olive oil, measured by the bath, is a tenth of a bath from each cor (which consists of ten baths or one homer, for ten baths are equivalent to a homer). Also one sheep is to be taken from every flock of two hundred from the well-watered pastures of Israel. These will be used for the grain offerings, burnt offerings and fellowship offerings to make atonement for the people, declares the Sovereign LORD. All the people of the land will be required to give this special offering to the prince in Israel. It will be the duty of the prince to provide the burnt offerings, grain offerings and drink offerings at the festivals, the New Moons and the Sabbaths — at all the appointed festivals of Israel. He will provide the sin offerings, grain offerings, burnt offerings and fellowship offerings to make atonement for the Israelites.

"'This is what the Sovereign LORD says: In the first month on the first day you are to take a young bull without defect and purify the sanctuary. The priest is to take some of the blood of the sin offering and put it on the doorposts of the temple, on the four corners of the upper ledge of the altar and on the gateposts of the inner court. You are to do the same on the seventh day of the month for anyone who sins unintentionally or through ignorance; so you are to make atonement for the temple.

"'In the first month on the fourteenth day you are to observe the Passover, a festival lasting seven days, during which you shall eat bread made without yeast. On that day the prince is to provide a bull as a sin offering for himself and for all the people of the land. Every day during the seven days of the festival he is to provide seven bulls and seven rams without defect as a burnt offering to the LORD, and a male goat for a sin offering. He is to provide as a grain offering an ephah for each bull and an ephah for each ram, along with a hin of olive oil for each ephah.

"'During the seven days of the festival, which begins in the seventh month on the fifteenth day, he is to make the same provision for sin offerings, burnt offerings, grain offerings and oil.

" 'This is what the Sovereign LORD says: The gate of the inner court facing east is to be shut on the six working days, but on the Sabbath day and on the day of the New Moon it is to be opened. The prince is to enter from the outside through the portico of the gateway and stand by the gatepost. The priests are to sacrifice his burnt offering and his fellowship offerings. He is to bow down in worship at the threshold of the gateway and then go out, but the gate will not be shut until evening. On the Sabbaths and New Moons the people of the land are to worship in the presence of the LORD at the entrance of that gateway. The burnt offering the prince brings to the LORD on the Sabbath day is to be six male lambs and a ram, all without defect. The grain offering given with the ram is to be an ephah, and the grain offering with the lambs is to be as much as he pleases, along with a hin of olive oil for each ephah. On the day of the New Moon he is to offer a young bull, six lambs and a ram, all without defect. He is to provide as a grain offering one ephah with the bull, one ephah with the ram, and with the lambs as much as he wants to give, along with a hin of oil for each ephah. When the prince enters, he is to go in through the portico of the gateway, and he is to come out the same way.

" 'When the people of the land come before the LORD at the appointed festivals, whoever enters by the north gate to worship is to go out the south gate; and whoever enters by the south gate is to go out the north gate. No one is to return through the gate by which they entered, but each is to go out the opposite gate. The prince is to be among them, going in when they go in and going out when they go out. At the feasts and the appointed festivals, the grain offering is to be an ephah with a bull, an ephah with a ram, and with the lambs as much as he pleases, along with a hin of oil for each ephah.

" 'When the prince provides a freewill offering to the LORD — whether a burnt offering or fellowship offerings — the gate facing east is to be opened for him. He shall offer his burnt offering or his fellowship offerings as he does on the Sabbath day. Then he shall go out, and after he has gone out, the gate will be shut.

" 'Every day you are to provide a year-old lamb without defect for a burnt offering to the LORD; morning by morning you shall provide it. You are also to provide with it morning by morning a grain offering, consisting of a sixth of an ephah with a third of a hin of oil to moisten the flour. The presenting of this grain offering to the LORD is a lasting ordinance. So the lamb and the grain offering and the oil shall be provided morning by morning for a regular burnt offering.

" 'This is what the Sovereign LORD says: If the prince makes a gift from his inheritance to one of his sons, it will also belong to his descendants; it is to be their property by inheritance. If, however, he makes a gift from his inheritance to one of his servants, the servant may keep it until the year of freedom; then it will revert to the prince. His inheritance belongs to his sons only; it is theirs. The prince must not take any of the inheritance of the people, driving them off their property. He is to give his sons their inheritance out of his own property, so that not one of my people will be separated from their property.'"

Then the man brought me through the entrance at the side of the gate to the sacred rooms facing north, which belonged to the priests, and showed me a place at the western end. He said to me, "This is the place where the priests are to cook the guilt offering and the sin offering and bake the grain offering, to avoid bringing them into the outer court and consecrating the people."

He then brought me to the outer court and led me around to its four corners, and I saw in each corner another court. In the four corners of the outer court were enclosed courts, forty cubits long and thirty cubits wide; each of the courts in the four corners was the same size. Around the inside of each of the four courts was a ledge of stone, with places for fire built all around under the ledge. He said to me, "These are the kitchens where those who minister at the temple are to cook the sacrifices of the people."

The man brought me back to the entrance to the temple, and I saw water coming out from under the threshold of the temple toward the east (for the temple faced east). The water was coming down from under the south side of the temple, south of the altar. He then brought me out through the north gate and led me around the outside to the outer gate facing east, and the water was trickling from the south side.

As the man went eastward with a measuring line in his hand, he measured off a thousand cubits and then led me through water that was ankle-deep. He measured off another thousand cubits and led me through water that was knee-deep. He measured off another thousand and led me through water that was up to the waist. He measured off another thousand, but now it was a river that I could not cross, because the water had risen and was deep enough to swim in — a river that no one could cross. He asked me, "Son of man, do you see this?"

Then he led me back to the bank of the river. When I arrived there, I saw a great number of trees on each side of the river. He said to me, "This water flows toward the eastern region and goes down into the Arabah, where it enters the Dead Sea. When it empties into the sea, the salty water there becomes fresh. Swarms of living creatures will live wherever the river flows. There will be large numbers of fish, because this water flows there and makes the salt water fresh; so where the river flows everything will live. Fishermen will stand along the shore; from En Gedi to En Eglaim there will be places for spreading nets. The fish will be of many kinds — like the fish of the Mediterranean Sea. But the swamps and marshes will not become fresh; they will be left for salt. Fruit trees of all kinds will grow on both banks of the river. Their leaves will not wither, nor will their fruit fail. Every month they will bear fruit, because the water from the sanctuary flows to them. Their fruit will serve for food and their leaves for healing."

This is what the Sovereign Lord says: "These are the boundaries of the land that you will divide among the twelve tribes of Israel as their inheritance, with two portions for Joseph. You are to divide it equally among them. Because I swore with uplifted hand to give it to your ancestors, this land will become your inheritance.

"This is to be the boundary of the land:

"On the north side it will run from the Mediterranean Sea by the Hethlon road past Lebo Hamath to Zedad, Berothah and Sibraim (which lies on the border between Damascus and Hamath), as far as Hazer Hattikon, which is on the border of Hauran. The boundary will extend from the sea to Hazar Enan, along the northern border of Damascus, with the border of Hamath to the north. This will be the northern boundary.

"On the east side the boundary will run between Hauran and Damascus, along the Jordan between Gilead and the land of Israel, to the Dead Sea and as far as Tamar. This will be the eastern boundary.

"On the south side it will run from Tamar as far as the waters of Meribah Kadesh, then along the Wadi of Egypt to the Mediterranean Sea. This will be the southern boundary.

"On the west side, the Mediterranean Sea will be the boundary to a point opposite Lebo Hamath. This will be the western boundary.

"You are to distribute this land among yourselves according to the tribes of Israel. You are to allot it as an inheritance for yourselves and for the foreigners residing among you and who have children. You are to consider them as native-born Israelites; along with you they are to be allotted an inheritance among the tribes of Israel. In whatever tribe a foreigner resides, there you are to give them their inheritance," declares the Sovereign Lord.

"These are the tribes, listed by name: At the northern frontier, Dan will have one portion; it will follow the Hethlon road to Lebo

Hamath; Hazar Enan and the northern border of Damascus next to Hamath will be part of its border from the east side to the west side.

"Asher will have one portion; it will border the territory of Dan from east to west.

"Naphtali will have one portion; it will border the territory of Asher from east to west.

"Manasseh will have one portion; it will border the territory of Naphtali from east to west.

"Ephraim will have one portion; it will border the territory of Manasseh from east to west.

"Reuben will have one portion; it will border the territory of Ephraim from east to west.

"Judah will have one portion; it will border the territory of Reuben from east to west.

"Bordering the territory of Judah from east to west will be the portion you are to present as a special gift. It will be 25,000 cubits wide, and its length from east to west will equal one of the tribal portions; the sanctuary will be in the center of it.

"The special portion you are to offer to the LORD will be 25,000 cubits long and 10,000 cubits wide. This will be the sacred portion for the priests. It will be 25,000 cubits long on the north side, 10,000 cubits wide on the west side, 10,000 cubits wide on the east side and 25,000 cubits long on the south side. In the center of it will be the sanctuary of the LORD. This will be for the consecrated priests, the Zadokites, who were faithful in serving me and did not go astray as the Levites did when the Israelites went astray. It will be a special gift to them from the sacred portion of the land, a most holy portion, bordering the territory of the Levites.

"Alongside the territory of the priests, the Levites will have an allotment 25,000 cubits long and 10,000 cubits wide. Its total length will be 25,000 cubits and its width 10,000 cubits. They must not sell or exchange any of it. This is the best of the land and must not pass into other hands, because it is holy to the LORD.

"The remaining area, 5,000 cubits wide and 25,000 cubits long, will be for the common use of the city, for houses and for pastureland. The city will be in the center of it and will have these measurements: the north side 4,500 cubits, the south side 4,500 cubits, the east side 4,500 cubits, and the west side 4,500 cubits. The pastureland for the city will be 250 cubits on the north, 250 cubits on the south, 250 cubits on the east, and 250 cubits on the west. What remains of the area, bordering on the sacred portion and running the length of it, will be 10,000 cubits on the east side and 10,000 cubits on the west side. Its produce will supply food for the workers of the city. The workers from the city who farm it will come from all the tribes of Israel. The entire portion will be a square, 25,000 cubits on each side. As a special gift you will set aside the sacred portion, along with the property of the city.

"What remains on both sides of the area formed by the sacred portion and the property of the city will belong to the prince. It will extend eastward from the 25,000 cubits of the sacred portion to the eastern border, and westward from the 25,000 cubits to the western border. Both these areas running the length of the tribal portions will belong to the prince, and the sacred portion with the temple sanctuary will be in the center of them. So the property of the Levites and the property of the city will lie in the center of the area that belongs to the prince. The area belonging to the prince will lie between the border of Judah and the border of Benjamin.

"As for the rest of the tribes: Benjamin will have one portion; it will extend from the east side to the west side.

"Simeon will have one portion; it will border the territory of Benjamin from east to west.

"Issachar will have one portion; it will border the territory of Simeon from east to west.

"Zebulun will have one portion; it will border the territory of Issachar from east to west.

"Gad will have one portion; it will border the territory of Zebulun from east to west.

"The southern boundary of Gad will run south from Tamar to the waters of Meribah Kadesh, then along the Wadi of Egypt to the Mediterranean Sea.

"This is the land you are to allot as an inheritance to the tribes of Israel, and these will be their portions," declares the Sovereign LORD.

"These will be the exits of the city: Beginning on the north side, which is 4,500 cubits long, the gates of the city will be named after the tribes of Israel. The three gates on the north side will be the gate of Reuben, the gate of Judah and the gate of Levi.

"On the east side, which is 4,500 cubits long, will be three gates: the gate of Joseph, the gate of Benjamin and the gate of Dan.

"On the south side, which measures 4,500 cubits, will be three gates: the gate of Simeon, the gate of Issachar and the gate of Zebulun.

"On the west side, which is 4,500 cubits long, will be three gates: the gate of Gad, the gate of Asher and the gate of Naphtali.

"The distance all around will be 18,000 cubits.

"And the name of the city from that time on will be:

THE LORD IS THERE."

INVITATION TO
HAGGAI

When Cyrus, king of Persia, conquered Babylon in 539 BC, he gave the exiled Jews permission to return to their homeland and rebuild the temple in Jerusalem. A group went back the next year and within two more years they'd laid and dedicated the temple foundation. But their work was then stopped by suspicious and resentful neighbors who had connections in the Persian court. Sixteen years later a new king, Darius, came to the throne and soon after this the prophet Haggai began urging the returned exiles to resume work on the temple. He called specifically on Zerubbabel, the appointed governor, and Joshua, the high priest, to lead the community in this project. They followed through and within four years the reconstruction was completed and worship resumed in the temple.

The book of Haggai records the messages he brought to the community during a strategic four-month period at the beginning of Darius's reign. The first message challenges the people to recognize that their crops haven't been blessed because they've left God's house in ruins. In response, they resume work on the temple. The second message encourages them in this work. Some of them, possibly including Haggai himself, had seen the temple the Babylonians destroyed over sixty years before. They may have been discouraged at how insignificant the new temple looked by comparison. But Haggai brought God's promise that the new temple's glory would be even greater than that of the original temple. The third message assures the people that from now on their crops will be blessed. The final message encourages Zerubbabel personally. He's the heir to the throne of David, and this message seems to be an intentional reversal of a word God spoke to Jehoiachin, the Judean king who was taken to Babylon as a hostage. Through Jeremiah, God told him, *Even if you, Jehoiachin son of Jehoiakim king of Judah, were a signet ring on my right hand, I would still pull you off* (see p. 286). But now, through Haggai, God says to Jehoiachin's successor, *I will make you like my signet ring, for I have chosen you*. The people are back in their land, and so is God's blessing.

HAGGAI

In the second year of King Darius, on the first day of the sixth month, the word of the LORD came through the prophet Haggai to Zerubbabel son of Shealtiel, governor of Judah, and to Joshua son of Jozadak, the high priest:

This is what the LORD Almighty says: "These people say, 'The time has not yet come to rebuild the LORD's house.'"

Then the word of the LORD came through the prophet Haggai: "Is it a time for you yourselves to be living in your paneled houses, while this house remains a ruin?"

Now this is what the LORD Almighty says: "Give careful thought to your ways. You have planted much, but harvested little. You eat, but never have enough. You drink, but never have your fill. You put on clothes, but are not warm. You earn wages, only to put them in a purse with holes in it."

This is what the LORD Almighty says: "Give careful thought to your ways. Go up into the mountains and bring down timber and build my house, so that I may take pleasure in it and be honored," says the LORD. "You expected much, but see, it turned out to be little. What you brought home, I blew away. Why?" declares the LORD Almighty. "Because of my house, which remains a ruin, while each of you is busy with your own house. Therefore, because of you the heavens have withheld their dew and the earth its crops. I called for a drought on the fields and the mountains, on the grain, the new wine, the olive oil and everything else the ground produces, on people and livestock, and on all the labor of your hands."

Then Zerubbabel son of Shealtiel, Joshua son of Jozadak, the high priest, and the whole remnant of the people obeyed the voice of the LORD their God and the message of the prophet Haggai, because the LORD their God had sent him. And the people feared the LORD.

Then Haggai, the LORD's messenger, gave this message of the LORD to the people: "I am with you," declares the LORD. So the LORD stirred up the spirit of Zerubbabel son of Shealtiel, governor of Judah, and the spirit of Joshua son of Jozadak, the high priest, and the spirit of the whole remnant of the people. They came and began to work on the house of the Lord Almighty, their God, on the twenty-fourth day of the sixth month.

In the second year of King Darius, on the twenty-first day of the seventh month, the word of the Lord came through the prophet Haggai: "Speak to Zerubbabel son of Shealtiel, governor of Judah, to Joshua son of Jozadak, the high priest, and to the remnant of the people. Ask them, 'Who of you is left who saw this house in its former glory? How does it look to you now? Does it not seem to you like nothing? But now be strong, Zerubbabel,' declares the Lord. 'Be strong, Joshua son of Jozadak, the high priest. Be strong, all you people of the land,' declares the Lord, 'and work. For I am with you,' declares the Lord Almighty. 'This is what I covenanted with you when you came out of Egypt. And my Spirit remains among you. Do not fear.'

"This is what the Lord Almighty says: 'In a little while I will once more shake the heavens and the earth, the sea and the dry land. I will shake all nations, and what is desired by all nations will come, and I will fill this house with glory,' says the Lord Almighty. 'The silver is mine and the gold is mine,' declares the Lord Almighty. 'The glory of this present house will be greater than the glory of the former house,' says the Lord Almighty. 'And in this place I will grant peace,' declares the Lord Almighty."

On the twenty-fourth day of the ninth month, in the second year of Darius, the word of the Lord came to the prophet Haggai: "This is what the Lord Almighty says: 'Ask the priests what the law says: If someone carries consecrated meat in the fold of their garment, and that fold touches some bread or stew, some wine, olive oil or other food, does it become consecrated?'"

The priests answered, "No."

Then Haggai said, "If a person defiled by contact with a dead body touches one of these things, does it become defiled?"

"Yes," the priests replied, "it becomes defiled."

Then Haggai said, "'So it is with this people and this nation in my sight,' declares the Lord. 'Whatever they do and whatever they offer there is defiled.

"'Now give careful thought to this from this day on — consider how things were before one stone was laid on another in the Lord's temple. When anyone came to a heap of twenty measures, there were only ten. When anyone went to a wine vat to draw fifty measures, there were only twenty. I struck all the work of your hands with blight, mildew and hail, yet you did not return to me,' declares the LORD. 'From this day on, from this twenty-fourth day of the ninth month, give careful thought to the day when the foundation of the LORD's temple was laid. Give careful thought: Is there yet any seed left in the barn? Until now, the vine and the fig tree, the pomegranate and the olive tree have not borne fruit.

" 'From this day on I will bless you.' "

The word of the LORD came to Haggai a second time on the twenty-fourth day of the month: "Tell Zerubbabel governor of Judah that I am going to shake the heavens and the earth. I will overturn royal thrones and shatter the power of the foreign kingdoms. I will overthrow chariots and their drivers; horses and their riders will fall, each by the sword of his brother.

" 'On that day,' declares the LORD Almighty, 'I will take you, my servant Zerubbabel son of Shealtiel,' declares the LORD, 'and I will make you like my signet ring, for I have chosen you,' declares the LORD Almighty."

ZECHARIAH

Shortly after the prophet Haggai began urging the returned exiles to complete the rebuilding of the temple, the prophet Zechariah joined him in challenging them to restore justice and true worship to their community. The book of Zechariah records the messages he brought to them beginning in the second year of King Darius of Persia (520 BC). Overall the book is collected into two main parts. The visions and prophecies of the first part focus on temple-building and renewed worship. The oracles of the second half of the book present a broader picture of a future leader and the coming of God's kingdom.

The book begins with a general call to repentance that Zechariah gave at the start of his ministry. It then records a series of eight symbolic visions he received a few months later. The message of this opening set of visions is that God has put in place everything that's needed for the temple to be rebuilt. They are intricately ordered:

: The first and last describe four differently-colored horses whose riders and drivers God sends throughout the earth. They report that conditions are peaceful and right for rebuilding.
: The second and third visions show that the hostile foreign powers that threatened the country have been neutralized.
: The sixth and seventh visions show that the sins of the people have been taken away.
: The two central visions (the fourth and fifth) depict God establishing the community leaders—Joshua the high priest and Zerubbabel the governor—in their positions of authority so they can lead the renewal. This authority is emphasized in an immediately following episode in which Joshua is given a crown.

The second sequence of prophecies in the first part of the book is also intricately structured. The temple was destroyed by the Babylonians some seventy years earlier, in the fifth month of the year. Ever since, the Jews have been fasting during that month to show their grief and sorrow. But now that the temple is being rebuilt, some of the returned exiles living in Bethel have sent messengers to inquire of the priests and prophets in Jerusalem whether they should continue this fast. God sends them an answer through Zechariah, in six parts:

: This answer begins by exposing how insincerely the people have been fasting in the fifth month, and also in the seventh month (when the Babylonian-appointed governor was assassinated).
: Zechariah then challenges the people to practice true justice as the fast that's acceptable to God, just as the earlier prophets had taught.
: He then offers God's assurances that the temple will be restored and God's presence will once again dwell there.
: In light of this last promise, the people are urged to *be strong* in rebuilding the temple.
: In response to the teaching about the nature of true fasting, they're then challenged to practice justice.
: And, finally, in response to the original question, they're told that all of their fasts (which also included the tenth month, when the siege of Jerusalem began, and the fourth month, when its walls were breached) will become joyful celebrations. In fact, people from all nations will come and join them in worshiping the true God.

The messages in the second main part of the book aren't dated, and they're not attributed directly to Zechariah like the others. They include poetic oracles rather than symbolic vision reports, and they address a different situation. The central concern is no longer with rebuilding the temple, but with the leadership of the community. The rulers of Judea are described as *shepherds* who prey on the flock instead of protecting and nourishing it. The speaker of the oracles has been a good shepherd, but he's now being rejected. He predicts that after a time of suffering under the bad shepherds, God will send a righteous king from the line of David to re-establish justice and restore the fortunes of the nation. The messages here, like those in the first section of the book, anticipate God's future definitive triumph over every enemy, when *the Lord will be king over the whole earth*.

ZECHARIAH

In the eighth month of the second year of Darius, the word of the Lord came to the prophet Zechariah son of Berekiah, the son of Iddo:

"The Lord was very angry with your ancestors. Therefore tell the people: This is what the Lord Almighty says: 'Return to me,' declares the Lord Almighty, 'and I will return to you,' says the Lord Almighty. Do not be like your ancestors, to whom the earlier prophets proclaimed: This is what the Lord Almighty says: 'Turn from your evil ways and your evil practices.' But they would not listen or pay attention to me, declares the Lord. Where are your ancestors now? And the prophets, do they live forever? But did not my words and my decrees, which I commanded my servants the prophets, overtake your ancestors?

"Then they repented and said, 'The Lord Almighty has done to us what our ways and practices deserve, just as he determined to do.'"

On the twenty-fourth day of the eleventh month, the month of Shebat, in the second year of Darius, the word of the Lord came to the prophet Zechariah son of Berekiah, the son of Iddo.

During the night I had a vision, and there before me was a man mounted on a red horse. He was standing among the myrtle trees in a ravine. Behind him were red, brown and white horses.

I asked, "What are these, my lord?"

The angel who was talking with me answered, "I will show you what they are."

Then the man standing among the myrtle trees explained, "They are the ones the Lord has sent to go throughout the earth."

And they reported to the angel of the Lord who was standing among the myrtle trees, "We have gone throughout the earth and found the whole world at rest and in peace."

Then the angel of the Lord said, "Lord Almighty, how long will you withhold mercy from Jerusalem and from the towns of Judah, which you have been angry with these seventy years?" So the LORD spoke kind and comforting words to the angel who talked with me.

Then the angel who was speaking to me said, "Proclaim this word: This is what the LORD Almighty says: 'I am very jealous for Jerusalem and Zion, and I am very angry with the nations that feel secure. I was only a little angry, but they went too far with the punishment.'

"Therefore this is what the LORD says: 'I will return to Jerusalem with mercy, and there my house will be rebuilt. And the measuring line will be stretched out over Jerusalem,' declares the LORD Almighty.

"Proclaim further: This is what the LORD Almighty says: 'My towns will again overflow with prosperity, and the LORD will again comfort Zion and choose Jerusalem.'"

Then I looked up, and there before me were four horns. I asked the angel who was speaking to me, "What are these?"

He answered me, "These are the horns that scattered Judah, Israel and Jerusalem."

Then the LORD showed me four craftsmen. I asked, "What are these coming to do?"

He answered, "These are the horns that scattered Judah so that no one could raise their head, but the craftsmen have come to terrify them and throw down these horns of the nations who lifted up their horns against the land of Judah to scatter its people."

Then I looked up, and there before me was a man with a measuring line in his hand. I asked, "Where are you going?"

He answered me, "To measure Jerusalem, to find out how wide and how long it is."

While the angel who was speaking to me was leaving, another angel came to meet him and said to him: "Run, tell that young man, 'Jerusalem will be a city without walls because of the great number of people and animals in it. And I myself will be a wall of fire around it,' declares the LORD, 'and I will be its glory within.'

"Come! Come! Flee from the land of the north," declares the LORD, "for I have scattered you to the four winds of heaven," declares the LORD.

"Come, Zion! Escape, you who live in Daughter Babylon!" For this is what the LORD Almighty says: "After the Glorious One has sent me against the nations that have plundered you—for whoever touches you touches the apple of his eye—I will surely raise my hand against them so that their slaves will plunder them. Then you will know that the LORD Almighty has sent me.

"Shout and be glad, Daughter Zion. For I am coming, and I will live among you," declares the LORD. "Many nations will be joined with the LORD in that day and will become my people. I will live among you and you will know that the LORD Almighty has sent me to you. The LORD will inherit Judah as his portion in the holy land and will again choose Jerusalem. Be still before the LORD, all mankind, because he has roused himself from his holy dwelling."

Then he showed me Joshua the high priest standing before the angel of the LORD, and Satan standing at his right side to accuse him. The LORD said to Satan, "The LORD rebuke you, Satan! The LORD, who has chosen Jerusalem, rebuke you! Is not this man a burning stick snatched from the fire?"

Now Joshua was dressed in filthy clothes as he stood before the angel. The angel said to those who were standing before him, "Take off his filthy clothes."

Then he said to Joshua, "See, I have taken away your sin, and I will put fine garments on you."

Then I said, "Put a clean turban on his head." So they put a clean turban on his head and clothed him, while the angel of the LORD stood by.

The angel of the LORD gave this charge to Joshua: "This is what the LORD Almighty says: 'If you will walk in obedience to me and keep my requirements, then you will govern my house and have charge of my courts, and I will give you a place among these standing here.

" 'Listen, High Priest Joshua, you and your associates seated before you, who are men symbolic of things to come: I am going to bring my servant, the Branch. See, the stone I have set in front of Joshua! There are seven eyes on that one stone, and I will engrave an inscription on it,' says the LORD Almighty, 'and I will remove the sin of this land in a single day.

" 'In that day each of you will invite your neighbor to sit under your vine and fig tree,' declares the LORD Almighty."

Then the angel who talked with me returned and woke me up, like someone awakened from sleep. He asked me, "What do you see?"

I answered, "I see a solid gold lampstand with a bowl at the top and seven lamps on it, with seven channels to the lamps. Also there are two olive trees by it, one on the right of the bowl and the other on its left."

I asked the angel who talked with me, "What are these, my lord?"

He answered, "Do you not know what these are?"

"No, my lord," I replied.

So he said to me, "This is the word of the LORD to Zerubbabel:

'Not by might nor by power, but by my Spirit,' says the LORD Almighty.

"What are you, mighty mountain? Before Zerubbabel you will become level ground. Then he will bring out the capstone to shouts of 'God bless it! God bless it!'"

Then the word of the LORD came to me: "The hands of Zerubbabel have laid the foundation of this temple; his hands will also complete it. Then you will know that the LORD Almighty has sent me to you.

"Who dares despise the day of small things, since the seven eyes of the LORD that range throughout the earth will rejoice when they see the chosen capstone in the hand of Zerubbabel?"

Then I asked the angel, "What are these two olive trees on the right and the left of the lampstand?"

Again I asked him, "What are these two olive branches beside the two gold pipes that pour out golden oil?"

He replied, "Do you not know what these are?"

"No, my lord," I said.

So he said, "These are the two who are anointed to serve the Lord of all the earth."

I looked again, and there before me was a flying scroll.

He asked me, "What do you see?"

I answered, "I see a flying scroll, twenty cubits long and ten cubits wide."

And he said to me, "This is the curse that is going out over the whole land; for according to what it says on one side, every thief will be banished, and according to what it says on the other, everyone who swears falsely will be banished. The LORD Almighty declares, 'I will send it out, and it will enter the house of the thief and the house of anyone who swears falsely by my name. It will remain in that house and destroy it completely, both its timbers and its stones.'"

Then the angel who was speaking to me came forward and said to me, "Look up and see what is appearing."

I asked, "What is it?"

He replied, "It is a basket." And he added, "This is the iniquity of the people throughout the land."

Then the cover of lead was raised, and there in the basket sat a woman! He said, "This is wickedness," and he pushed her back into the basket and pushed its lead cover down on it.

Then I looked up—and there before me were two women, with the wind in their wings! They had wings like those of a stork, and they lifted up the basket between heaven and earth.

"Where are they taking the basket?" I asked the angel who was speaking to me.

He replied, "To the country of Babylonia to build a house for it. When the house is ready, the basket will be set there in its place."

I looked up again, and there before me were four chariots coming out from between two mountains—mountains of bronze. The first chariot had red horses, the second black, the third white, and the fourth dappled—all of them powerful. I asked the angel who was speaking to me, "What are these, my lord?"

The angel answered me, "These are the four spirits of heaven, going out from standing in the presence of the Lord of the whole world. The one with the black horses is going toward the north country, the one with the white horses toward the west, and the one with the dappled horses toward the south."

When the powerful horses went out, they were straining to go throughout the earth. And he said, "Go throughout the earth!" So they went throughout the earth.

Then he called to me, "Look, those going toward the north country have given my Spirit rest in the land of the north."

The word of the LORD came to me: "Take silver and gold from the exiles Heldai, Tobijah and Jedaiah, who have arrived from Babylon. Go the same day to the house of Josiah son of Zephaniah. Take the silver and gold and make a crown, and set it on the head of the high priest, Joshua son of Jozadak. Tell him this is what the LORD Almighty says: 'Here is the man whose name is the Branch, and he will branch out from his place and build the temple of the LORD. It is he who will build the temple of the LORD, and he will be clothed with majesty and will sit and rule on his throne. And he will be a priest on his throne. And there will be harmony between the two.' The crown will be given to Heldai, Tobijah, Jedaiah and Hen son of Zephaniah as a memorial in the temple of the LORD. Those who are far away will come and help to build the temple of the LORD, and you will know that the LORD Almighty has sent me to you. This will happen if you diligently obey the LORD your God."

In the fourth year of King Darius, the word of the LORD came to Zechariah on the fourth day of the ninth month, the month of Kislev. The people of Bethel had sent Sharezer and Regem-Melek, together with their men, to entreat the LORD by asking the priests of the house of the LORD Almighty and the prophets, "Should I mourn and fast in the fifth month, as I have done for so many years?"

Then the word of the LORD Almighty came to me: "Ask all the people of the land and the priests, 'When you fasted and mourned in the fifth and seventh months for the past seventy years, was it really for me that you fasted? And when you were eating and drinking, were you not just feasting for yourselves? Are these not the words the Lord proclaimed through the earlier prophets when Jerusalem and its surrounding towns were at rest and prosperous, and the Negev and the western foothills were settled?' "

And the word of the Lord came again to Zechariah: "This is what the Lord Almighty said: 'Administer true justice; show mercy and compassion to one another. Do not oppress the widow or the fatherless, the foreigner or the poor. Do not plot evil against each other.'

"But they refused to pay attention; stubbornly they turned their backs and covered their ears. They made their hearts as hard as flint and would not listen to the law or to the words that the Lord Almighty had sent by his Spirit through the earlier prophets. So the Lord Almighty was very angry.

" 'When I called, they did not listen; so when they called, I would not listen,' says the Lord Almighty. 'I scattered them with a whirlwind among all the nations, where they were strangers. The land they left behind them was so desolate that no one traveled through it. This is how they made the pleasant land desolate.' "

The word of the Lord Almighty came to me.

This is what the Lord Almighty says: "I am very jealous for Zion; I am burning with jealousy for her."

This is what the Lord says: "I will return to Zion and dwell in Jerusalem. Then Jerusalem will be called the Faithful City, and the mountain of the Lord Almighty will be called the Holy Mountain."

This is what the Lord Almighty says: "Once again men and women of ripe old age will sit in the streets of Jerusalem, each of them with cane in hand because of their age. The city streets will be filled with boys and girls playing there."

This is what the Lord Almighty says: "It may seem marvelous to the remnant of this people at that time, but will it seem marvelous to me?" declares the Lord Almighty.

This is what the Lord Almighty says: "I will save my people from the countries of the east and the west. I will bring them back to live in Jerusalem; they will be my people, and I will be faithful and righteous to them as their God."

This is what the Lord Almighty says: "Now hear these words, 'Let your hands be strong so that the temple may be built.' This is also what the prophets said who were present when the foundation was laid for the house of the Lord Almighty. Before that time there were no wages for people or hire for animals. No one could go about their business safely because of their enemies, since I had turned everyone against their neighbor. But now I will not deal with the remnant of this people as I did in the past," declares the Lord Almighty.

"The seed will grow well, the vine will yield its fruit, the ground will produce its crops, and the heavens will drop their dew. I will give all these things as an inheritance to the remnant of this people. Just as you, Judah and Israel, have been a curse among the nations, so I will save you, and you will be a blessing. Do not be afraid, but let your hands be strong."

This is what the Lord Almighty says: "Just as I had determined to bring disaster on you and showed no pity when your ancestors angered me," says the Lord Almighty, "so now I have determined to do good again to Jerusalem and Judah. Do not be afraid. These are the things you are to do: Speak the truth to each other, and render true and sound judgment in your courts; do not plot evil against each other, and do not love to swear falsely. I hate all this," declares the Lord.

The word of the Lord Almighty came to me.

This is what the Lord Almighty says: "The fasts of the fourth, fifth, seventh and tenth months will become joyful and glad occasions and happy festivals for Judah. Therefore love truth and peace."

This is what the Lord Almighty says: "Many peoples and the inhabitants of many cities will yet come, and the inhabitants of one city will go to another and say, 'Let us go at once to entreat the Lord and seek the Lord Almighty. I myself am going.' And many peoples and powerful nations will come to Jerusalem to seek the Lord Almighty and to entreat him."

This is what the Lord Almighty says: "In those days ten people from all languages and nations will take firm hold of one Jew by the hem of his robe and say, 'Let us go with you, because we have heard that God is with you.'"

A prophecy:

> The word of the Lord is against the land of Hadrak
> and will come to rest on Damascus—
>
> for the eyes of all people and all the tribes of Israel
> are on the Lord—
>
> and on Hamath too, which borders on it,
> and on Tyre and Sidon, though they are very skillful.

Tyre has built herself a stronghold;
she has heaped up silver like dust,
and gold like the dirt of the streets.

But the Lord will take away her possessions
and destroy her power on the sea,
and she will be consumed by fire.

Ashkelon will see it and fear;
Gaza will writhe in agony,
and Ekron too, for her hope will wither.

Gaza will lose her king
and Ashkelon will be deserted.

A mongrel people will occupy Ashdod,
and I will put an end to the pride of the Philistines.

I will take the blood from their mouths,
the forbidden food from between their teeth.

Those who are left will belong to our God
and become a clan in Judah,
and Ekron will be like the Jebusites.

But I will encamp at my temple
to guard it against marauding forces.

Never again will an oppressor overrun my people,
for now I am keeping watch.

Rejoice greatly, Daughter Zion!
Shout, Daughter Jerusalem!
See, your king comes to you,
righteous and victorious,

lowly and riding on a donkey,
on a colt, the foal of a donkey.

I will take away the chariots from Ephraim
and the warhorses from Jerusalem,
and the battle bow will be broken.

He will proclaim peace to the nations.
His rule will extend from sea to sea
and from the River to the ends of the earth.

As for you, because of the blood of my covenant with
you,
I will free your prisoners from the waterless pit.

Return to your fortress, you prisoners of hope;
even now I announce that I will restore twice
as much to you.

I will bend Judah as I bend my bow
and fill it with Ephraim.

I will rouse your sons, Zion,
against your sons, Greece,
and make you like a warrior's sword.

Then the Lord will appear over them;
his arrow will flash like lightning.

The Sovereign Lord will sound the trumpet;
he will march in the storms of the south,
and the Lord Almighty will shield them.

They will destroy
and overcome with slingstones.

They will drink and roar as with wine;
they will be full like a bowl
used for sprinkling the corners of the altar.

The Lord their God will save his people on that day
as a shepherd saves his flock.

They will sparkle in his land
like jewels in a crown.

How attractive and beautiful they will be!
Grain will make the young men thrive,
and new wine the young women.

Ask the Lord for rain in the springtime;
it is the Lord who sends the thunderstorms.

He gives showers of rain to all people,
and plants of the field to everyone.

The idols speak deceitfully,
diviners see visions that lie;
they tell dreams that are false,
they give comfort in vain.

Therefore the people wander like sheep
oppressed for lack of a shepherd.

"My anger burns against the shepherds,
and I will punish the leaders;
for the Lord Almighty will care
for his flock, the people of Judah,
and make them like a proud horse in battle.

From Judah will come the cornerstone,
from him the tent peg,

from him the battle bow,
from him every ruler.

Together they will be like warriors in battle
trampling their enemy into the mud of the streets.

They will fight because the LORD is with them,
and they will put the enemy horsemen to shame.

"I will strengthen Judah
and save the tribes of Joseph.

I will restore them
because I have compassion on them.

They will be as though
I had not rejected them,

for I am the LORD their God
and I will answer them.

The Ephraimites will become like warriors,
and their hearts will be glad as with wine.

Their children will see it and be joyful;
their hearts will rejoice in the LORD.

I will signal for them
and gather them in.

Surely I will redeem them;
they will be as numerous as before.

Though I scatter them among the peoples,
yet in distant lands they will remember me.

They and their children will survive,
and they will return.

I will bring them back from Egypt
and gather them from Assyria.

I will bring them to Gilead and Lebanon,
and there will not be room enough for them.

They will pass through the sea of trouble;
the surging sea will be subdued
and all the depths of the Nile will dry up.

Assyria's pride will be brought down
and Egypt's scepter will pass away.

I will strengthen them in the LORD
and in his name they will live securely,"

declares the LORD.

Open your doors, Lebanon,
so that fire may devour your cedars!

Wail, you juniper, for the cedar has fallen;
the stately trees are ruined!

Wail, oaks of Bashan;
the dense forest has been cut down!

Listen to the wail of the shepherds;
their rich pastures are destroyed!

Listen to the roar of the lions;
the lush thicket of the Jordan is ruined!

This is what the LORD my God says: "Shepherd the flock marked for slaughter. Their buyers slaughter them and go unpunished. Those who sell them say, 'Praise the LORD, I am rich!' Their own shepherds do not spare them. For I will no longer have pity on the people of the land," declares the LORD. "I will give everyone into the hands of their neighbors and their king. They will devastate the land, and I will not rescue anyone from their hands."

So I shepherded the flock marked for slaughter, particularly the oppressed of the flock. Then I took two staffs and called one Favor and the other Union, and I shepherded the flock. In one month I got rid of the three shepherds.

The flock detested me, and I grew weary of them and said, "I will not be your shepherd. Let the dying die, and the perishing perish. Let those who are left eat one another's flesh."

Then I took my staff called Favor and broke it, revoking the covenant I had made with all the nations. It was revoked on that day, and so the oppressed of the flock who were watching me knew it was the word of the LORD.

I told them, "If you think it best, give me my pay; but if not, keep it." So they paid me thirty pieces of silver.

And the LORD said to me, "Throw it to the potter"—the handsome price at which they valued me! So I took the thirty pieces of silver and threw them to the potter at the house of the LORD.

Then I broke my second staff called Union, breaking the family bond between Judah and Israel.

Then the LORD said to me, "Take again the equipment of a foolish shepherd. For I am going to raise up a shepherd over the land who will not care for the lost, or seek the young, or heal the injured, or feed the healthy, but will eat the meat of the choice sheep, tearing off their hooves.

"Woe to the worthless shepherd,
who deserts the flock!
May the sword strike his arm and his right eye!
May his arm be completely withered,
his right eye totally blinded!"

A prophecy: The word of the LORD concerning Israel.

The LORD, who stretches out the heavens, who lays the foundation of the earth, and who forms the human spirit within a person, declares: "I am going to make Jerusalem a cup that sends all the surrounding peoples reeling. Judah will be besieged as well as Jerusalem. On that day, when all the nations of the earth are gathered against her, I will make Jerusalem an immovable rock for all the nations. All who try to move it will injure themselves. On that day I will strike every horse with panic and its rider with madness," declares the LORD. "I will keep a watchful eye over Judah, but I will blind all the horses of the nations. Then the clans of Judah will say in their hearts, 'The people of Jerusalem are strong, because the LORD Almighty is their God.'

"On that day I will make the clans of Judah like a firepot in a woodpile, like a flaming torch among sheaves. They will consume all the surrounding peoples right and left, but Jerusalem will remain intact in her place.

"The LORD will save the dwellings of Judah first, so that the honor of the house of David and of Jerusalem's inhabitants may not be greater than that of Judah. On that day the LORD will shield those who live in Jerusalem, so that the feeblest among them will be like David, and the house of David will be like God, like the angel of the LORD going before them. On that day I will set out to destroy all the nations that attack Jerusalem.

"And I will pour out on the house of David and the inhabitants of Jerusalem a spirit of grace and supplication. They will look on me, the one they have pierced, and they will mourn for him as one mourns for an only child, and grieve bitterly for him as one grieves for a firstborn son. On that day the weeping in Jerusalem will be as great as the weeping of Hadad Rimmon in the plain of Megiddo. The land will mourn, each clan by itself, with their wives by themselves: the clan of the house of David and their wives, the clan of the house of Nathan and their wives, the clan of the house of Levi and their wives, the clan of Shimei and their wives, and all the rest of the clans and their wives.

"On that day a fountain will be opened to the house of David and the inhabitants of Jerusalem, to cleanse them from sin and impurity.

"On that day, I will banish the names of the idols from the land, and they will be remembered no more," declares the LORD Almighty. "I will remove both the prophets and the spirit of impurity from the land. And if anyone still prophesies, their father and mother, to whom they were born, will say to them, 'You must die, because you have told lies in the Lᴏʀᴅ's name.' Then their own parents will stab the one who prophesies.

"On that day every prophet will be ashamed of their prophetic vision. They will not put on a prophet's garment of hair in order to deceive. Each will say, 'I am not a prophet. I am a farmer; the land has been my livelihood since my youth.' If someone asks, 'What are these wounds on your body?' they will answer, 'The wounds I was given at the house of my friends.'

> "Awake, sword, against my shepherd,
> against the man who is close to me!"
> declares the Lᴏʀᴅ Almighty.
>
> "Strike the shepherd,
> and the sheep will be scattered,
> and I will turn my hand against the little ones.
>
> In the whole land," declares the Lᴏʀᴅ,
> "two-thirds will be struck down and perish;
> yet one-third will be left in it.
>
> This third I will put into the fire;
> I will refine them like silver
> and test them like gold.
>
> They will call on my name
> and I will answer them;
> I will say, 'They are my people,'
> and they will say, 'The Lᴏʀᴅ is our God.' "

A day of the Lᴏʀᴅ is coming, Jerusalem, when your possessions will be plundered and divided up within your very walls.

I will gather all the nations to Jerusalem to fight against it; the city will be captured, the houses ransacked, and the women raped. Half of the city will go into exile, but the rest of the people will not be taken from the city. Then the Lᴏʀᴅ will go out and fight against those nations, as he fights on a day of battle. On that day his feet will stand on the Mount of Olives, east of Jerusalem, and the Mount of Olives will be split in two from east to west, forming a great valley, with half of the mountain moving north and half moving south. You will flee by my mountain valley, for it will extend to Azel. You will flee as you fled from the earthquake in the days of Uzziah king of Judah. Then the Lᴏʀᴅ my God will come, and all the holy ones with him.

On that day there will be neither sunlight nor cold, frosty darkness. It will be a unique day — a day known only to the Lᴏʀᴅ — with no distinction between day and night. When evening comes, there will be light.

On that day living water will flow out from Jerusalem, half of it east to the Dead Sea and half of it west to the Mediterranean Sea, in summer and in winter.

The LORD will be king over the whole earth. On that day there will be one LORD, and his name the only name.

The whole land, from Geba to Rimmon, south of Jerusalem, will become like the Arabah. But Jerusalem will be raised up high from the Benjamin Gate to the site of the First Gate, to the Corner Gate, and from the Tower of Hananel to the royal winepresses, and will remain in its place. It will be inhabited; never again will it be destroyed. Jerusalem will be secure.

This is the plague with which the LORD will strike all the nations that fought against Jerusalem: Their flesh will rot while they are still standing on their feet, their eyes will rot in their sockets, and their tongues will rot in their mouths. On that day people will be stricken by the LORD with great panic. They will seize each other by the hand and attack one another. Judah too will fight at Jerusalem. The wealth of all the surrounding nations will be collected — great quantities of gold and silver and clothing. A similar plague will strike the horses and mules, the camels and donkeys, and all the animals in those camps.

Then the survivors from all the nations that have attacked Jerusalem will go up year after year to worship the King, the LORD Almighty, and to celebrate the Festival of Tabernacles. If any of the peoples of the earth do not go up to Jerusalem to worship the King, the LORD Almighty, they will have no rain. If the Egyptian people do not go up and take part, they will have no rain. The LORD will bring on them the plague he inflicts on the nations that do not go up to celebrate the Festival of Tabernacles. This will be the punishment of Egypt and the punishment of all the nations that do not go up to celebrate the Festival of Tabernacles.

On that day HOLY TO THE LORD will be inscribed on the bells of the horses, and the cooking pots in the LORD's house will be like the sacred bowls in front of the altar. Every pot in Jerusalem and Judah will be holy to the LORD Almighty, and all who come to sacrifice will take some of the pots and cook in them. And on that day there will no longer be a Canaanite in the house of the LORD Almighty.

INVITATION TO
Joel

The book of Joel was written for a specific occasion, and it uses this occasion to deliver a powerful spiritual message. A swarm of locusts has overrun the land of Judah and eaten everything in sight. The book begins with a description of this devastation, observing that not enough remains even for grain and wine offerings in the temple. After calling for the people to repent in response to this disaster, the book then offers a detailed description of the locust swarm itself. It describes the locusts as if they were an invading army, with God at their head. Joel asserts that the *day of the Lord*, the day of judgment many of the other prophets also warned about, has arrived. He renews his call for repentance through fasting, community prayer and heartfelt contrition. He promises that in response, God will not only drive the locusts away, but restore even more than the locusts have eaten. And he foretells even greater blessings. God will defeat all the nations that are opposing his people, and pour out his Spirit on *the survivors* in Judah. If the people will *return to the Lord* with all of their hearts, they'll not only see the return of their prosperity, they'll experience unprecedented spiritual blessings as the *day of the Lord* arrives.

While the occasion of the book of Joel is clear, its exact date is difficult to determine. Unlike most prophetic works, it isn't situated in the reign of one or more kings. What historical references it does make seem to fit a number of different periods. Joel provides no information about himself other than that he was the *son of Pethuel*. Conclusions about when he prophesied depend largely on what evidence is considered. The placement of the book in the Hebrew Bible between Hosea and Amos, for example, would suggest that Joel was one of the earliest prophets. However, the book of Joel may have been put just before Amos because it says near its end that *the Lord will roar from Zion and thunder from Jerusalem*, and the beginning of Amos says *the Lord roars from Zion and thunders from Jerusalem*. Literary evidences within the book of Joel itself suggest a much later date. Joel is filled with phrases that are characteristic of other prophets, and if these are quotations or allusions, they may be intended to show that the entire prophetic tradition lies behind his message of warning and promise. This would mean that he came after most of the other prophets, and from this perspective, he may have been roughly a contemporary of Malachi.

JOEL

T he word of the LORD that came to Joel son of Pethuel.

> Hear this, you elders;
>   listen, all who live in the land.
> Has anything like this ever happened in your days
>   or in the days of your ancestors?
> Tell it to your children,
>   and let your children tell it to their children,
>   and their children to the next generation.
> What the locust swarm has left
>   the great locusts have eaten;
> what the great locusts have left
>   the young locusts have eaten;
> what the young locusts have left
>   other locusts have eaten.
>
> Wake up, you drunkards, and weep!
>   Wail, all you drinkers of wine;
> wail because of the new wine,
>   for it has been snatched from your lips.
> A nation has invaded my land,
>   a mighty army without number;
> it has the teeth of a lion,
>   the fangs of a lioness.
> It has laid waste my vines
>   and ruined my fig trees.
> It has stripped off their bark
>   and thrown it away,
>   leaving their branches white.
>
> Mourn like a virgin in sackcloth
>   grieving for the betrothed of her youth.

Grain offerings and drink offerings
are cut off from the house of the Lord.

The priests are in mourning,
those who minister before the Lord.

The fields are ruined,
the ground is dried up;

the grain is destroyed,
the new wine is dried up,
the olive oil fails.

Despair, you farmers,
wail, you vine growers;

grieve for the wheat and the barley,
because the harvest of the field is destroyed.

The vine is dried up
and the fig tree is withered;

the pomegranate, the palm and the apple tree—
all the trees of the field—are dried up.

Surely the people's joy
is withered away.

Put on sackcloth, you priests, and mourn;
wail, you who minister before the altar.

Come, spend the night in sackcloth,
you who minister before my God;

for the grain offerings and drink offerings
are withheld from the house of your God.

Declare a holy fast;
call a sacred assembly.

Summon the elders
and all who live in the land

to the house of the Lord your God,
and cry out to the Lord.

Alas for that day!
For the day of the Lord is near;
it will come like destruction from the Almighty.

Has not the food been cut off
before our very eyes—

joy and gladness
from the house of our God?

The seeds are shriveled
beneath the clods.

The storehouses are in ruins,
the granaries have been broken down,
for the grain has dried up.

How the cattle moan!
The herds mill about

because they have no pasture;
even the flocks of sheep are suffering.

To you, Lord, I call,
for fire has devoured the pastures in the wilderness
and flames have burned up all the trees of the field.

Even the wild animals pant for you;
the streams of water have dried up
and fire has devoured the pastures in the wilderness.

Blow the trumpet in Zion;
sound the alarm on my holy hill.

Let all who live in the land tremble,
for the day of the Lord is coming.

It is close at hand—
a day of darkness and gloom,
a day of clouds and blackness.

Like dawn spreading across the mountains
a large and mighty army comes,

such as never was in ancient times
nor ever will be in ages to come.

Before them fire devours,
behind them a flame blazes.

Before them the land is like the garden of Eden,
behind them, a desert waste—
nothing escapes them.

They have the appearance of horses;
they gallop along like cavalry.

With a noise like that of chariots
they leap over the mountaintops,

like a crackling fire consuming stubble,
like a mighty army drawn up for battle.

At the sight of them, nations are in anguish;
every face turns pale.

They charge like warriors;
they scale walls like soldiers.

They all march in line,
not swerving from their course.

They do not jostle each other;
each marches straight ahead.

They plunge through defenses
without breaking ranks.

They rush upon the city;
they run along the wall.

They climb into the houses;
like thieves they enter through the windows.

Before them the earth shakes,
the heavens tremble,

the sun and moon are darkened,
and the stars no longer shine.

The Lord thunders
at the head of his army;

his forces are beyond number,
and mighty is the army that obeys his command.

The day of the Lord is great;
it is dreadful.
Who can endure it?

"Even now," declares the Lord,
"return to me with all your heart,
with fasting and weeping and mourning."

Rend your heart
and not your garments.

Return to the Lord your God,
for he is gracious and compassionate,

slow to anger and abounding in love,
and he relents from sending calamity.

Who knows? He may turn and relent
and leave behind a blessing—

grain offerings and drink offerings
for the Lord your God.

Blow the trumpet in Zion,
declare a holy fast,
call a sacred assembly.

Gather the people,
consecrate the assembly;

bring together the elders,
gather the children,
those nursing at the breast.

Let the bridegroom leave his room
and the bride her chamber.

Let the priests, who minister before the Lord,
weep between the portico and the altar.

Let them say, "Spare your people, Lord.
Do not make your inheritance an object of scorn,
a byword among the nations.

Why should they say among the peoples,
'Where is their God?'"

Then the Lord was jealous for his land
and took pity on his people.

The Lord replied to them:

"I am sending you grain, new wine and olive oil,
enough to satisfy you fully;

never again will I make you
an object of scorn to the nations.

"I will drive the northern horde far from you,
pushing it into a parched and barren land;

its eastern ranks will drown in the Dead Sea
and its western ranks in the Mediterranean Sea.

And its stench will go up;
its smell will rise."

Surely he has done great things!
Do not be afraid, land of Judah;
be glad and rejoice.

Surely the LORD has done great things!
Do not be afraid, you wild animals,
for the pastures in the wilderness are becoming green.

The trees are bearing their fruit;
the fig tree and the vine yield their riches.

Be glad, people of Zion,
rejoice in the LORD your God,

for he has given you the autumn rains
because he is faithful.

He sends you abundant showers,
both autumn and spring rains, as before.

The threshing floors will be filled with grain;
the vats will overflow with new wine and oil.

"I will repay you for the years the locusts have eaten —
the great locust and the young locust,
the other locusts and the locust swarm —

my great army that I sent among you.
You will have plenty to eat, until you are full,
and you will praise the name of the LORD your God,
who has worked wonders for you;

never again will my people be shamed.

Then you will know that I am in Israel,
that I am the LORD your God,
and that there is no other;

never again will my people be shamed.

"And afterward,
I will pour out my Spirit on all people.

Your sons and daughters will prophesy,
your old men will dream dreams,
your young men will see visions.

Even on my servants, both men and women,
I will pour out my Spirit in those days.

I will show wonders in the heavens
and on the earth,
blood and fire and billows of smoke.

The sun will be turned to darkness
and the moon to blood

before the coming of the great and dreadful day
    of the LORD.

And everyone who calls
on the name of the LORD will be saved;

for on Mount Zion and in Jerusalem
there will be deliverance,
as the LORD has said,

even among the survivors
whom the LORD calls.

"In those days and at that time,
when I restore the fortunes of Judah and Jerusalem,

I will gather all nations
and bring them down to the Valley of Jehoshaphat.

There I will put them on trial
for what they did to my inheritance, my people Israel,

because they scattered my people among the nations
and divided up my land.

They cast lots for my people
and traded boys for prostitutes;
they sold girls for wine to drink.

"Now what have you against me, Tyre and Sidon and all you regions of Philistia? Are you repaying me for something I have done? If you are paying me back, I will swiftly and speedily return on your own heads what you have done. For you took my silver and my gold and carried off my finest treasures to your temples. You sold the people of Judah and Jerusalem to the Greeks, that you might send them far from their homeland.

"See, I am going to rouse them out of the places to which you sold them, and I will return on your own heads what you have done. I will sell your sons and daughters to the people of Judah, and they will sell them to the Sabeans, a nation far away." The LORD has spoken.

Proclaim this among the nations:
Prepare for war!

Rouse the warriors!
Let all the fighting men draw near and attack.

Beat your plowshares into swords
and your pruning hooks into spears.

Let the weakling say,
"I am strong!"

Come quickly, all you nations from every side,
and assemble there.

Bring down your warriors, Lord!

"Let the nations be roused;
let them advance into the Valley of Jehoshaphat,
for there I will sit
to judge all the nations on every side.
Swing the sickle,
for the harvest is ripe.
Come, trample the grapes,
for the winepress is full
and the vats overflow—
so great is their wickedness!"

Multitudes, multitudes
in the valley of decision!
For the day of the Lord is near
in the valley of decision.
The sun and moon will be darkened,
and the stars no longer shine.
The Lord will roar from Zion
and thunder from Jerusalem;
the earth and the heavens will tremble.
But the Lord will be a refuge for his people,
a stronghold for the people of Israel.

"Then you will know that I, the Lord your God,
dwell in Zion, my holy hill.
Jerusalem will be holy;
never again will foreigners invade her.

"In that day the mountains will drip new wine,
and the hills will flow with milk;
all the ravines of Judah will run with water.
A fountain will flow out of the Lord's house
and will water the valley of acacias.
But Egypt will be desolate,
Edom a desert waste,
because of violence done to the people of Judah,
in whose land they shed innocent blood.

Judah will be inhabited forever
and Jerusalem through all generations.

Shall I leave their innocent blood unavenged?
No, I will not."

The Lord dwells in Zion!

INVITATION TO
MALACHI

The rebuilding of the temple under Zerubbabel and Joshua, inspired by the prophecies of Haggai and Zechariah, was completed in 516 BC. The new temple was meant to be the centerpiece of a community where there was true justice and genuine worship. Unfortunately, as the years went by, the people of Judah fell farther and farther away from this ideal. By the middle of the next century, their worship had become cold, formal and corrupt, and their society was plagued with injustice. Malachi challenged the people to honor God properly in their worship and in their dealings with one another. If they did, he promised, their prosperity and honor would be restored. (Malachi means "my messenger," so it could be either the prophet's name or his title.)

Malachi brought his challenges to the people in a distinctive style. He first offered an abrupt charge; then he voiced the objections he anticipated in response; and finally he answered those objections. Through this means he addressed:

: the people's doubts that God still favored them;
: their offering of blemished animals in sacrifice, and the priests' partiality in interpreting the law;
: the vital importance of the marriage covenant;
: the sense that evildoers prospered;
: the people's failure to bring tithes to support the priests and the temple;
: their complaints that it was futile to serve God.

The book of Malachi records how some of the people repented in response to his challenges, and how God said he'd spare them when he came to judge the earth. The book reminds the people to keep the law of Moses, and ends with God's promise to send the prophet Elijah back before the *great and dreadful day of the* Lord. Yet for those who revere God's name *the sun of righteousness will rise with healing in its rays*.

MALACHI

A prophecy: The word of the LORD to Israel through Malachi.

"I have loved you," says the LORD.

"But you ask, 'How have you loved us?'

"Was not Esau Jacob's brother?" declares the LORD. "Yet I have loved Jacob, but Esau I have hated, and I have turned his hill country into a wasteland and left his inheritance to the desert jackals."

Edom may say, "Though we have been crushed, we will rebuild the ruins."

But this is what the LORD Almighty says: "They may build, but I will demolish. They will be called the Wicked Land, a people always under the wrath of the LORD. You will see it with your own eyes and say, 'Great is the LORD—even beyond the borders of Israel!'

"A son honors his father, and a slave his master. If I am a father, where is the honor due me? If I am a master, where is the respect due me?" says the LORD Almighty.

"It is you priests who show contempt for my name.

"But you ask, 'How have we shown contempt for your name?'

"By offering defiled food on my altar.

"But you ask, 'How have we defiled you?'

"By saying that the LORD's table is contemptible. When you offer blind animals for sacrifice, is that not wrong? When you sacrifice lame or diseased animals, is that not wrong? Try offering them to your governor! Would he be pleased with you? Would he accept you?" says the LORD Almighty.

"Now plead with God to be gracious to us. With such offerings from your hands, will he accept you?"—says the LORD Almighty.

"Oh, that one of you would shut the temple doors, so that you would not light useless fires on my altar! I am not pleased with you," says the LORD Almighty, "and I will accept no offering from your hands. My name will be great among the nations, from where the sun rises to where it sets. In every place incense and pure offerings will be brought to me, because my name will be great among the nations," says the LORD Almighty.

"But you profane it by saying, 'The Lord's table is defiled,' and, 'Its food is contemptible.' And you say, 'What a burden!' and you sniff at it contemptuously," says the LORD Almighty.

"When you bring injured, lame or diseased animals and offer them as sacrifices, should I accept them from your hands?" says the LORD. "Cursed is the cheat who has an acceptable male in his flock and vows to give it, but then sacrifices a blemished animal to the Lord. For I am a great king," says the LORD Almighty, "and my name is to be feared among the nations.

"And now, you priests, this warning is for you. If you do not listen, and if you do not resolve to honor my name," says the LORD Almighty, "I will send a curse on you, and I will curse your blessings. Yes, I have already cursed them, because you have not resolved to honor me.

"Because of you I will rebuke your descendants; I will smear on your faces the dung from your festival sacrifices, and you will be carried off with it. And you will know that I have sent you this warning so that my covenant with Levi may continue," says the LORD Almighty. "My covenant was with him, a covenant of life and peace, and I gave them to him; this called for reverence and he revered me and stood in awe of my name. True instruction was in his mouth and nothing false was found on his lips. He walked with me in peace and uprightness, and turned many from sin.

"For the lips of a priest ought to preserve knowledge, because he is the messenger of the LORD Almighty and people seek instruction from his mouth. But you have turned from the way and by your teaching have caused many to stumble; you have violated the covenant with Levi," says the LORD Almighty. "So I have caused you to be despised and humiliated before all the people, because you have not followed my ways but have shown partiality in matters of the law."

Do we not all have one Father? Did not one God create us? Why do we profane the covenant of our ancestors by being unfaithful to one another?

Judah has been unfaithful. A detestable thing has been committed in Israel and in Jerusalem: Judah has desecrated the sanctuary the LORD loves by marrying women who worship a foreign god. As for the man who does this, whoever he may be, may the LORD remove him from the tents of Jacob—even though he brings an offering to the LORD Almighty.

Another thing you do: You flood the LORD's altar with tears.

You weep and wail because he no longer looks with favor on your offerings or accepts them with pleasure from your hands. You ask, "Why?" It is because the Lord is the witness between you and the wife of your youth. You have been unfaithful to her, though she is your partner, the wife of your marriage covenant.

Has not the one God made you? You belong to him in body and spirit. And what does the one God seek? Godly offspring. So be on your guard, and do not be unfaithful to the wife of your youth.

"The man who hates and divorces his wife," says the Lord, the God of Israel, "does violence to the one he should protect," says the Lord Almighty.

So be on your guard, and do not be unfaithful.

You have wearied the Lord with your words.

"How have we wearied him?" you ask.

By saying, "All who do evil are good in the eyes of the Lord, and he is pleased with them" or "Where is the God of justice?"

"I will send my messenger, who will prepare the way before me. Then suddenly the Lord you are seeking will come to his temple; the messenger of the covenant, whom you desire, will come," says the Lord Almighty.

But who can endure the day of his coming? Who can stand when he appears? For he will be like a refiner's fire or a launderer's soap. He will sit as a refiner and purifier of silver; he will purify the Levites and refine them like gold and silver. Then the Lord will have men who will bring offerings in righteousness, and the offerings of Judah and Jerusalem will be acceptable to the Lord, as in days gone by, as in former years.

"So I will come to put you on trial. I will be quick to testify against sorcerers, adulterers and perjurers, against those who defraud laborers of their wages, who oppress the widows and the fatherless, and deprive the foreigners among you of justice, but do not fear me," says the Lord Almighty.

"I the Lord do not change. So you, the descendants of Jacob, are not destroyed. Ever since the time of your ancestors you have turned away from my decrees and have not kept them. Return to me, and I will return to you," says the Lord Almighty.

"But you ask, 'How are we to return?'

"Will a mere mortal rob God? Yet you rob me.

"But you ask, 'How are we robbing you?'

"In tithes and offerings. You are under a curse — your whole nation — because you are robbing me. Bring the whole tithe into the storehouse, that there may be food in my house. Test me in this," says the LORD Almighty, "and see if I will not throw open the floodgates of heaven and pour out so much blessing that there will not be room enough to store it. I will prevent pests from devouring your crops, and the vines in your fields will not drop their fruit before it is ripe," says the LORD Almighty. "Then all the nations will call you blessed, for yours will be a delightful land," says the LORD Almighty.

"You have spoken arrogantly against me," says the LORD.

"Yet you ask, 'What have we said against you?'"

"You have said, 'It is futile to serve God. What do we gain by carrying out his requirements and going about like mourners before the LORD Almighty? But now we call the arrogant blessed. Certainly evildoers prosper, and even when they put God to the test, they get away with it.'"

Then those who feared the LORD talked with each other, and the LORD listened and heard. A scroll of remembrance was written in his presence concerning those who feared the LORD and honored his name.

"On the day when I act," says the LORD Almighty, "they will be my treasured possession. I will spare them, just as a father has compassion and spares his son who serves him. And you will again see the distinction between the righteous and the wicked, between those who serve God and those who do not.

"Surely the day is coming; it will burn like a furnace. All the arrogant and every evildoer will be stubble, and the day that is coming will set them on fire," says the LORD Almighty. "Not a root or a branch will be left to them. But for you who revere my name, the sun of righteousness will rise with healing in its rays. And you will go out and frolic like well-fed calves. Then you will trample on the wicked; they will be ashes under the soles of your feet on the day when I act," says the LORD Almighty.

"Remember the law of my servant Moses, the decrees and laws I gave him at Horeb for all Israel.

"See, I will send the prophet Elijah to you before that great and dreadful day of the LORD comes. He will turn the hearts of the parents to their children, and the hearts of the children to their parents; or else I will come and strike the land with total destruction."

A WORD ABOUT
THE NIV

The goal of the New International Version (NIV) is to enable English-speaking people from around the world to read and hear God's eternal Word in their own language. Our work as translators is motivated by our conviction that the Bible is God's Word in written form. We believe that the Bible contains the divine answer to the deepest needs of humanity, sheds unique light on our path in a dark world and sets forth the way to our eternal well-being. Out of these deep convictions, we have sought to recreate as far as possible the experience of the original audience — blending transparency to the original text with accessibility for the millions of English speakers around the world. We have prioritized accuracy, clarity and literary quality with the goal of creating a translation suitable for public and private reading, evangelism, teaching, preaching, memorizing and liturgical use. We have also sought to preserve a measure of continuity with the long tradition of translating the Scriptures into English.

The complete NIV Bible was first published in 1978. It was a completely new translation made by over a hundred scholars working directly from the best available Hebrew, Aramaic and Greek texts. The translators came from the United States, Great Britain, Canada, Australia and New Zealand, giving the translation an international scope. They were from many denominations and churches — including Anglican, Assemblies of God, Baptist, Brethren, Christian Reformed, Church of Christ, Evangelical Covenant, Evangelical Free, Lutheran, Mennonite, Methodist, Nazarene, Presbyterian, Wesleyan and others. This breadth of denominational and theological perspective helped to safeguard the translation from sectarian bias. For these reasons, and by the grace of God, the NIV has gained a wide readership in all parts of the English-speaking world.

The work of translating the Bible is never finished. As good as they are, English translations must be regularly updated so that they will continue to communicate accurately the meaning of God's Word. Updates are needed in order to reflect the latest developments in our understanding of the biblical world and its languages and to keep pace with changes in English usage. Recognizing, then, that the NIV would retain its ability to communicate God's Word accurately only if it were regularly updated, the original translators established the Committee on Bible Translation (CBT). The Committee is a self-perpetuating group of biblical scholars charged with keeping abreast of advances in biblical scholarship and changes in English and issuing periodic updates to the NIV. The CBT is an independent, self-governing body and has sole responsibility for the NIV text. The Committee mirrors the original group of translators in its diverse international and denominational makeup and in its unifying commitment to the Bible as God's inspired Word.

In obedience to its mandate, the Committee has issued periodic updates to the NIV. An initial revision was released in 1984. A more thorough revision process was completed in 2005, resulting in the separately published TNIV. The updated NIV you now have in your hands builds on both the original NIV and the TNIV and represents the latest effort of the Committee to articulate God's unchanging Word in the way the original authors might have said it had they been speaking in English to the global English-speaking audience today.

Translation Philosophy

The Committee's translating work has been governed by three widely accepted principles about the way people use words and about the way we understand them.

First, the meaning of words is determined by the way that users of the language actually use them at any given time. For the biblical languages, therefore, the Committee utilizes the best and most recent scholarship on the way Hebrew, Aramaic and Greek words were being used in biblical times. At the same time, the Committee carefully studies the state of modern English. Good translation is like good communication: one must know the target audience so that the appropriate choices can be made about which English words to use to represent the original words of Scripture. From its inception, the NIV has had as its target the general English-speaking population all over the world, the "International" in its title reflecting this concern. The aim of the Committee is to put the Scriptures into natural English that will communicate effectively with the broadest possible audience of English speakers.

Modern technology has enhanced the Committee's ability to choose the right English words to convey the meaning of the original text. The field of computational linguistics harnesses the power of computers to provide broadly applicable and current data about the state of the language. Translators can now access huge databases of modern English to better understand the current meaning and usage of key words. The Committee utilized this resource in preparing the 2011 edition of the NIV. An area of especially rapid and significant change in English is the way certain nouns and pronouns are used to refer to human beings. The Committee therefore requested experts in computational linguistics at Collins Dictionaries to pose some key questions about this usage to its database of English — the largest in the world, with over 4.4 billion words, gathered from several English-speaking countries and including both spoken and written English. (The Collins Study, called "The Development and Use of Gender Language in Contemporary English," can be accessed at *http://www.thenivbible. com/about-the-niv/about-the-2011-edition/*.) The study revealed that the most popular words to describe the human race in modern U.S. English were "humanity," "man" and "mankind." The Committee then used this data in the updated NIV, choosing from among these three words (and occasionally others also) depending on the context.

A related issue creates a larger problem for modern translations: the move away from using the third-person masculine singular pronouns — "he/him/his" — to refer to men and women equally. This usage does persist in some forms of English, and this revision therefore occasionally uses these pronouns in a generic sense. But the tendency, recognized in day-to-day usage and confirmed by the Collins study, is away from the generic use of "he," "him" and "his." In recognition of this shift in language and in an effort to translate into the natural English that people are actually using, this revision of the NIV generally uses other constructions when the biblical text is plainly addressed to men and women equally. The reader will encounter especially frequently a "they," "their" or "them" to express a generic singular idea. Thus, for instance, Mark 8:36 reads: "What good is it for someone to gain the whole world, yet forfeit their soul?" This generic use of the "distributive" or "singular" "they/ them/their" has been used for many centuries by respected writers of English and has now become established as standard English, spoken and written, all over the world.

A second linguistic principle that feeds into the Committee's translation work is that meaning is found not in individual words, as vital as they are, but in larger clusters: phrases, clauses, sentences, discourses. Translation is not, as many people think, a matter of word substitution: English word x in place of Hebrew word y. Translators must first determine the meaning of the words of the biblical languages in the context of the passage and then select English words that accurately communicate that meaning to modern listeners and readers. This means that accurate translation will not always reflect the exact structure of the original language. To be sure, there is debate over the degree to which translators should try to preserve the "form" of the original text in English. From the beginning, the NIV has taken a mediating position on this issue. The manual produced when the translation that became the NIV was first being planned states: "If the Greek or Hebrew syntax has a good parallel in modern English, it should be used. But if there is no good parallel, the English syntax appropriate to the meaning of the original is to be chosen." It is fine, in other words, to carry over the form of the biblical languages into English—but not at the expense of natural expression. The principle that meaning resides in larger clusters of words means that the Committee has not insisted on a "word-for-word" approach to translation. We certainly believe that every word of Scripture is inspired by God and therefore to be carefully studied to determine what God is saying to us. It is for this reason that the Committee labors over every single word of the original texts, working hard to determine how each of those words contributes to what the text is saying. Ultimately, however, it is how these individual words function in combination with other words that determines meaning.

A third linguistic principle guiding the Committee in its translation work is the recognition that words have a spectrum of meaning. It is popular to define a word by using another word, or "gloss," to substitute for it. This substitute word is then sometimes called the "literal" meaning of a word. In fact, however, words have a range of possible meanings. Those meanings will vary depending on the context, and words in one language will usually not occupy the same semantic range as words in another language. The Committee therefore studies each original word of Scripture in its context to identify its meaning in a particular verse and then chooses an appropriate English word (or phrase) to represent it. It is impossible, then, to translate any given Hebrew, Aramaic or Greek word with the same English word all the time. The Committee does try to translate related occurrences of a word in the original languages with the same English word in order to preserve the connection for the English reader. But the Committee generally privileges clear natural meaning over a concern with consistency in rendering particular words.

Textual Basis

For the Old Testament the standard Hebrew text, the Masoretic Text as published in the latest edition of *Biblia Hebraica*, has been used throughout. The Masoretic Text tradition contains marginal notations that offer variant readings. These have sometimes been followed instead of the text itself. Because such instances involve variants within the Masoretic tradition, they have not been indicated in the textual notes. In a few cases, words in the basic consonantal text have been divided differently than in the Masoretic Text. Such cases are usually indicated in the textual footnotes. The Dead Sea Scrolls contain biblical texts that represent an earlier stage of the transmission of the Hebrew text. They have been consulted, as have been the Samaritan Pentateuch and the ancient scribal traditions concerning deliberate textual changes. The translators also consulted the more important early versions. Readings from these versions, the Dead Sea Scrolls and the scribal traditions were occasionally followed where the Masoretic Text seemed doubtful and where accepted principles of textual criticism showed that one or more of these textual witnesses appeared to provide the correct reading. In rare cases, the translators have emended the Hebrew text where it appears to have become corrupted at an even earlier stage of its transmission. These departures from the Masoretic Text are also indicated in the textual footnotes. Sometimes the vowel indicators (which are later additions to the basic consonantal text) found in the Masoretic Text did not, in the judgment of the translators, represent the correct vowels for the original text. Accordingly, some words have been read with a different set of vowels. These instances are usually not indicated in the footnotes.

The Greek text used in translating the New Testament has been an eclectic one, based on the latest editions of the Nestle-Aland/United Bible Societies' Greek New Testament. The translators have made their choices among the variant readings in accordance with widely accepted principles of New Testament textual criticism. Footnotes call attention to places where uncertainty remains.

The New Testament authors, writing in Greek, often quote the Old Testament from its ancient Greek version, the Septuagint. This is one reason why some of the Old Testament quotations in the NIV New Testament are not identical to the corresponding passages in the NIV Old Testament. Such quotations in the New Testament are indicated with the footnote "(see Septuagint)."

Footnotes and Formatting

Footnotes in this version are of several kinds, most of which need no explanation. Those giving alternative translations begin with "Or" and generally introduce the alternative with the last word preceding it in the text, except when it is a single-word alternative. When poetry is quoted in a footnote a slash mark indicates a line division.

It should be noted that references to diseases, minerals, flora and fauna, architectural details, clothing, jewelry, musical instruments and other articles cannot always be identified with precision. Also, linear measurements and measures of capacity can only be approximated (see the Table of Weights and Measures). Although *Selah*, used mainly in the Psalms, is probably a musical term, its meaning is uncertain. Since it may interrupt reading and distract the reader, this word has not been kept in the English text, but every occurrence has been signaled by a footnote.

As an aid to the reader, sectional headings have been inserted. They are not to be regarded as part of the biblical text and are not intended for oral reading. It is the Committee's hope that these headings may prove more helpful to the reader than the traditional chapter divisions, which were introduced long after the Bible was written.

Sometimes the chapter and/or verse numbering in English translations of the Old Testament differs from that found in published Hebrew texts. This is particularly the case in the Psalms, where the traditional titles are included in the Hebrew verse numbering. Such differences are indicated in the footnotes at the bottom of the page. In the New Testament, verse numbers that marked off portions of the traditional English text not supported by the best Greek manuscripts now appear in brackets, with a footnote indicating the text that has been omitted (see, for example, Matthew 17:[21]).

Mark 16:9−20 and John 7:53−8:11, although long accorded virtually equal status with the rest of the Gospels in which they stand, have a questionable standing in the textual history of the New Testament, as noted in the bracketed annotations with which they are set off. A different typeface has been chosen for these passages to indicate their uncertain status.

Basic formatting of the text, such as lining the poetry, paragraphing (both prose and poetry), setting up of (administrative-like) lists, indenting letters and lengthy prayers within narratives and the insertion of sectional headings, has been the work of the Committee. However, the choice between single-column and double-column formats has been left to the publishers. Also the issuing of "red-letter" editions is a publisher's choice — one that the Committee does not endorse.

The Committee has again been reminded that every human effort is flawed — including this revision of the NIV. We trust, however, that many will find in it an improved representation of the Word of God, through which they hear his call to faith in our Lord Jesus Christ and to service in his kingdom. We offer this version of the Bible to him in whose name and for whose glory it has been made.

The Committee on Bible Translation

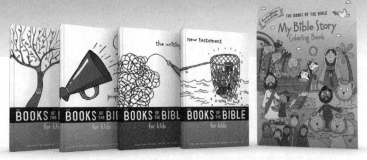

Kids, Read the Bible in a Whole New Way!

The Books of the Bible is a fresh way for kids to experience Scripture! Perfect for reading together as a family or church group, this 4-part Bible series removes chapter and verse numbers, headings, and special formatting. Now the Bible is easier to read, and reveals the story of God's great love for His people, as one narrative. Features the easy-to-read text of the New International Reader's Version (NIrV). Ages 8-12.

Look for all four books in *The Books of the Bible*:

Covenant History
Discover the Beginnings of God's People 9780310761303

The Prophets
Listen to God's Messengers Tell about Hope and Truth 9780310761358

The Writings
Learn from Stories, Poetry, and Songs 9780310761334

New Testament
Read the Story of Jesus, His Church, and His Return 9780310761310

My Bible Story Coloring Book
The Books of the Bible 9780310761068

The Books of the Bible Children's Curriculum
9780310086161

These engaging lessons are formatted around relatable Scripture references, memory verses, and Bible themes. This curriculum has everything you need for 32 complete lessons for preschool, early elementary, and later elementary classes.